SETTING THE DESERT ON FIRE

BY THE SAME AUTHOR

The Bow Group: A History

SETTING THE DESERT ON FIRE

*T. E. Lawrence and
Britain's Secret War in Arabia,
1916–18*

JAMES BARR

BLOOMSBURY

First published in Great Britain 2006

Bloomsbury Publishing Plc,
36 Soho Square,
London W1D 3QY

A CIP catalogue record for this book
is available from the British Library

ISBN 0 7475 7986 5
ISBN-13 9780747579861

10 9 8 7 6 5 4 3 2 1

Typeset by Hewer Text UK Ltd, Edinburgh
Printed in Great Britain by Clays Ltd, St Ives plc

Bloomsbury Publishing, London, New York and Berlin

The paper this book is printed on is certified by the © 1996 Forest Stewardship
Council A.C. (FSC). It is ancient-forest friendly. The printer holds
FSC chain of custody SGS-COC-2061

FSC
Mixed Sources
Product group from well-managed
forests and other controlled sources

Cert no. SGS-COC-2061
www.fsc.org
© 1996 Forest Stewardship Council

CONTENTS

LIST OF ILLUSTRATIONS

The declaration of jihad on 14 November 1914 in Constantinople. (*Informations und Dokumentationszentrum Armenien, Berlin*)

The Holy Mosque in Mecca. (*Imperial War Museum Q73539*)

The Hijaz Railway under construction, near Amman. (*University of Istanbul, image no 90590/18*)

Two Bedu. (*Imperial War Museum Q60079*)

Sharif Husein ibn Ali in December 1916. (*Imperial War Museum Q59888*)

Three men, three pledges: Sir Henry McMahon (*Permission British Library 592/5(28)*), Arthur Balfour (*Imperial War Museum Q30737*) and Sir Mark Sykes (from *Mark Sykes, His Life and Letters* by Shane Leslie, Cassell & Co, London, 1923 (a division of the Orion Publishing Group, London))

Council of war at Jeddah, October 1916. (*Imperial War Museum Q58706*)

A jovial Abdullah. (*Imperial War Museum Q59956*)

Sharif Feisal ibn Husein at the Paris peace conference. (*Imperial War Museum Q105615*)

T.E. Lawrence, David Hogarth and Alan Dawnay in Egypt, 1918. (*Imperial War Museum Q59595*)

The British enter Jerusalem, 11 December 1917. (*Imperial War Museum Q12616*)

Going their separate ways. Victorious Bedu fighters and Turkish prisoners pass in the street, Damascus, 1918. (*Imperial War Museum Q12367*)

Feisal leaves the Victoria Hotel in Damascus, 3 October 1918. (*Imperial War Museum Q12364*)

An exhausted Lawrence, on 3 October 1918 in Damascus. (*Imperial War Museum Q75534*)

NOTES ON THE KEY FIGURES IN THIS BOOK

Abdullah ibn Husein (1882–1951) Husein's second son. The ambitious power behind his father, his own aspirations hinged on joining the Hijaz to Yemen and staving off the threat posed by Ibn Saud. Recognised by the British as Emir of Transjordan in May 1923, he was assassinated in Jerusalem.

Allenby, Sir Edmund (1861–1936) Commander-in-chief of the British Third Army in France from October 1915. Sent to Egypt in June 1917 following his perceived failure at Arras, he brought a sense of purpose to the demoralised Egyptian Expeditionary Force. Best known for capturing Jerusalem in December 1917. He served as High Commissioner in Egypt in difficult circumstances after the war, from March 1919.

Asquith, Herbert (1852–1928) British Liberal Prime Minister, 1908 until December 1916.

Auda abu Tayi (died 1924) Sheikh of the Huwaytat. Auda was an infamous raider well known to pre-war European travellers to the region. Outlawed by the Ottomans after he had murdered two tax collectors, to the British he seemed a natural supporter of the Arab revolt.

Balfour, Arthur (1848–1930) Former Prime Minister (1902–5) whom Lloyd George brought back as Foreign Secretary in December 1916. Published the Balfour Declaration in November 1917. Resigned in 1922.

Brémond, Edouard (1868–1948) Commanded an infantry unit in France before he was wounded, and then nominated as Chief of the French Military Mission to the Hijaz in August 1916, on the strength of his extensive pre-war experience in North Africa. Recalled December 1917.

Chamberlain, Sir Austen (1863–1937) Secretary of State for India May 1915 to July 1917. Initially against British intervention in the Hijaz, he increasingly feared the consequences if the Ottomans recaptured Mecca, and supported sending British troops. Forced to resign in July 1917 over a damning report into the failed Indian Army expedition to Baghdad which had met with disaster at Kut in 1916.

Clayton, Gilbert (1875–1929) Director of Military Intelligence at British Army Headquarters, 1914–16; in charge of the Arab Bureau and Hijaz operations 1916–17; Chief Political Officer in Egyptian Expeditionary Force 1917–18. Cautious, firm believer in the threat to Egypt posed by the Ottoman declaration of jihad.

Fakhreddin ('Fakhri') Pasha, (1868–1948) Ottoman commander who was sent to defend Medina in late May 1916, following suspicions that a revolt was imminent. He held out until January 1919.

Feisal ibn Husein (1886–1933) Third son of Sharif Husein. The recipient of British support after showing a willingness to help the British that contrasted with the attitude of his two elder brothers. Forced out of Syria by the French in July 1919. Proclaimed King of Iraq in Baghdad by the British in August 1921.

Grey, Sir Edward (1862–1933) British Foreign Secretary, 1905–16. A dutiful, but increasingly uncertain, politician who willingly delegated responsibility for dealing with Sharif Husein to Henry McMahon in Cairo in 1915.

Haidar, Ali (1866–1935) Appointed Emir of Mecca by the Ottoman government in June 1916 to replace Sharif Husein. Returned to Lebanon in March 1917 after eight months in Medina.

Hogarth, David (1862–1927) Arrived in Egypt in August 1915. Director of the Arab Bureau from its creation in spring 1916 until that autumn. Hogarth was a veteran archaeologist who volunteered his services following the outbreak of war. He was instrumental in bringing Lawrence into intelligence work in Cairo. He opposed large-scale intervention in the Hijaz.

Husein ibn Ali (1853–1931) Appointed Emir of Mecca in 1908 by Sultan Abdul Hamid. Revolted against the Ottoman government in June 1916. Recognised as King of Hijaz in 1916, he abdicated in favour of his eldest son, Ali, in 1924. After Abdul Aziz ibn Saud overran the Hijaz in 1925, he spent the rest of his life in exile.

Ibn Saud, Abdul Aziz (1880–1953) Sultan of Najd, in central Arabia. Having captured Riyadh in 1902, he was allied to, and received assistance from, the British during the war. He defeated his rivals Ibn Rashid, 1921–2, and Sharif Husein's son Ali, in 1925.

Jafar Pasha al Askari (1885–1936) Ottoman Army officer, held prisoner of war in Cairo. He had been captured by the British in February 1916 during their suppression of the Senussi's revolt, in which he was an *agent provocateur*. He was persuaded to serve with the Arab rebels, whom he joined in the summer of 1917. Born in Baghdad, he served twice as Prime Minister of Iraq, and several times as Minister of Defence between 1923 and 1936, when he was murdered in a coup.

Jaussen, Antonin (1871–1962) French priest turned archaeologist who had travelled in the Hijaz extensively before the war. He was unsurprisingly sucked into intelligence work during the war.

Jemal Pasha, Ahmed (1872–1922) Commander of the Ottoman Fourth Army and Military Governor of Syria from December 1914. A secretive man, he orchestrated efforts to win Sharif Husein's support for an invasion of Egypt and then, when these failed, a crackdown on nascent Arab nationalism in Syria, which earned him the soubriquet 'The Blood-letter'. Recalled following the loss of Jerusalem, December 1917.

Joyce, Pierce (1878–1965) Egyptian Army officer. Arrived at Rabigh in November 1916, tasked with protecting the new British airfield, and effectively defending the village against Ottoman attack. Joyce rapidly became the organisational linchpin of operations in the Hijaz and at Aqaba. He was an adviser to the Iraqi Army after the war.

Kitchener, Herbert (1850–1916) Secretary of State for War, 1914–16. Supported British encouragement of Sharif Husein's plans to revolt. His death at sea in June 1916 robbed the Arab revolt's enthusiasts of a key ally in Whitehall just when the revolt had run out of momentum.

Lawrence, Edward (T.E.) (1888–1935) Intelligence officer in Egypt, from December 1914 until November 1916 when he was formally transferred to the Arab Bureau to work on Hijaz operations. Lawrence was drawn into British intelligence following his work as an archaeologist in the region before the war. He was sent to the Hijaz in October 1916 to assess the deteriorating situation following contradictory reports.

Liman von Sanders, Otto (1855–1929) German commander of the Ottoman Fifth Army. Originally sent to Constantinople in December 1913 at the head of a German military mission to improve the Ottomans' armed forces, Liman von Sanders was given command of the combined Turkish and German forces in Palestine in February 1918.

Lloyd, George (1879–1941) Elected MP for West Staffordshire in 1910, Lloyd was attached to the Mediterranean Expeditionary Force and a Turkish-speaking intelligence officer in November 1914. Intermittently involved in the Arab Bureau, Lloyd took a close interest in economic and financial matters and was a fervent imperialist.

Lloyd George, David (1863–1945) Minister for Munitions May 1915–July 1916, Secretary of State for War July–December 1916. Lloyd George achieved his ambition when he became Prime Minister in December 1916 (to October 1922), his energy attracting Conservative and Unionist support. Hoping to colonise Palestine, his support for an advance towards Jerusalem first served to help the Arabs, but would ultimately let them down.

McMahon, Sir Henry (1862–1949) High Commissioner in Egypt 1914–16. Pursued a policy of ambiguity and procrastination when tasked with coming to an agreement with Sharif Husein by London in 1915.

Murray, Sir Archibald (1860–1945) Commander-in-chief of the Egyptian Expeditionary Force, January 1916–June 1917. Tasked with sending as many men as possible back to France to fight, he was vehemently opposed to sending British troops to the Hijaz to support Husein. He was eventually undone by conflicting political and military pressures and, following the unsuccessful second battle of Gaza, was recalled to Britain in June 1917.

Robertson, Sir William (1860–1933) Chief of the Imperial General Staff (January 1915–February 1918). Trenchant opponent of any military venture which might distract resources and attention from the Western Front. Once the Arabs made headway north, he became marginally less sceptical.

Said, Nuri (1888–1958) Arab Ottoman Army officer. Joined Arab revolt in July 1916, acting as Jafar Pasha's chief of staff. He remained loyal to Feisal after the war, and – testimony to the region's political instability – served as Prime Minister of Iraq fourteen times between 1930 and 1958, when he was murdered in a coup.

Shaalan, Nuri (born *c.* 1845) Sheikh of the north Arabian Rwala Bedu. The Rwala were an important and wide-ranging constituent of the large Aniza tribe. Nuri Shaalan had murdered two brothers to assume his title. He was sought as an important, if volatile, ally by both Ottomans and British.

Stirling, Francis (1880–1958) Intelligence officer, who had been sent back to Egypt after being shell-shocked at Gallipoli in 1915. He served with the Arabs in the final stages of their campaign in July 1918.

Storrs, Ronald (1881–1955) Oriental Secretary at the British High Commission in Cairo 1909–17. Cerebral, early enthusiast for encouraging Sharif Husein to revolt and seize the Caliphate. Appointed 'stopgap' Military Governor of Jerusalem in December 1917.

Sykes, Sir Mark (1879–1919) British MP for Hull (from 1911) and government adviser on Middle East (from spring 1915). Closely involved in the discussions on the future of the Ottoman Empire in 1915, he was tasked with pursuing the agreement with France and Russia over the division of the Ottoman Empire in which France was allotted present-day Syria and Lebanon.

Weizmann, Chaim (1874–1952) A scientist for the British government, Weizmann was appointed Head of the Zionist Commission to Palestine in 1918. He met Feisal that May and eventually became the first President of Israel, 1949–1952.

Wemyss, Rosslyn (1864–1933) Appointed Commander of the Egyptian Squadron of the Royal Navy in January 1916 after service at Gallipoli. Supported efforts to supply the Arabs during the early stages of the revolt. Recalled to London in July 1917, where he was made First Sea Lord.

Wilson, Cyril (1873–1938) Appointed Britain's 'Pilgrimage Officer' at Jeddah in June 1916, after serving as Governor of the Red Sea Province of Sudan. Bluntly rejected Wingate's call for troops to be sent to help Husein, an intervention prompted by his overriding sense of duty to Britain.

Wilson, Sir Henry (1864–1922) A corps commander with the British Expeditionary Force in France in 1916 Wilson's lucid explanation of complex military issues and political awareness endeared him to Lloyd George, who promoted him to replace Robertson as Chief of the Imperial General Staff in February 1918. Retired February 1922 and assassinated that June by Irish republicans.

Wingate, Sir Reginald (1861–1953) Governor-General of the Sudan, and Sirdar of the Egyptian Army 1899–1916. Appointed High Commissioner of Egypt, October 1916. Insistently proposed sending British troops to the Hijaz when the revolt's momentum failed. Replaced by Allenby in 1919.

Young, Sir Hubert (1885–1950) Assistant political officer and logistics officer in Mesopotamia 1915–18. Transferred to help the Arabs in Syria in March 1918. Easily irascible, he served after the war in the Foreign and Colonial Offices.

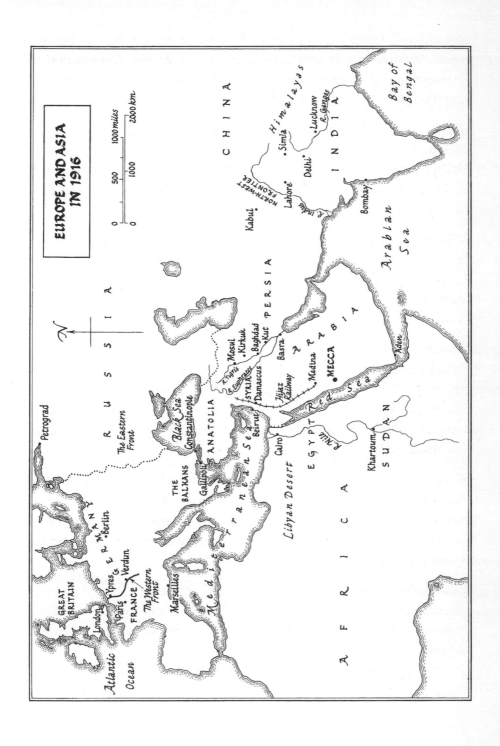

EUROPE AND ASIA
IN 1916

0   500   1000   1000 miles
0   1000   2000 km

N

GREAT BRITAIN

Atlantic Ocean

London
Paris
Ypres
Verdun
FRANCE
The Western Front

G E R M A N Y
Berlin

Marseilles

Petrograd

R U S S I A
The Eastern Front

THE BALKANS

Gallipoli

Black Sea

Constantinople

ANATOLIA

Mediterranean Sea

Beirut
Damascus
SYRIA
Mosul
Kirkuk
Baghdad
Kut
Basra
R. Tigris
R. Euphrates

PERSIA

Kabul

NORTH-WEST FRONTIER

Simla
Lahore
Delhi
Lucknow
R. Ganges

I N D I A

Bombay

Arabian Sea

Bay of Bengal

Himalayas

C H I N A

Hijaz Railway
Medina
MECCA

A R A B I A

Red Sea

Aden

Cairo
EGYPT
R. Nile
Libyan Desert
Khartoum
SUDAN

A F R I C A

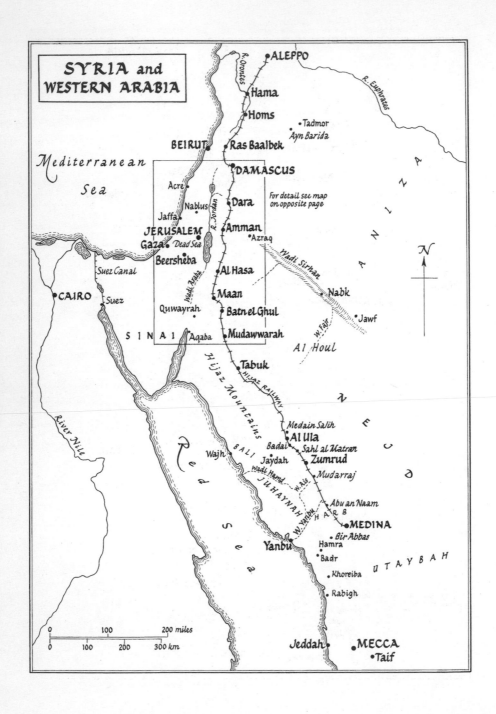

SYRIA and WESTERN ARABIA

Mediterranean Sea

ALEPPO

R. Orontes

R. Euphrates

Hama

Homs

Tadmor

Ayn Barida

BEIRUT

Ras Baalbek

DAMASCUS

A N I Z A

Acre

For detail see map on opposite page

Nablus

Dara

Jaffa

R. Jordan

Amman

JERUSALEM

Azraq

Gaza

Dead Sea

Wadi Sirhan

Beersheba

Suez Canal

Al Hasa

Nabk

CAIRO

Maan

W. Fajr

Suez

Jawf

Quwayrah

Batn el Ghul

SINAI

Aqaba

Mudawwarah

Al Houl

Wadi Araba

N

Tabuk

Hijaz Mountains

HIJAZ RAILWAY

N

River Nile

Medain Salih

Al Ula

E

Badai

Sahl al Matran

Red

Wajh

BALI

Jaydah

Zumrud

J

D

Wadi Hamd

Mudarraj

J U H A Y N A H

W. Ais

Sea

W. Yanbu

Abu an Naam

H A R B

MEDINA

W. Yanbu

Bir Abbas

Yanbu

Hamra

Badr

U T A Y B A H

Khoreiba

Rabigh

100   200 miles

0   100   200   300 km

Jeddah

MECCA

Taif

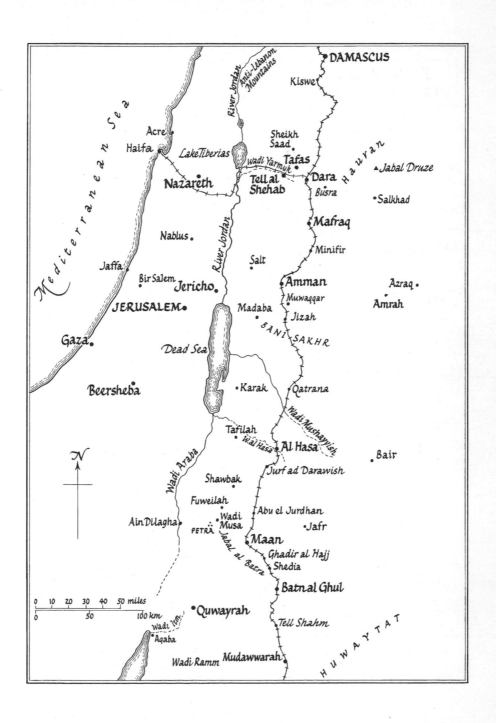

A NOTE ON THE TEXT

Due to the difficulty of transliterating Arabic words into English, the names of Arabs and places in this narrative were spelt in a wide variety of ways by the British at the time. I have standardised place and personal names to a single form across the text and the quotes to avoid confusion, and dropped the definite article 'Al' in many cases for simplicity. Major places are referred to by their Anglicised names. The spelling of all other place-names follows the most recent *Times* Atlas, minus the diacritical marks or accents. Like the British at the time, I have used the words 'Ottoman' and 'Turk' interchangeably.

All dialogue is quoted directly from official minutes or the reports and memoirs of those who witnessed the conversation. Its accuracy cannot be proven, but it is the best record we have of what was said at the time.

The effect of inflation means that £1,000 in 1916 is worth about £55,000 today.

PROLOGUE

On 26 March 2005, I found what I had been looking for. In a stony valley in the Hijaz mountains of western Saudi Arabia, one hundred miles north of Medina, stands a rust-brown steam engine. It rests ten yards off the railway embankment it once plied, its wheels half sunk in the drifting desert sand, pointing north. Further up the line ahead of it, its tender is heading in the opposite direction. A jumble of upside-down, skewed wheels are all that remains of two more carriages. Like the railway track itself, their wooden sides have long since disappeared. Here, among some stunted thornbushes and under the silty blue desert sky, is an unsettling scene of headlong disaster.[1]

A closer look among the wreckage provides a likely cause for this catastrophe. A brutal dent in the back of the firebox – still hot to the touch, though now from the heat of the ferocious midday sun – and below it a chunk of missing floor where the stoker would have stood, both suggest that an explosion beneath the wheels blasted this engine off the track: this train was probably mined. Today, it is one of only four remaining wrecks along the vanished railway line, slowly disintegrating memorials to a secret war, directed by the British, that began in June 1916.

Seven hundred miles further north and three years earlier, in a back street of the ancient city of Damascus – the capital of modern Syria – I had seen a line of similar, elderly steam engines, woven to some sidings by dry grass growing through their wheels. It was this glimpse that first sparked my curiosity. These were the shunting yards of the

northern terminus of the Hijaz Railway, which once linked Damascus
with the holy city of Medina, where the Prophet Muhammad, founder
of Islam, is buried.

Begun in 1900, the Hijaz Railway was the brainchild of the Ottoman
sultan, Abdul Hamid, and it attracted British suspicions from the start.
Before it was even finished, the hawkish foreign editor of *The Times*,
Valentine Chirol, described the project as an effort by the Sultan to 'link
up the seat of his temporal power as Sultan at Constantinople with the
seat of his spiritual power as Caliph of Mecca'. The Sultan's strategy,
Chirol claimed, was designed to enhance 'throughout the Mahomedan
world the spiritual authority to which he lays claim as heir to the
Caliphate of Islam'.[2] The Caliph – the deputy or successor to the Prophet
Muhammad – was the title conferred on Muhammad's closest followers
after his death; the Caliphate the extensive empire they had conquered.
The title was appropriated by the Ottomans in the fifteenth century.
Even at the beginning of the twentieth century the Ottoman sultan
maintained a sway as Caliph among Sunni Muslims that mesmerised the
British. Chirol, who like many other Britons treated Muslims as a
potentially fanatical mass, believed that the Sultan's power as Caliph
gave him a disturbing and disruptive influence worldwide. In particular,
the British feared the Sultan would use his position to upset the stability
of Britain's eastern Empire, home to 100 million of the global population
of nearly 300 million Muslims.

The Sultan encouraged donations from Muslims around the world
towards the railway. Muslims in India, the British government took note,
gave generously. According to one official estimate five million rupees
were sent from India towards the scheme, at a time when the average
income of a Bombay family was fifty-two rupees a month.[3] Donations
paid for one-third of the cost of the railway, which reached Medina in
1908, a year ahead of schedule. For eight years afterwards the Hijaz
Railway transformed travel through a lawless land. A forty-day desert
march or an expensive voyage by sea down through the British-controlled
Suez Canal now took just three days by train. The Sultan, as a
consequence, basked in the gratitude of Muslims worldwide. His grip,
which had been waning, seemed renewed; his influence, once limited,

suddenly appeared to extend far beyond the crumbling borders of the shrinking Ottoman Empire.

Chirol predicted trouble. 'The completion of the Hijaz Railway,' he foresaw, 'will in a large measure relieve the Sultan from the galling dependence upon friendly relations with Great Britain which the maintenance of his main line of communications with Arabia now necessitates.'[4] And he was right. At the outbreak of war in 1914 the Ottomans joined the Germans' side. Encouraged by the Germans, who were convinced that Muslim unrest could turn the advantage of the British Empire's enormous size into a terrible liability, that November the Sultan made an incendiary announcement. 'Know that our state is today at war with the Governments of Russia, England and France and their allies, who are the mortal enemies of Islam,' his spokesman dramatically proclaimed from Constantinople. 'The commander of the Faithful, the Caliph of the Muslims, summons you to the jihad!'[5]

Desperate to avert a Muslim insurrection in Egypt and in India, which would divert British forces from the crucial Western Front, the British conceived an astonishing and unprecedented response to blunt the force of the Sultan's call to holy war. They decided to intervene in Arabian tribal politics and foment a revolt designed to divide Islam by giving the Hijaz – the holiest region of the Muslim world – its independence. At dawn one summer morning in 1916, in the sacred city of Mecca, that uprising finally began.

A PARTING OF THE WAYS

(February 1914–October 1915)

At the epicentre of the Muslim world, Mehmed Zia was crouched on the floor of the town hall in Mecca because it was too dangerous to stand up. Now and then bullets splurted through the building's tall wooden shutters and spat over his head. They left dust in the air, splinters of silvery sun-bleached timber on the floor and an unfamiliar constellation of holes through which the molten daylight squinted. It was early in the morning of 10 June 1916.

Zia, the Turkish commander of Ottoman forces in the holy city, considered his situation. Three weeks earlier, news had reached Mecca that the Ottomans' enemy, the British, had just begun to blockade the Red Sea. The great war now raging in Europe had pitted the two powers, once allies, against each other and to Zia this latest action must have seemed a symptom of the war's inexorable spread worldwide. Reports of Britain's move had sparked a panic about food in Mecca. The Grand Mufti – Mecca's highest authority on religious matters – then issued an apocalyptic warning to the inhabitants that they would starve unless they threw the Turks out of their city. Not entirely surprisingly, from then on relations between the Ottomans and the townspeople abruptly deteriorated. Gunfire had finally erupted at half-past three that morning, just after the call to prayer at dawn had ululated through the city's close streets.

During the winter Zia might have had enough troops to stop the violence. But it was now the height of an Arabian summer, and over half the Ottoman soldiers who normally garrisoned Mecca were taking refuge from the ferocious summer heat forty miles east and 4,000 feet higher in the mountain resort of Taif, up in the chain of sandpapery mountains along the western edge of modern Saudi Arabia which gave the region its daunting name: the Hijaz, Arabic for barrier.

Down in Mecca, where by mid-afternoon the temperature might reach forty-five degrees Celsius, Zia had been left behind to preserve order with about a thousand men. Almost all of these were across town in barracks on the Jeddah road, but there was also a handful of soldiers in the Jiyad fortress which dominated the city from the south. However, sometime before dawn the previous day the water to the fortress and the telegraph cables to Jeddah, Medina and Taif had all been cut. So too, Zia now discovered, had the telephone line from the barracks. When he resorted to sending orders by hand to his forces there, his messenger was shot within yards of leaving the town hall. The man now sprawled dead, his blood soaking into the earthen street outside.

Having gingerly examined the bullet holes perforating his office, Zia decided that the gunfire originated from the amphitheatre of rocky, ochre hills above the city and that the Bedu, the wild nomadic tribesmen of the desert, were consequently responsible. Life in the Hijaz was violent – 'The only things made in Mecca are swords, daggers and slippers for Arabs,'[1] one visitor remarked – and unrest among the Bedu was commonplace, especially since the Hijaz Railway had reached Medina eight years earlier. The railway had improved the Ottomans' grip over this, the most southerly and significant arm of their empire. It also made the pilgrimage to Mecca faster, cheaper and safer than before. Yet all these advantages had brought the Ottomans into mounting conflict with the Bedu. The tribesmen's livelihood depended on hiring out camels and guides to travellers, with protection rackets and robbery related subsidiary lines of business. This was a way of life now threatened by the train, the competing demands of the Ottoman taxman, and the diseases that followed in the wake of the railway, like cholera, which devastated close-knit tribal families. Although disturbances by the Bedu punctuated life in the Hijaz with growing frequency, Zia knew that some concessions to the tribesmen would normally ensure a ceasefire. So he tugged the telephone towards himself to ring Number One Mecca and speak to Sharif Husein.[2]

As his telephone number suggested, if anyone could call the tribesmen off, it was Husein. The Emir, or Governor, of Mecca, Husein was also a sharif, one of about 800 men from two families, the Aoun and the Zaid, whose rivalry resulted from their common claim to direct descent from the Prophet Muhammad. An Aoun himself, Husein had championed – and probably secretly orchestrated – the local tribesmen's violent campaign to stop the railway being extended from Medina to Mecca. And averse as he was to the forces of progress, he also loved using the telephone.

'I called up the Emir,' Zia remembered, 'and asked what this all meant, saying at the same time, "The Bedouins have revolted against the Government; find a way out." '[3]

'Of course we shall,' Husein replied enigmatically, before cutting Zia off.

Since the Sultan, Abdul Hamid, had appointed him Emir at the age of fifty-five, eight years earlier, Sharif Husein had found himself increasingly isolated. Abdul Hamid had been deposed in 1909 and the new 'Young Turk' regime which took over viewed his appointee in Mecca with suspicion. Knowing that the Ottomans balked at forcing out a descendant of Muhammad, Husein played heavily on his ancestry to head off jealous relatives and encroaching Ottoman interference. He would speak slowly yet obscurely and dress austerely in a black robe and tarbush, around which a fine white turban was tightly swirled. The turban and his silky, almost pure white beard framed large brown eyes and a solemn, inscrutable expression.

Husein cemented his position with grand displays of largesse, receiving and giving coffee to as many as 3,000 Meccans in a day.[4] In private, when it suited him, he would reach across the divide he had fashioned, patting his guests with his hand or putting his arm around their shoulder and calling them 'Ibni' – my son – or 'Habibi' – my dear.[5] 'Such a nice old man, with a charming twinkle in his eye,' wrote one man fooled by these deliberately disarming tactics.[6] But another, more perceptive visitor dryly described a man who loved 'to deal first hand with affairs'.[7] For behind Husein's otherworldly façade lurked an obsessive patriarch whose four sons, Ali, Abdullah, Feisal and Zeid, signed themselves off in their letters to him as his 'slaves', who had reputedly ordered the murder of some of his opponents and kept others chained to the floor of a foul prison beneath his palace.[8] Subsequently, it emerged that it was Husein himself who had fired the single shot that triggered the crackle of gunfire across the city early on that cloudless morning.

Behind this uprising lay the as-yet invisible hand of Britain. British overtures to Husein dated back two years to a brief flirtation which took place in Cairo early in 1914. Pre-war Cairo was just as hectic, cosmopolitan and filthy as it is today. 'The streets are full of Greeks, Dagos, and French people of all sorts from merchants to *petites dames*, sour and haughty Germans, Yids of every degree, a sprinkling of Yankees and the omnipresent English,' one wide-eyed visitor observed.[9] Old Cairo was a medieval bastion of Islamic thought where beturbaned Arab scholars in flowing robes jostled their way past ragged labourers in the winding, dark bazaars. Across town in the new city, local businessmen gathered on the veranda of the Turf Club at sundown to drink gin and criticise the government. At the Gezira Sporting Club, on an island in the Nile, the tennis courts were crowded and the race meetings busy. Séances were in vogue at the time, and in Cairo, fancy-dress balls the rage. Ronald Storrs, a balding young British diplomat on his first foreign posting, could never forget how the Archbishop of the Autocephalous Church of Mount Sinai, Porphyrios II, had turned up at one disguised as himself. Storrs, who, in the opinion of a onetime secretary of the Gezira Club, was 'thoroughly unscrupulous',[10] had an untaxing job, involving moderate amounts of work and much excess. One particular instant at another party when a glamorous European *comtesse* had flashed the golden coronet embroidered on her knickers in front of his face to prove her noblesse was indelibly seared in his memory.

Into this maelstrom in April 1914, Sharif Husein's son Abdullah had appeared, as if from another world, bemoaning the difficulties his father was experiencing with his Ottoman overlords. He presented the British with an unusual request. 'I found myself . . . being asked categorically whether Great Britain would present the Grand Sharif with a dozen, or even half a dozen machine guns,' remembered Storrs, who was given the task of meeting Abdullah.[11] He rebuffed Abdullah's appeal to help his father resist the Ottomans, but in terms that did not preclude a later change of mind: 'We could never entertain the idea of supplying arms to be used against a Friendly Power,' Storrs had explained, choosing this last phrase carefully. 'Abdullah can have expected no other reply, and we parted on the best of terms.'

Storrs's sly point was that by 1914 the Ottomans were no longer a Friendly Power in more than name. Sixty years earlier, the relationship between the two powers had been so different. In 1854 Britain had gone to war with Russia in the Crimea to preserve the integrity of the Ottoman Empire as a buffer against Russian expansion. At that time, although their empire was beginning to fragment, the Ottomans still controlled much of the eastern Mediterranean. Their possessions included their Anatolian heartland and much of the Balkans to the west, and Libya and Egypt to the south. At the eastern end of the sea, Syria – including Palestine – and Iraq were also Ottoman, as were the coastal fringes of Arabia. Greeks, Slavs, Armenians, Kurds, Jews, Circassians and Arabs: all were ruled from Constantinople by a government dominated – from the Sultan downwards – by Turks. Ambitious Arabs in particular felt increasingly aggrieved at their limited opportunites within the Ottoman Empire.

Yet the Ottoman sultan depended increasingly on Arabia. Not only did Islam provide a unifying force within his disparate empire, its leadership – through the Caliphate and control of the Hijaz – gave him an influence among Muslims throughout the world. The British encouraged him, in the belief that the Ottoman Empire was a stabilising influence in an otherwise volatile region, and that their highly publicised friendship with the Sultan might improve relations with their Muslim subjects, particularly the sixty million living in British India, who were wrongly but generally perceived to have been behind the mutiny of 1857.

By the 1870s, however, British relations with the Ottomans had begun to cool. From its opening in 1869 the Suez Canal provided a bypass through the increasingly troubled Ottoman Empire, which defaulted on its loans in 1876. When Russia invaded Ottoman territory in the Balkans two years later, Britain did not intervene as forcefully as before. And the price of British willingness to help the Ottomans through their overwhelming financial problems was high. Britain took over Cyprus in 1878 and annexed Egypt four years later – when Storrs was a year old – after a breakdown in law and order directly threatened the security of the canal, by now a key strategic asset as Britain's economic and military dependence on India continued to grow.

Britain and the Ottoman Empire were growing apart, but most of the British Empire's Muslims still regarded the Sultan as the Caliph and would follow him unquestioningly. 'The Caliph holds the sacred places and the noble relics,' stated one Egyptian in a disturbing letter which one of Storrs's predecessors had carefully filed away. 'Though the Caliph were hapless as Bayazid, cruel as Murad or mad as Ibrahim,* he is the shadow of God, and every Moslem must leap up at his call as the willing servant to his master's work.'12 When Greece clashed with the Ottomans in 1897, British officials in India observed with alarm how, even on the remote North-West Frontier, Muslims backed their co-religionists against the Greeks.

Appreciating how Muslims might destabilise the British Empire, the Germans now also encouraged the Ottomans to stress the Caliphate. 'The Sultan and the three hundred million Muslims who revere him as their leader should know that the German Emperor is their friend forever,' declared the Kaiser on a visit to Damascus in 1898.13 To prove the point, and reveal a questionable sense of taste, he also gave the city an overblown gilt wreath to bolt on to the tomb of Saladin, the Muslim warrior lionised for defeating the Crusaders seven centuries before. Fancy metalwork continued to play an important role in the burgeoning German–Ottoman friendship: Germany supplied the engineering expertise needed by the Sultan to build the Hijaz Railway, its rails, and many of the trains that ran on them.

At the outbreak of the war in August 1914 the Ottomans hesitated before declaring their support for Germany and the Austro-Hungarian Empire to form an alliance ranged against Britain, France, Italy and

---

* Three Ottoman sultans: Bayazid I (1389–1402) had plans to capture Constantinople which were disrupted by the unexpected appearance of Tamerlaine, who enslaved him; Murad IV (1623–40) restored stability to the Ottoman state by killing 20,000 opponents; Ibrahim I (1640–8) was a lunatic.

Russia. Now that the Ottomans were an enemy of Britain, Storrs's earlier proviso to Abdullah immediately lapsed. Faced with the threat of jihad, Storrs turned his devious mind to ways of causing trouble by stoking Arab disaffection towards the Turks. One idea in particular caught his imagination: an ancient tenet – downplayed by the Ottomans because they did not meet it – that the Caliph should come from the Quraysh, the Prophet Muhammad's own tribe, of which Abdullah and his father Sharif Husein were both members.[14]

Fears of a pan-Islamic backlash if Britain were caught meddling with the Caliphate deterred some officials, however,[15] and Storrs was forced to proceed with care: 'I am strongly against any tinkering or jerrymandering with the Caliphate,' he later declared, entirely disingenuously, 'and equally strongly convinced that it must and will turn towards the Sharifate of Mecca, and that we should do our all to help it in that direction and to prevent it from lapsing to any other.'[16] Storrs's idea was taken up at the highest level because his former boss, the British Agent in Egypt, Lord Kitchener, had now been appointed Secretary of State for War in London. Anticipating the Sultan's call for jihad by a few days, at the end of October 1914, Kitchener dispatched an enticing message to Husein via Storrs: 'Till now we have defended and befriended Islam in the person of the Turks: henceforward it shall be in that of the noble Arab. It may be that an Arab of true race will assume the Caliphate at Mecca or Medina, and so good may come by the help of God out of all the evil which is now occurring.'[17] But Husein had responded warily, and for a time the British did not further press the possibility Kitchener had now raised.

The issue rapidly resurfaced early in 1915, after the British government agreed to launch an offensive designed to knock the Ottomans out of the war. The plan was to seize the Ottoman Empire by the throat by a landing in the Dardanelles strait, 150 miles south-west of Constantinople. British forces would fight their way up the Gallipoli peninsula and into the capital, forcing the Ottomans to surrender and opening a new southern front against Austria and Germany in the process. Paying exemplary, if somewhat optimistic, attention to post-war planning, the British decided that once they had deposed the Sultan the obvious successor to the Caliphate would be Sharif Husein. But the plans came to nothing. Premature naval action alerted the Ottomans to British intentions, and with too little preparation, surprise or firepower, the mainly Australian and New Zealander force that landed at Gallipoli on 25 April suffered heavy casualties and was quickly fought to a standstill.

Searching for a way to end the deadlock, the British commander at Gallipoli cast around for ways to undermine the Ottomans. Believing that Arab troops comprised a substantial proportion of the force he faced, he raised the question of reviving contact with Sharif Husein. Kitchener's replacement in Cairo, Sir Henry McMahon – who now held the title High Commissioner as Britain had turned Egypt into a protectorate when war broke out – remembered what happened next: 'I was begged by the Foreign Office to take immediate action and draw the Arabs out of the war.'[18]

At the end of May McMahon contacted Husein, telling him that the British government wanted to communicate secretly with him.[19] Cairo also authorised an aerial drop of a leaflet denouncing the jihad over Jeddah during June. 'Surely every true Mahometan must regard with loathing this cynical employment of his religion as an instrument to be used by a foreign power for the furtherance of its own selfish ambitions,' proclaimed the airborne propaganda, which had clearly been drafted by someone with a rich sense of irony. The 'Arabian peninsula', the leaflet continued, would remain independent: 'We shall not annex one foot of land in it, nor suffer any other Power to do so.'[20] In the meantime, Husein's reservations had faded. Worried about his own security, he was now much keener to conclude a deal with Britain.

Husein had been watching nervously as, immediately east of the Hijaz, a powerful rival emerged. Abdul Aziz Ibn Saud was a young, belligerent chieftain who had forged his reputation in 1902 by seizing the central Arabian town of Riyadh – then a collection of adobe forts, today the soulless skyscraper capital of modern Saudi Arabia. From Riyadh, Ibn Saud began to promote Wahabism, a strongly puritanical form of Islam, across a swathe of central Arabia.

By 1915, Husein was increasingly exercised about the spread of Wahabi ideas.[21] Come November, when Arabia's winter rains began to replenish the seasonal wells and revive the plants which provided widespread grazing, the Harb and Utaybah tribesmen from around Mecca would wander deep into the desert.* There they would come into contact with the Saudis who offered them money, rifles and land if they took up the Wahabi faith espoused by Ibn Saud. In difficult times, the Bedu would naturally gravitate towards the strongest tribal leader and they had wandered increasingly widely in recent years, which had been unusually dry.[22] Amid drought, and the disease and economic turmoil caused by the arrival of the railway in the Hijaz, Husein worried that, to the tribesmen, Ibn Saud looked richer and stronger than he.

As the ruler of Mecca and Muhammad's descendant, Husein was also under growing pressure from the Ottoman government to endorse the call for a jihad that it had first issued on 14 November 1914, days after joining the war on the Germans' side. Aware of Ottoman plans to dispense with him if he refused, to play for time Husein sent his son Feisal to Constantinople to confront the government. Husein also instructed his son to discuss supporting the jihad with Ahmed Jemal Pasha, the new governor of Syria, but not to concede anything. While in Damascus Feisal was approached by members of a secretive Arab cabal in Syria begging Husein to champion the Arab fight for greater recognition within the Ottoman Empire, demands which he passed on to his father in Mecca. Husein was quite willing to adopt the Arab nationalists' modern vocabulary of rights, decentralisation and home rule, if it helped him strengthen his own dynastic struggle in the Hijaz.

Husein also liked the idea of a realm encompassing Syria because it promised the self-sufficiency which the Hijaz had never had. Reliant throughout its history on the outside world – in particular, India – for food and pilgrims, the Hijaz was badly affected by a war in which the British cut off both. Sugar trebled in price; rice and coffee almost disappeared.[23] In India, much of the available shipping was requisitioned for military usage by the authorities who, disturbed by the Sultan's call for holy war, were in any case extremely reluctant to allow pilgrims to go anywhere they might

---

* The Harb and the Utaybah were rival tribes, the Harb being about twice as numerous as the Utaybah. The Harb roamed widely between the Hijaz, Hail, in central northern Arabia, and Riyadh, and were known for being tough, clannish fighters.

pick up subversive ideas. By 1916, the number of pilgrims arriving in the Hijaz from abroad had fallen to less than a quarter of pre-war levels, and the revenue they generated correspondingly fell away.[24] Petrol was still imported to Arabia from abroad and, as it and timber were scarce, Meccans were reduced to selling off their furniture and the ornately carved wooden doors and windows of their houses, for firewood to feed themselves.[25]

A devout man, Husein believed divine anger lay behind the signs of economic decline. 'Islam' itself means 'submission' and many Muslims took a fatalistic view of government, believing that Allah sent bad rulers to punish those who had displeased Him. Before he became Emir, Husein had spent many years living in Constantinople, and felt that the social change he had witnessed there went against the teaching of the Quran. Women working in the post office, for instance, were one example of 'an evil that will greatly injure us if it increases'.[26] The question was, how should he react? Muslim scripture was absolutely clear: to rise against the Sultan-Caliph was to rebel against Allah Himself.[27] But the distinction between the Sultan, and the 'Young Turk' ruling party, which had seized most of the Sultan's powers in 1909, offered Husein a loophole. While remaining loyal to the Sultan, the choice, he later explained, was 'either to please the gang who rule the Ottoman Empire and provoke the anger of God, or to provoke their anger and please God'.[28]

Husein made up his mind on 13 July 1915 when, on the first day of Ramadan, he discovered that Ottoman soldiers in the Hijaz had been excused the obligation of observing the month-long daytime fast.[29] Afterwards he would criticise this violation of one of Islam's five essential acts of faith, but soldiers serving on the frontline are excused the duty of fasting and it may simply have dawned on him that what he had seen revealed the Ottomans' belief that he was their enemy. The following day he wrote to Sir Henry McMahon, aggressively repeating the demands made to him by the Syrians his son Feisal had met. To secure Arab friendship, the British would have to recognise 'the independence of the Arab countries'.[30] According to Husein, these included, in today's terms, the entire Arabian peninsula (except Aden, which was then British), Israel, Jordan, Iraq, Lebanon and Syria, as well as a horizontal sliver of southern Turkey running between the Mediterranean and the Iranian border. Britain would also have to agree to an Arab caliphate, receiving preferential economic treatment in return. In a covering note which more accurately reflected the weakness of his position, Husein's son Abdullah pleaded for the resumption of the annual tributes of grain traditionally sent by the government of Egypt to the Hijaz for the poor of Mecca and Medina.

When he received Husein's letter in August McMahon, a slight, bespectacled and cautious man who had spent much of his life demarcating the wilder frontiers of India, refused to take its demands seriously. Husein's 'pretensions are in every way exaggerated, no doubt considerably beyond his hope of acceptance', he informed the British Foreign Secretary, Sir Edward Grey, 'but it seems very difficult to treat with him in detail without seriously discouraging him'.[31] Worried about either over-committing the British government or disappointing Husein, McMahon decided that the safest option was to procrastinate. He delegated to Storrs the task of drafting a response, telling Husein that it was too early to discuss the future settlement of an area still under Ottoman control.

What McMahon's dilatory answer lacked in encouragement, Storrs tried to make up for with flowery style: 'To the excellent and well-born Sayyid, the descendant of the Sharifs, the Crown of the Proud, Scion of Muhammad's Tree and Branch of the Qurayshite Trunk . . .' the opening of his reply began.[32] Husein, unsurprisingly, skimmed this wordy greeting and, in his answer, accused McMahon of being lukewarm and reluctant to get down to details: 'The fact is,' he added, 'the proposed frontiers and boundaries represent not the suggestions of one individual whose claim might well await the conclusion of the War, but the demands of our people who believe that those frontiers form the minimum necessary to the establishment of the new order for which they are striving.'[33]

Husein's dramatic claim to represent wider Arab demands, which was based only on the approaches Feisal had received, might have sounded exaggerated to the British had not a young Arab deserter from the Ottoman Army arrived in Cairo before his reply reached McMahon. Muhammad al Faruqi was a junior staff officer at Gallipoli who had given himself up to the British. He claimed that nine out of ten Arab officers in the Ottoman Army were members of a powerful and well-funded underground movement capable of action against the Turks at any time. Complete rubbish though this was – there were, it has since been established, never more than ninety Arab activists within the Ottoman Army and they had been widely dispersed by the Ottoman High Command as soon as their disloyalty was suspected – Faruqi's credibility soared when he disclosed that he knew that McMahon was negotiating with Husein.[34] When he described the Arabs as being on the brink of a decision on whether to back the British or the Germans, the British were unnerved. Crucially, they convinced themselves that the very invisibility of the movement which Faruqi had described was proof of its sophistication rather than an indication of its insignificance.

Another developing problem made Faruqi's revelations about a united Arab network even more explosive. Early in September the Foreign Office circulated a secret memorandum which considered for the first time the consequences of a British withdrawal from Gallipoli. The paper warned that if the British abandoned the peninsula, the Ottomans would be free to attack the Suez Canal again. They had already tried to do so – unsuccessfully – that February, but intelligence reports revealed that they had since improved their transport infrastructure in southern Palestine and would now be able to attack in much greater numbers: a figure of 200,000 was later raised. In the meantime, Gallipoli had challenged the conventional wisdom that the Ottoman Empire was close to collapse and the British Empire nigh on invincible. Might the Egyptian population support the Ottomans if they attacked the canal a second time? the paper's author wondered.

Storrs laughed blackly at this fear. He told his servant 'that upon the first attempt of him, or of his colleagues, to cut my throat (or even Cheetham's*), their wages [would] be reduced by half: dismissal to follow upon the second offence'.[35] But he did not deny that an uprising in Cairo was possible and his papers include several examples of inflammatory leaflets urging jihad which had fallen into his hands. The novelist John Buchan, who was working in the Foreign Office in

---

* Milne Cheetham was another British official working in Cairo. He was senior to Storrs.

London at the time, vividly conveyed this tense atmosphere in *Green-mantle*, which he started writing at the end of 1915. In the book Buchan described how, following the Sultan's call for jihad, there was 'a dry wind blowing through the East and the parched grasses wait the spark'.[36]

Greenmantle's fictional Foreign Office mandarin went on to encapsulate Britain's dilemma if the call for jihad precipitated a Muslim revolt: 'The war must be won or lost in Europe. Yes; but if the East blazes up, our effort will be distracted from Europe and the great *coup* may fail. The stakes are no less than victory and defeat.'[37]

There were signs that the parched grasses were already alight in places. Besides the news that spring of massacres of Christian Armenians by Ottoman troops, during the summer of 1915 reports appeared that in the desert west of Cairo the Senussi – a tribe known for its religious fanaticism – were about to begin a disruptive campaign against the British, backed by Ottoman military advisers, guns and money.[38] Even before this began, there were concerns in Cairo that the government in London was not treating the threat of Muslim unrest sufficiently seriously. When the General Staff asked the genial head of intelligence in Egypt, Bertie Clayton, for a note on the information he had gleaned from Faruqi, Clayton recognised he had been given a golden opportunity to make this point. 'I shall take the opportunity of rubbing in the fact that if we definitely refuse to consider the aspirations of the Arabs,' he told his boss Sir Reginald Wingate, 'we are running a grave risk of throwing them into the arms of our enemies which would mean that the jihad which so far has been a failure would probably become a reality.'[39]

This dire warning from the normally unflappable Clayton could not be ignored. His memorandum was wired to Kitchener immediately. 'You must do your best to prevent any alienation of the Arabs' traditional loyalty to England,' Kitchener replied the following day.[40] Then on 18 October McMahon received Husein's reply. Faruqi's story corroborated Husein's claim that he was not simply speaking for himself and McMahon was forced to reconsider his previously dismissive view of the Sharif. He immediately wired the Foreign Office to say that Husein was unhappy with his reply and that he had no choice but to negotiate. McMahon met Faruqi immediately to discuss what terms the Arabs might be willing to accept. 'From further conversation with Faruqi,' McMahon told Grey in another telegram that day: 'it appears evident that Arab party are at parting of the ways and unless we can give them immediate assurance of nature to satisfy them they will throw themselves into the hands of Germany.'[41]

2

WILL THIS DO?

(October 1915–June 1916)

McMahon's stark warning that the Arabs were on the verge of backing the Germans had an immediate effect in London. When the Dardanelles Committee, an unwieldy coalition of British politicians steering the war effort, next met at 10 Downing Street on 20 October, it was forced to decide how McMahon should respond to Husein. Circumstances conspired against a careful consideration of the problem. The Prime Minister, Herbert Asquith, was ill with overwork, and the loyalty of the Arabs was an arcane intrusion into an agenda dominated at that time by an argument over whether conscription should be introduced, which was tearing Asquith's Liberal Party apart. It seems as if it was only during discussion of the matter that day that the Foreign Secretary, Sir Edward Grey, hurriedly drafted instructions for McMahon. Grey too was suffering from the strain of war. His eyesight was failing and since the outbreak of hostilities he had increasingly doubted whether he could make much difference to the war effort. The urgency of McMahon's request offered him the chance to pass the buck.

Today Grey's brief handwritten advice can be found among the papers of the National Archive, at Kew in the London suburbs. 'The important thing is to give our assurances that will prevent Arabs from being alienated, and I must leave you discretion in the matter as it is urgent and there is not time to discuss an exact formula,' Grey proposed telling McMahon. 'The simplest plan would be to give an assurance of Arab independence saying that we will proceed at once to discuss boundaries if they will send representatives for that purpose, but if something more precise than this is required you can give it.' But it is Grey's hastily scribbled pencil message above these words, which he must have added just before he passed the note down the table to his colleague Kitchener, that is most revealing: 'Lord K,' it reads, 'will this do? EG.'[1]

Kitchener evidently thought it would. After the meeting the two politicians had a short and very British discussion. Should they pass the Sharif 'warm' or 'cordial' assurances? Kitchener, who had met Husein's son Abdullah before the war, favoured 'warm'; Grey, who had not, preferred the starchy 'cordial'. Later the same day Grey wired McMahon instructing him to give the Sharif cordial assurances. With that, he delegated McMahon the responsibility for coming to an arrangement with Husein.

Grey's decision was an odd one because McMahon saw himself only as a caretaker for the duration of Kitchener's absence from Cairo. He studiously avoided taking on more responsibility than he had to and relied heavily on his advisers, one of whom described him as, with one exception, 'quite the laziest man I have met'.[2] Other men who knew him were only slightly more charitable. 'He is a nice man and I like him very much, but his ability is of a very ordinary type,' observed another former colleague.[3] Despite these reservations, Grey had now given McMahon what Clayton interpreted as 'a free hand'.[4]

One British official had some advice to offer on the conduct of the negotiations that Grey had now authorised McMahon to open: 'the position must be clearly understood from both the French and the Arab side from the outset, or we shall be heading straight for serious trouble.'[5] But neither did McMahon inform the French of his dealings with the Sharif; nor, quite deliberately, did he ever make clear beyond doubt what he was offering to the Arabs. Having decided, presumably, that Faruqi was the Arabs' representative, McMahon ignored Grey's advice to hold talks. In a letter dated 24 October 1915 he gave Husein a hazy declaration that Britain would recognise the majority of the area he demanded, but which excluded two of its most fertile zones. One was the bridgehead at the northern end of the Persian Gulf, which was already occupied by the Indian Army. The other was a sketchily defined coastal portion of Syria, of which only the inner edge was loosely drawn. This line followed a string of four Syrian towns from Damascus, through Homs and Hama, to Aleppo which Faruqi had insisted were integral to a future Arab state. He also added a further general qualification, the aim of which he then explained to Grey.

'I am not aware of the extent of French claims in Syria, nor of how far His Majesty's Government have agreed to recognise them,' McMahon reminded Grey two days after writing to Husein:

> Hence, while recognising the towns of Damascus, Hama, Homs and Aleppo as being within the circle of Arab countries, I have endeavoured to provide for possible French pretensions for those places by a general modification to the effect that His Majesty's Government can only give assurances in regard to these territories 'in which she can act without detriment to the interests of her ally France'.[6]

This final phrase was a carefully crafted ambiguity, with which McMahon and Storrs were clearly delighted. Although from the Arab point of view, it could be read as a confirmation that Britain was free to commit Syria to the Arabs, in reality the phrase made McMahon's offer provisional on the resolution of France's expansive but as yet undefined territorial ambitions in the Levant. Of the scope of these, McMahon preferred to remain ignorant so that he could preserve his ability to make an offer to Husein which, as he implied to Grey, he never expected the British would have to honour in full.[7]

McMahon's assumption that he could afford to be vague, based on his belief that his work was a temporary expedient rather than a long-term commitment, was widely shared. 'After all, what harm can our acceptance of his [Husein's] proposals do?' asked Sir Reginald Wingate, a pocket-sized Machiavelli who was Governor-General of Sudan and Sirdar, or commander, of the Egyptian Army. 'If the embryonic Arab State comes to nothing, all our promises vanish and we are absolved from them – if the Arab State becomes a reality, we have quite sufficient safeguards to control it . . . In other words the cards seem to be in our hands and we have only to play them carefully.'[8]

Husein was more immediately preoccupied by the threats posed by his neighbour Ibn Saud and by an imminent Ottoman crackdown on his powers than the exact extent of a future Arab state in Syria, and because of this he made an unsuitable spokesman for the Syrian Arabs. Softened by the gift of £20,000 that McMahon dispatched with a further letter in December, at the beginning of 1916 Husein told McMahon that, though he still did not accept the British exclusion of the Syrian coast, he did not want to strain the Anglo-French alliance and that the dispute could be resolved after the war. 'Great Britain may rest assured, that we shall adhere to our resolve . . . which was made known to Storrs – that able and accomplished man – two years ago,' declared the Sharif, in a hint at his violent plans: 'We are only waiting for an opportunity in consonance with our situation.'[9]

Ottoman pressure on Husein was growing all the time. That February, 1916, both Jemal, the Governor of Syria, and Enver, the Ottoman Minister for War and architect of the policy of holy war, took the train south to Medina to press Husein to deliver the troops he had promised for the jihad. Just as the British feared, the Ottomans had plans for a second attack on the Suez Canal, in which it was hoped that an Arab force would play an important role in destabilising the Arab population in Cairo. 'My greatest desire,' Jemal later recalled of this time, 'was to do anything and everything to prevent the revolutionary tendencies displayed by Sharif Husein from developing and to persuade him to send an auxiliary force to Palestine under the command of one of his sons.'[10] Enver also had plans to drive the jihad into eastern Africa, where an uprising among the Muslims in the Horn of Africa might assist the German forces fighting the British for control of East Africa. Their joint mission smacked of desperation, but Husein saw it as a threat. Alarmed by Enver's proposal, believing – possibly wrongly – that the real reason for sending troops was to overthrow him, on 18 February Husein appealed to McMahon for food, £50,000 in gold, weapons and ammunition. In return, he promised that his son Feisal could raise a revolt of 'not less than 100,000 people' in Syria.[11]

For Clayton, Husein's list of requests was a crucial turning point. 'The Sharif has definitely decided that his interests lie with the Allies and not with the Turks,' he wrote at the beginning of March, before adding a telling indication of the limited importance he attached to McMahon's correspondence: 'Whatever may be the outcome of the negotiations, it seems they have at least had the effect of preventing him from throwing in his lot on the side of our enemies.'[12] A fortnight later Husein wrote again, raising his estimate of his supporters in Syria to 250,000. He suggested that the British might land on the Syrian coast to assist them and to cut the railway to ease the pressure the Ottomans could exert on him. It was now that he asked the British to blockade the Hijaz coast, hoping that he could blame their action on the Ottomans' presence in the region, and bully the merchants of Jeddah – who were firmly pro-Ottoman – into supporting him. After further promises from Husein that a revolt was imminent, on 1 May the British secretly shipped 5,000 Japanese rifles and over two million rounds of ammunition to the Hijaz, expecting the revolt to begin later in the month. They also began smuggling large quantities of gold ashore. But there was no news of an uprising from Husein.

Although he was unaware of the large-scale smuggling operation which had begun to the Hijaz, Jemal had other evidence of Arab separatist activity on which he now decided to act. From letters left behind by the French consul, François Georges-Picot, who had hurriedly left Beirut at the outbreak of the war, he had known for eighteen months that some Arab nationalists had asked for French assistance to help them liberate Syria. 'Judging by these documents,' he later explained, 'there was not the slightest doubt that the Arab revolutionaries were working under French protection.'[13] He began to order the arrest of those implicated by the letters shortly afterwards but he was reluctant to prosecute them. Many of the authors were well known and he feared that to pursue them would 'endanger the success of the Islam unity movement' which was the basis for jihad.[14] Perhaps that was why, when Jemal eventually authorised prosecutions, one of the Christians behind the plot was initially singled out. In the spring of 1916, Joseph Hani, a Christian Arab who had written a number of the letters to Picot, was convicted of treason and hanged in Beirut.

A secretive man, Jemal gave no explicit reason for the timing of his change of mind, but it seems likely that he was frustrated that the jihad

had failed to succeed because his patience with Husein was also wearing thin. Shortly afterwards, he pressed Husein again for the dispatch of the 'Mujahideen' regiment which Feisal – still in Damascus – had promised, and which was supposed to be mustering at Medina. Then in May he ordered the trial of a larger group of well-known and mostly Muslim Arabs.

Husein then overreached himself. With the new trial in progress he wired Enver with demands he wanted satisfied before he would support a holy war with troops. Husein's message, Jemal recalled after the war, 'ran more or less as follows. If you want me to remain quiet, you must recognise my independence in the whole of the Hijaz – from Tabuk to Mecca – and create me hereditary prince there. You must also drop the prosecution of the guilty Arabs and proclaim a general amnesty for Syria and Iraq.'[15]

Summoning Feisal to see him, Jemal showed him Enver's reply. 'You will not see your son Feisal again unless you send the volunteers to the front as you promised,' Enver had apparently threatened Husein.[16] 'Feisal feverishly read the telegram and turned pale,' recalled Jemal, who then reminded Feisal that his father was in a weak position in which it was best 'to avoid doing or saying anything' which might help his enemies in Constantinople, many of them relatives, to undermine him.[17] He could not pardon the 'traitors', Jemal then replied to Husein, adding that to ask for a hereditary title just at that moment 'does not seem to me to be well chosen'. Early in the morning of 6 May twenty-one Arabs, convicted of association with the nationalist movements, were hanged in public. They were not typical freedom fighters. By nine in the morning several local politicians, a newspaper proprietor, a magistrate, a barrister and others dangled from gallows erected overnight in the main squares of Beirut and Damascus. The hangings convinced Husein that he could not delay action any longer. Suspecting his son was also now in danger, he recalled Feisal from Damascus.

Feisal gave Jemal the flimsy excuse that he was needed in Medina to meet the Arab force being collected for the attack on Suez, and left Damascus in a hurry. It was only now that Jemal sensed trouble. 'It never struck me as possible that a man of Sharif Husein's experience, a greybeard, with one foot in the grave, could be so egotistical and ambitious,' he claimed after the war.[18] At his orders the Turkish authorities in Mecca now made local grandees swear an oath of allegiance and handed out money to various sheikhs – supposedly as gifts to the poor – in a thinly veiled effort to buy tribal loyalties. Just as Husein had wanted, news of the British blockade of Jeddah, which began on 15 May, provoked uproar and in Mecca the skeleton garrison's commander, Mehmed Zia, was ordered to reinforce Jeddah. 'Seeing a feeling of extreme dissatisfaction towards the troops,' Zia later recalled, he also moved soldiers into the Jiyad fort in Mecca after sunset on the same day.[19]

Early the following morning, Zia's telephone in the town hall rang; it was Sharif Husein. Why, Husein had asked, had sentries been posted around the city and the shops in the city's bazaar been forced to close? Ghalib Pasha, the Governor of the Hijaz, who was up the road in Taif, initially replied that the move was a precautionary measure designed to preserve food stocks. But he then backed down later the same day. The volte-face only encouraged local ill-feeling, and predicting the inevitable, Zia began to stockpile food for his men.

With no news that the situation in the Hijaz was returning to normal, on 22 May Jemal ordered Fakhreddin Pasha, the commander of the Ottoman Army's Twelfth Corps, to move to Medina. A zealous, intimidating man, Fakhri, as he was known to the British, had infamously been involved in the organisation of the massacres of Armenians in southern Anatolia the year before. He was proud to have been given responsibility for the holy city and he promised he would report on the situation once he arrived. Disturbed by the atmosphere he found there on arrival, on 2 June he called Jemal to pass on his impressions.

'I had an unmistakable foreboding that I was about to get bad news,' Jemal remembered after the war.[20]

'It seems to me certain that the railway will be attacked tonight or tomorrow morning at the latest,' Fakhri told Jemal. 'Please don't leave us without reinforcements!'[21]

Reacting to the news that Fakhri and his men were on their way to Medina, Husein had sent a staccato message asking the British for more money, which arrived in Cairo on 23 May. At Suez, on a Sunday evening five days later Ronald Storrs quietly boarded a ship which would take him to the Hijaz. His luggage was unusual: two strong wooden boxes, each containing £5,000 in gold, two cartons of cigarettes for Abdullah and Feisal and a sack of specially printed newspapers, entitled *Haqiqat*, or *Truth*: optimistically perhaps, given that they were written and edited by British Intelligence.

At an agreed rendezvous, a desolate beach several miles south of Jeddah, early in the morning of 6 June Storrs was carried ashore on the shoulders of some Arab slaves, his white suit trousers splashing in the Red Sea surf. In a dark tent on the shoreline he met Zeid, Husein's youngest son, and his cousin, Shakir. Zeid was about twenty, Storrs guessed, with flaccid features and 'evidently attempting to encourage the growth of a somewhat back-ward beard . . . obviously the Benjamin of the family', he reported, unimpressed.[22] Storrs skimmed the list of requests with which Zeid had presented him: among them, a demand for £70,000 stood out.

Storrs explained that he could pay no money until he knew that the revolt had begun.

'I am then happy to be able to announce to you that it began yesterday at Medina,' Zeid replied, slightly too quickly.[23]

Reluctant to spend more time than he had to in enemy territory, Storrs took Zeid at his word, gave him the two boxes of coins and, in a moment of cavalier generosity, removed his gold watch and fastened it to Zeid's wrist. Then he invited Zeid and Shakir back aboard ship. While the two Arabs were shown 'the wireless, which appeared to fascinate them, the guns, the Captain's bathroom and other wonders of the deep', Storrs went below to compose a telegram.[24]

> Satisfactory meeting with Zeid and his cousin this morning. Rising began yesterday Monday at Medina but as all communications in Hijaz are cut no news. Other towns to rise on Saturday. Arabs hope to induce 800 Turks at Jeddah, 1,000 at Mecca, and 1,200 at Taif to surrender; otherwise they will kill them . . . Please dispatch immediately 50,000 pounds now definitely promised but not payable until revolt satisfactorily ascertained to have begun.[25]

But the rising which had begun the day before was not going to plan. Fakhri had been ready when the Arabs' attack on Medina finally came on 5 June. There was not much support within the walls for Husein or his family in a city which, due to the new railway, was as close to Damascus as it was to Mecca. And, unlike Mecca, the old city of Medina was walled, more self-reliant for food, and well defended by thousands of troops who were supported by artillery and machine guns in concrete, ziggurat-like forts dotted around the plain surrounding the city. Against these, the camel-mounted tribesmen led by Ali, Husein's eldest son, had an array of antique flintlocks and rifles, often with twisted barrels or held together with wire. Moreover, the elderly Japanese rifles the British had supplied in May belatedly revealed a disconcerting tendency to burst on firing.[26] Some of the ammunition turned out to be the wrong calibre.

To the north of Medina, Feisal tried to attack the railway connecting the Hijaz with the north but, with no explosives to hand, all his tribesmen could do was tear up the track or pile rocks on the rails.[27] Since the Ottoman government still hoped to extend the railway further southwards, there was a large hoard of rails and sleepers in Medina. Using these where necessary, engineers in an armoured train quickly repaired the damage, so that specialist reinforcements could be dispatched to the city.[28] Ali and Feisal rapidly withdrew to a safe distance from the city. They had no money. To lend the opposite impression, Feisal later admitted, he had filled a chest with stones, and had it locked and guarded constantly.[29]

In Taif, above Mecca, the uprising also stalled. By the time Husein's son Abdullah arrived there on 9 June, the town was buzzing with rumours that violence was imminent and many people had packed their belongings and were hurrying away. The Turks were fortifying the town, digging trenches outside the walls. Against advice Abdullah went to see Ghalib Pasha, the Governor of the Hijaz, in his office, leaving two friends outside the door. 'If there was any trouble I was to shoot the *vali* in the room, and they were to dispatch anyone who tried to interfere outside,' he wrote in his memoirs.[30] He tried to convince Ghalib that he was on a tribal raid beyond the town but the *vali* did not believe him, turning grey and mumbling that he wished he had stayed in Mecca. Abdullah's attack shortly after midnight failed to capture the town, but it did succeed in stopping the Turkish forces in Taif from going down to Mecca to help their colleagues. As darkness fell the following day, Abdullah recalled, 'We lit bonfires on the hills and kept up a continuous shouting and beating of drums to make the enemy believe that the tribes were gathering in great numbers.'[31]

The same day two British ships, the *Fox* and the *Hardinge*, arrived off Jeddah, having been alerted by Storrs's telegram to Cairo. Neither represented the cream of the Royal Navy: according to her short and energetic commander, 'Ginger' Boyle, the *Fox* was 'almost the slowest and oldest ship commanded by a Captain in the Navy' while the *Hardinge* had been loaned from the Royal Indian Marine.[32] As planned, at nine o'clock that night both ships turned on their searchlights and began to shell the Turkish positions outside the town, which a force of about 4,000 Harb tribesmen then attacked early the next day. 'We were horrified at the Arab method of attack – they were simply advancing in a mass, quite openly some of them firing their rifles in the air,' a British sailor recalled. 'The Turks simply waited and then poured a withering fire into their ranks.'[33] Trying to help the Arabs regain the initiative, the British became unwittingly embroiled in the port's highly factional politics when Boyle invited a local tribal leader aboard the *Fox* to point out possible targets inside the town that he could shell. Boyle became suspicious when the man identified some unlikely-looking buildings. 'Months after I heard that my picturesque sheikh was in reality a merchant of the town,' he later wrote, surmising that the man 'had taken advantage of this opportunity to rid himself of trade rivals'.[34]

Fifty miles east, in Mecca, the Ottoman troops in the Jiyad fortress above Mecca began to bombard the Kaaba, the sacred stone cube at the centre of the Holy Mosque. The first shell left a foot-long gash in the building, while the explosion of a second set fire to the Kiswa, the Kaaba's black covering embroidered with extracts from the Quran.[35] Several worshippers in the central open area of the mosque were killed by flying shrapnel.

In Constantinople, the Ottoman government quickly established that what had happened was not one of the disturbances that punctuated

Hijazi life, but a full-scale uprising. On a pine-clad estate just outside the city, a seven-year-old girl named Musbah Haidar was agonising over her French verbs. It was a hot morning and, distracted by the tempting cries of a street vendor outside, she had been daydreaming about a cold ice cream when suddenly her father Ali appeared. Sharif Ali Haidar came from the rival Zaid branch of Muhammad's descendants: he was the obvious replacement for Husein. The Grand Vizier, he explained to his daughter, had just asked him to become the new emir of Mecca, and he had accepted.[36] On 16 June Haidar was driven through the streets of the Ottoman capital in an open landau drawn by four horses which only the Sultan ever used. Dressed in the tasselled white turban of a Zaid sharif and a long black robe adorned with golden, twirling leaves, he sat beneath a green banner embroidered in Arabic *Allahu Akbar* – God is Great. A plumper, glitzier version of Husein, Haidar left Constantinople for Medina three days later. On 21 June, further reinforcements followed him.

Kitchener did not live to hear the news that the revolt had broken out. On 5 June, the same day that the uprising began in Medina, the ship on which he was sailing to Russia sank off Orkney, north of Scotland, taking the hero of Khartoum with her. His body was never found. Kitchener's abrupt death deprived the Arabs of their greatest advocate in London, and without his influence other, more sceptical politicians began to question why Britain should be embroiled in the revolt at all.

Husein's uprising, so long in the planning, had started to go badly wrong.

3

A STRANGE UNCANNY PLACE

(June–September 1916)

News of British involvement in the uprising was badly received in India. From his summer office overlooking the emerald lawns of Simla the Viceroy, Lord Chelmsford, dispatched an angry telegram to London on 13 June. He used one of the ruder phrases the strangled intercourse of British diplomacy would permit. 'We are greatly disturbed by report of British naval activity off Jeddah,' he complained, asking for the news to be carefully suppressed in light of the impact it might have on Muslim opinion. 'It appears very difficult to reconcile action taken with the pledge formally given,' he observed, referring to the promise not to violate the Hijaz that Britain had made when war broke out. He was, he added, opposed to any further action that would break the spirit of this commitment.[1]

In Cairo, British officials took the opposite view. They wanted news of the revolt spread widely because they believed they could blunt the jihad by manufacturing a split between the Sultan and Sharif Husein. Only if that divide were public would Muslims ask themselves whether, if Husein, scion of the Prophet and ruler of Mecca, rejected the Sultan's call, the jihad could possibly be justified.

Cairo won. Briefed by one of McMahon's advisers in Egypt, on 21 June Reuters reported that an uprising had begun in the Hijaz. 'Startling' news of the 'Great Arab Revolt', as the British depicted Husein's local uprising, was reported in *The Times* the following day. Faced with the now impossible task of stopping the news from seeping into the subcontinent, on 23 June the Government of India was forced to confirm that a rebellion in Mecca had broken out.

Muslims in India reacted vociferously. On the North-West Frontier, the governor reported how Husein was being publicly cursed in the mosques for bringing violence on the Hijaz by revolting.[2] On 27 June in Lucknow, the All-India Muslim League met and condemned the Sharif's action with a vitriolic resolution, the strength of which took Lord Chelmsford aback.[3] More disturbingly still, the Bombay Muslim League suggested that Husein's actions had given real cause for jihad.

The Muslim press called on the British not to intervene. On 30 June the Lahore newspaper, *Kisan*, said: 'In these circumstances, the utmost that we can expect from our Government is that it will avoid making any interference in the matter and will take no step to encourage the Sharif of Mecca.'[4] Later the same day in Jeddah the British landed explosives, 3,000 more rifles, six machine guns, 1.2 million rounds of ammunition, almost 600 tons of food and a first batch of mountain guns. With these McMahon sent Egyptian gunners. 'Care of course would be taken not to send anyone with religious scruples,' he reassured the Foreign Office.[5]

The arrival of large quantities of supplies belied the fact that the organisation of the revolt was in chaos. 'The last two weeks we have lived in the middle of a storm of telegrams and conferences and excursions,' one British officer in Cairo wrote at the beginning of July.[6] Wingate, in Khartoum, was not impressed. Fed up with being 'bombarded with telegrams from all parts, none of which quite tally with each other', he dispatched one of his officials, Colonel Cyril Wilson, to establish exactly what was going on.[7] The delivery of the food and weapons gave Wilson an excuse to go ashore in Jeddah. Framed by mauve hills behind, from a distance in the fierce sunlight the port looked as if it was carved from ivory, though its minarets, one of which tilted precariously, broadcast the town's decay to seaborne visitors. Built on commerce, unlike Mecca or Medina, Jeddah was clustered around its central market, but under the saggy awnings in the bazaar there was almost nothing to buy. 'Everyone stares at you fixedly and silently,' noted another visitor, who described Jeddah as a 'strange uncanny place which breathes danger and death'.[8]

Unusually for modern Saudi Arabia, the old quarter of Jeddah today retains a flavour of the architecture and a strong sense of the dilapidated feel which Wilson must have experienced ninety years ago. The tall houses list unsteadily: dead coral, though abundant, has never been an ideal building material, and overbearing redwood balconies, intricate fretwork and ornately carved doors and shutters add to the claustrophobic air. Old men in white robes and red *keffiyehs* lounge on chairs on the streetside and – a constant reminder of the slave trade which thrived across the Red Sea until recently – black African faces mingle with Arab. Scrawny cats root among the dustbins and everywhere there is the fruity smell of sewage. Choice in the characterless central bazaar has hardly improved, though alongside endless ranks of leather sandals and women's outer clothing – have any colour *abaya* you like, so long as it's black – there was one stall at which you could buy gnarled sprigs of a woody plant used, so its owner explained, to induce childbirth.

Wilson walked through the narrow, eerily silent streets, where dust danced in the shards of sunlight penetrating between the tall houses, until he arrived at the British consulate. A short man, dressed in khaki and wearing his pith helmet, he pushed open the door, seemingly the first person to enter the consulate since it had been hurriedly abandoned at the onset of the war. Save for a few old chairs and some cupboards it was empty, and it needed a lick of paint.

Bluntly, Wilson described what he had found in the town. The Sharif seemed to have started his revolt 'without sufficient preparation and somewhat prematurely', he decided.[9] Nor did 'intrigue among his own people, which appears to be rampant . . . make matters easier for him'. There were at least two factions in Jeddah: the Harb tribesmen who had captured the town, led by the wiry Sharif Mohsen, a former smuggler with a penchant for torture, and the merchants, represented by Mohammed Nessif, a portly trader who wore gold-rimmed spectacles. Nessif lived in the centre of Jeddah in a palatial house topped with plaster crenellations, which it is possible to look around today. In the privacy of one of the darkened, grand upstairs rooms, furnished with Persian carpets and divans, Nessif confided to the British that he dreaded being ruled by Husein because 'the Sharifs in the country were all corrupt and unreliable'.[10]

Wilson decided that Faruqi, who had been dropped in Jeddah by the British at the first opportunity, was at the root of the problems. The young Arab was reportedly stirring up anti-British sentiment and his attempts to protect his role as go-between vis-à-vis the Sharif and the High Commissioner irritated Wilson who urged change. 'Unless there is some permanent British representative at Jeddah the present confusion of the continual requests for supplies . . . will continue,' he warned, inadvertently recommending himself for the job.[11]

The last pocket of Turkish resistance in Mecca was subdued by the Egyptian gunners on 10 July. With the Turks removed from the holy city, the Pilgrimage, lifeline of the Hijaz, could now be resumed. The same day, the War Committee approved paying Husein £125,000 a month for the next four months to help him meet its costs. At the end of July, it was in the guise of 'Pilgrimage Officer', a title calculated by Storrs to be colourless enough not to invite similar diplomatic representatives from France or Italy, that Wilson returned to Jeddah to stay. Over the British consulate, a tatty Union Jack billowed languorously once again. The Pilgrimage was now just eight weeks away, and from Cairo Storrs, who considered himself lucky to have been passed over for Wilson's job, couched the need to make it a success in box-office terms. He wanted Husein's 'first independent season to open as brilliantly as possible; any row, scandal, or epidemic, would react swiftly and discreditably upon the management, and discourage or even annihilate subsequent bookings'.[12]

Wilson had longer-term ideas. 'The British Government has the whip hand over the Sharif as he probably could not exist without money or supplies,' he argued, in decidedly undiplomatic terms. It was time 'to make a start in introducing British influence on the lines – presumably already roughly decided on – along which British relations with the Sharif's Government will run in future after the war'.[13]

As these opinions suggested, Wilson was a strange choice for what was essentially a demanding diplomatic role. A professional soldier turned provincial governor in Sudan, he did not speak much Arabic and, though only in his early forties, had been worn down by years of intermittent dysentery. 'I've never forgotten that illness Cyril had at Erkowit,' his forceful wife Beryl fretted.[14] But when three years earlier he had been told to retire to Britain Wilson had stubbornly refused.[15] Possibly Wingate, no genius himself, picked a man whom he knew would not outshine him. Perhaps Wilson, who had never escaped the cool shadow of his father, Sir Charles, who had retired a major-general, jumped gratefully at an opportunity to advance himself. In the words of a colleague, he 'looked tired, like a man grappling ceaselessly with insoluble problems . . . he had a thankless task, which was performed with unfailing good humour'.[16]

Within days of Wilson's arrival, on the evening of 1 August the Ottoman government's new choice of Emir, Ali Haidar, stepped off the train in Medina. Led from the station through crowds of onlookers, Ali Haidar's first destination was the Mosque of the Holy Tomb, Muhammad's place of burial, where he stopped to pray. Behind him a caravan followed bringing the tents and carpets needed by a tribal leader as well as the water filters and medicines required to pre-empt and ease the inevitable internal consequences of living in the East. He had also, strangely, been given a number of furs by the Sultan, who had evidently never visited the Hijaz in summer. As yet unknown to Wilson, Ali Haidar's arrival would dramatically change the situation in the Hijaz, reinvigorating Turkish attempts to break out of Medina and recapture Mecca before the Pilgrimage at the beginning of October.

Two days after Ali Haidar's arrival, Fakhri launched a counterattack against Sharif Husein's forces on the road south towards Mecca. The running battle that followed lasted over twenty-four hours. Coincidentally, the following day in the Sinai desert a Turkish force of about 18,000 – double the number the British anticipated – clashed with British forces only twenty-five miles east of the Suez Canal. The British defeated the Turkish force, but at a cost of over 1,100 men killed and wounded. Worried about the febrile atmosphere Ottoman agents had worked up inside Egypt, the general in charge of the defence of the canal, Sir Archibald Murray, ordered the Ottoman prisoners of war to be marched through the streets of Cairo to try to stop the spread of rumours of an imminent Ottoman invasion.[17]

In Cairo, the British hastily concocted a plan to relieve the pressure on the Sharif. Pre-war reconnaissance of the Hijaz Railway by Antonin Jaussen, a jovial roly-poly French priest with an interest in ancient

hieroglyphs and amateur espionage, had revealed two weak points along
the line. The better of the two – it was more accessible – was the
escarpment at Batn al Ghul, sixty miles east of the port of Aqaba at the
foot of modern Jordan.

Intrigued by Jaussen's observation that 'it would be relatively easy to
cause serious damage to this descent',[18] in September 2004, I left my car
beside the modern road which runs parallel to the railway towards the
Saudi border, and climbed for ten minutes up a flint-strewn hillside to a
vantage point above the railway line. Below me in a hollow, only the
foundations of Batn al Ghul station remained. But the curving line of the
railway remains clearly visible until it enters a narrow cutting and snakes
off the steppe of southern Syria down into the black and sharp yellow
sands of Arabia in the distance.

There is no doubt that the railway was vulnerable at this point. But the
only way to reach Batn al Ghul was from Aqaba, across territory roamed
by the Huwaytat and the Bani Atiyah, two tribes well known for their
treachery and violence.[19]

Sir Archibald Murray was initially ambivalent about a raid from
Aqaba. But he was pressured into investigating the possibility further by
the War Committee in London, which had been lobbied by Bertie
Clayton, then on a short visit to the capital.[20] After summoning up some
enthusiasm for the scheme, Murray ordered a naval reconnaissance of
Aqaba. As he admitted, he was 'surprisingly short of topographical
information' about the area.[21] Closer inspection revealed that the port –
then a run-down fort and a few houses among a shoreline palm grove –
was better defended than expected. 'Bullets were whizzing over the
bridge like angry bees,' recalled one man aboard a British ship sent on the
mission.[22]

Murray remained ambivalent. And Murray's boss, the Chief of Imperial General Staff, Sir William Robertson, was vehemently opposed to a
landing at Aqaba, seeing it as a diversion from more important fronts.
'My sole object is to win the war,' he later stated, 'and we shall not do that
in the Hijaz nor in the Sudan.'[23] Preferring to leave the Foreign Office
with a problem of their own creation, Robertson had already advised
Murray against taking control of British support for the revolt. When he

sensed growing pressure on Murray to mount an expedition, he wrote again in August, directing Murray to 'give the Turks a good hiding in the Sinai Peninsula'[24] and warning him that, 'We cannot go to Aqaba merely for the sake of helping the Sharif. We must be sure that the operations will give us some definite advantage over the Turk, with special reference to the defence of Egypt . . . One never knows where these little expeditions may not lead us.'[25]

At the same time Robertson wrote to Wingate – whom he suspected to be behind the drive to commit troops to the Hijaz – to reject his offer to move the centre of operations supporting the revolt to his own fief in Khartoum. In his letter, he took the opportunity to remind Wingate that in Europe a different scale of warfare was under way: 8.5 million rounds of ammunition had been fired by artillery since the beginning of the Somme offensive a little more than a month earlier, Robertson explained, adding for good measure the range of calibres of the field guns used.[26] It cannot have escaped Wingate's notice that the heaviest field guns he had available were about the smallest in use on the Somme.

In Medina, Ali Haidar deftly exploited the political problems of Britain's support for Husein. On 9 August he issued a proclamation in which he accused Husein of naïvety for accepting British help and of 'trying to place the House of God, the Qibla* of Islam, and the tomb of the Prophet, under the protection of a Christian Government'.[27]

Haidar left the British with a difficult choice. To send troops would play into his hands; not to, risked the collapse of the revolt since Wilson did not think that the Arabs alone could resist the Ottoman forces. The potential after-effects of either option were also fiercely debated. From India, one provincial governor warned the British government that 'a flame of fire [would] undoubtedly be lit in India' if any British soldier set foot in the Hijaz.[28] To Wingate, who was worried about the loyalty of the Sudanese, the danger of doing nothing was just as great. 'You know just as well as I do,' he warned Clayton, 'that the collapse of the Sharif's movement will be a far more serious blow to British prestige in the

---

* Qibla: the direction of prayer for all Muslims – towards Mecca.

Islamic world than our failure in the Dardanelles or the surrender at Kut'
– a reference to the Mesopotamian town where, earlier that year, part of
the Indian Army had been forced to surrender after being encircled by the
Ottomans.[29] In a crisis, Wingate expected the Sharif to allow British
troops to land: 'Religious prejudices, nationalistic considerations and
personal feelings go to the winds when the individual concerned is faced
at close quarters with the alternatives of success or defeat,' he believed.[30]

Wilson decided to sound out Husein's son Feisal on whether or not
British troops would be welcomed, but Husein refused to let him travel
up the coast to meet his son. Husein, indeed, was being generally
difficult. He would not allow explosives to be offloaded, probably – the
British speculated – because he feared an international backlash for
ordering the destruction of the Hijaz Railway, for which so many
Muslims had raised money a few years before. And he maintained an
obsessive interest in Wilson's activities. One hot, humid afternoon at the
quayside, Wilson found himself having to help assemble harnesses for the
animals towing the artillery which had begun to arrive. 'None of us had
ever seen a gun team harnessed,' he admitted, before gamely describing
how it had taken three and a half hours to attach a team of mules to one
gun.[31] Throughout the process, the telephone had rung at half-hourly
intervals. It was Husein in Mecca, demanding a regular update on
progress.[32] Only when the harness was complete did Wilson establish
that the guns were too heavy to cope with the mountain track to Taif or
the sandy coastal path to Yanbu, 180 miles to the north; they were
useless.

Eventually Sharif Husein relented and allowed Wilson to go to Yanbu,
the dilapidated little port where Feisal was based at the time. The
decision was a relief for Wilson, who was finding the pace of work in
Jeddah a strain. 'I'm thankful to be going on this trip,' he wrote to
Wingate, before adding that he blanched at the attire which Husein
insisted he wear while out of town. 'The Sharif is sending me down a silk
scarf and the Bedouin rope thing which I will wear over my helmet,' he
reluctantly conceded. But 'I absolutely refuse to disguise myself as an
Arab,' he declared: 'if I'm scuppered I propose to be scuppered in my own
uniform.'[33]

Wilson arrived off Yanbu on 27 August. He was the first British officer to meet Feisal. It must have been an odd contrast: the short, trenchant Wilson, borrowed *keffiyeh* draped over his helmet, giving him the appearance of wearing an enormous red bonnet, beside the finely robed Feisal, a tall thin man in his early thirties whose long face, and the curved Arab dagger belted to his waist, gave him a medieval appearance. Wilson immediately liked Feisal.

Feisal explained to Wilson how he had left his tribesmen about forty miles east of Yanbu at Bir Abbas, a well in the last pass through the mountains separating Medina from the coast, through which the Turks were most likely to come. Hinting that he was rapidly losing face, he told Wilson that he would not return to his men until he could promise them men, money and explosives to help them destroy the railway.

Feisal should blame his father for the shortage of dynamite, Wilson frankly replied: '60 odd boxes of bombs had been on board a warship for weeks,' he explained. 'Feisal,' Wilson observed, 'went as near cursing his saintly father as I suppose a son of a Grand Sharif could.'[34]

'My father tries to do everything but is not a soldier,' Feisal commented, with a sigh.

'Having had a month's experience of the old gentleman,' Wilson wrote afterwards, 'I was able to agree cordially.'

In Cairo, McMahon read Wilson's telegraphed report on his meeting with Feisal with a surging sense of despair. He had been led to understand that Feisal was a natural leader, but Wilson's portrayal of their conversation suggested a man who could not 'stand the racket', he believed.[35] Though Wilson reported that Feisal had asked for 300 men, McMahon raised this figure to 1,000. However, finding such a large number of Muslim troops would not be easy. Wingate – in his role as Sirdar of the Egyptian Army – immediately volunteered his own Sudanese troops, provided these were replaced by regular British soldiers. But London saw through this self-serving offer and instantly rejected it.

The only other Muslim troops were either serving in East Africa or were Indians whose deployment in the Hijaz the Government of India would presumably veto. That left the Arab prisoners of war captured by the British in Mesopotamia. After a trawl through the prison camps in

India, about 700 Arab former Ottoman soldiers were sent to the Hijaz in mid-July under Nuri Said, a young, elfin Iraqi officer who had defected to the Allies at the start of the war. They were 'a scummy lot', said Wingate,[36] disappointed by the fact that many of these former prisoners arrived in the Hijaz under the impression that they were being resettled, and proved unwilling to take up arms against the Ottomans.[37] Besides the brave few who did offer their services – risking their and their families' lives if they were captured – there were also some volunteers from Mecca. As Wilson admitted towards the end of August, 'the whole business of giving the Sharif military assistance bristles with difficulties; he has started, in a military sense, practically from bedrock'.[38]

There was little time to train what recruits to Husein's cause there were. On 10 September Cairo received a report that Turkish forces in Medina were building up, and that a mahmal* had arrived in the city, suggesting that the Turks hoped to recapture Mecca in time for the Pilgrimage at the beginning of October. 'I reckon that this will be all over by the middle of October,' wrote Bertie Clayton the same day, though what he thought the final outcome might be he left unsaid.[39] Two days later, McMahon convened a conference in Egypt to review the escalating crisis. There, Wilson – who had made the journey up from Jeddah specially – met McMahon and Murray for the first time. Admiral Wemyss, commander of the Red Sea fleet, Clayton and Storrs were also present.

As unusually frank minutes of what was said at this meeting survive, it is possible to eavesdrop on the row that followed. 'Something drastic' was needed, McMahon suggested, 'to ensure that the Arabs keep their tails up through this critical period, which is not likely to, and cannot, last very long'.[40] Wilson opened the discussion by describing the deteriorating situation in the Hijaz. 'What Feisal and the Arabs are very keen on,' he explained, 'is to see some regular troops.' He went on to suggest a figure of between two and three thousand.

When he heard Wilson's estimate, Murray – usually a reserved and thoughtful man – exploded. He had just received another demand for

---

* A richly embroidered ceremonial litter used to transport the new Kiswa, the black cloth covering the Kaaba, which was replaced each year during the Pilgrimage.

nearly 3,000 troops to serve on the Balkan front and this additional request was the final straw. Accusing Wilson of being 'completely out of touch', Murray reminded the others present that his orders were to reduce the number of British troops in Egypt. Then he moved briskly on to other requests from the Hijaz he had recently received. 'Take the telegram asking for two aeroplanes,' he snapped at Wilson: 'You talk as if two aeroplanes were two swallows, as if they could simply drop down there and do anything else you require.'

When Murray had finally finished, McMahon began to speak. 'It was the most unfortunate date in my life when I was left in charge of this Arab movement,' he complained, 'it is nothing to do with me: it is a purely military business.' Summing up the situation, he declared that it was time to weigh the consequences of the Sharif's success or failure. Husein's success, he felt, would have very far-reaching results. 'His failure – and this I want to emphasise, for it is not a matter of purely civil concern – would affect the Mohammedans throughout the world. The effect in India would be enormous; I do not know how many troops it would take to clear that up.'

The spectre McMahon had raised, of having to send thousands of troops to save India, seemed to calm Murray. Murray replied that he had finished grumbling, and now wanted to arrive at some numbers of the troops he might be able to put on standby to help if necessary. Clayton enquired about the Sudanese troops whom Wingate had offered. Murray must have seen a flicker of concern cross Wilson's face, because he interrupted: 'I think Colonel Wilson is right,' he said. 'If you are going to do it, do it with the proper coloured men; use white men.'

'Of course there is a great religious difficulty about that,' McMahon replied.

'I do not believe in sending black troops,' said Murray. 'They won't realise that the British Government is behind them unless they see British troops – white faced soldiers walking about and smoking.'

'There is one more thing,' McMahon added, bringing the discussion to a close. 'If I cannot get these troops from the British Government I am reduced to getting them from the French. I could get them tomorrow but I do not want to do so. That is the alternative.'

'I think we all learnt each other's minds and cleared the atmosphere somewhat,' Wemyss noted in his diary.[41] But the fundamental question remained unanswered. Which was more risky: to send troops or to watch the revolt fail? Then there was the problem of dealing with the French, who had just arrived in Egypt. And, unknown to the British, there was another development, of which they were only just about to become aware.

4

FOREIGN INFLUENCES

(June 1915–October 1916)

On 15 September the Viceroy, Lord Chelmsford, warned London of a disturbing discovery in India. Two weeks before, British Intelligence in Delhi had been passed three letters written on yellow silk which had been surrendered to the authorities in north-west India. The Silk Letters, as they became known, had been written at the beginning of July in the Afghan capital, Kabul. They detailed progress on plans to recruit an Islamic 'army of salvation' designed 'to create a Union among Islamic kings' for the benefit of an addressee in the Hijaz.[1]

Under interrogation, the courier of the Silk Letters identified their author as Obeidullah Sindhi and the man to whom he was writing as Mahmud Hasan. Hasan's name was familiar to Cyril Wilson, who had heard that he was behind much of the anti-British intrigue in the Hijaz. The names of both men were well known to the authorities in Delhi. Hasan was the principal of a hardline Muslim theological college in northern India, and a man with a substantial following. Obeidullah, one of his former students, was one of the most wanted Muslim subversives, who had been missing for more than a year. What was most disturbing was how he had suddenly appeared in Kabul, where a German military mission was known to be trying to provoke anti-British feeling on the North-West Frontier. 'There is no doubt,' Chelmsford remarked, 'that a conspiracy is afoot in Kabul, with tentacles in Hijaz and India, which though fantastic in details might have serious developments if unchecked.'[2]

The Silk Letters provided the first news about Obeidullah Sindhi and

Mahmud Hasan in over a year. Obeidullah had given British Intelligence the slip in Lucknow in June 1915, and had not been seen since. Hasan was last seen boarding a ship in Bombay which would take him to the Hijaz. At the time the city's Commissioner of Police had expressed his doubts: he could not help suspecting, he said, that Hasan's departure was 'due to something more than the mere desire to perform the Hajj'.[3] He was right: the courier now filled in the details from the missing year. Having met in the Hijaz, at the end of their pilgrimage Obeidullah and Hasan had gone on to Medina. There in February 1916 they met the two senior Turkish politicians, Jemal and Enver, who were in the city on their fruitless quest to press Husein to back the jihad. Having secured a letter signed by Ghalib, the Governor of the Hijaz, advocating holy war against the British Obeidullah had then returned overland to Afghanistan. But Hasan, the Silk Letters proved, had stayed in the Hijaz. Obeidullah now wanted Hasan to pass on his proposals to the Ottoman government 'because this is the only way of inflicting an effective blow against the infidels in India'.[4] He also wanted to recruit Sharif Husein as one of the leaders of his army: a hope which, though optimistic, nevertheless caused concerns in India in case Husein reciprocated. Yes, Obeidullah's scheme seemed improbable, the Director of Intelligence in India, Sir Charles Cleveland, admitted, but 'wherever he deals with the facts, he is, I should say, almost always accurate'.[5] The Silk Letters forced the Government of India to recognise that it could no longer simply wish the revolt had never happened. With its support, Cyril Wilson in Jeddah was charged with the task of finding and arresting Mahmud Hasan.

McMahon, meanwhile, was worrying about foreign influence from another quarter. On 1 September a French military mission had arrived in Egypt. It was led by Colonel Edouard Brémond, a tall, broad-shouldered bear of a man with a grey beard almost as long as his service in French North Africa. McMahon had only received sketchy details from the Foreign Office about the French mission, its members and its purpose. As far as he was aware, a 'Colonel Bredus' was on his way, who had no plans to venture closer to Arabia than Cairo. Displaying a touching faith in the *Entente Cordiale*, he believed this. Brémond rapidly corrected both his name and his remit on arrival, when he announced that he would be sailing to Jeddah in the middle of the month. Less than a fortnight later, a second French delegation followed. This transpired to be a flock of several hundred, mainly distinguished, North African pilgrims led by the Moroccan sultan's head of protocol, a man named Si Kaddour Ben Ghabrit, whom Storrs described as a former spy with 'a clever agreeable [and] utterly false face'.[6] They were to follow Brémond to Jeddah.

Brémond made it clear that the French were ready to send troops to support the Sharif, an offer that unnerved McMahon. The same day that the French pilgrims arrived – and the day after the acrimonious meeting with General Murray at which he had raised the possibility that he might be forced to turn to the French for support – McMahon sent a panicky telegram to London. Describing the British as 'morally committed' to support Husein and likely to 'be held in a large measure responsible for his failure', he requested a brigade – just over 4,000 men – to send to the coastal village of Rabigh, a hundred miles north of Jeddah, to stiffen Arab resistance. Were Britain unable to assist, he went on, 'I know French Government is ready to offer to send French Moslem troops to Hijaz and this I greatly deprecate, as it will rob us of very great political advantages which Sharif's success will hereafter give us.'[7] Bertie Clayton disagreed. 'I do not share this fear myself,' he wrote to a sympathetic colleague in London, 'as feeling in those parts is distinctly anti-French and likely to remain so, especially when the terms of the Sykes-Picot arrangement become known.'[8]

Even an official as senior as Clayton had not found out about the terms of the 'Sykes-Picot arrangement' until early that summer. The arrangement was a secret deal between the British and French governments named after its negotiators. Sir Mark Sykes was a young, rumbustious Tory Member of Parliament and witty caricaturist; François Georges-Picot, the tall, thin former consul in Beirut who had inadvertently betrayed the Arab nationalists by leaving his correspondence files behind in his hurry to escape Syria at the outbreak of war. Their agreement, thrashed out over the winter of 1915–16 and approved by the Russians in May 1916, was the victors' blueprint for the division of the Ottoman

Empire after the war, which offered the simplistic clarity that McMahon's reluctant, sketchy commitments to the Arabs lacked.

Sykes had sealed his reputation as an expert on the Middle East in 1915 with the publication of a doorstopper history of the Ottoman Empire, based on several visits he had made to the region before the war. Brought into the War Office by Kitchener, he was rapidly dubbed 'the Mad Mullah' for his whirlwind approach to policy-making.[9] Having learned of McMahon's plans to reach an understanding with Husein while he was visiting Cairo, he returned to London to argue that the French had ambitions in Syria and would be suspicious of any British deal with Husein. He proposed reaching a settlement with the French before any agreement with the Arabs was finalised. The War Committee agreed, and instructed him to achieve it. But they did not tell Cairo, nor, in any case, did McMahon want to know.

On 16 December 1915, Sykes returned to 10 Downing Street with a characteristically sweeping proposal. What he wanted, he told the War Committee, was 'a belt of English-controlled country between the Sharif of Mecca and the French',[10] which would split the Ottoman Empire in two, link the British bridgehead in Mesopotamia to the Mediterranean and keep Husein, whom he favoured as the next Caliph of Islam, out of the clutches of Paris. When asked exactly where the frontier would lie, Sykes sliced his finger across a map of the Middle East from the Mediterranean to the Persian frontier. 'I should like to draw a line from the "e" in Acre to the last "k" in Kirkuk,' he said. Sykes knew that this conflicted with the territory claimed by Husein but, like McMahon, was unconcerned. As one entry in the index of his book – 'Arab character: *see also* Treachery'[11] – light-heartedly makes clear, he saw little need to keep faith with the Arabs, whose ambitions he did not expect to be realised. 'I am confident,' he told a colleague, 'that the suzerainty of the Sharif in Arabia proper will in practice be purely honorary.' This assumption shaped his plan 'to get Arabs to concede as much as possible to French'.[12]

Concessions would come, not just from the Arabs but also from the British. Picot was a robust and unyielding negotiator whose main tactic was to portray himself as a sympathetic moderate unfortunately held hostage by the French public's chauvinism over Syria. 'Syria was very near the heart of the French,' he told the British at the second meeting convened to discuss a settlement, adding regretfully that 'now, after the expenditure of so many lives, France would never consent to offer independence to the Arabs, though at the beginning of the war she might have done so.'[13] He went on to say that he was not convinced by the strength of the Arab movement and resolutely rejected the British plans to win the Arabs over, which in Cairo McMahon was already putting into action. Officials from the Foreign Office who attended this meeting were infuriated by Picot, whom they privately denounced as 'extreme', but their frustration arose from the realisation that they would have no choice but to accept what he said. Although Sykes was able to force Picot to accept that McMahon's overtures to Husein were necessary to reduce the possibility that Britain would have to withdraw thousands of troops from the Western Front to deal with an uprising in India, he ultimately had to recognise France's extensive interests in Syria, almost in full.[14]

At the beginning of 1916 with Picot, Sykes overlaid a veneer of imperial influence, if not actual control, on the area which had just been committed by McMahon to Husein. The Sykes-Picot agreement divided the Arab 'confederation' along the diagonal line Sykes had proposed into northern and southern areas under French and British protection respectively. Adjacent to each area would be zones of control where Britain and France would be free to establish 'such direct or indirect administration or control as they desire'.[15] The 'Blue' French zone filled the Syrian coastal area disputed by Husein and mushroomed north into Anatolia, while the 'Red' British zone capped the Persian Gulf like the head of an unlit match. At Russian insistence, Palestine would be internationally administered. It was designated the colour brown.

Sykes's scheme found few supporters in London, where the general opinion was that he had prematurely surrendered too much of the region to the French. 'It seems to me we are rather in the position of the hunters who divided up the skin of the bear before they had killed it,' the Director of Military Intelligence in London remarked.[16] Questions over whether Sykes's agreement was compatible with what McMahon had offered Husein were raised even before the terms of the Sykes-Picot accord were formally communicated to Cairo on 27 April 1916. It was presumably doubts of this kind which explain why, days earlier, Wingate suddenly revisited his copies of McMahon's correspondence with Husein. He decided that McMahon's offer was 'sufficiently vaguely worded as to admit of the eventual extension of French influence in these regions'.[17] When Clayton returned to London in July 1916, he argued that the Sykes-Picot 'understanding' should remain informal and unpublished, in case it torpedoed what McMahon had achieved with Husein. But he acknowledged that it was only a matter of time before the agreement became common knowledge.[18]

The fact that the Sykes-Picot agreement remains known by the names of its negotiators, rather than by its official title – the Anglo-French Agreement – reflects the success of Clayton and others in depicting it as a private arrangement between the two men, rather than the binding accord between the two nations they represented. Low expectations of the likelihood of Arab success meant that worries that McMahon's and Sykes's respective commitments were contradictory could be ignored for the time being. 'If the Arab scheme fails, the whole scheme will also fail and the French and British Governments would then be free to make any new claims,' a Whitehall summary of the situation concluded with an unmistakable note of hope.[19]

Nor did the French rate the strength of the Sykes-Picot agreement that highly, as Brémond's arrival in Egypt on 1 September reflected. The French War Office had given the revolt only a guarded welcome, describing it as 'favourable to French interests to some extent', in that it might help pave the way for French intervention and hinder the Turks.[20] In general the French viewed Arab success in the Hijaz more cautiously than the British. France's North African colonies were also Arab, and the French government worried that if Husein succeeded they might find themselves 'in the presence of an Arabised Islam that draws from its conquests new strength to expand and resist Christian power'.[21] Nor did the idea that the Sharif might assume the Caliphate enchant them: Moroccans regarded the Sultan of Morocco as their caliph, an arrangement the French did not want to disturb.

Brémond mentioned none of these worries on his arrival in Cairo at the start of September. When he met General Murray, he simply explained how the French hoped to fix the notoriously volatile costs of the Hajj to help their pilgrims and, by using a deputation of Muslim officers who could enter Mecca, establish directly from Husein exactly what he required.[22] Outwardly, Murray welcomed French support. But later the same day he wrote to Robertson, admitting that he would 'be sorry if for political reasons the French render the Sharif material assistance', because if they did, the pressure on him to send British troops would consequently increase.[23]

On 15 September Brémond left Egypt for Jeddah together with the religious delegation, which took rose water for washing the Kaaba – a much sought-after task. The French received a rapturous reception when they arrived off Jeddah five days later. Brémond soon spoke on the telephone to Husein, who immediately organised a dinner in his honour in the port the following night. It was a lavish occasion, held in an enormous room decorated with French, British and the crimson Sharifian flags, and the hundred guests sat around a low table on borrowed carpets. Over the telephone Husein – who did not come down for the dinner – relayed more good news to Brémond. The Ottomans had just surrendered at Taif, in the mountains above Mecca. This not only removed the final obstacle to the Pilgrimage by eliminating the threat posed by the closest Ottoman troops to Mecca, but it also freed Abdullah to go north to help his brothers contain the Turks in Medina. Brémond happily relayed the message to Egypt, announcing that other pilgrims waiting in Egypt could depart for the Hijaz. Three days later a large tricolour was hoisted over the French consulate.

The fact that the French had instantly gained access to the Sharif disturbed the British. In Cairo, McMahon's adviser Ronald Storrs decided it was time to make another trip down the Red Sea. Annoyed by Arab intermediaries whom he believed could not pass on a message verbatim, Storrs was sufficiently anxious to speak to the Sharif directly that he thought it might 'even be worth the journey to Jeddah to talk with him awhile over the Jeddah–Mecca telephone'.[24] An opportunity to do so arose when Storrs was detailed to accompany the Egyptian mahmal down to Jeddah aboard the Red Sea fleet's largest ship, HMS *Euryalus*. The

British aim was clear: to land the mahmal with enough pomp to awe the Arabs and to trump the French.

Boarding the *Euryalus* on 22 September, Storrs discovered that he had been allotted the best berth aboard by the admiral, 'Rosy' Wemyss. Early the following day, he had his bath to the sound of the Egyptian brass band doing their morning practice. To break up the monotony of the voyage, each day Storrs played chess with Wemyss on deck. The admiral, who wore a monocle, turned out to be a formidable opponent. In the background, his grey parrot cawed 'damn the Kaisah, damn the Kaisah' raucously.[25] Wemyss won every game; Storrs blamed the parrot for distracting him.

The *Euryalus* arrived off Jeddah on 26 September, joining a flotilla of British and French ships anchored off the port. Wemyss and Storrs went ashore the following morning, welcomed to the Hijaz first by a salute fired from some ancient mortars and then by a cluster of local dignitaries led by Sharif Mohsen. Among these were two familiar faces who, Storrs recorded, 'appeared really glad to see us'.[26] It was Wilson and Ruhi, Storrs's secret agent, whom he had lent to Wilson. After several stops for coffee and for what Wemyss described as the exchange of 'flowery compliments', they called on Colonel Brémond, and then headed for the British consulate.

Behind closed doors inside the consulate, Wilson assured Wemyss that the welcome, though elaborate, was genuine, and expressed his delight at the impact of the admiral's visit to Storrs. Wilson's own position, Storrs reported, had been 'raised in a manner he had up to now scarcely dared to dream possible'.[27] Despite the general expectation that the Pilgrimage would trigger a Turkish attempt to recapture Mecca, Wilson also seemed happier about the military situation as well. He 'no longer believes in a Turkish advance south of Medina, and even speaks of reported with-drawals', noted Storrs in his diary. 'If this means that it will no longer be necessary to send an English Brigade or French Batteries to Rabigh, it is a very deep relief to me.'[28]

Like Brémond, Admiral Wemyss was invited to dinner with Mohsen, the Harb sheikh, by Sharif Husein the following night, but as he and Storrs were anxious to visit Rabigh, Wemyss thought it best to decline. Storrs spotted his opportunity to speak to Husein and went to the telephone to ring Number One Mecca. 'After a short pause, I distinguished what I rightly took to be the tones of the Grand Sharif himself, bidding me a warm and affectionate welcome to Jeddah, and anxiously asking me whether the Admiral would accept his hospitality,' he remembered.[29] But then 'three or four other voices became audible on the wire, and I remarked to the Sharif that in my opinion we were being tapped'. Impossible, replied Husein, until he too heard the voices. He called through to the operator, Storrs recalled, 'in stronger language than I had expected from so holy a man, ordering them to cut off everybody's instrument in the Hijaz excepting his own and mine for the next half-hour. This was instantly done and we conversed henceforth in a silence of death.'

Back aboard *Euryalus* Wemyss also gave Sharif Mohsen and his retainers a tour of their flagship: 'The big guns struck them so much that they could not at first believe them to be guns at all,' observed Storrs, while 'the size, comfort and cleanliness of the Admiral's cabin came in for admiring comment'. But, he decided contentedly at the end of that day, 'it was the guns in the end which produced the greatest effect'.[30] Having performed their prayers on the stern deck, Mohsen and his 'most disreputable looking guard' departed 'in a state of mind divided between awe, and intense satisfaction at having demonstrably espoused the winning cause'. One of the party confided to Storrs that he had not, until then, believed that such a large ship could float.

The following morning the mahmal was landed in Jeddah. 'Thousands . . . crammed the streets,' said Brémond: 'There was joy everywhere. "The Harvest" had returned.'[31] From a rooftop in the town one of Wilson's staff surveyed the scene. The boxes containing the Kiswa were brought ashore 'amidst a scene of wildest confusion',[32] he would later recall, before the mahmal was loaded on to a camel and carried jauntily through the jostling spectators, many of whom carried black umbrellas to protect themselves from the morning sun. The procession set out for Mecca the following morning, with 'the stately mahmal and then the long string of dust-coloured camels passing into the pearly desert in the half light of dawn'.

Leaving the *Euryalus* behind in Jeddah harbour for maximum effect,

Wemyss and Storrs transferred to a smaller ship and headed for Rabigh, one hundred miles north of Jeddah. 'Very hot, damp, windless and oppressive'[33] was Storrs's verdict on the fuggy climate of the desolate plain on which Rabigh stood, by the edge of a lagoon in which sharks were occasionally spotted. This nondescript location belied the strategic importance of the village, because its abundant supplies of fresh water made it a vital stopping point on the line of a Turkish advance towards Mecca.

Rabigh today is unrecognisable, having grown into a bland coastal town. The spit which separates the lagoon from the sea, once an empty whaleback of sand, is now crowned by an enormous oil terminal. What has not changed is the view inland. To the north-east, across the gently corrugated coastal plain, a distinctive two-horned mountain poking through the dirty desert haze indicates the direction from which the Turks, in 1916, were expected to come.

Wemyss and Storrs were visiting to survey the village's defences and find a site for an aerodrome because, despite Murray's fulmination a fortnight earlier, at McMahon's insistence biplanes were now waiting to be sent to the Hijaz to buoy up tribal morale. Wemyss, in particular, wanted to know whether his ships' guns could support the Arab forces who were camped a few miles inland, and as the party walked away from the seashore, Storrs silently counted his paces. Alfred Parker, another officer travelling with the pair, who then stayed on in Rabigh, summarised the importance of the village in a message to Egypt two days later: 'Arab cause is successful if Mecca is denied to Turkish force . . . According to all reports force must come by Rabigh and therefore if Rabigh is held Arab cause is won.'[34]

Whether or not to send troops to help hold Rabigh was high on the agenda back in London, following McMahon's formal request for soldiers. The Chief of the Imperial General Staff and the War Committee's main military adviser, Sir William Robertson, remained trenchantly opposed to the idea, describing a landing in the Hijaz as a 'leap in the dark',[35] and so the committee decided to ask the principal British officials around the region what they thought would happen if the Sharif failed.

Primed by Robertson to oppose intervention, Maude, the commander of the Indian Expeditionary Force in Mesopotamia, thought that the effect of the recapture of Mecca in Iraq would be minor. From Egypt, Murray argued that the Sharif's failure might 'have as little effect as evacuation of Gallipoli or surrender at Kut'[36] – a deliberate reference to two raw defeats he hoped would discourage the politicians from intervening. Although he did not rule out the possibility of serious upheaval, Murray was willing to run the risk until the end of the campaigning season in France, when battle-weary troops could be sent out to Egypt to bolster its defences against civil unrest. In India the Viceroy, Lord Chelmsford, worried by the discovery of the Silk Letters, produced five reasons not to send troops which focused on the resentment which such an action would cause in the subcontinent, the danger that it might spark a jihad in Afghanistan, and the likelihood that the Sharif's claim to the Caliphate would be ruined if he was discovered to be relying on British soldiers. When asked whether Husein was in real danger Wilson breezily replied, 'No, not at the moment', though he added that if the Turks defeated the Arab forces in the Hijaz mountains and advanced closer to Rabigh, then the situation could become critical.[37] Against all of these, McMahon and Wingate, who warned London of Muslim agitation in Egypt, the Sudan and India if the Sharif were crushed, sounded rather isolated, particularly as news came in that the Pilgrimage had gone well and that the Egyptian mahmal, and not its Turkish competitor, had reached the Kaaba.

Murray's view seems to have been particularly decisive in the discussions which were then held in London. Wingate subsequently heard from one of George V's private secretaries, with whom he shared a passion for golf, how 'after the Dardanelles and Mesopotamia the General Staff are rather shy about these commitments in the East. Their argument is that if we send a Brigade it may expand into a Division, then an Army Corps, and eventually an Expedition.'[38] If the Sharif was so precarious, the opponents of military action asked, was a brigade of 4,000 men enough to save him? Swayed by these arguments, and unconvinced by pessimistic assessments made by McMahon and Wingate, on 3 October the War Committee concluded that the replies it had received 'all pointed to the undesirability of sending any reinforcements to Rabigh beyond a flight of aeroplanes and

such guns as might be eventually available'.[39] Since Wemyss's reconnaissance had demonstrated that Rabigh could be protected by naval barrage,
the committee decided that naval assistance would be 'sufficient if the local
defence was properly organised'.

Yet these decisions were far from final. As one official in London
astutely observed, the War Committee had acted on the understanding
that the situation in the Hijaz was improving. In fact, the state of affairs
in Arabia was already deteriorating. The Turks began to attack the Arab
positions at Bir Abbas on the road from Medina the same day, a
development which was relayed two days later to Jeddah by Parker,
the officer now based permanently in Rabigh. The situation, Parker
added in his telegram, was 'not good at present'.[40] There was no sign of
Abdullah, who was supposed to be moving from Taif to Medina, and
with Feisal to the north, and Abdullah 'entirely out of touch', Parker
warned Wilson that if the Turks attacked Rabigh, they would capture
the village and its water supply.

At the same time, the War Committee also decided to give Wingate
full responsibility for supporting the Sharif, effectively taking the burden
off McMahon. Oddly, given his earlier desire to be shot of the problem,
McMahon was stung by the implication that he was not up to the task. In
a telegram to London, he now attacked Wingate. 'The Sirdar shows a
generous disposition to assume both political and military responsibilities which in my opinion his geographical position and the dearth of
military resources rendered him and still render him incapable of
discharging,' he wrote, copying this view to Wingate for good measure.[41] The government in London disagreed. On 9 October, encouraged
by Murray, Grey told McMahon to give Wingate whatever political
authority he needed. Two days later, Wingate was also secretly offered
McMahon's job as High Commissioner in Egypt.

Flexing his new power from Khartoum, on 11 October Wingate seized
on the report of the fighting at Bir Abbas to recommend 'a British Brigade
being at once placed under orders for Rabigh and all arrangements made
for its immediate conveyance to that port'.[42] He also announced his
intention to see Rabigh for himself. It was a decision that would indirectly
make another man, as yet unknown, a household name.

5

ALL CLAWS AND TEETH

(October–November 1916)

A gunshot and the tinkle of broken glass hitting the ship's deck abruptly ended Storrs's brief siesta.[1] It was his third trip down the Red Sea in five months, when he had been banking on no more than one. The spur had been Wingate's sudden suggestion four days earlier on 11 October that a delegation should visit Jeddah and Rabigh. Wingate's own hopes of visiting Arabia had been squashed in London, where Grey feared that the appearance of so senior an official would only fuel Arab suspicions of Britain's imperial ambitions in the Hijaz.[2] Clayton might have gone but his new-born son was desperately ill and he was juggling his never-ending workload with looking after his wife and child. That left Storrs, who was at best a reluctant adventurer.

The ship, the *Lama*, which was carrying supplies to the Hijaz, was 'loaded with coal, ammunition etc over 2 feet above safety line', Storrs noted in his diary.[3] Nor did the departure date inspire much confidence. Friday 13 October was, as the ship's captain admitted, an ominous day to sail. Within ten minutes of this observation two of the *Lama*'s boilers had burst, making full steam impossible and adding an extra day to a journey Storrs knew from experience he would find interminably boring. A prickly man, Storrs hated the inane company to which he was subjected on the voyages down the Red Sea and he had been looking forward to conversation with the 'super-cerebral' companion from the Intelligence Department with whom he was travelling this time. But the intelligence officer had proved uninterested in joining in a discussion about the merits of Debussy with Storrs and an Egyptian former Ottoman Army officer, Aziz Ali al Masri, and infuriatingly, so far as Storrs was concerned, he was amusing himself by shooting at a line of bottles balanced on the ship's handrail instead.

At twenty-eight, this man was young, too short to be a regular Army officer, with fair hair and electric-blue eyes. Everyone always noticed his eyes. 'Very, very blue', remembers Diana Elles who, as a teenager, met him over seventy years ago. He had 'a very keen face. You could see the pressure behind it.'[4] In his right hand he held a large Browning pistol, which he raised deftly again to eye-level. Another shot: another bottle evaporated from the rail. His name was Ned Lawrence and he would eventually become known to the world as 'Lawrence of Arabia'. But at the time he was almost unknown. Looking back, Storrs commented that mentions of Lawrence's name in his diary up to that point occurred 'with what must now seem a ludicrous infrequency and inadequacy' because Lawrence was too junior to have been part of the inner circle of officials directing British involvement in the revolt.[5]

Storrs had only got to know Lawrence four months earlier, when he wanted to design some stamps for the newly independent Hijaz in time for the Pilgrimage. The idea was typical of Storrs: in his own words, 'self-paying and incontrovertible' proof that the revolt had happened, which would be spread throughout the Muslim world by pilgrims' letters home.[6] Storrs had approached Husein for a design, but was disappointed by the secular image that the Sharif had sent back to him, which could be mistaken for an Ottoman design. So he sought the advice of the map-making section of the Intelligence Department that July, 1916. It was there that he first encountered Lawrence, who was interested in printing. According to Storrs, the pair spent an afternoon wandering the corridors of the Arab Museum in Cairo in search of arabesque motifs appropriate for the Hijaz. The first stamps, cobalt-blue and each worth one piastre, were issued that August.[7]

Lawrence was delighted to be asked to help. He was bored by the work allotted to him in the Intelligence Department, where he seemed to spend too much of his time answering the telephone, and longed for the British to take a more buccaneering approach within the region. In particular he wondered whether the tribesmen he had met on his travels as an archaeologist in Syria before August 1914 might help win the war in that part of the world. 'I want to pull them all together, & to roll up Syria by way of the Hijaz in the name of the Sharif,' he wrote to his mentor, the Oxford University professor and Middle East expert, David Hogarth, early in 1915. It was not just the Ottomans he hoped to remove: with Husein as a figurehead, Lawrence believed, 'we can rush right up to Damascus, & biff the French out of all hope of Syria', a part of the world he believed was not French by right.[8]

Lawrence appreciated the origin of the French 'hope of Syria' from his research into crusader castles as an undergraduate seven years before. Aged twenty, and armed with a camera and a Mauser pistol, he had set out for Beirut to assess the architectural relationship between the castles of Syria and Europe. He spent a summer on foot touring the chain of citadels built by the French seven centuries earlier to defend the same tranche of fertile seaboard, in what is today Lebanon and western Syria, over which McMahon and Husein now argued. His radical conclusion, that 'all that was good in Crusading architecture hailed from France or Italy', not only overturned the prevailing assumption that Crusader castles had borrowed stylistically from the Byzantine East, helping to earn him a first-class degree, but also made him instinctively understand the medieval roots of the French belief that Syria was theirs.[9] France's determination to return to Syria was an ambition Lawrence was determined to ruin.

Years after university, Lawrence's near-obsession with the medieval world continued to inform his thinking. In a report he wrote on 'The Politics of Mecca' in February 1916, Lawrence compared the effects of an armed uprising in Mecca with the fourteenth-century papal schism.

If we can arrange that this political change shall be a violent one, we will have abolished the threat of Islam, by dividing it against itself, in its very heart. There will then be a Khalifa in Turkey and a Khalifa in Arabia, in theological warfare, and Islam will be as little formidable as the Papacy when Popes lived in Avignon.[10]

His chief, Bertie Clayton, loved this analysis. 'Lawrence is quite excellent on this and many other subjects, and you may take his stuff as being good,' he told the Director of Intelligence in London.[11]

By then Lawrence had begun moonlighting for the Arab Bureau, which was run out of a suite of rooms in the Savoy Hotel in Cairo by Hogarth who, having found Lawrence a job in the War Office at the outbreak of war, had then been sucked into intelligence work himself. The Bureau's role was twofold, an uneasy combination of intelligence-gathering and analysis, and policy-making. Its staff routinely condensed intelligence from around the Arab world into a frequent digest, the *Arab Bulletin*, which was issued to a small circle interested in the region. Its other, harder task was to try to unite the divergent Middle Eastern policies pursued from London, Cairo and Delhi. 'There is no kind of touch between us except rather bad tempered telegrams,' admitted one of the Bureau's members, the red-haired, chain-smoking Gertrude Bell, before she herself was sent to try to improve the estranged relationship between Cairo and the Government of India.[12] Her mission, however, was not a success and the Government of India remained doggedly opposed to the Arab Bureau's plans to help the Sharif.

Given his fluent advocacy of the Arab revolt in his February memorandum, Lawrence was asked in March to follow Bell to Basra to put the case to the Indian Army officers and test the water locally for signs of the Arab nationalist feeling described by Faruqi, the Gallipoli deserter. He had also been authorised to spend up to £1 million in an attempt to bribe the Turks to end their siege of the 11,000-strong British force at Kut on the Tigris. Originally Lawrence planned to take both Faruqi and Aziz Ali al Masri with him, but the commander of the Indian Army in Mesopotamia had objected, fearing that the two men might destabilise the local Arab population.[13] Lawrence had another even more secret agenda which he had probably devised with Clayton, whom he later described as working 'like water, or permeating oil, creeping silently and insistently through everything'.[14] This was to denigrate the Indian Army's intelligence capability and to find evidence in their files to shore up the Arab Bureau's case for backing Sharif Husein.

Outwardly, Lawrence's visit to Mesopotamia was a failure. He returned to Cairo in May 1916 having been unable to buy the freedom of the British force at Kut, and having established that the Arab nationalist party in Basra was 'about 12 strong'.[15] But, for the surreptitious purposes he and Clayton had also intended, the trip had been a success. Lawrence had uncovered a letter in the files in Basra which would be particularly useful in undermining the Government of India's opposition to the Bureau's determination to interfere in the Hijaz. 'If the Sultan of Turkey were to disappear,' one Indian Army officer who had lived with Ibn Saud believed, 'the Caliphate by common consent of Islam would fall to the family of the Prophet, the present representative of which is the Sharif of Mecca. In this case he would command the support of the Ibn Saud.'[16] Lawrence had also seen enough to write a devastating critique of the intelligence department in Basra. Witheringly, he described its head, a Colonel Beach, as 'very excellent but he has never been in Turkey, or read about it, and he knows no Arabic. This would not necessarily matter, but unfortunately his staff do not supply the necessary knowledge.'[17]

The contents of Lawrence's report rapidly assumed a legendary notoriety in Cairo. 'It was a violent criticism,' recalled another intelligence officer, Frank Stirling: 'We dared not show it to the C-in-C, but had to water it down till it was considered fit for the great man's perusal.'[18] Having tasted the excitement of a more active role, on his return to Cairo Lawrence also embarked on a campaign of pedantry designed to ensure he could transfer permanently from the Intelligence Department to the Bureau. 'I was all claws and teeth, and had a devil,' he later admitted of this period.[19] By the time he set out for Jeddah with Storrs, the Intelligence Department was glad to see the back of him and he had a well-deserved reputation as a hatchet-man. Lawrence, Storrs wrote approvingly, liked 'nonsense to be treated as nonsense, and not civilly or dully accepted or dismissed'.[20] This time Lawrence's task was to prove that it was unnecessary to send troops to the Hijaz and to undermine the newly arrived Colonel Brémond, head of the French military mission to the Hijaz.

Storrs and Lawrence finally landed at Jeddah early on Monday, 16 October. The French consulate on the quayside would have been immediately distinguishable by its flag, though Lawrence ignored it in his later description of their arrival. 'When at last we anchored in the outer harbour, off the white town hung between the blazing sky and its reflection in the mirage . . . then the heat of Arabia came out like a drawn sword and struck us speechless.'[21]

Before the war Lawrence had been planning to write two books, one on the Crusades, the other on his travels in the Middle East, which he had already decided would be entitled *Seven Pillars of Wisdom* after a phrase in the Book of Proverbs.[22] Once in the Hijaz he made detailed notes of the people he met, incidents and his surroundings in a slim army notebook. In the back of this book he kept an elegiac newspaper cutting from *The Times* about his younger brother. Will Lawrence, a Royal Flying Corps observer, had been missing since being shot down over France a year earlier. In the piece, Will's Oxford tutor mourned the loss of so many of his students: 'One by one they fall; great and strong and wise, they sleep deep the long sleep of death in gallant company,' he wrote, describing his former student anonymously as 'one of the noblest – if it be not a treason to discriminate – of all the dead one has known who have died for England'.[23] By the time he arrived in Jeddah, Lawrence had lost two brothers: the other was Frank, who had been killed earlier in 1915. Their deaths seem to have been a significant spur to him: 'They were both younger than I am,' he wrote to a friend, 'and it doesn't seem right, somehow, that I should go on living peacefully in Cairo.'[24]

Seven Pillars of Wisdom became Lawrence's story of what happened to him after he was first sent to Arabia. It was a book originally born out of his frustration with the unsatisfactory outcome of the revolt, which in time he softened into a private souvenir of a small war. Just 200 copies were initially printed, most for subscribers who each paid thirty guineas for a copy. 'It does not pretend to be impartial,' Lawrence wrote in a brief foreword in 1926, advising his readers to 'take it as a personal narrative pieced out of memory'. Despite this caveat, *Seven Pillars of Wisdom* remains an outstanding memoir, its accuracy usually corroborated by the other sources, both contemporary and subsequent, which have since come to light.

Lawrence found the atmosphere in the narrow streets of Jeddah close and tense. His own uniform turned a deeper khaki from his sweat. In front of him Storrs was, as usual, wearing his white tropical suit, oblivious to the fact that it was stained dark red from the scarlet leather of the armchair in which he had spent the preceding three days reclining. At the British consulate Wilson ushered them into a dark room, shuttered against the heat. He did not trust Storrs and his only previous contact with Lawrence had been a run-in over whether British officers should wear Arab dress about the town.

The day before, Wilson had learned through a telegram from Wingate that the government had decided not to send troops or aeroplanes after all. He had been under the impression all along that troops were being held in readiness, had told the Sharif several times that aircraft were on their way, and was annoyed that his ignorance was about to be embarrassingly exposed. The fact that it was Lawrence, a junior, amateur soldier, who was able to reveal to him the political badminton which had led to the dispatch of the brigade being sanctioned and cancelled more than once, irritated Wilson further. 'Lawrence wants kicking and kicking *hard* at that then he would improve,' he fulminated to Clayton, describing Lawrence as 'a bumptious young ass who spoils his undoubted knowledge of Syrian Arabs etc by making himself out to be the only authority on war, engineering, running HM's ships and everything else. He put every single person's back up I've met, from the Admiral down to the most junior fellow.'[25]

The feeling was mutual. Both Storrs and Lawrence quickly formed the impression that Wilson's judgement was poor and that the information he was passing back to Cairo was unreliable. 'There are some personal remarks here about Colonel Wilson which I won't write down,'[26] Lawrence wrote to Clayton, reminding him to put 'a few leading questions' about Wilson to Storrs on his return. We can guess what Storrs said from the comments he wrote in his diary. Wilson, he thought, was 'irritable and aggressive, and totally unsuited for anything beyond provincial administration'.[27] Terrified of being asked to replace Wilson, however, he kept his fiercest criticism private. Though 'a good old boy who keeps British prestige fairly high in the Hijaz', Wilson, he told a friend, was 'very stupid and knows no Arabic' and reminded him of 'a very low geared bicycle working at full speed day and night'.[28]

Like Wilson, however, Storrs was mortified by the telegram cancelling the aeroplanes, particularly as the ship carrying them had already arrived off Rabigh. Storrs was going to meet Abdullah later that day for the first time since that first pregnant encounter in 1914. It would be a symbolic occasion, at which Storrs had been hoping to establish what Abdullah needed, not to tell him what he could not have. Instead, 'It was our privilege,' he wrote sarcastically, 'to announce to Abdullah that the Brigade, more than once promised by HMG would not be sent; and that the flight of aeroplanes, promised and despatched to Rabigh was being withdrawn.'[29] Nor could he provide the £10,000 Abdullah had asked for. 'I felt myself therefore somewhat poorly equipped for the role of a *Deus ex Machina*,' he later reminisced.[30]

Wilson read the news he had received aloud to Abdullah. 'It was a lengthy telegram,' Abdullah later recalled, 'and the gist of it was that news of the Arab revolt had been received in India with the greatest indignation and that agents or friends of the Germans and the Turks there had made capital out of it, maintaining that the Allies had occupied sacred Muslim areas.'[31] The British government, Wilson continued, could not risk trouble in India and had decided to restrict its help to arms, supplies and money as before. Neither the troops, nor the aircraft, would now be sent. This news 'was a heavy blow to me', Abdullah wrote afterwards, 'as we desperately needed aircraft, gunners and engineers'.[32]

'Pardon me,' Abdullah said, looking directly at Storrs, 'it was your letter and your messages that began this thing with us, and you know it from the beginning.'[33] Abdullah 'had us on toast now and then',[34] Wilson reported to Clayton, but there was nothing more that either he or Storrs could do. Abdullah was forced to telephone his father with the bad news. After Abdullah had finished listening to his father's railing at the British change of mind, he handed the receiver to Storrs. 'Storrs in full blast was a delight to listen to,' wrote Lawrence, 'a lesson to every Englishman alive on how to deal with suspicious or unwilling Orientals.'[35] Within minutes, he had managed to persuade the Sharif that Lawrence should be allowed to visit his younger son Feisal to assess the situation, having hinted that with better information about the situation it might be possible to reverse the British government's decision.

That evening Husein rang back. Would Storrs and his colleagues like to hear a recital by the Turkish brass band captured at Taif? 'Sharif Husein laid his receiver on the table of his reception hall, and we, called solemnly one by one to the telephone, heard the band in the Palace at Mecca forty-five miles away,' Lawrence recalled.[36] That night he and Storrs dined with Brémond.

Abdullah met Brémond early the following morning and told him the news that the British had withdrawn the aeroplanes and refused to send troops.

'I have heard nothing about this,' Brémond told Abdullah, surprised that nothing had been said at dinner the previous evening. 'It is rather serious. What are you going to do?'

'It means concluding peace,' Abdullah apparently replied.[37]

Storrs's admission that the British would not be sending aeroplanes could not have been worse timed. Later that day, Abdullah received a message from his brother Feisal, who was up in the hills on the road to Medina, telling him that he was now being bombed by Turkish aircraft. At about midday, Sharif Husein made the first of many calls to Storrs, begging him to reverse the British government's decision. He continued 'pitilessly without intermission to dominate and interrupt us', Storrs wrote at the end of that day, 'till I had to remind him that we had not, unfortunately, got the British Army drawn up in the Consulate back garden'.[38] When Storrs heard from Brémond that Abdullah had threatened to sue for peace, he rapidly arranged for McMahon to confirm to the Sharif that supplies of food, weapons and ammunition would continue to be sent. Abdullah, fortunately, saw this as a victory when, in fact, it was simply a restatement of the existing British policy.

Dinner that evening was a painful experience. Abdullah arrived with the bandsmen – 'scarecrows', Lawrence described them – whom Husein had sent down to entertain the British. Reviews of the performance, which included a rendition of *Deutschland Über Alles*, were unanimous. 'Somewhat discordant', was Wilson's verdict.[39] 'Excruciating,' said Wilson's colleague, Young.[40] 'Our ears ached with the noise,' remembered Lawrence.[41] 'After a while Aziz Ali [al Masri] said there was a piece called *The Echo* they could render with great skill,' Storrs, who had moonlighted as an opera critic before the war, recalled: 'The result was two notes of an ineffable *tristesse* on the trombone, followed by a pause in which we consumed more than half a course. Then a few more disjointed and incoherent notes from the rest of the orchestra, and so on *da capo*. Even the Egyptians – indeed all but Abdullah – were stricken with the horror of the melody.'[42] Storrs himself was almost doubled up with laughter, desperately trying not to catch Lawrence's eye.

'Is not this the music that is played for the dead?' one Egyptian officer asked. 'Storrs saved situation,' Lawrence noted, as his colleague skilfully made light of the comment, causing everyone to laugh.[43]

Lawrence was impatient. In a telegram that day to Clayton he brusquely summarised the day's discussions: 'Nobody knew real situation Rabigh so much time wasted.'[44] He would head for Rabigh the following day with Aziz Ali al Masri, who thought that it was neither necessary nor wise to send British troops. According to Lawrence, Masri's view was that British staff should be landed at Rabigh to deal directly with Ali and Feisal, bypassing Husein 'of whom they are all respectfully afraid'[45] and who was 'frightfully jealous of his purse-strings, and keeps his family annoyingly short'.[46] Lawrence believed that the British should supply some funds to Husein's sons directly to circumvent their father's tight-fistedness, but this would never be sanctioned until someone had completed a more penetrating assessment of each of their personalities than Wilson's, which only tended to reveal their author's reliance on degrees of the adjective 'nice'. Lawrence spotted an opportunity for himself: 'There is great need of some Intelligence work being done at Jeddah,' he told Clayton. 'If one stayed there, and worked, one would be able to appreciate the Hijaz situation quite well.'[47]

Lawrence arrived in Rabigh on 19 October to meet Ali before riding inland to find Feisal. Ali was suffering from a relapse of his tuberculosis. He looked 'a little old already', felt Lawrence, and though conscientious, was 'without force of character, nervous and rather tired'.[48] But he was also extremely reluctant to allow Lawrence to head up-country, and he only relented on condition that Lawrence spoke to no one along the way. The local sheikh had an unresolved blood feud with Sharif Husein, and was correctly suspected to be in league with the Turks. With two guides from a friendly local tribe Lawrence – dressed up in an Arab headscarf and cloak that Ali had lent to him to disguise his uniform – set out for Feisal's camp in the mountains after dark on 21 October. He was well aware that he was about to embark on a dangerous journey. He also knew how some German sailors, who had attempted to travel up the Hijaz coast some months earlier, had afterwards been discovered trussed up like chickens and minus their heads.

Life as a desk officer in Cairo had barely prepared Lawrence for the slow journey by camel. Even in October, his fair skin quickly blistered with sunburn and his eyes ached from the glare of the sun reflecting off the coastal plain, the Tihamah.

Bar the fast new highway that now follows the coast, the Tihamah has not changed in the intervening years. Unremittingly flat and bleak despite being so close to the sea, its miles of monotonous gravel flats are alleviated only by the occasional thorn tree, black as if scorched by the fierce sun. The only signs of life are the gangs of Pakistani labourers shovelling hot tarmac on to the road. Hell would be being a roadbuilder in Saudi Arabia.

Halfway up the coastal leg of the ride, Lawrence learned from the guides that there were wells inland at Khoreiba, only twenty-five miles north-east of Rabigh. This was a significant discovery, undermining the basis for Parker's belief in the importance and security of Rabigh, which Lawrence would emphasise in his report on his return.

The guides led Lawrence east up Wadi Safra, a narrowing rocky valley in which he passed through a series of settlements. Finally, after two days' riding, on a bend in the valley by now perhaps 300 yards wide he reached Hamra, a large village surrounded by small gardens and a dense grove of date palms. Now tumbledown and more or less deserted, in 1916 the mud houses of Hamra teemed with Feisal's supporters, who were camped there. Lawrence was led to one of the larger houses, where his guide spoke to a black slave standing guard with a sword, who in turn led Lawrence into an inner courtyard. There, in a dark doorway, Lawrence remembered, was 'a white figure waiting tensely for me. This was Feisal.'[49] Feisal's dark hair, black hooded eyes and strong nose reminded Lawrence of someone. Later he would describe the Sharif's son as looking 'very like the monument of Richard I, at Fontevraud'.[50]

'Do you like our place here in Wadi Safra?' Feisal asked.

'Well,' replied Lawrence: 'but it is far from Damascus.' After the war he would boast that this double-edged phrase fell on Feisal and his advisers 'like a sword in their midst'.[51] There was a pause as the Arabs considered the ambition and reproach implied by his answer. Then Feisal looked up at Lawrence, smiled, and replied: 'Praise be to God, there are Turks nearer us than that.'[52]

'I felt at first glance,' Lawrence wrote afterwards, 'that this was the man I had come to Arabia to seek.'[53]

Back on the coast in the decrepit seashore town of Yanbu two days later, Lawrence considered what he had seen. He began by writing up his impressions of each of the Sharif's four sons. The youngest, the half-brother of the others, Zeid, he curtly dismissed: 'His mother is Turkish and he takes after her.'[54] Tuberculosis ruled out Ali. Abdullah, Lawrence decided, though likeable, was too ambitious to be trustworthy. 'The Arabs consider him a most astute politician, and a far-seeing statesman,' he admitted, before adding, 'he has possibly more of the former than of the latter in his composition'.[55]

'Tall, graceful, vigorous, almost regal in appearance': Feisal was Lawrence's obvious preference.[56] Though Feisal had a hot temper, a short attention span and a tendency to be rash, he also had 'far more personal magnetism and life than his brothers' and, promisingly, was 'perhaps not over scrupulous'. And he too had ambition: 'full of dreams', was Lawrence's phrase, 'with the capacity to realise them'. This last trait was crucial, because what the revolt lacked, Lawrence had decided, was 'leadership: not intellect, nor judgement, nor political wisdom, but the flame of enthusiasm that would set the desert on fire'.[57]

Lawrence also began to develop his ideas about the way the Arabs would need to fight in future. Go just up the road beyond Hamra, the village where Lawrence first met Feisal, and ahead you can see two spiky peaks which dominate the climbing road to Medina. Lawrence, who saw this imposing view, argued that the Hijaz mountains presented a formidable barrier to Turkish ambitions to recapture Mecca. Wiry and independent, the Bedu were 'cheerful snipers', who he argued – on the basis of a day up at Hamra – were ideally suited to warfare in the mountains.[58] They had their limitations: they would only serve under their own sheikhs and near their homes, and they found artillery and aeroplanes terrifying. But they were 'not afraid of bullets, or of being killed – it is just the manner of death by artillery that they cannot stand', he explained, in a reference to Muslims' belief in bodily resurrection on the Day of Judgement, which being blown to pieces would prejudice.

This tribute to the Bedu's unorthodox military skills immmediately met with scepticism. It was, Alfred Parker commented, 'a delightful theory' which did not bear clear reasoning. He believed that Lawrence exaggerated the advantage the Bedu enjoyed in the mountains. 'In India,' Parker recalled from his own experience, 'it has proved that provided a force can move quickly enough it can carry out its objective in the face of the opposition of a hill tribe, a more efficient enemy than the Arab.'[59]

Lawrence was determined to drive home the point that this war was, for the British, entirely new: 'The Hijaz war is one of dervishes against regular troops – and we are on the side of the dervishes,' he wrote from Yanbu. 'Our text books do not apply to its conditions at all.'[60] This was provocative, and true. Both Wingate and Wilson had been involved in fighting the dervishes at the end of the previous century, and the classic handbook on irregular warfare, *Small Wars*, made its loyalties clear from the start: the forces opposing regular troops, its author, Charles Callwell, stated, 'whether guerrillas, savages or quasi-organized armies, will be regarded as the enemy'.[61] Though the book was already two decades old, Callwell had a timeless warning for his readers: 'Guerrilla warfare is what the regular armies always have to dread, and when this is directed by a leader with a genius for war, an effective campaign becomes well-nigh impossible.'[62]

When, on 1 November, the *Suva* picked up Lawrence from Yanbu, its captain squinted at his disreputable-looking passenger. 'I had heard of a Captain Lawrence being on the coast,' 'Ginger' Boyle wrote in his memoirs: 'I had assumed he was one of the military officers sent over and was a little astonished when a small, untidily dressed and most unmilitary figure strolled up to me on board the ship I was temporarily commanding and said, hands in pockets and so without a salute: "I am going over to Port Sudan in this ship." '63

6

CRISIS OVER RABIGH

(November–December 1916)

In Jeddah, Colonel Wilson was in a panic. On 29 October he had received a telegram from Abdullah, informing him that his father had been unanimously recognised as 'King of the Arab Nation' by the people of Mecca. Wilson was stunned. The news, he told McMahon, had come as a 'complete surprise', and was 'all the more astonishing in view of the very strong representation against any such action which Mr Storrs informed me he had made to Emir Abdullah' a fortnight earlier.[1]

The French had unwittingly made matters worse. Some of their Muslim soldiers had been summoned to witness the announcement, which was made by a dignitary with frequent prompting from Abdullah. Unable to follow what was being said, the soldiers had assumed the ceremony was connected to the Islamic New Year the day before and, at its end, had followed the lead of the rest of the audience and cheered. It was only hours later that they found that 'the talk of the town was that they had congratulated the Sharif on becoming King in the name of the French Republic', Wilson reported frantically days later.[2] The senior French Muslim officer, he added, had 'now gone to bed with "fever" until the decision of the French Government as to recognition is received'.

Further confusion followed when Wilson angrily telephoned Abdullah to ask him why he had not discussed his intention beforehand. Abdullah claimed that negotiations on the announcement had been going on in secret between him and McMahon. This reply threw Wilson, and from London, Sir Edward Grey demanded an explanation. Unravelling the mystery in Cairo, Clayton discovered that in July Faruqi had told Husein that McMahon was willing to offer him the title 'King of the Arabs'.[3] 'To increase his own importance', Faruqi, Clayton established, was 'apt to record purely imaginary conversations with the High Commissioner and sometimes to attribute to him somewhat remarkable statements'.[4] This was an extraordinarily embarrassing admission because it was on information offered by Faruqi a year earlier that Clayton had based his shrill warning of the threat of jihad, which had in turn galvanised the War Committee into approving McMahon's approach to Husein. Moreover, it transpired that the Arab Bureau, which had been able to decipher Faruqi's coded telegrams since the beginning of July, knew about the approach, but when Husein had replied dismissively, the Bureau assumed the matter was closed. Until then, in line with his justification that he was rebelling against the Committee of Union and Progress rather than the Sultan, he had rejected the idea, because by making himself King he was implicitly challenging the Sultan's authority. It was only when Abdullah raised the idea again to counter Ali Haidar's accusation that Husein was a British puppet, and threatened to give up the revolt unless the announcement was made, that Husein had given in. Abdullah worked through the night after the announcement, telegraphing allied and neutral governments with the news, and concocting ready-made telegrams of congratulation to be distributed among the merchants in Jeddah for them to sign and return.

Abdullah's snap announcement left the British with a problem. It was impossible not to acknowledge the Sharif after the Russian, Serbian and Italian governments rapidly offered their congratulations to the new monarch. Indeed, as Wilson recognised when he had recovered from the shock of the news, to recognise Husein in some way might help weaken the enemy claim that the British planned to rule the Hijaz. While it was agreed that, for the time being, Husein should be called 'His Majesty the Sharif', the question of what to call him in the long run was a complicated one.

In London officals at the India Office said they did not mind recognising Husein as 'King of the Arabs', since the title conveyed a national, rather than territorial, claim, which did not impinge on their ally Ibn Saud. But the French, opposed to any title which might convey sovereignty over their Arab colonies in North Africa, preferred 'King of the Holy Places'. This the India Office rejected because it hinted at a spiritual supremacy too close to the Caliphate for their comfort. Wingate meanwhile suggested 'King of the Arabs in Hijaz', which McMahon boiled down to the 'King of the Hijaz', the formula which was finally agreed and eventually announced to the wider world on 1 January 1917.[5] It was the first sign of the true limits of McMahon's commitment to Husein.

Lawrence reached Khartoum on 6 November, the day that Wingate's promotion to High Commissioner of Egypt was made public. He was determined to make the case to Wingate for a new form of irregular war. He told Wingate that, following his discovery that there were wells at Khoreiba, Rabigh could not be secured by the presence of British ships offshore: a large Turkish force could either outflank Rabigh altogether or use Khoreiba to launch an overwhelming attack on the Arabs at Rabigh. But Wingate twisted Lawrence's analysis, using it in a report to the Foreign Office to reinforce his own belief that it was necessary to land at least a brigade to defend Rabigh.[6]

When he reached Cairo, Lawrence described what he had seen to Clayton. Clayton was under immense pressure. His new-born son had just died and, following a turf war within Army Headquarters in Egypt, almost all the military intelligence functions had been wrested from him, leaving him running the Bureau, which was being attacked from all sides for its amateurish management of the revolt. Wingate was furious that neither he nor Wilson had been informed earlier about the decision not to send troops and criticised the Arab Bureau for its failure to forward relevant telegrams from London to him. 'Unfortunately our clerical staff consists almost entirely of ladies who are not used to Government work,' the Bureau's deputy director explained to Wingate.[7] The secretaries at the Bureau do not all appear to have been employed for their shorthand. 'One of our typists, Miss MacKenzie, was the success of the evening,' Hogarth told his wife, of a dance held earlier that month.[8] Of the others, Miss Clay was 'very pretty', Miss Mason's qualifications included a spell as 'a show-off skating girl for a rink', while Miss James, a 'very cheeky' 'honeypot', had instantly fallen for one of the new officers who had joined the Bureau to improve logistics.[9] 'The confusion last month was great,' the Bureau's deputy director confessed that November, adding that his staff were learning – although 'by experience of many mistakes'.[10]

Meanwhile the situation in the Hijaz was worsening. Shortly after Lawrence left him, Feisal abandoned his camp at Hamra and retreated further down Wadi Safra towards the coast. From off Rabigh on 1 November Admiral Wemyss alerted McMahon that the Turks had followed Feisal down the wadi, and were now just three days' march from Rabigh. At about the same time, Wilson reported that Brémond had just told him that French troops earmarked for service in the Hijaz would arrive in Egypt in the middle of the month, which only increased the pressure on Britain to match their ally's commitment, just as Murray had predicted it would. The fear that the French offer of help would lead to Britain being blamed if the revolt collapsed provoked the War Committee in London to entertain Wingate's repeated demands that a force should be sent to Rabigh to stop the Turkish advance to Mecca. Reluctant to allow foreign troops to land, but painfully aware that the military situation was deteriorating, Husein vacillated. Believing that the Sharif would eventually concede and permit troops, Wingate kept up the pressure, but his insistence provoked spirited opposition from Robertson and Murray, backed by the beleaguered Arab Bureau, which believed that the arrival of British troops there would fatally compromise the Arab movement. 'Rabigh', as their increasingly bitter argument quickly became abbreviated, would only disappear as an issue when it finally became clear that neither French troops nor the expected Turkish advance towards Mecca would be forthcoming.

The end of the argument over Rabigh was still nine weeks away when, on 10 November, the War Committee asked Robertson to assess how many men would be needed to defend Rabigh. Robertson, who had assumed that he had successfully buried the issue a month earlier, was dismayed to witness the change in the mood in London, where the politicians were increasingly sensitive to the likelihood that, if they did nothing and the revolt failed, they could be accused of having let the Arabs down. Even Sykes, who had been firmly opposed to the dispatch of troops, seemed to be changing his mind. He had been lobbied by Norman Bray, a member of Wilson's staff who had returned to London after visiting Rabigh to argue that a brigade of soldiers was needed to defend the village.[11] In an attempt to discourage intervention, when Robertson reported to the War Committee on 13 November he suggested that it would be necessary to send 15,000 troops, a force the same size as the Turkish garrison in Medina, and more than three times the number Bray, and Wingate, had advised.

Murray was similarly concerned by the mounting political pressure for large-scale military intervention in the Hijaz. What he found most galling was that Wingate's assessment of the situation depended on Wilson and Parker, two men in whose judgement he had no faith whatsoever.[12] Not surprisingly, when he heard that Lawrence had returned from Rabigh, he asked for a report on Lawrence's findings that he could then pass on to Robertson in London. Under siege for the Bureau's inept handling of the revolt, Clayton was only too happy to oblige.

Amid the confusion of the Arab Bureau's office Lawrence wrote up his impressions of the situation in the Hijaz so that Clayton could pass them to Murray. In – his own words – 'a violent memorandum', he attacked the arguments made for sending British troops to Rabigh one by one. The tribesmen, he said, were the backbone of the revolt and, so long as they held out in the mountains, no British reinforcements were needed. If the tribesmen's resistance on the mountain road did collapse, unreliable communications with the Arabs and the fact that the Turks were within one hundred miles of Rabigh meant that the British would have too little notice to ship troops to Rabigh and deploy them in the time it would take the Turks to advance to the coast. Any British attempt to pre-empt this sequence of events by landing a large number of troops while the Arabs were still holding out would have the opposite effect intended, Lawrence argued, because the Arabs were deeply suspicious of Britain's imperialist intentions in the Hijaz: 'If the British, with or without the approval of the Sharif, disembarked an armed force at Rabigh powerful enough to take possession of the groves and organise a position there, they would, I am convinced, say "We are betrayed" and scatter to their tents.'[13] Having arrived in Rabigh, the British would be left holding a position on the coast, which the Turks, thanks to the wells at Khoreiba, could easily bypass. This, Lawrence argued, was exactly what the French wanted, because they did not want the Arab revolt to spread and challenge their own claim to Syria. 'They say,' Lawrence elaborated, ' "Above all things, the Arabs must not take Medina. This can be assured if an allied force lands at Rabigh. The tribal contingents will go home, and we will be the sole bulwark of the Sharif in Mecca. At the end of the war we will give him Medina as a reward." '[14] Believing that the reasons for Arab animosity towards Christians' presence in the Hijaz were political, and not religious, Lawrence recommended restricting British assistance to the aeroplanes which had been withdrawn and a handful of instructors who would represent no threat to the independence of the Hijaz.

Robertson welcomed this helpful second opinion from Lawrence, whom Murray recommended as 'an officer of great experience and knowledge of Arabs, who has just returned from a visit to Feisal's camp and also Rabigh'.[15] He incorporated Lawrence's conclusions in a further report on 19 November. This covered plans to launch an offensive against the Turks in the Sinai, which was designed to reduce the pressure on the Arabs in the Hijaz, and in it, Robertson repeated his warning that a British force should not be sent to Rabigh. Convinced by Lawrence's depiction of Brémond's agenda, officials in London pressed the French government on the behaviour of its representative in the Hijaz and on 27 November the French commander-in-chief, Joffre, wired Brémond a message informing him that the French government supported the capture of Medina and telling him to change his attitude. However, as Brémond observed, this order was not followed by any of the artillery he had requested for Ali and Feisal. 'One cannot capture a town with a telegram,' he mused afterwards.[16]

Clayton's astute support of Murray bolstered his own precarious situation. Storrs told a friend admiringly how Clayton's 'shares after having been forced down almost to zero . . . have now risen again together with those of the Arab Bureau, and are for the moment in some estimation'.[17] Wingate, in the meantime, was forced to defend himself when the Foreign Office questioned the disparity between the opinion he had attributed to Lawrence in his telegram of 7 November and the views Lawrence had then expressed in his own report ten days later, which Murray had then circulated widely. 'I understood him to agree that in such an emergency the Arabs would welcome this help,'[18] Wingate weakly replied on the 23rd. He must have been ruing his decision days earlier to overrule Clayton, who wanted Lawrence back in Cairo, and, having warmly endorsed Robertson's suggestion that Lawrence return to the Hijaz to assist with intelligence-gathering, it was too late for him to change his mind.[19] Furious at the way in which he had been out-manoeuvred, Wingate could only reveal his feelings to Wilson in private, disparaging Lawrence in a letter the following day as 'a visionary' whose 'amateur soldiering has evidently given him an exaggerated idea of the soundness of his views on purely military matters'.[20] He was, he told Wilson, 'annoyed in all this matter, not so much on account of the apparent want of straightness on the part of certain people who should be above that sort of thing, but on account of the huge loss of time when I am working at very high pressure, morning, noon and night'.

By 2 December Lawrence was back in Yanbu, the run-down port one hundred miles north of Rabigh. During his absence Feisal had retreated from Hamra and that night he set out with a guide from the local Juhaynah tribe and rode through the night to find Feisal, who was now north-east of the port, in the fertile Wadi Yanbu.

Feisal's tribesmen were not far inland and Lawrence reached their camp much sooner than he expected, in the middle of the night. 'When we got near we saw through the palm trees the flame and smoke of many fires, and the whole valley was full of shouting, and rifle shots, and the roaring of camels,' he wrote in his diary. 'I have never seen so many camels together and the mess was indescribable.'[21] Following his guide, Lawrence pressed through the crowds of men and animals and found Feisal sitting on a carpet in the middle of the wadi, reading reports and writing orders by the light of a lamp. Barely had the two men greeted one another when a bundle of hay fell off the back of a camel behind them, and they were engulfed by an avalanche of straw. The incident was almost allegorical for Feisal then explained what had happened in the mountains, where he had left his younger brother Zeid to guard the pass into Wadi Safra. Under pressure from a Turkish advance, Zeid's force had disintegrated. His men, Lawrence would write, had become, 'a loose mob of fugitives' who were now either 'riding wildly through the night towards Yanbu' or heading for their homes to protect their families from the Turks.[22]

The Turks' headway south-west from Medina was serious news, as it meant that they had effectively driven a wedge between Feisal's and Ali's forces at Yanbu and Rabigh respectively. Having talked with Feisal almost until dawn, Lawrence then tried, and failed, to sleep. After an hour he got up: 'it was too cold to do anything else'.[23] The mist had come down into the wadi, he was saturated and, as Feisal's intelligence depended on the scattering tribesmen, wild, contradictory reports were coming in about Turkish movements. The Harb and Juhaynah, the two tribes on whom Feisal depended, were demoralised; their camp, Lawrence observed, was 'not far off panic'.[24]

After sunrise, Feisal moved further down the wadi towards the sea. The next day, he offered Lawrence an odd gift. It was a British Lee-Enfield rifle which had been captured by the Turks at Gallipoli, engraved in golden Arabic: 'Part of our booty in the battles for the Dardanelles' and then given by the Ottomans to Feisal. Lawrence carved the date – 4 December 1916 – into the stock and, apparently, carried the rifle throughout the rest of the war.[25] But he made no mention of the weapon in any of the reports he wrote immediately afterwards, perhaps recognising that the gift was a rather barbed one. Feisal also asked Lawrence to wear Arab garments, giving him some white silk robes embroidered with gold: wedding garments sent to him by an aunt in Mecca. Among the Bedu, who dressed in russet, brown and indigo-dyed robes, these made Lawrence anything but inconspicuous – they were designed to give Lawrence a status that would make his permanent presence in the camp unquestionable.

Lawrence stayed two days with Feisal before returning to Yanbu. Back at the port, on 5 December he wrote to Hogarth with a downbeat report on Feisal's position, wondering whether his pessimism might be attributable to the fact that he had slept for a total of three hours in the previous three nights. 'All the same,' he admitted, 'things are bad.'[26]

There were telltale signs that Feisal's tribal coalition was under strain. The Juhaynah chiefs, Lawrence reported, were jealous of the influence Feisal was exerting on their kinsmen, and Feisal worried that the Harb and Juhaynah might turn on each other. Feisal himself, said Lawrence, was fast becoming a 'tribal leader not a leader of tribes', a phrase that Wingate speedily appropriated to advance his own case for sending troops.[27] The fact that the tribesmen were now drifting away, Lawrence admitted frankly, meant that 'the shield of Rabigh on which, in my old report, I relied for all the defensive work is now gone'.[28] Nothing now stood in the Turks' way except Ali's force in Rabigh, which Lawrence dismissed as 'anaemic', and the threat posed to their supply line and rear by the Harb in the mountains and Feisal in Wadi Yanbu. In his own notebook, Lawrence noted Feisal's bleak appraisal of the impact of the Turkish advance on the ambitious ideas they had discussed: 'Impossible go S[outh] Syria while Turks free attack Mecca: he would chuck the N[orth] and go south with Bisha and Hudheil to die in its defence' – a reference to two tribes Feisal felt he could trust in the last resort.[29] Feisal 'has now swung round to the belief in a British force at Rabigh,' Lawrence reported to Hogarth early in December, admitting that 'I see myself that the arguments have force'.[30]

Bad news followed Lawrence down to the sea. The day after he had left Feisal, the Turks had attacked. While the artillery the British had supplied made 'an immense noise, most excellent for tribal work', according to Lawrence, the guns had not been supplied with sights nor any of the range-finding equipment needed to make them effective and the ancient shells that came with them had fuses damp with fungus.[31] Cosmetic in value, the artillery proved little use in the battle that followed. The tribesmen were routed and Feisal was forced to flee for Yanbu. When asked by Feisal why his Juhaynah tribesmen had retreated, Abdel Kerim replied that his men were tired and thirsty and wanted to brew some coffee. After the war, Lawrence remembered his reaction to this excuse: 'Feisal and I lay back and laughed: then we went to see what could be done to save the town.'[32]

Faced with an imminent Turkish attack, in Yanbu the Arabs were frantically trying to improve the town's defences. Coordinating the defence was Herbert Garland, a tall, sardonic metallurgist, who had worked before the war preserving ancient Egyptian tools. In wartime the conservationist had metamorphosed into bomb-maker. Thousands of 'Garland grenades' – a type of mortar shell – were manufactured and shipped to Gallipoli. Garland himself was shipped to the Hijaz in September 1916 to assist in training the Bedu in the use of explosives. 'The barren, jagged, uninviting mountains of the Hijaz do not . . . display any apparent attractions which would indicate why Muhammad, or any less important person, should wish to visit them,' he dryly observed, noting of his pupils that 'A robber in the Hijaz has his lot cast amongst such experts that his profession must be difficult to follow.'[33]

The Bedu, who deemed hard work beneath them, rounded up the townspeople of Yanbu to dig a trench in front of the town. Garland found an old Turkish cannon at the fort, but as it 'was apt to fire astern instead of forward we relied on its warlike appearance to help us scare off the Turks'.[34] More usefully, out at sea behind the town, five ships sent by Boyle scoured the Yanbu plain with their searchlights by night. One of the Turks' Bedu guides later admitted that the Turks had faltered when the slow sweep of the searchlights revealed the barren openness of the plain they would have to cross to attack the little port.[35]

Lawrence also found an unwelcome letter from Cyril Wilson awaiting him in Yanbu. Wingate, Wilson explained, wanted Lawrence to manage the supplies into the port, a task Lawrence found deeply uncongenial, since he regarded himself as 'primarily Intelligence Officer, or liaison with Feisal'.[36] Lawrence tried to wriggle out. 'I do not quite understand what the Sirdar can mean by my superintending the "supply question",' he replied to Wilson, arguing – rather inconsistently – that the Arabs were best left to manage supplies themselves and that Garland was better qualified for the role. To emphasise the point he added that he was so bogged down by 'coding and decoding, and local work that I have been unable to write a word of a report . . . on my visit to Feisal'.[37] In fact he had already written in detail on the precarious situation for Hogarth's benefit the day before.

In his letter to Wilson Lawrence also requested an urgent aerial reconnaissance of Wadi Safra by the British aeroplanes which had now returned to Rabigh. Wadi Safra was too far from Rabigh to be reached in a return trip by the aircraft, and reconnaissance of the area only became possible once Lawrence had organised a makeshift airstrip at Yanbu, at which the biplanes could refuel before flying back to Rabigh. Even so, Lawrence was determined that the Royal Flying Corps should not make him superfluous. Days later he offended the head of the flight, Major Ross, by claiming that the value of aerial photography 'is very great in organised warfare, but the results are of no use to us here'.[38] It was a strange criticism, given that the aircraft could supply accurate and up-to-date information on Turkish movements which had so far been lacking. On 9 December from Rabigh, Colonel Joyce sent Wilson a series of aerial photographs taken the previous day over Wadi Safra. These revealed that a small Turkish force had reached the wells at Bir Said, about twenty miles from the sea, and just forty-five from Yanbu. It looked, Joyce decided, as if the Turks had made up their minds to 'dispatch Feisal'.[39]

Pierce Joyce had arrived at Rabigh a month earlier in command of a detachment of 450 Egyptian troops whose job was to protect the new British airfield beside the lagoon. A brusque, west-coast Irishman, a 'giant of a man' at over six feet four inches tall, Joyce was a professional soldier who walked stiffly as a result of a bad wound he had received during the Boer War. He had been tasked by Wingate with deciding how best to defend Rabigh, and he was unimpressed by what he found there. The trenches dug by the Arabs were 'mere scratchings', he wrote to Wilson in Jeddah, and his men were having to sleep under blankets because the '*Minerva* brought us 10 tents *minus* the poles so of course they are useless'.[40] With frequent heavy rain and hail at night, the lack of shelter was a serious problem: 'I'd like to wring somebody's neck over it for it simply means that someone has been damn careless and we suffer in consequence.'

Joyce had little faith in his own Egyptian troops if the Turks made it to Rabigh. The British, Brémond thought, always answered 'Yes' a little too fast when he asked them if they trusted the Egyptians.[41] Nor was Joyce happy about the other Arab troops in the camp which Ali, whom

Joyce branded 'a little shit',[42] would not allow him to visit. They were 'doubtful allies putting up the rottenest fight',[43] he complained, who would 'melt away like snow when a few Turks appear' while the 'so-called regular troops are so eaten up with intrigue that it is very doubtful if they will fight either, or on which side'. Rampant intrigue was the most obvious of the Arabs' problems, but not the only one. At the end of January 1917, Joyce put in an order for 10,000 mercury pills to treat the syphilis rife among Ali's men.[44]

Further flights revealed that there was a large Turkish force in Wadi Yanbu, and other troops moving south from Bir Said, a village halfway between Wadi Yanbu and Wadi Safra, control of which enabled the Turks to tie Feisal's troops in Yanbu and cut them off from Rabigh.[45] When Storrs visited Yanbu on 13 December he reported 'a regular panic ashore' and that Feisal had taken up residence aboard HMS *Hardinge*.[46] The Egyptian soldiers based in Yanbu under Garland were also nervous. 'We cannot . . . defend this town,' they told Joyce, unless they were reinforced by a sizeable regular force, to compensate for the likelihood of the Arabs running away when the shooting began.[47]

7

TURNING POINT

(December 1916–January 1917)

'Rabigh has been a perfect nuisance during the last few weeks but I have
been as stubborn as a donkey and so far have succeeded in getting my
way,' Sir William Robertson wrote to Murray on 1 December.[1] He spoke
too soon. The weakness of Lawrence's arguments had been rudely exposed
by news that the Turks were nearing the coast. The Turks' advance and
political crisis in London combined to revive the case for sending a force
to the Hijaz. When, on 5 December, Herbert Asquith resigned as Prime
Minister following a collapse in confidence over his conduct of the war,
the Secretary of State for India, Sir Austen Chamberlain, immediately
buttonholed Asquith's energetic replacement, David Lloyd George,
about whether to send troops to Rabigh.[2] 'I disliked stirring up the
Sharif,' Chamberlain wrote in a private minute to his advisers, 'but since
he was egged on by Lord Kitchener and Egypt, I dislike still more the
prospect of seeing him go under.'[3]

Chamberlain was a political heavyweight whose views Lloyd George
could not ignore. 'Rabigh again discussed,' Robertson wearily warned
Murray on 11 December, of a meeting of Lloyd George's newly created
War Cabinet earlier that day.[4] Unwilling to appear to be doing nothing,
the War Cabinet cautiously agreed that if Husein applied for troops in
writing, then a force could in principle be sent. 'We do not wish to land
troops in Hijaz except in last extremity, but Sharif must be saved from
destruction if possible,' the Foreign Office informed Wingate later the
same day, adding that if a brigade was enough to hold Rabigh, 'we
authorise you to despatch these troops from Suez whenever you receive a

request from Sharif . . . but you must be satisfied that the force is sufficient and that it can be supplied with water and all necessities.'[5]

By chance, in Khartoum Wingate had received just such an appeal from the Sharif, who had reluctantly handed Wilson a request for help in Jeddah the night before. He immediately telegraphed the Foreign Office early on 11 December to say that Husein had finally asked for 6,000 men. Husein would prefer Muslims, Wingate reported, but if none were available, he had no objection to British troops instead.[6] His telegram crossed with the Foreign Office message authorising dispatch.

Overnight, however, Husein changed his mind. He had been swayed by a report in the Medina-based Turkish propaganda newspaper, *Hijaz*, which alleged that he had already promised the region to the British after the war,[7] and was unwilling to play further into the hands of his would-be replacement, Ali Haidar. At three o'clock on the afternoon of the 12th, Wingate was obliged to ask London to ignore his earlier message, explaining that Husein preferred to keep a force – which must comprise Muslim troops alone – on standby at either Suez or Port Sudan. Angry with the Sharif, that night he drafted a telegram asking Wilson to try to force Husein to acknowledge his responsibility, should the Turks recapture Mecca.[8] He also asked for, and received, permission from London to issue an ultimatum to Husein, telling him that he had to accept troops now, or never. Husein, however, refused to be brow-beaten.

Storrs arrived in Jeddah the same day. He was in buoyant mood, having remembered to bring a gramophone with him on his latest voyage and, with the cool boom of Wagner in the background, had this time defeated the ship's paymaster 'dreadfully' at chess.[9] Arriving ashore, Storrs wandered through the city's twisting streets to the tall, white-washed palace where Husein was staying. Pushing his way through the large and noisy crowd that had gathered outside, he went inside with Wilson to meet Husein for the first time.

Husein was taller and more impressive than Storrs had expected. He had 'a captivating sincerity of utterance, enhanced by a benignant, noble simplicity of demeanour', recorded Storrs, a man who was rarely lost for words.[10] Under the fierce glare of an acetylene lamp, Wilson and Storrs discussed the military situation with Husein late into the night. Wilson presented Husein with Feisal's latest prediction – reported by Lawrence – that the revolt would collapse within three weeks.[11] But the Sharif was in combative mood. Referring to the somewhat speculative request he had first made that March, he reproached Storrs for Britain's failure to land in Syria and cut the Hijaz Railway to support him. Gripping the young diplomat by the lapels of his jacket, Husein reminded Storrs of the importance of McMahon's letters. 'The High Commissioner is the justification of my action,' he said, 'and wherever I meet him I will grasp him like his, claiming him as my witness.'[12] It was becoming clear to the British that Husein invested considerably more faith in the correspondence than they did. And he did so from a position of considerable power. Husein was, wrote another British officer, 'quite acute enough to realise that he . . . is rendering important services to the British in this theatre of the war' by 'immobilising the best part of two Turkish divisions', and expected to be treated if not as an equal then as more than 'a mere suppliant in receipt of favours'.[13]

Husein's realisation that the Turks were winning the propaganda war did, however, lead him to acknowledge to Wilson the problem that the Indians were causing in Mecca. The British had already established that the Turkish governor of the Hijaz, Ghalib Pasha, who was now a prisoner of war, had met Mahmud Hasan before the outbreak of the revolt and signed a declaration of support for the holy war, which was then dispatched to Afghanistan.[14] But when Wilson asked Husein to sanction Hasan's arrest, at first the Sharif had 'demurred as he nearly always did when asked to do something helpful, saying that it was inadvisable to treat so saintly a man in such rough fashion'.[15] It was only when Wilson patiently explained to Husein that Hasan was advocating his murder that the Sharif rapidly agreed that the Indian should be ejected from Mecca. Hasan was arrested on 18 December, sent down to Jeddah and exiled to Malta early the following month.[16] The Silk Letters plot, instrumental in persuading the Government of India to take a closer interest in the Hijaz, had finally been broken up.

For other reasons, as yet unknown to the British, the situation was moving in their favour. The Turkish Minister for War, Enver Pasha, had planned to send an expeditionary force to the Hijaz but, according to the chief German military adviser to the Ottoman government, Otto Liman von Sanders, the 'organisation of this expedition, in which Christians could not be permitted to participate, was found so difficult by the Turks, that it was dropped in the fall'.[17] As he expected the British to attack Palestine in January 1917, Liman von Sanders urged Jemal in Syria to concentrate all his available resources on repelling that offensive. Disregarding the religious significance of holding on to the holy city, he took the view that Medina had no strategic value whatsoever and told Jemal to forget Fakhri, whose frequent pleas for supplies he dismissed as 'customary Turkish exaggeration'.[18]

Supplies to Medina began to dwindle. In the city, Ali Haidar complained that there was barely enough food for the townspeople and that the army's pack animals were starving.[19] Outside the city, the Turks' foraging in the mountains between their front line and Medina incurred hostility from the local Harb tribesmen, whose livestock the Turks were pilfering.[20] The Harb increasingly raided Turkish supply lines, which stretched for more than fifty miles through the mountain passes, on one occasion capturing 300 camels.[21]

Without hard currency, the Turks had trouble bolstering waning tribal support. Their paper money had no buying power compared to the vast quantity of British gold which was now arriving in Jeddah. By the beginning of 1917, the Sharif had been paid nearly £1 million in gold sovereigns and there are plenty of anecdotes to suggest that the Hijaz was awash with British coin.[22] Captain Boyle watched an Arab offer one of his men a sovereign in exchange for a packet of cigarette papers: 'the sailor, although surprised, rose to the occasion', he remembered, followed swiftly by 'other members of the boat's crew who were fortunate enough to have cigarette papers on them'.[23]

It was 'the fattest time the tribes have ever known', stated Lawrence.[24] The Bedu were understandably determined to milk the willingness of both sides to pay them for as long as possible. One sheikh told the Turks that the Arabs commanded considerably more support than was in fact the case, apparently to draw out the conflict, in which the Turks were paying him as an informant.[25] As a result, the Turks believed that substantial numbers of British, Egyptian and Algerian troops had already landed at Rabigh. They certainly knew from spies that Feisal had a British adviser.[26] They may also have thought that their enemy was well fortified since, in a moment of desperation, Wingate had deliberately wired a report saying that he had sent barbed wire to Rabigh *en clair* in the hope that the Turks might intercept it.[27]

The British too were encouraged to believe that the forces ranged against them were of a higher calibre than they really were. From Medina, the picture looked a little different. The Turkish force – a camel corps – which was so feared by Feisal and Lawrence, was 'short of food and money' in Ali Haidar's opinion, and was eventually forced to turn back due to malnutrition and disease.[28] Late in December Fakhri toured his frontline troops at Hamra and in Wadi Yanbu. Concerned by their condition and their vulnerability to bombing by British seaplanes operating from off Yanbu, on 23 December he ordered his men to withdraw to positions around Medina.[29]

It was not immediately clear that Turkish orders had changed, partly because the Turks who had been in Wadi Yanbu were first ordered south, towards Rabigh. From there, Colonel Joyce reported, he believed that the enemy was 'coming on slowly and systematically'.[30] When they met Wilson off Yanbu on 27 December to discuss the emergency measures needed to defend Rabigh, Feisal and Lawrence knew only that the Turks had withdrawn from Wadi Yanbu. Wilson had passed through Rabigh on his way up from Jeddah, and must have been aware of Joyce's pessimistic assessment of his chances of fending off a Turkish attack on the village. When Feisal raised the possibility of attacking Wajh, a small port 180 miles north of Yanbu, to reduce the pressure on Rabigh to the south by exposing the railway – the Turks' supply line – to attack, Wilson unexpectedly agreed. The British had considered, and then shelved, the same plan three months earlier, because they deemed then situation at Rabigh too uncertain to risk a leap up the coast. Feisal now believed that it was time to take the risk. Wilson, who increasingly took the view that Wingate's effort to pressurise the Sharif into accepting troops was misguided, was willing to help him. He offered to mass as much naval support off Rabigh as possible to discourage a Turkish advance while Feisal marched northwards. The decision was taken to

attack Wajh on the day after the next moonless night. So the assault was
scheduled for 23 January.

That afternoon, Feisal and Lawrence began to plan an overland march
designed to demonstrate their strength to the country through which
they would pass en route to Wajh. Feisal then left the coast for Wadi Ais,
an inland valley running towards the railway, eighty miles north of
Yanbu, where he hoped to meet his brother Abdullah, who had left
Mecca by the inland road to Medina weeks earlier. Abdullah had been
slow to set out, because he was worried that his mainly Utaybah
tribesmen would clash with his brother Ali's Harb contingent.[31] Feisal
now hoped to inform his brother of his plans.

On 3 January Lawrence set off with a small party of Harb tribesmen
towards Hamra to establish whether the Turks had evacuated Wadi
Safra. Having climbed the dangerously rotten strata of Jabal Dhifran, a
mountain overlooking the road towards Hamra, the following morning they saw Turkish tents far below them. A few pot shots at the
campsite raised the Turkish garrison; seeing he was outnumbered,
Lawrence led the tribesmen away down into the valley back to Yanbu,
where they surprised two Turkish soldiers. They were 'much unbut-
toned, disturbed at their first morning duty', Lawrence sniggered
later.[32] It was his first encounter with the enemy in the Hijaz, and he
was heartened by it: 'They were the most ragged men I have ever seen,
bar a British tramp and surrendered at once.'[33] Their physical condition and, under interrogation, description of the sickness afflicting
the Ottoman forces clearly persuaded Lawrence that his plans to head
north could now be resurrected. On 5 January he asked the Arab
Bureau for four maps covering Syria and Mesopotamia.[34] It was a
significant request.

Oddly, despite the improvement in the Arabs' situation, on 5 January
Wilson received a telephone call from one of Husein's officials suggesting
that the Sharif would be willing to accept troops if Wingate advised that
course of action. He reported the approach to Wingate, who seized on the
news. Newly installed as the High Commissioner in Cairo, having just
taken over from McMahon, Wingate informed the Foreign Office the

following day that he had received 'a formal application'[35] for help from Husein, and that he would now send troops to Rabigh.

Murray was surprised by this unexpected development. 'I need hardly say what a blow your letter and the Sharif's telegram are to me,' he wrote to Wingate the same day, openly accusing him of making Husein feel 'more or less obliged to accept this assistance'.[36] At the eastern edge of the Sinai, his forces – already under-strength in his opinion – were on the point of launching an attack designed to drive the Turks back into Palestine. Deploying troops to the Hijaz now would, Murray insisted, 'seriously hamper my operations if not entirely bring them to a stand-still'. Wingate pressed on regardless. Orders were drafted for the 'General Officer Commanding, Rabigh', instructing him 'that the Sharif is to be maintained and Mecca secured at all costs'.[37] But they were never issued, largely due to Wilson's unexpected intervention.

When he heard what Wingate had told the Foreign Office Wilson contacted the Arab Bureau. 'I consider it most dangerous to send British troops to Hijaz on strength of a telephone message from an Arab Government official which the Sharif can easily repudiate,' he ventured: 'I much regret this decision.' If troops were to be sent, Wilson argued that Husein should be asked how much time he needed to pave the way for their arrival.[38]

Wingate tried to suppress Wilson's opinion but in the Arab Bureau Hogarth, who was vehemently opposed to sending troops, ensured that Wilson's views were transmitted to London, exposing the reality behind Wingate's assertion that the Sharif had asked for troops. At the India Office a senior adviser, Sir Arthur Hirtzel, was critical of Wingate. 'HMG have not been too well served by Sir Reginald Wingate in this most important matter,' he commented, explaining, for the record, that 'but for the fact that Sir Archibald Murray was sufficiently obstinate not to move without confirmation from the War Office, HMG would not have known that this "formal application" was nothing more than a telephone message in which the whole respon-sibility was thrown on us. Knowing it, the War Cabinet declined to act.'[39] Already bruised by this episode, Wingate was then forced to admit on 12 January that Wilson had just received a further letter from the Sharif, 'to the effect that he does not desire us to land British troops in the Hijaz at present'.[40]

Murray now took full advantage of the fact that Wingate had over-stretched himself. 'Things seem to be going so well in the Hijaz,' he told the High Commissioner on 19 January, that he saw no further need to keep the brigade on standby for Rabigh, when it could more usefully be employed in his approaching offensive in Sinai.[41] With no troops to deploy, Wingate was forced to concede. On 24 January he wrote to Arthur Balfour, the new Foreign Secretary, to try to draw a line under the affair. While the Turks' contraction around Medina was good news, he said, the final removal of the menace of a Turkish advance on Mecca depended on Britain's ability 'to help the Arabs permanently to destroy the Turkish railway communications with the Hijaz'. It was to this end, Wingate suggested, that 'all our energies should now be directed'.[42]

During the argument over troops, Lawrence had been making prep-arations for the march up the coast to Wajh which, Feisal hoped, would advertise the strength of his support, bringing more tribesmen on to his side and possibly forcing the surrender of Wajh without a fight. On 17 January, he landed at Umm Lajj, nearly a hundred miles up the coast from Yanbu, with Boyle and Charles Vickery to meet Feisal to finalise tactics. Major Vickery was the first of a small mission of regular officers summoned by Wingate to advise the Arabs on destroying the railway. A professional soldier of sixteen years' experience, he made no effort to hide his disdain for the disorganisation of the campaign, which he attributed to the disproportionate role amateurs like Lawrence and Garland had played in it so far. But the professionals were about to take over: the meeting was to be Lawrence's last task before he handed over to another member of the mission, Colonel Stewart Newcombe, and returned to Cairo. 'I wish I had not to go back to Egypt,' he had ended a letter to his mother the previous evening. 'Any way I have had a change.'[43]

Boyle, Vickery and Lawrence rode to Feisal's camp and arrived in time for lunch. 'It was a greasy stew,' remembered Boyle, 'out of which we helped ourselves to pieces of meat with our fingers. Feisal handed me choice morsels and I understood that this was a special mark of favour to

his principal guest, so I felt obliged to eat them.'[44] Boyle was aching from
his camel ride – 'Except as a child at the Zoo, or going to the Pyramids as
a tourist, I had never mounted one' – and the reek of sun-warmed human
faeces on the ground around him put him off the thought of food.
Vickery was similarly put off. He 'saved the situation by producing a
large flask of whisky, a proceeding frowned upon by Lawrence, but
laughed at by Feisal, and the contents were very welcome', Boyle wrote in
his memoirs.[45] Lawrence, who did not drink, slated Vickery's action as
'tactless' given the Muslim company, and put it down to years of living in
the Sudan, which 'took the fine edge off some Englishmen'.[46]

After lunch Feisal suggested that Vickery should muster a force of
several hundred Bedu on the island of Al Hasani, off Umm Lajj, and from
there sail up the coast and wait off Wajh until he arrived from the south.
The question was how long his army would take to cover the distance, a
journey of one hundred miles.

The coastal plain between Umm Lajj and Wajh, hemmed to the east
by low hills and bounded on the west by the turquoise stripe of the Red
Sea, was then, as now, a desiccated, empty place. Its monotony was only
broken in places by a few stunted, flat-topped trees, their branches cowed
and black as if scorched by the hot onshore wind. It was doubtful whether
a force of almost 6,000 men, two to a camel, and a further 5,000 on foot,
would find enough water along the way to sustain itself. The decision
hinged on whether the wells two-thirds of the way to Wajh at Abu
Zuraybat were full, though heavy rain encouraged the Arabs to think that
there might be pools along the way, lessening the importance of the
wells.[47] If not, the force would have to travel more slowly to survive,
missing the date of the attack. Feisal decided to take the risk. As a
precaution, Boyle agreed to drop twenty tons of water at a point a short
distance south of Wajh at Habban, which Feisal's force should reach on
22 January, the day before the proposed assault on Wajh. The British
decided to give Brémond no warning of their plans to attack.[48]

Newcombe, however, had been delayed and Lawrence's exit from the
campaign was postponed. As Feisal intended to set out for Wajh early the
next day, Lawrence realised to his delight that it would be impossible to
complete the handover. Realising nevertheless that he had not impressed

Vickery, he decided to take the opportunity to win Newcombe round to his own way of thinking. He had surveyed the eastern Sinai with Newcombe before the war and wrote to his old colleague that night. 'This show is splendid: you cannot imagine greater fun for us, greater fury and vexation for the Turks. We win hands down if we keep the Arabs simple . . . to add to them heavy luxuries will only wreck this show, and guerilla does it,' he gushed, before pre-empting criticism of his approach.

> Vickery had a funny idea that nothing had yet been done out here. It's not true! May I suggest that by effacing yourself for the first part and making friends with the head men before you start pulling them about, you will find your way very much easier? . . . After all, it's an Arab war, and we are only contributing materials – and the Arabs have the right to go their own way and run things as they please. We are only guests.[49]

The following morning Feisal's force set out for Wajh, arrayed in two wings, which took turns to sing to one another. Newcombe, who had arrived shortly after they set out, rapidly caught up, but he did not send Lawrence back to the coast, preferring to travel with him for the following week. The Arabs' style of marching was 'rather splendid and barbaric', Lawrence wrote days earlier, as the force moved from Yanbu. Then, Lawrence rode behind Feisal, dressed in the white wedding clothes and a scarlet headdress he had been given. Next to Lawrence, also in a red headcloth, was Feisal's cousin Sharraf, who was wearing the henna-dyed robe and black cloak typical of a Juhaynah. Behind them were

> three banners of faded crimson silk with gilt spikes, behind them the drummers playing a march, and behind them again the wild mass of twelve hundred bouncing camels of the bodyguard, packed as closely as they could move, the men in every variety of coloured clothes and the camels nearly as brilliant in their trappings, and the whole crowd singing at the tops of their voices a warsong in honour of Feisal and his family.[50]

As Feisal predicted, to march in such numbers marked a profound change for the Bedu, who were more used to raiding in parties which rarely comprised more than a dozen of their kinsmen. 'We are no longer Arabs but a nation,' observed one of the Juhaynah's leaders, Abdel Kerim, somewhat gloomily, as he looked down from his tent at the hundreds of camp-fires below him one night during a halt in the march. Awed by what he saw, another tribesman declared: 'It is not an army but a world which is moving on Wajh.'[51]

8

WAJH AND AFTER

(*January–February 1917*)

There was no sign of Feisal's Arabs when, on 22 January as agreed, the *Hardinge* arrived off Habban with the emergency water supply. With no moon that night, the British had their best chance of slipping inshore unnoticed by a Turkish garrison rumoured to be 800-strong and Wemyss decided to press on to Wajh regardless. He was anxious to put ashore as fast as possible the 400 Arabs on board who had been collected from Al Hasani island, one hundred miles to the south. As he had little faith in the Arabs' willingness to fight if the Turkish garrison did not surrender first, he had also cobbled together a landing party comprising the *Hardinge*'s marines and its stokers, led by Vickery.[1]

A black night gave way to dawn fog on 23 January. 'Our little fleet steamed slowly northward like grey ghosts to take up their fighting positions,' remembered Vickery's right-hand man, Norman Bray.[2] Vickery decided to go ahead with a landing on the north side of Wajh, which had been planned on the assumption that Feisal would be approaching simultaneously from the south. Just after seven o'clock that morning the silence was interrupted by the rattle of chains, as the *Hardinge* dropped its anchors, and landing boats packed with Juhaynah tribesmen in their damp and smelly camel-hair cloaks were jerkily lowered into the glassily calm sea and rowed ashore unseen.

Wajh today is a much larger town than it was in 1917, boasting its own small airport. A few once-smart merchants' houses and the old mosque, with its fat, stubby minaret, are all that remain of the little walled port which Wemyss decided to attack that chilly morning in

January 1917. Foreigners are unusual here and, judging by the few unfriendly stares I attracted, not especially welcome. The town council has optimistically dotted the seafront with gaudily painted benches – all empty when I went past in March 2005 – which perch on the edge of an odd coral plateau which hangs over the beach below like a petrified breaking wave.

Scrambling from the beach up the crumbling crest of this plateau ninety years ago, Bray found that the mist had cleared. To the south, the tops of some of the whitewashed houses in the town of Wajh, which in 1917 was mostly squeezed between the headwall of the plateau and the shoreline, were visible. 'We have often wanted to know how the Arabs fight,' he reported afterwards: 'The result now observed was highly interesting.'[3] Many of the Arabs refused to go any further, but a small group of about a hundred advanced at 'a very sharp pace' straight at the Turks. When the Turks began shooting from about 1,000 yards away, the Juhaynah took no notice: 'They appeared,' Bray observed incredulously, 'to be out for a constitutional.' The Arabs finally stopped thirty yards from the Turks and began shooting back. 'When the Turks fell they showed not the least emotion or satisfaction and merely said "*mayit*"', the Arabic word for 'dead'. Overrunning the Turkish defences and leaving their own dead on the plain, the tribesmen disappeared into Wajh.

Bray returned to the shore to see what the *Hardinge* could do to help the tribesmen. But the distance from the ships to the shore was so short that shells fired from the British ships simply ricocheted screaming off the rocks before or behind the town to detonate in the hills beyond. The naval party landed, but appeared to him to be at sea on land.

'What would you advise us to do?' its leader asked Bray.

'Well, you are commanding here and not I,' Bray retorted.

'Yes, yes, I know. But what would you do if you were I?'[4]

Following the Arabs into Wajh, Bray found mayhem. 'The dead were still lying about, the houses had been ransacked from roof to floor, papers everywhere, boxes and cupboards cut open and even the mattresses cut open to find hidden treasure.'[5] Kapok was blowing down the streets. The Arabs had moved from house to house, shooting and looting, 'eating their

way into the bowels of the town'.[6] By the end of that day, the remaining
Turks had taken refuge in a few houses and the mosque at the southern
end of Wajh.

The following morning the Arabs sent one of the Turkish prisoners
with a white flag to offer his comrades the chance to surrender. Exactly
what happened next is unclear. In Bray's official report he mentioned no
resistance, describing only how under a white flag Vickery had then
entered the empty town. Yet in his memoirs, he described a spirited
defence which ended only when, from out at sea in the *Fox*, Boyle decided
to shell the mosque: 'A huge gaping hole was blown in the wall, and
fifteen very bewildered and very dusty and begrimed men staggered out
without their weapons, in token of surrender.'[7] Although this later
account undoubtedly plays up the drama of the event, the fact that Feisal
afterwards criticised Boyle for the damage he had done to the town
suggests that more force was used than Bray admitted at the time. By
mid-afternoon on 24 January, the British were in control of the town.
They had lost one man. Stewart, the observer in one of the seaplanes
directing the naval bombardment, was leaning forward in his cockpit to
send a radio message when he was hit by a bullet and killed. He was
buried at sea that evening.

Feisal arrived the following day with his force of more than 10,000
tribesmen. Progress up the gravel plain beside the sea had been slow and
he had reached Habban two days later than planned on 24 January, by
which time the attack on Wajh was into its second day. Stung by
his failure, Feisal immediately dispatched men to participate in the
mopping-up operation, but he had arrived too late.

The political consequences of the delay were severe, Lawrence realised
when he arrived in Wajh. The townspeople, who had stayed despite
Feisal's warning a week earlier that he was coming, were furious at what
the Bedu and the British had done to their town. All their dhows, vital
for the trade they maintained with Egypt, had been destroyed in the
bombardment, which had 'punched large holes in all walls', Lawrence
noted.[8] And while the Arabs' almost twenty killed was a negligible loss
as far as either Vickery or Bray – who had both seen action in France –
were concerned, in Lawrence's opinion they were unnecessary casualties:

'Our rebels were not materials, like soldiers, but friends of ours, trusting in our leadership. We were not in command nationally, but by invitation; and our men were volunteers, individuals, local men, relatives, so that a death was a personal sorrow to many in the army.'9

On 27 January, having spent two days supervising the offloading of stores in Wajh, Lawrence left for Cairo with Wilson to decide what to do next. As his letter to Newcombe suggested, he was worried that Vickery thought he was incompetent and he may have feared that he was vulnerable in the report that Vickery would inevitably write on the operation. Lawrence probably raised his fear to Feisal, who rapidly wrote to his father about his concern 'that Lawrence should not return [to] Cairo as he has given such very great assistance'. The Sharif raised the letter with Wilson, who in turn reported the request that Lawrence be allowed to stay to Clayton.10

Lawrence was right: Vickery was scathing. 'Although it only embarked on a four days' march, due north, parallel to the coast line, and within twenty miles of it, a great part of Feisal's army lost its way and arrived at the rendezvous two days late,' Vickery commented.11 Bray – piqued in later life that he had never basked in the glory Lawrence had enjoyed – would write how 'the excuse was "lack of water", but there was nothing to have prevented five hundred men being pushed on ahead to Wajh', a failure, he believed, which 'was a reflection, both on Feisal's leadership and still more on his British advisers'.12 The real reason Lawrence did not admit until after the war. The day after he set out for Wajh, Feisal received news that his brother Abdullah had ambushed a Turkish column near the railway, capturing its commander, artillery and a substantial sum of money. The Arabs had stopped for some impromptu, exuberant celebrations for this major coup, and were delayed as a consequence.

On his return to Cairo, Lawrence spent several days helping to correct the draft of the *Handbook of Hejaz* – the Arab Bureau's embryonic guidebook to the region – and furiously writing up his impressions of the tribal situation and the attack on Wajh. In meetings with Hogarth, Storrs and Wingate he stressed the dividend which Feisal's march was paying: news of the revolt and recognition of Feisal's strength were beginning to spread far to the north into Syria. Tewfiq Majali, a member of the family implicated in a violent uprising against Ottoman rule in the southern Syrian town of Karak in 1910, was one of those who now contacted Husein. The same day that Feisal arrived in Wajh leaders of the Bali tribe came south to offer him their allegiance. Members of the Aida, Fuqarah and Wuld Suleiman tribes from east of the Hijaz Railway would also quickly join Feisal in Wajh.[13] All three were satellite clans of the Aniza, the dominant tribe in northern Arabia. Their arrival raised hopes that Nuri Shaalan, the leading sheikh of the largest Aniza subtribe, the Rwala, might also join the revolt. In his seventies, Shaalan was, in Lawrence's words, 'not a very attractive person',[14] who had killed two of his brothers to seize control of his tribe. He had, however, been imprisoned by the Turks before the war and one of his close friends had been hanged in the May 1916 executions which had accelerated Husein's decision to revolt, and was thought by Lawrence to be 'worth buying'.[15] But widespread famine in Syria meant that when Feisal approached Shaalan late in 1916, the elderly chieftain had explained that he depended on Turkish goodwill for grain. 'Nothing prevents us from joining you but the lack of food and arms', was Shaalan's tantalising reply.[16]

Clayton and Lawrence briefly considered flying supplies to Nuri Shaalan's home at Jawf, nearly 300 miles east of Aqaba. They were encouraged by the local commander of the newly formed Royal Flying Corps, who saw no reason why this wild scheme could not succeed, 'providing . . . misfortune, such as an engine failure, does not interfere',[17] but Jawf was too remote, and the plan was eventually abandoned. Clayton and Lawrence knew that Feisal's revolt would dramatically expand in scope if Shaalan could be persuaded to support Feisal, because the Aniza were camel breeders who ranged widely between the northern Hijaz, Syria and Mesopotamia, and enjoyed correspondingly far-reaching influence. The Turks shared this view of Shaalan's importance. Ali Haidar had given the sheikh a gold watch when he met him en route for Medina the previous summer. Jemal had then awarded him a medal for loyalty and advanced his son part of a large reward for capturing Feisal dead or alive.[18]

On 3 February Lawrence met Brémond, who was also in Cairo. The bear-like Brémond suggested to Lawrence that the British join the French in an attack on Aqaba, followed by an attempt to seize the railway near Maan. Lawrence, who had visited the port before the war, knew that the beach was surrounded by several ranks of rising cliffs which would give the Turks a great defensive advantage. Brémond's scheme not only ran the risk of degenerating into a second Gallipoli, but also, Lawrence suspected, by landing European troops at the northern end of the Hijaz, would stop the Arabs' revolt spreading northwards into Syria, which the French hoped to rule uncontested after the war. He told Brémond he opposed the plan. When Brémond announced that he would put the idea to Feisal anyway, Lawrence decided to get to Feisal first; he did not trust Feisal not to refuse Brémond's offer.

A bemused Hogarth watched his former student hurriedly depart for Wajh the following day. 'I've just seen TEL off again to his wilds and I'm afraid that this time it may be for long enough. But don't tell his mother,' he warned his wife Laura, who lived half a mile from Lawrence's parents in Oxford. 'It is a queer venture he has gone off upon and I'm sure no Insurance Co. would accept a policy on his life. But if anyone will, he'll come through.'[19]

On his return to Wajh, Lawrence found Herbert Garland making preparations to lead a party to attack the railway. From the port it would be possible to raid anywhere along a lonely 250-mile stretch of the Hijaz Railway, from Tabuk in the north past Al Ula to Mudarraj in the south. Being that much further from Medina, the region east of Wajh was also a marginally less sensitive area into which British officers might travel. Early in February, Garland finally received permission from Feisal to go inland himself.

Garland had little information about the Hijaz Railway. Among Wingate's papers, kept today in the university library beside the Norman cathedral at Durham, is an intriguing report on the railway's stations and bridges, dated 1907, illustrated with photographs taken from a moving train, and written by someone who self-effacingly identifies himself only as 'G' – probably *The Times'* correspondent Philip Graves.[20] But 'G' had only been allowed to travel as far as the gateway to the Hijaz – Madain

Salih – and the section further south had not yet been completed in any case. The only Briton known to have travelled the length of the line was Arthur Wavell, an enterprising young Army officer who disguised himself as a pilgrim to enter Mecca early in 1909. Wavell shared none of 'G''s reticence about publicity. In his hilarious book on his escapade, published in 1912, however, he mentioned only in passing that the stations south of Madain Salih were fortified with trenches and barbed wire to protect them against marauding tribesmen disadvantaged by the railway. He was killed fighting the Germans in East Africa before he could share any further details with the Arab Bureau.[21]

The question was what to attack along the railway line. As the earlier debate over whether to attack the railway from Aqaba had highlighted, there were few obvious targets within striking distance. The railway, a single, narrow-gauge track which ran for over 800 miles between Medina and Damascus, was an unflashy piece of German engineering, running through just two tunnels, and over two viaducts both of which were far to the north, in Syria. The railway's many other bridges – which had been exhaustively catalogued by 'G' – were expected to be vulnerable, but on closer inspection they turned out to be stubby, massive constructions which were not only very solidly built but, being low to the ground, were also relatively easy to repair temporarily with heaps of ballast. The forts which studded the railway every twenty miles seemed unsuitable, since – following Wavell – they were assumed to be well defended and even today it is possible to see the zigzag lines of trenches around them. But George Lloyd, a Conservative MP who had taken a close interest in the railway since its conception and who had now been sucked into the Arab Bureau as well, believed that the best targets were the railway's locomotives. These had all been imported from Europe before the war and were irreplaceable due to the British blockade of the Mediterranean and Red Sea coasts and the fact that the railway from Constantinople through Turkey to Damascus was not yet complete. On his expedition to the railway Garland hoped to mine a train.

Even before he reached the railway, Garland faced a hazardous journey. 'I must confess,' he admitted afterwards, 'that before the war took me to the Hijaz, the Moslem Holy Land, I . . . knew little about it, except that Medina and Mecca were situated somewhere there.'[22] Although the British tended to exaggerate European ignorance about the Hijaz – the French archaeologists Jaussen and Savignac had in fact travelled in the northern Hijaz extensively before the war – it was certainly a wild and inhospitable region, the southern half of which was barely known. The chain of sabre-toothed peaks which erupt fifty miles inland was a fearsome barrier which helped preserve fierce local hostility to outsiders, particularly non-Muslims. 'Knowing as we did that few professing Christians had penetrated the Hijaz, except in a subterranean sense, those of us who set out for the interior, in the early days of the Revolt, did so with some trepidation,' Garland explained sardonically afterwards.[23]

Garland decided to head south-east from the Red Sea coast up Wadi Hamd to the railway: a distance of almost exactly 150 miles. Even if it had already been available, the *Handbook of Hejaz*, which Lawrence had just been proofreading, would have been no use to him: 'South of Wadi Hamd . . . is ill-known to us, and the Wadi Hamd . . . has never been described by any explorer', was all the thin guidebook had to say.[24] Its brief comments on the type of people Garland might meet along the way were no more comforting. The tribes 'are of exceptionally predatory character, low morale, and disunited organisation', the *Handbook* explained, adding that 'the nomads are individually less to be trusted in Hijaz than in almost any other Arabian province', and that 'safe conducts given, in all sincerity, by their Sheikhs, have less validity and less local range'.[25] Waiting until after nightfall on 12 February, amid thunder, lightning and heavy rain, Garland left the little port of Wajh and headed eastwards into the unknown.

Garland's guide for this foray was the cheerful 26-year-old Abdel Kerim, who had led Lawrence up Wadi Yanbu the previous December and then accompanied Feisal on the march to Wajh. A leading light among the Juhaynah and a sharif descended from the Prophet, Abdel Kerim was deemed the best man to ensure Garland would return in one piece. But the deference the young tribesman's ancestry attracted, which had led Lawrence to recommend him, was – Garland felt – an unfortunate drawback. Next time, he made a mental note, he would take a less important guide because it was inconvenient to travel with a 'Sharif who finds his chief pleasure in dismounting to be kissed by passing kinsmen'.[26]

Garland knew his presence deep in the Hijaz was extraordinary. In one of the long, black and cream Bedu tents he visited, he overheard a woman hidden behind a screen promise to let her child see 'the Christian' if it stopped wailing. Instantly there was silence, and Garland turned to see 'a little brown head . . . with eyes very wet and wide open' appear above the partition for a moment.[27] In other places, his guide referred to him as a Turkish prisoner for his own safety. Nor was he left in any doubt about the basis for the loyalty of the Juhaynah, who were disconcertingly fascinated by gold teeth. 'It's alright now,' one of them told Garland, 'we are friends. We realise that the English are good people with much gold, more than the Turks. But if I'd met you in the desert six months ago, I should have cut your head off, and taken it to Mecca as a reward.'[28]

Constantly at the mercy of the elements, the Bedu were a careworn people, Garland felt, who would eat ravenously, not out of greed but from uncertainty. Once he watched a tribesman eat an entire sheep in a single sitting, using his right hand – the left, being unclean, is never used for eating – to roll the rice boiled inside the carcass into a ball which he then tossed into his mouth. Animals were only killed to eat at times of celebration; normally, the tribesmen lived on a diet of rice and dates, buttermilk, cheese and *semn*, a flour milled from the red seed of a plant which flowered intermittently in the desert. Bread was baked hard in the ash of the dying fire. 'One was always hungry,' another officer remembered, years later.[29] When finally the embers died, and the fireside talk of past feuds and raids trailed off, each man in Garland's party – over fifty in all – would sleep in the lee of his kneeling camel for protection from the bitter desert wind. 'The animal spends the night chewing,' Garland discovered: 'A camel's head, with its drooping bottom lip, its ill-proportioned ears, and its shaggy eyebrows, is never a thing of beauty, but seen by moonlight when one is only half awake it seems like an animated gargoyle.'[30]

Although fear and hunger slowed the hours in Garland's mind, his journey was undoubtedly an unhurried one. The year before had been the driest in the region since 1895 but the winter rains had now revived the rocky hills.[31] A sparse fur of pale green, and the single, pearly grass stalks shooting up here and there through the stones may have seemed unimpressive to him, but looked verdant to the Bedu, who were determined to let their camels roam to graze. Garland begged Abdel Kerim to quicken the pace: 'I cajoled, urged, pleaded . . . but all my efforts to get him to increase our rate of progress, which was about 10 miles a day, were quite unavailing.'[32] The Bedu refused to push their camels faster than their natural jaunty lope.

Though the wadi appeared empty, its sandy base was plaited by animal tracks and the Bedu frequently diverted to follow marks left by gazelles, hyena, wolves, jackals, or even the occasional leopard. 'The echoes in the hills were wonderful,' recalled Garland: 'in some places a single rifle shot resounds time after time exactly like a roll of thunder.'[33]

Even today the Bedu retain astonishing abilities as huntsmen. In southern Jordan I watched my Bedu guide Attayak Ali, who was driving our jeep, stamp on the brakes and leap from the cab to scoop up a chikor partridge he had spotted at the wayside. In the Hijaz in 1917 both partridge and sand grouse, in the words of another British officer, made 'a valuable addition to the stock pot'.[34]

There were also hidden dangers: the brackish water in the wadi, in which luminous green algae bloomed, not only had a salty taste defying 'tea, whiskey, lime juice or any other beverage',[35] but also attracted snakes, scorpions and spiders – which the Bedu are deft at flicking into the fire. And all around, all the time, there was the infuriating swarm of dozens of flies, a constant, low and inexplicably sinister hum.

As they neared the railway Garland and Abdel Kerim argued over tactics. Garland wanted to lay the mine and stay close on a nearby hill to see if it worked. Not wanting to be caught by the Turkish patrols that guarded the line, Abdel Kerim flatly refused. He wanted to plant the mine and be away as fast as possible. When, on the night of 20 February, they finally reached the stony, blasted valley through which the railway ran, Garland won, though not through force of argument. As he explained afterwards to his envious colleagues, 'The approach of the train five minutes after starting work settled the matter.'[36]

9

THE FIRST RAILWAY RAIDS

(February–April 1917)

Trains on the Hijaz Railway were not supposed to run at night.

When, through the darkness, he heard the shriek of a whistle followed by the squeal of metal wheels biting the railway track, Herbert Garland, who was kneeling beside the rails, jerked upright with surprise.[1] He hesitated for a moment. Then he scrabbled for the five-pound cartons of gelignite on the ground beside him. At a pinch, he could squeeze three of them into the hollow he had partially excavated under the rail.

From one of the pockets of the khaki jacket he wore under his black cloak Garland pulled the action of an old Martini Henry rifle. Its barrel had been sawn off and the trigger guard removed so that all that was left was an oblong of brown steel from which the trigger protruded, exposed. This he loaded with a thick, old-fashioned bullet the size of his thumb, fished from another pocket. Swivelling the mechanism so that the trigger was upper-most, he carefully wedged it into the hole, barrel pointing into the explosive, trigger – tightened beforehand for his own safety – brushing the rail above. The lights of the engine were now clearly visible, 200 yards away, coming towards him at – he guessed – twenty-five miles per hour, which left him fifteen seconds. He got up and ran. Round his legs his jellaba swirled, seemingly determined to trip him up. Beneath his bare feet the stony ground felt like 'carving knives, bayonets and tin tacks'.

'I wished I had devoted more time to physical training in my youth,' Garland, who had a weak heart, laconically recalled after the war.[2]

As the locomotive's front wheels passed over the mine, nothing happened.

But, a split second later, as the heavier driving wheels flexed the track, they crushed the hidden trigger below. There was a searing yellow flash. Momentarily it revealed Garland's silhouette, Arab robes flapping, as he sprinted away from the railway past the woody plants that could endure this wilderness. Instantaneously, there was an enormous explosion, the engine bucked, then blackness returned. Through the darkness came the 'clanking, whirling, rushing' noise of the stricken train, the shouts and screams of those inside it as it corkscrewed off the stony embankment, and the lethal patter of debris returning to earth.[3]

On a low hill overlooking the track, Garland stopped running and, swearing vehemently between gasps for breath, turned to survey his handiwork by the sliver of light from the waning moon. Satisfied, he turned and headed back towards the group of chattering Arabs whose cigarettes glowed in the blackness. It was 20 February 1917, 'the first time that the Turks have had a train wrecked', he reported later,[4] and, it would seem, the first ever act of sabotage committed by the British Army behind enemy lines.

Six days later, Garland was back in Wajh. Yet far from being exhilarated, he was furious. In a damning report on his return he described his guide Abdel Kerim as 'absolutely incapable of action, criminally haphazard and careless . . . responsible for all the delays of the party and none of its success'.[5] While Lawrence relished the challenge of fitting in with the Arabs – 'I want to rub off my British habits,' he told a colleague[6] – Garland hated the Arab clothing Lawrence recommended he wear to gain acceptance and to avoid standing out. It was 'most annoying and encumbering', he said, having found that the slightest breeze caused the ends of his headscarf to flick the cigarettes out of his mouth.[7]

While Garland was up at the railway, Lawrence had been in Wajh. Realising that he would now be permanently attached to Feisal, Lawrence decided to take the young sharif into his confidence. To explain Brémond's anti-Arab motives he revealed the gist of the Sykes-Picot agreement to Feisal for the first time. It is not clear exactly how much Lawrence knew about the agreement – he had been away in Mesopotamia in April 1916 when its terms were first transmitted to Cairo – but it appears that he knew of its existence and had given some thought to its implications. He advised Feisal that, to foil French ambitions in Syria, they must develop plans to spread the revolt far to the north, because Lawrence believed that only the Arabs' right by conquest would overturn a French claim based on historic influence in the region: Feisal had to reach Damascus before the end of the war. 'One night we all swore not go Mecca till after we had seen Damascus. Great fun when I insisted on taking the oath too,' Lawrence jotted shortly afterwards in his notebook.[8]

To win the support he needed to fulfil his ambition to reach Damascus, Lawrence also knew he had to reassure his colleagues about Feisal. Feisal's belated appearance in Wajh had hardly been a good advertisement for his reliability and, although Lawrence himself had made his mind up that Feisal was the most useful of Sharif Husein's sons, his view was not necessarily accepted in Cairo. Clayton had always been rather doubtful about the ultimate loyalties of Feisal, because of Feisal's close contact with Enver during the negotiations over whether Husein would endorse the jihad. Even Lawrence had been taken aback when, having made sympathetic noises about the Arab nationalists hanged at Jemal's order in 1916, Feisal replied that their punishment as traitors seeking foreign intervention was just. But now, Feisal's position appeared to be changing. From his conversations with Lawrence, it appeared that Feisal believed a *rapprochement* with the Turks was 'most improbable', although he said he had no personal grudge against the Ottomans if they left the Arabs alone. According to Feisal, the divide between the Arabs and the Turks was widening. His father Husein's position towards the Turks was hardening, and he himself found it hard to see how even Turks opposed to the current government could accept the Arabs' plans because the Arabs' aims inevitably involved the destruction of the Ottoman Empire.[9] This was a substantial step from many Arab nationalists' restricted desire for greater autonomy within the Ottoman Empire.

Tribesmen continued to arrive in Feisal's camp on the high ground above Wajh to pledge their support. Lawrence thought that the influx would help bolster morale amongst the local tribe, the Bali, who were threatening to leave the camp, by creating competition for the money the British were offering. 'The whole country is full of envoys and volunteers, and great sheikhs coming in to swear allegiance,' Lawrence wrote at the time: 'Nawaf and Auda are both very well, and waiting for us.'[10] Nawaf's father was Nuri Shaalan. Auda abu Tayi was a legendary outlaw, with a reputation for savagery infamous even by the high standards of the Hijaz, whom Lawrence had recently heard had been killed.[11] Lawrence wanted to use Auda's tribe, the Huwaytat, who had, according to Gertrude Bell, 'a resounding name for devilry and reckless courage', to attack the railway near Maan.[12] Both Auda and Nuri Shaalan played significant parts in the plans he was developing, and he was delighted to hear that Auda was alive.

After a detour via Aqaba, Brémond arrived from Egypt in Wajh on 18 February to meet Feisal. With him was Antonin Jaussen, the priest who was France's foremost expert on the Hijaz. Although Lawrence, having already poisoned Feisal's mind about Brémond's agenda, seems to have made himself scarce for the meeting, his influence over Feisal did not go unnoticed. Jaussen reported that Lawrence 'shares and maintains Feisal and his people's natural hostility towards foreign intervention in Arabia' and that Feisal seemed to hold Lawrence's friendship in high regard.[13] Brémond presented Feisal with the first of six machine-guns and offered the young sharif a French staff officer to advise him. The gift failed to soften Feisal, who told Brémond that he disapproved of his Aqaba plan, and rejected the need for a military adviser on the grounds that 'scientific military knowledge' was not needed in tribal warfare.[14]

Later that day, Feisal told Lawrence what he had said to Brémond. He had claimed that it was his lack of artillery which had driven him to move to Wajh so that he could more easily threaten the railway. 'Had he had French guns to reply to the guns which the French had supplied to the Turks, he would have gone straight for Medina,' Feisal had teased Brémond, explaining that instead he now planned to use his mobility and growing numbers to defeat the enemy.[15] There was, Lawrence noted exultantly, 'really no saying where this protraction of his front would end!'

Having seen Brémond off, Lawrence immediately returned to Cairo. He had been working with Feisal on the elongation of the revolt northward, to which Nuri Shaalan and Auda abu Tayi were key, and he now wanted to brief Clayton with an ambitious plan he had devised with Feisal. 'Feisal's present intention is to raise all the nomad tribes from the Huwaytat at Jurf ad Darawish north of Maan, to Medina. This involves combining the Auda abu Tayi, Ibn Jad, Ibn Jazi, and Abu Togeiga Huwaytat; the Bani Atiyah; the Bali; the Moahib; the Fuqarah; the Aida; the Wuld Suleiman and the Juhaynah,'[16] he wrote, listing a welter of tribal names, as much to demonstrate his mastery of the complex web of alliances that would be needed as to enlighten his chief. Feisal had received promises of support from most of these tribes, Lawrence reported, and other Arabs – from the area to the east of the Dead Sea in present-day Jordan, the Hauran east of Damascus in Syria, and as far north as the Lebanon – had also been in touch. But as most of these were settlers who owned land, and were consequently nervous of reprisals by the Ottoman government if they joined the revolt, Feisal had told them to bide their time. Clayton was impressed but, for the moment, cautious, because he felt the plan was a distraction from the main objective of Britain's continuing support for the Arabs in the Hijaz, which was the capture of Medina. 'This *is* important,' he wrote on Lawrence's report, together with a simple further instruction: 'File'.

In Rabigh, where the pressure on Joyce was already lifting – days earlier he had ordered more footballs for his men – news of Garland's raid dramatically improved morale. In Jeddah, the French observed that the hard-pressed staff of the British Agency found time to practise their golf.[17] Reports that a train leaving the city had been mined also had a dramatic effect in Medina. The atmosphere there was already panicky following an explosion days earlier, possibly due to sabotage, which destroyed one of the city's barracks. The families of government officials were being evacuated to Syria by the time Garland was approaching the railway. Though Garland believed he had hit a train full of troops, it may in fact have been one of these trains, crowded with women and children, which he had mined in the darkness on 20 February. Small wonder then that crucifixion was rumoured to be the punishment for any British officer caught by the Turks.[18]

As Medina was turned to a war footing, the Holy Mosque was commandeered as a store for ammunition and military equipment. Within the city a shortage of supplies and requisitioning by Fakhri's men drove up prices. Traders in the city's souk stopped accepting the paper notes the soldiers were paid in, and demanded hard currency instead. 'An occasional train with a meagre quantity of supplies would arrive from Damascus and bring slight relief to the famished garrison,' recalled Ali Haidar, whose hopes of replacing Sharif Husein as Emir had been frustrated. 'The military situation stagnated, and a general feeling of uncertainty pervaded all.'[19]

One day at the end of February, Fakhri burst into Ali Haidar's quarters. He was 'in a state of great distress', according to Haidar, because he had just received orders from Damascus that he was to evacuate the city immediately.[20] 'The news horrified me,' Haidar recollected. 'I sent a strongly-worded telegram to Jemal in which I said that the very idea of deserting the Holy Tomb was utterly shameful, and that it should be protected to the last man, if necessary.'

Three days later Fakhri appeared again. The two men saw each other infrequently, as each suspected that the other was conspiring against him. 'Jemal has cancelled orders for the evacuation,' Fakhri excitedly explained. 'He was in a considerable state of emotion and I, in my joy, clasped and embraced him,' recalled Haidar: 'From that moment we became friends . . . I saw so much deep religious faith in him that I found it quite easy to forgive the past.'[21] Their *rapprochement* was short-lived. Soon afterwards, Ali Haidar received a telegram recalling him to Syria. Early in March he bid farewell to Fakhri. 'The protection of this Tomb is in the hands of God, but you are His instrument,' Haidar told the beleaguered general: 'I leave it in your care. Be worthy of the trust.'[22] Having locked his own belongings in a mosque, Haidar left for Damascus.[23] He would spend the rest of the war reunited with his family in an isolated palace in the Lebanese hills.

Wingate first heard a rumour that Fakhri had been ordered to withdraw from Medina on 5 March. As far as he was concerned, the timing of this news could not have been worse. On the eastern edge of the

Sinai desert, the British were preparing to attack the small town of Gaza at the end of the month. But their force had been depleted by the withdrawal of another full division, of 17,000 men, to France that February and Wingate was alarmed that, if Fakhri heard news of the British attack, he would hurry north to help defend Gaza. Believing the information to have come from 'an absolutely reliable source', he wired an order to Jeddah for Lawrence and Newcombe the following day. They were to keep up the pressure on the railway and to cut the telegraph wire to Medina, which followed the railway track, as far to the north as possible.[24]

By the time that Wingate's demand arrived, Newcombe had already reached the railway at Dar al Hamra, a station 110 miles north-east of Wajh. A tall man whose hawkish stare radiated determination, Newcombe had a reputation for recklessness: 'He runs his head into wasps' nests,' Hogarth believed.[25] But he was also rather dashing. In a satchel he always carried were two packets, tied with ribbons, of letters from two girls he had met while fighting in France.[26] Having spent two days watching the line, and having decided that demolitions further south had clearly been ineffective since trains were running in both directions more or less daily, Newcombe opted for a three-pronged attack on the station.[27] His guide, the young and well-respected Sharif Nasir, hoped that the attack would help persuade the numerous Arabs the Ottomans employed on the railway to desert. But the assault on the station on 3 March was a failure, though demolitions each side of the station destroyed at least a mile of track, and isolated one of the working parties tasked with checking the line each day. They were, reported Newcombe, '8 most delighted prisoners'.[28]

To Lawrence, Wingate's demand was music to his ears. All this time he had been stuck in Wajh, tasked with supervising the offloading of cars and with erecting a radio mast, both jobs he loathed. 'Did 369 things in all today,' he wrote sarcastically on 5 March, jealously recording news that Abdullah had blown up a section of the long bridge at Abu an Naam on the railway seventy miles north-west of Medina.[29] Wingate's demand for urgent railway demolitions gave him the excuse he needed to escape. Since Newcombe was out of reach and

Feisal wanted to stay on the coast to ensure that the fractious camp at Wajh stayed calm, no one else could carry out Wingate's demand. So, in a letter to Wilson, Lawrence outlined a plan – 'spur of the moment', he admitted – in which he would attack the stations where water was stored at the same time as destroying as many rails as possible. The volume of water the Turks would then need to transport to run repair trains to fix the line would paralyse their efforts to leave Medina *en masse*. 'If we can cut the line on such a scale that they cannot repair it, or smash their locomotives, the force will come to a standstill . . . If only we can hold them up for ten days.'[30]

The following night, Lawrence set out south-eastwards for Abdullah's camp in Wadi Ais with a disparate group of local tribesmen, a few Ageyli* and a Moroccan named Hamed. But he was succumbing to dysentery and his journey quickly assumed a nightmarish quality. At the end of the second day, in a remote valley north of Wadi Ais, Lawrence was lying down recovering from an agonising day's riding, when suddenly there was a shot. That was not unusual in itself since the Bedu frequently fired into the air – but then Suleiman, an Utaybah with the party, took Lawrence to the other side of the wadi where one of the Ageyli was lying dead, shot at close range in the forehead. Given the friction there had been between the Ageyli and the Hijazi tribesmen in Wajh, Lawrence immediately suspected Suleiman, until another tribes-man vouched that he had been collecting wood with Suleiman when the shooting happened.

The only person missing was the Moroccan, Hamed. It was Lawrence who found him, collecting his belongings in an apparent bid to escape. Covering him with his pistol, Lawrence shouted for the other Arabs, who clustered round the pair. Hamed admitted shooting the Ageyl following an argument, leaving Lawrence with a terrible dilemma. To do nothing raised the risk of a blood-feud escalating between the Ageyli and the Moroccans once they were back at Wajh. The alternative – in line with tribal justice – was to kill Hamed. Shooing the Moroccan into a dank

---

* Young townsmen from the Qasim area of central Arabia who made a living out of desert trade, from breeding and selling camels to escorting caravans across the desert. Often they had fled the religious strictures imposed by the Wahabi Saudis.

gully in the side of the wadi, Lawrence gingerly shot him once, twice, a third time before he finally stopped moving. In his notes he drew a rough map, marking the gully with a heavily incised > and the word 'Death-crack' and a terse label:

Camped here.
Awful night.
Shot.[31]

Lawrence's physical condition continued to deteriorate over the next three days. His boils, aggravated by riding, worsened. The Hijaz was forged by volcanic activity, and riding across the crazed pavement of disintegrating, brown-black lava field was desperately painful. 'This halt is wonderful,' he wrote during one break from riding: 'Am lying under a low thin thorn tree with tiny buds of leaves sprouting out at the bases of its plentiful thorns . . . The air round us is full of the humming of insects and lively with flies. Heat and a faint cool wind.'[32] Back on his camel the torture resumed: he would afterwards describe how 'puffs of feverish wind pressed like scorching hands against our faces', cracking his lips and drying out his throat until he was hoarse.[33] After five terrible days, on 15 March he arrived at Abdullah's camp, a cluster of yellow tents the French had privately dubbed 'the Camp of the Cloth of Gold', due to their similarity to knights' pavilions and the lifestyle Abdullah had adopted.[34] Once a tent had been pitched for him next to Abdullah's, Lawrence crawled inside to lie down.

Lawrence would spend most of the next ten days in the tent. With hindsight after the war, he described how he used this time profitably, honing his strategy of guerrilla warfare, but this seems unlikely. Not only had he already developed many of these ideas but, as consecutive entries in his diary – written feebly in pencil – show, he was very ill. 'Fever bad,' he wrote on 17 March; 'Fever still very heavy'; 'Fever better; boil worse'; 'Got up today. Pretty bad'; 'Got up today. Fever bad'; 'In bed all day; boil v bad.' That day he wrote to his colleagues in Wajh, explaining he had been unable to do anything due to illness and urging them to beg Feisal to come up to the railway, where his influence would be much greater. In the entry for Friday, 23 March, after a week in and around his tent, his diary reads: 'Better – decided start on Sunday.' But on Saturday he relapsed: 'Still hope to start tomorrow; am beastly ill, really.' And the following day, there is the plaintive 'In Wadi Ais: was unable to get off.'[35]

While Lawrence was languishing in Abdullah's camp, Newcombe returned to Wajh, discovered Wingate's order, and turned immediately back towards the railway. On his return to the railway line, Newcombe was dismayed to find that the Turks had unearthed all five mines his party had laid on his previous expedition and had repaired what damage he had done to the track in just four days. The unexpected speed of these repairs meant that the British would have to cut the line every two to three days to keep it out of action, Newcombe calculated. This was a rate that he knew it would be impossible to maintain, particularly as the tribesmen proved increasingly uninterested in destroying the track. Worried that the Bedu would kill Arabs working on the railway, Feisal had decided to pay a sovereign for every prisoner brought back to Wajh alive. This, Newcombe discovered, created an incentive to take prisoners rather than blow up the railway, which it was almost impossible to reverse. Even his guide, Mirzuq, who as a camel merchant by trade should have had a strong vested interest in destroying the track, preferred the thought of the quick reward from taking captives. Mirzuq's leadership depressed Newcombe. 'His method is to hear everyone's views,' the veteran soldier complained to Wilson: 'Bedouin talking all day, wanting to capture prisoners, Ageyl wanting to destroy the line by night and so avoid the dreaded aeroplane and Bisha more or less ready to do as they are told, if some *bakhshish* is forthcoming. I manage occasionally to get a word in to make Mirzuq keep to the point, i.e. prevent trains running.'[36]

Lawrence ran into problems at Abdullah's camp. 'Who is this "red" newcomer and what does he want?' one tribesman asked Abdullah.[37] 'I did not like his intervention as I was suspicious of his influence among the tribes,' Abdullah later recalled of Lawrence. Although he tried to explain Lawrence's role to his followers, he observed that 'the general dislike of Lawrence's presence was quite clear' and he made no great effort to change this.[38] Once he had recovered, Lawrence did not stay long. On

26 March, the same day that the British offensive against Gaza began, he
set off down Wadi Ais towards the railway with a party of Utaybah
tribesmen led by Sharif Shakir, a young man of about the same age as
Lawrence, who – like many Bedu – plaited his black hair into six pigtails
kept glossy with frequent applications of camel urine.[39] By the 28th, the
raiders were lying on a hill west of Abu an Naam station, 'like lizards in
the long grass'.[40] It was Lawrence's first sight of the railway: through his
binoculars he could see a long bridge of nineteen squat arches guarded by
a small outpost on a dark knoll, and to the south, the water tower and two
station buildings of Abu an Naam itself, all built of lead-grey local basalt.
Slightly nearer in the foreground was a small, nondescript building, in
fact a mosque, surrounded by white tents sleeping about 300 soldiers in
all. There were too many, Lawrence reckoned, to dare a direct attack of
the sort he had suggested to Wilson before setting out.

The artillery attack was, from the Arabs' point of view at least, a
Lawrence opted instead to mine the track either side of the station that
night and, at dawn the following day, to bombard the station with the
field gun the raiders had brought with them. Under cover of darkness he
headed south to lay a mine. Having done so, he left some tribesmen with
a machine-gun in some nearby bushes to mow down any escaping
passengers and, a little further down the line, shinned up a telegraph
pole to cut the wires. The recoil of the pole when he cut the third and
final wire was so great that he was shaken off, landing in a heap on a
tribesman named Mohamed who tried to break his fall. They only had an
hour's sleep before dawn; Mohamed got his revenge when he bellowed
the call to prayer in Lawrence's ear.

The artillery attack was, from the Arabs' point of view at least, a
spectacular success. Shells hit both the station buildings and pierced the
tank crowning the water tower. A further hit on a wagon in a siding
started a fierce fire; its locomotive uncoupled and started south to escape.
'We watched her hungrily as she approached our mine,'[41] Lawrence
recalled, before there was a puff of dust, a loud bang, and the engine came
to a standstill. But there was no machine-gun fire: the Bedu gunners had
already given up and disappeared. The drivers were able to jack the
locomotive back on to the track and head onwards, albeit at snail's pace.
Taking advantage of the thick black smoke which had begun to boil from

the burning wagon, the tribesmen advanced towards the station, shoot-ing some Turkish soldiers who tried to surrender. Realising that it would be unwise to go any closer to the chaos, Lawrence watched from a distance. The bombardment had caused the Turks seventy casualties, he estimated, and the Arabs took a further thirty prisoners. Traffic was held up for three days.

Sharif Shakir led the celebrations in Abdullah's camp when he returned with Lawrence. From the darkness outside the circle of tribes-men squatting round the fire, Lawrence watched as, in the centre, Shakir sang, raising his hands and throwing back his head at the end of each phrase, while the tribesmen beat time with their hands.

Disappointed by the mine he had laid at Abu an Naam, Lawrence set out again on 3 April for the railway with Dakhilallah, a sheikh with 'the manner and appearance of a toad', who nevertheless commanded respect among the Juhaynah as a judge.[42] This time, Lawrence headed towards Mudarraj station, thirty-five miles north of Abu an Naam. Furious, dark-blue clouds hid the summits of the mountains and the following day the party was engulfed by a dust spout, and then torrential rain, which turned the dust that had covered the men to mud and made the narrow mountain paths so treacherous that one tribesman slipped to his death.

After the bugle had blown at Mudarraj to call the Turks in for dinner that night, Lawrence laid a mine under the track where it crossed the bleak pass just to the south of the station, before retreating up the rough hillside to wait among the crags. From this position the following morning, he watched as a Turkish patrol scoured the track and the sand each side for signs of tampering. But although the Turks could see signs of the raiders – 'we left the whole bank and the sandy plain each side . . . as though a school of elephant had danced on it,' Lawrence reported – they failed to find the mine.[43] Then, to Lawrence's horror, from the south appeared a train crowded with women and children: evacuees from Medina. The train reached the top of the pass and began to accelerate downhill towards Mudarraj. Then it passed over the point where Lawrence had set the mine.

Nothing happened.

'They were not quite the prize we had been hoping for,' wrote

Lawrence; but his relief rapidly turned to irritation.[44] Not only had his mine failed again but behind him the Juhaynah had surged to the edge of the outcrop like spectators. From Mudarraj, the Turks spotted the tribesmen on the skyline and began shooting, ineffectively due to the long range. Now worried that the Turks might cut off their line of retreat to Wadi Ais, Lawrence sent the heavy German machine-gun he had brought with him away, and returned towards the rails with Dakhilallah. To provide cover, Dakhilallah led the evening call to prayer on the track itself. 'It was probably the first prayer of the Juhaynah for a year or so,' Lawrence reported, 'and I was a novice, but from a distance we passed muster, and the Turks stopped shooting in bewilderment.'[45] With the prayers over, and once it was dark, Lawrence began an uneasy hunt for the primed trigger. After some nervous scrabbling among the ballast, he finally found it, reset it, and left for the south. He paused along the way to demolish a bridge and cut about 200 rails using guncotton charges, before heading for safety as fast as possible. A distant boom the following day suggested that the mine had finally worked. Lawrence headed back to Abdullah's camp and from there to Wajh.

10

DIFFERENCES OVER TACTICS

(April–May 1917)

Pierce Joyce was struck by the change in Feisal he saw when he moved from Rabigh to Wajh in late March. 'Feisal's whole attention is now turned northwards and he considers the actual taking of Medina the work of Abdullah, Ali and Zeid,' he told Wilson shortly after his arrival.[1] Unaware of what Lawrence had secretly told Feisal, Joyce was mystified by Feisal's sudden focus on Syria, and his loss of interest in the Hijaz. 'He cares little about Medina,' Joyce reported a week later, adding that he suspected that Feisal's ambitions stretched as far as Damascus. 'I have endeavoured to confine Feisal to local ambitions and Military operations,' he added, 'but from somewhere he has developed very wide ideas.'[2]

Joyce was irritated by the disappearance of Lawrence, whose most valuable skill was his ability to steer Feisal, who was increasingly nervous about French ambitions in Syria. 'Lawrence is still out with Abdullah. I will show him your letter when he returns. I have no power to order him anywhere,' he explained to Newcombe, who had written to Lawrence urging him to bring Feisal up to the railway.[3] Joyce then decided to show Newcombe's letter directly to Feisal. The move was not a success. 'Sharif Feisal much upset by your letter but is really doing everything possible only he has not got the camels,' Joyce wrote to Newcombe the following day, admitting: 'I'm fed up.'[4]

Lawrence reappeared in Wajh the next day, 14 April, after thirty-four days away. In his absence Wajh had become the centre of British operations. Soldiers in shorts and pith helmets unloaded stores at the quayside, armoured Rolls-Royce and Crossley cars had been landed, and two British armourers, brought in to service the tribesmen's – frequently antique – rifles and weapons, had succeeded in training thirty Arabs in machine-gunning, entirely by mime. The aeroplanes and pilots of the small Royal Flying Corps detachment had arrived from Yanbu in mid-March. Six days later the flight's leader, Major Ross, set out up Wadi Hamd, with four spare tyres strapped to the side of his car, to hunt for a forward airstrip which would give his biplanes the range to reconnoitre and bomb the railway, one hundred miles away.

On his return, Lawrence criticised British tactics: 'The blowing up of culverts is waste of time and explosive'[5], he suggested, and although he thought the mines 'have had a most powerful moral effect on the drivers and on the Turks generally, who are terrified of them', he was disappointed that they were 'not set off till the driving wheels pass over them . . . and the damage thus tends to be too far back'.[6] He felt that the Arabs should fight a war which made the most of their mobility and unpredictability, targeting the railway, but not the Turks themselves. 'We might be a vapour, blowing where we listed,' he later described his philosophy, as hard for the Turks to beat as 'eating soup with a knife'.[7] He argued that 'a constant series of petty destructions' was the best way to keep the railway out of action, so that the garrison in Medina were neither able to advance towards Mecca nor retreat to Damascus: 'The Turk was harmless there. In prison in Egypt he would cost us food and guards.'

Newcombe strongly disagreed with Lawrence's desire for an inconclusive war. By the beginning of May, when he returned to Wajh, he had spent most of the previous two months attacking the railway north-east of Wajh and he was not impressed by Lawrence's advice, based as it was on ten days' experience. Taking a sideswipe at the style of Lawrence's reports – 'It does not help us to win the war merely to collect scraps of information about Bedouins, unless we also hurt the Turk. But hurting the Turk seems too risky for most Arabs'[8] – he argued that a different approach was needed to obtain a decisive result. 'Either all of us are wasting our time here, instead of getting on with the war, or an entirely new line must be taken, of making camel corps and training Bisha [tribesmen]' to execute attacks on a much greater scale.[9]

Unlike Newcombe, who – according to Wilson – arrived in the Hijaz
with the impression he was to be the Arabs' commander-in-chief,[10]
Lawrence always knew that he was an adviser, rather than a leader. And
he knew that there was no way of changing the Bedu's style of fighting.
The difficulty of surviving in the Hijaz meant that, for the sake of their
families, the tribesmen would always rather flee and live to fight another
day unless their honour within the tribe was at stake. To force them to
stand and fight, as Newcombe wished he could, would be entirely self-
defeating: 'An individual death was like a pebble dropped in water. Each
might make only a brief hole, but rings of sorrow widened out from
them. We could not afford casualties.'[11] Lawrence relished finding virtue
where his colleagues only saw vice: 'The Harith are not a large clan,' he
wrote of one set of arrivals to Wajh, 'but have been robbers for
generations, and so capable men of action.'[12]

Newcombe had been joined by another young engineer, Henry
Hornby, at the beginning of April, and Lawrence criticised his and
Newcombe's handling of the Arabs. 'Hornby spoke little Arabic; and
Newcombe not enough to persuade, though enough to give orders; but
orders were not in place inland.'[13] On his last raid, Newcombe had been
shot at by his own tribesmen. This extreme reaction, Lawrence believed,
had been prompted 'only out of disgust at his hardness, always wanting
to ride when they wanted to stop and eat. Also hard on water and food'.
His own conclusion from Newcombe's troubles was blunt: 'Mem: Don't
attempt too much.'[14] Ultimately, it was this reality which partly shaped
Lawrence's support for guerrilla tactics. His other motive was a desire to
turn the revolt northwards into Syria, which could not be achieved if the
Arabs focused their efforts on trying to capture Medina.

Two important men had also arrived during Lawrence's expedition
inland. The day after his return, Lawrence was sitting in Feisal's tent
catching up on news when there was a call from outside the tent and
Feisal, Lawrence remembered, 'turned to me with shining eyes, trying to
be calm, and said, "Auda is here" '.[15] Auda abu Tayi was the man whom
Lawrence had wanted to meet since February. With him was Mijlen
Shaalan, Nuri Shaalan's nephew.

Auda abu Tayi was infamous. A Czech traveller in the region a few years earlier incredulously recorded how Auda was known for having 'cut the heart from a wounded enemy and bit at it',[16] but in fact, as Richard Burton discovered when he passed through the Hijaz in 1853, the custom of trying a dead rival's gore had once been widespread[17] and Auda's continuing attachment to the practice simply marked him out as a traditionalist. So it was not surprising that Auda had taken an instant dislike to the Ottoman taxmen who appeared in the region following the construction of the Hijaz Railway. In 1908, he had fallen out with the Ottomans over payment of tax. After Auda shot dead two officials sent to bring him to Maan, a warrant was issued for his arrest.[18] Since then, he had become an outlaw, 'a tall, strong figure, with a haggard face, passionate and tragic',[19] who dramatically rushed out of Feisal's tent to smash his false teeth with a stone when he realised they were Turkish-made. In one contemporary photograph Auda, wearing a European suit jacket over a patterned Arab robe, stares unnervingly straight at the camera. He instantly mesmerised Lawrence.

The plan which Feisal then put to Lawrence bore the hallmarks of Auda's overpowering influence. It developed the general ideas which Lawrence had reported to Clayton that February but in a way which strongly benefited Auda's tribe, the Huwaytat, and bolstered Auda's prestige. Led by Auda, Lawrence would ride north-east from Wajh far beyond the railway into northern Arabia to buy 1,000 camels and arrange food and forage at Jafr, thirty-five miles north-east of Maan, for a force of about 600 regular troops led by Feisal, who would follow late in June. The decision to search for food and transport in this area was designed mainly to reward the Huwaytat, who roamed the area between Maan and Aqaba, and were said to be starving.[20] While Lawrence and Auda were dealing with the logistics, the British would move arms, ammunition, explosives and food to a point just south-west of Tabuk. Using the camels Lawrence would acquire, these supplies would then be shuttled up to Jafr, an operation which Feisal hoped to complete by 10 July.

From Jafr, the entire force would then head north to Azraq, a tumbledown castle hidden in a remote oasis fifty miles east of Amman, where Nuri Shaalan could frequently be found. From Azraq, Feisal would try to stir the Druses to the north into revolt and launch operations against the railway.[21] The Druses had revolted against the Turks twice in recent memory, in 1895 and 1910. Both uprisings had been violently suppressed by the Turks. Feisal calculated that it would not be difficult to stoke up Druse feeling again. Auda also had another plan. Having first asked the British to capture Aqaba that February, he now hoped that by causing trouble around Maan, he could force the Turks in Aqaba into surrender. The occupation of Aqaba itself, which Feisal planned to achieve by a landing of tribesmen late in July, would open the port as a route for supplies to ensure that the Huwaytat could not be starved by the Turks. This perfectly suited Lawrence's own agenda of turning the revolt northwards. It also solved the major problem Lawrence could see with a seaborne attack on Aqaba, since Auda intended to surprise the Turks by attacking from the landward side. Lawrence's own hopes that Aqaba would be easily overthrown were raised on 20 April when, in an opportunistic raid on the port, a British landing party snatched nine Ottoman soldiers. Of the nine, six were Arabs who wanted to join Feisal.[22]

The main obstacle to this plan was Lawrence's own chief, Clayton. Reviewing Feisal's intentions, Clayton noted that the scheme 'must not be allowed to interfere with the business which is already in hand, viz, the defeat of the Turks at Medina, Al Ula and Madain Salih, which should be cleared up in order to make the Northern move fully effective'.[23] It was only later that Clayton revealed his true objections to the plan. In his opinion Aqaba would be critical to Britain's future defence of Egypt and he feared that its occupation by tribesmen 'might well result in the Arabs claiming that place hereafter'.[24]

Lawrence had his own ulterior motives for supporting the scheme. He did not believe that the Arabs were likely to capture Medina quickly and he worried that time wasted trying to do so would only boost Abdullah's ambitions and benefit the French, who wanted to keep the revolt locked in the Hijaz, at the expense of Feisal's northern plans and his own intention to 'biff the French out of all hope of Syria'. Moving the centre of operations to Aqaba would irreversibly tip the centre of balance of the revolt to the north.

To undermine his colleagues' faith in Abdullah and the Arabs' ability to capture Medina, Lawrence turned to his favourite weapon, a venomous report. In a letter to Wilson on 16 April, he accused Abdullah of being complacent, lazy, profligate and incompetent. 'He considers the Arab position as assured with both Syria and Iraq irrevocably pledged to the Arabs by Great Britain's signed agreements, and for himself looks particularly to the Yemen,' Lawrence observed, in a tone suggesting that Abdullah's assurance was ill-founded.[25] Abdullah spent his day 'reading the Arabic newspapers, in eating, in sleeping and especially in jesting'. It was the amount of time allocated daily to this last activity, of which the camp's muezzin was normally the butt, that particularly riled Lawrence, who wrote while he was in Wadi Ais that he was 'not in the mood' for all the jollity.[26] The day before he had arrived, Lawrence reported to Wilson, Abdullah had apparently shot a coffee pot balanced on the muezzin's head three times from twenty yards, in exchange for £30. Abdullah's tribesmen, meanwhile, had gone two months unpaid, 'simply through *laisser faire*, for the gold was present in the camp to pay them up in full'. Suppressing his opinion when he was with Abdullah that, compared to Feisal's camp, 'things here are more businesslike', Lawrence concluded: 'He is incapable as a military commander and unfit to be trusted alone, with important commissions of an active sort.'

In fact, Abdullah was anything but incapable. The Arabs' one outstanding success so far – the ambush of the Turkish column led by Ashraf Bey outside Medina that January – was achieved under Abdullah's leadership. What Lawrence feared was that, if the British gave Abdullah the tools, he would complete the job of capturing Medina all too quickly. Feisal had warned him early that year that, though his brother was 'inclined to be lazy', he was 'quick when he does move'.[27] Abdullah had thought through how he would impose his father's authority on the other major Arabian sheikhs after the capture of Medina. As Lawrence told Wilson, 'This sounds a large operation, but Abdullah is convinced of its practicability, and has even worked out the details of his actions.' Wilson would have agreed. He was already concerned that Abdullah would turn on his Arab rivals if Medina were captured and chaos would ensue. In May he recommended that Feisal should be encouraged to begin operations as far north up the Hijaz Railway as was possible. Wingate agreed, and Clayton, though still personally reluctant, was instructed to investigate how best to support the move.

A series of events far beyond the Hijaz had helped sway opinion in Cairo in favour of pushing the Arabs northwards. On 11 March, British forces occupied Baghdad after a two-month-long campaign. Four days later, after large-scale strikes and then a mutiny in the city of Petrograd thrust a spanner into the works of Russia's industrial machine, Tsar Nicholas II abdicated. From Britain, the spectacle of what was happening in Russia disturbed the Prime Minister, David Lloyd George. Growing public opposition to the war was not confined to Russia and, worried that British workers might follow the Russians' example, Lloyd George urgently wanted a victory to revive public morale and fend off the possibility of labour unrest, which might paralyse Britain like Russia. Deeply anti-Turkish, Lloyd George had for some time nursed an interest in a British offensive into Syria which, as Prime Minister, he was now in a stronger position to pursue. Rather than treating the capture of Gaza as the final move in the existing policy of a belligerent defence of Egypt, he began to envisage the capture of the seaside town as the first stage of a push into Palestine.[28] Was there a more resonant target than Jerusalem, last in Christian hands in 1187, to reflect the rightness of Britain's cause?

The combination of the capture of Baghdad, the likely Russian collapse and an increasingly attractive offensive into Palestine all had an impact on the Arab revolt. If Russia made peace, pressure on the Ottomans' northern front would disappear and the chances of the Ottoman Empire surviving the war intact would dramatically increase. The consequent danger was twofold. Perhaps the Arabs would make peace with the Turks: the very outcome British support for the Arab revolt had been designed to prevent. Certainly the Ottomans would be able to move more troops to the Mesopotamian and Palestine fronts, a threat which in the short term would suck British troops from the Western Front, and in the long run could upset Britain's post-war plans for the region. Even before the outcome of the Russian revolution became clear, Feisal's plans to head northwards already appealed to Archibald Murray, who increasingly viewed his own and the Arabs' fortunes as positively linked: 'If I can gain a further success against the troops in front of me,' he told Robertson in February in advance of his attack on Gaza, 'it will immensely help the Arab Movement, and I *may* yet see them in force in the neighbourhood of Maan – an additional security to southern Sinai.'[29]

The fall of Baghdad and the Tsar, and the possibility of an offensive into Palestine also raised questions over the validity of the Sykes-Picot agreement, which would need to be addressed in the months ahead. Although, after he entered Baghdad, General Maude announced that the British came not 'as conquerors or enemies, but as liberators', the Indian Army's involvement in the capture of that city triggered an argument between Whitehall and Delhi over quite how liberating British rule in Mesopotamia after the war should be. Yet whatever the outcome of this debate, it was a domestic matter Britain intended to decide without reference to the French, or anyone else. If, as the third signatory to the agreement, Russia withdrew from the war – a possibility that looked increasingly likely – then the Sykes-Picot agreement would arguably be void. And if Britain advanced into Palestine, conquest would supersede the treaty's theoretical placement of Palestine under international control, just as the capture of Baghdad already raised the question of the status of Mesopotamia. That spring, a committee chaired by the former Viceroy, and arch-imperialist member of the War Cabinet, Lord Curzon, provided some simple answers to two of the three issues. It decided that it would be in Britain's best interests to control both Mesopotamia and Palestine after the war.

On 26 March – the same day that Lawrence set out for Abu an Naam – the British had attacked Gaza but failed to capture the town. Eight days later, Lloyd George called Mark Sykes in to see him. Sykes was about to leave for Cairo, having been appointed Chief Political Officer to the Egyptian Expeditionary Force in anticipation that the Gaza attack would open questions about the treaty he had negotiated with François Picot which he was the obvious candidate to consider. Sykes told Lloyd George how he hoped to develop relations with the various tribes in Palestine 'and, if possible, to raise an Arab rebellion further north in the region of Jabal Druse with a view to attacks on the Turkish lines of communication, particularly against the railway between Aleppo and Damascus'.[30]

Lloyd George was alarmed by this. He told Sykes it was vital not to commit the British government to any agreement with the tribes which would be prejudicial to British interests and might upset the French. He had also had breakfast that morning with the leading British Zionist Chaim Weizmann and, with the meeting fresh in his mind, now warned Sykes of the 'importance of not prejudicing the Zionist movement and the possibility of its development under British auspices'.[31] Many Jews in Britain, Weizmann had told Lloyd George that morning, knew Palestine well and might usefully be employed in the theatre.

As the former Minister for Munitions, Lloyd George knew how crucial Weizmann's scientific expertise had been in finding a way round the shortage of acetone, a key ingredient in the production of cordite – the smokeless explosive behind every bullet and shell the British forces fired – and he was inclined to agree with Weizmann that the Jews might be of use. The Jews, Lloyd George suggested to Sykes, 'might be able to render us more assistance than the Arabs'. He was also keen to take advantage of the Russians' disarray and told Sykes to do his best to add Palestine – which the Russians had insisted should be internationally administered – to the British sphere of influence. Before Sykes left, Lloyd George repeated his initial warning. There should be no 'political pledges to the Arab, and particularly none in regard to Palestine'. This demand effectively hobbled Sykes but he set out for Egypt nevertheless. By the time he arrived there towards the end of April, a second attempt by the British to take Gaza had also been repelled by the Turks.

On 4 May Sykes arrived in Jeddah to see Husein. He was hoping to reassure the Sharif about French ambitions in Syria by arguing that an Arab confederation had been agreed by both the British and the French in his treaty.[32] Husein was not the only one with growing suspicions about the French. British disquiet about French activities in the Hijaz had been growing since the beginning of the year. In January, Lawrence reported that Brémond had told Feisal 'that the firmness and strength of the present bonds between the allies did not blind them to the knowledge that these alliances were only temporary and that, between England and France, England and Russia, lay such deep and rooted seeds of discord that no permanent friendship could be looked for'.[33] The French officer also seemed to have been working on Abdullah. According to Lawrence, Abdullah had recently received a letter from Brémond pointing out that 'the English were surrounding the new Arabic kingdom on all sides, quoting Aden, Baghdad, and Gaza as instances'.[34] Brémond's reported behaviour raised anxiety in London. When the French asked if they could provide Sharif Husein with banking facilities, wireless equipment and doctors the British government objected. The 'French seem to have stolen a march on us in a region where hitherto they have had no influence', complained Sir Austen Chamberlain.[35] The Foreign Secretary, Arthur Balfour, told Wingate to ensure that, in future, the Sharif dealt through 'one channel only and that British' and that British officers anticipated and met Husein's needs as far as possible.[36]

Sykes met Husein for the first time on 5 May. In a cartoon he drew of their three-hour meeting, he depicted himself in his army uniform with sweat dripping off his brow while Husein sat cross-legged on a divan looking at him enigmatically. Behind the pair, a thermometer registered 120 degrees Fahrenheit. Sykes had passed Husein a message from King George V, welcoming Husein's efforts in the 'cause of Arab peoples whose ultimate enfranchisement from persecution will mark an epoch in development of civilisation and prosperity in Asia'.[37] Guff like this failed to impress the Sharif, who replied that unless Arab independence was assured 'he feared that posterity would charge him with assisting in the overthrow of the last Islamic power without setting up another in its place' and that if France annexed Syria he would be open to the charge of breaking faith with the Muslims of Syria 'by having led them into a rebellion against [the] Turk in order to hand them over to [a] Christian power'.[38] Sykes tried to reassure Husein about French ambitions in Syria, and claimed that he had persuaded Husein 'to admit at last, but only after lengthy argument, that it was essential to Arab development in Syria' to accept over-arching French influence there.[39]

It was an unconvincing argument, and Sykes himself was not convinced. He had realised that Brémond's continuing presence in Jeddah was doing little to help his cause. 'I am convinced that the sooner the French military mission is removed from Hijaz the better,' he told Wingate in a telegram that evening: 'The French officers are without exception anti-Arab . . . Their line is to crab British operations to the Arabs, throw cold water on all Arab actions to the British, and make light of the King to both,' he railed, before attacking 'the deliberately perverse attitude and policy followed by Colonel Brémond and his staff'.[40] Days later, the British ambassador in Paris complained to the French government about Brémond's conduct.[41]

In Cairo, Clayton was also sceptical. He did not believe Sykes's version of his discussions with Husein, and warned that the Sharif was likely to go back on his word once Sykes had left. He also reacted with surprise to Husein's response. The British, he said, had assured Husein that Arabia would be formed of 'a series of more or less independent states or confederations which would be loosely bound into an Arab federation'. Now, he claimed, 'The Sharif has perverted these assurances into a support of himself as supreme ruler.'[42] While it was true that the British had never explicitly committed themselves to supporting Husein except against the Ottomans, it was hardly surprising that Husein believed that he could count on the British to endorse his claim to political leadership of the Muslim world, given the suggestive message sent to him at the beginning of the war by Lord Kitchener.

FIGHTING FOR US ON A LIE

(May–June 1917)

It is still possible to visit the old pilgrim caravanserai of Qalaat Zorayb which stands in a secluded valley a little way inland from Wajh, as long as you don't mind crawling under the wire fence which the Saudi Department for Antiquities has recently erected around the site. The *qalaat* is an elegant building, a hundred yards square with high walls which meet at neat round towers, built from a warm, smooth stone which contrasts with the rough hills around. It was from here that Lawrence set out on 10 May 1917 on the first leg of his mission with Auda to secure food and camels for Feisal's planned march north. Over the back of his camel sagged a 45-pound sack of flour which had to last him six weeks, and in his saddle bag he carried £1,000 in gold which Feisal had given to him the day before as a reserve in addition to the £22,000 the baggage camels were carrying.

Three days earlier, Lawrence had met Sykes for the first time. Besides the brief entry in Lawrence's diary, there is no record of their meeting, but it seems likely that Lawrence challenged Sykes to reveal the terms of his treaty with Picot in full. The details which Sykes now revealed to him had stunning implications which he would thrash out in the lonely weeks ahead. It may even be that the meeting was the catalyst for a hasty decision to depart northwards. It is hard to believe, from the strength of the comments Lawrence went on to write during the journey, that he already knew all the details of the Sykes-Picot agreement before his meeting with its British co-author. He was, when the agreement was signed in May 1916, a junior officer responsible for tracking movements of Ottoman Army units, and there was certainly no need for him to know its secret details. Another intelligence officer appears only to have been aware from the beginning of 1918 that the French would get Syria, and possibly Palestine.[1] But, like others, Lawrence was aware that an agreement existed, and he seems to have guessed, accurately, that McMahon's vagueness over the future of northern Syria and the French sensitivities Sykes had been tasked with mollifying were in some way interconnected. What he heard from Sykes directly not only horrified him but spurred him into action.

Feisal chose Sharif Nasir, at twenty-seven about a year younger than Lawrence, to lead the expedition, most probably because Nasir commanded widespread respect as a descendant of the Prophet. The brother of the Emir of Medina and, unusually in the Hijaz, a Shia Muslim, Nasir had also previously accompanied Newcombe to the railway. Nesib al Bakri, a member of one of Damascus's leading families and an Arab nationalist whose help would be needed to spread the revolt northwards, also joined them. Lawrence took two servants, whose stories reflected the origins and aims of the revolt. Like Auda, one, named Gasim, was a tax exile from the Maan district, who was wanted for killing an Ottoman official. The other was Mohammed, a villager from the Hauran, where Feisal wanted to incite revolt. To protect them on the journey came seventeen Ageyli, the young townsmen from central Arabia, whose camels were slung with red and blue woollen saddle bags with scarlet tassels which reached the animals' knees. They were 'nice fellows, large-eyed, cheery, a bit educated, catholic, intelligent, good companions on the road', said Lawrence.[2] They had a talent for telling long verse stories about war, love, travel and magic. 'Needless to say,' commented another British officer, 'the love stories were unexpurgated.'[3]

Days of incessant, roasting sunshine had replaced the variable weather of springtime in the Hijaz. Heat pulsed off the ground in nauseating waves and flies buzzed in the stagnant air. Lawrence quickly suffered a rapid and debilitating relapse of his fever. 'Tired and sorry,' he wrote in his diary after a day in the saddle, 'v. sick', the following day, and 'pain and agony today', the day after that.[4] The party stopped for two days to let Lawrence's fever pass, before heading on to Abu Raqah, a valley of variegated sandstone that glowed pink at dawn and dusk. There, Lawrence persuaded a local Bedu to part with his two servants, Ali and Othman. 'Othman soft-looking. Ali fine fellow. Both apparently plucky, and Mohammed and Gasim are so useless that I must have extra men.'[5] Ali and Othman appeared inseparable. 'They were an instance of the eastern boy and boy affection which the segregation of women made inevitable,' he would write after the war. Their love was not sexual, he believed, but a 'manly love of a depth and force beyond our flesh-steeped conceit'. Lawrence took them on 'mainly because they looked so young and clean'.[6]

At a time when descriptions of homosexuality were vigorously censored, Lawrence wrote openly in *Seven Pillars of Wisdom* – initially for the very small audience of subscribers who supported the book's publication – about the Arabs in the desert who avoided the 'raddled meat' of women, preferring 'indifferently to slake one another's needs in their own clean bodies'.[7] He described how 'some began to justify this sterile process, and swore that friends quivering together in the yielding sand, with intimate hot limbs in supreme embrace, found there hidden in the darkness a sensual coefficient of the mental passion which was welding our souls and spirits in one flaming effort.'[8] But he distanced himself from these acts by adding: 'I was sent to these Arabs as a stranger, unable to think their thoughts or subscribe to their beliefs.'

Indeed Lawrence was repelled by sexual activity in general, 'holding procreation and evacuation alike as inevitable movements of the body'.[9] He made fun of the Arabs for their obsession with 'our comic reproductive processes not as merely an unhygienic pleasure, but as a main business of life'.[10] Partly, this attitude was shaped by inexperience. Even later in life, Lawrence admitted that the only sensation which the thought of sex aroused was dread. Describing his refusal after the war to accompany other soldiers to brothels, he admitted to his post-war confidante Charlotte Shaw his fear of 'seeming a novice in it . . . it's because I wouldn't know what to do, how to carry myself, where to stop. Fear again: fear everywhere.'[11] Others noticed his distaste. Lawrence appeared 'as hostile to sex as to the French', suggested one man who knew him.[12] Designed though this remark was to amuse, it seems to corroborate the impression that Lawrence had little sympathy for sexual relationships with either men or women.

The day after Lawrence hired Ali and Othman, 17 May, the Arab party headed on towards the railway. Near the track Lawrence bumped into Hornby, the Royal Engineer who had been brought in to assist in demolitions. The same age as Lawrence and renowned in Wajh for his singing, Hornby made up with tenacity for what he lacked in ability to speak Arabic: 'Arabs told me . . . that Hornby would worry the metals with his teeth when guncotton failed,' Lawrence joked afterwards.[13]

After his first, stilted meeting with Husein, Sykes returned to Cairo to discuss the administration of Syria with Picot and put an idea to him which reflected a change in the political weather. The previous month, the United States had joined the war against Germany. But when he announced his government's decision, the American President, Woodrow Wilson, launched a much more general attack on the conduct of European foreign policy which had led to war. He attacked the 'little groups of ambitious men who were accustomed to use their fellow men as pawns and tools', and declared: 'We have no selfish ends to serve. We desire no conquest, no dominion.' The United States, Wilson concluded, would 'fight for the things which we have always carried nearest our hearts – for democracy, for the right of those who submit to authority to have a voice in their own governments, for the rights and liberties of small nations'.[14] Rhetoric of this kind made Sykes feel decidedly uncomfortable. Unsurprisingly, when Wilson's foreign-policy adviser, Edward House, found out about the Sykes-Picot treaty, he was blunt. 'It is all bad, and I told Balfour so,' he wrote.[15] Sykes sensed a hostile turn in the mood towards British and French imperialist war aims, and now began to argue that the administration of Mesopotamia should be placed in Arab hands. He also suggested to Picot that France might match this stance in Syria.

On 18 May, Sykes returned to Jeddah with Picot and Feisal, whom he had picked up from Wajh on his way south. This time, he intended to make Husein realise 'the inevitable fact of French influence in Syria' by giving him full details of the Sykes-Picot agreement. In the clearest indication that the message Sykes was about to give conflicted with what McMahon had led the Sharif to believe, the Foreign Office agreed that Sykes could sugar the bitter pill by telling Husein that the British government would increase his monthly subsidy by £75,000 to £200,000 with immediate effect. The government dangled a further carrot in front of Husein. He would earn an additional £125,000 bonus if Medina was captured.[16]

Sykes and Picot went ashore in separate launches for a lunchtime meeting with Sharif Husein. Sykes showed Husein a prototype Arab flag, which comprised three horizontal stripes representing the Arab dynasties – 'Abbasid black, Omayad white, Alid green', Sykes explained[17] – unified by a red triangle on the hoist side, representing the Sharif. Husein preferred scarlet to the dark red Sykes proposed, but otherwise approved Sykes's design which again strongly suggested that Britain saw him as the dominant force among the Arabs.

It was the first time Husein had met Picot, and the conversation rapidly turned to the status of coastal Syria, over which McMahon and the Sharif had disagreed. Picot explained that France would recognise the principle of an autonomous Arab government in its sphere of influence, but that a French 'adviser' would possibly reside at Damascus. In the Blue area on the Syrian coast, which came under French control, a Franco-Arab administration would be formed where French and Arab flags would be flown. The French, Sykes added, had not ruled out the principle of fusing the government of the Blue area with that of the adjacent Arab state under French influence, though whether this would result in French annexation or Arab independence he did not specify. Husein did not like what he heard, frequently calling breaks for prayers which Sykes suspected were simply designed to give him time to consult his advisers without either Sykes or Picot in earshot. 'The interview closed most inconclusively, and was adjourned until the following morning, M. Picot being rather unfavourably impressed by the King,' Sykes told Wingate.[18] Wemyss, who was also present, described how the discussion started badly and 'at one moment [it] looked as though conversations would be broken off without any result',[19] before it was agreed that

Husein should come aboard Sykes's ship, *HMS Northbrook*, the following day.

Sykes worked on both Husein and Picot overnight. Having persuaded Picot to accept his proposal that Syria and Mesopotamia should be governed similarly, he then put the idea to Husein, suggesting that his acceptance of the formula would break the impasse.[20] Also under pressure to take the increased British subsidy, Husein agreed.

Aboard the *Northbrook* the following day 'Matters took a decidedly more favourable turn,' reported Wemyss afterwards, because 'the King verbally agreed to cooperate with the French in their sphere on the understanding that the French policy towards the Arabs should be similar to the British policy in the British sphere'.[21] Husein's and Picot's apparent agreement 'greatly improved the atmosphere', according to Sykes, who was pleased with the devious solution he had brokered.[22] Husein was delighted. During his correspondence with McMahon he had proposed that the British lease Mesopotamia from him for a set period prior to handover. Not wanting to upset Husein, McMahon had never dismissed this idea outright, arguing disingenuously that the issue required 'fuller and more detailed consideration than the present situation and the speed with which these negotiations are being conducted permit'.[23] Under the impression his idea remained a viable option, naïvely perhaps Husein now interpreted Picot's agreement as a commitment to extend the proposal to include Syria.[24] Picot had no idea of the leaseback scheme. He simply believed that British plans for Baghdad involved annexation, just as France intended with Syria, and was happy to accept the formula on that basis. He must have been puzzled by Husein's enthusiastic response. What is not clear is whether Sykes introduced the formula simply because he knew that it had a different, agreeable meaning for each party, or whether, motivated by his recognition that annexation was 'quite contrary to the spirit of the time', he thought he could draw Picot into an agreement which would ultimately benefit the Arabs when Britain accepted the need for Arab self-government in Mesopotamia, for which he was now arguing.

The agreement was a temporary palliative which became the source of increasing embarrassment as it became clear that Britain had no plans to allow Arab self-government in Mesopotamia. 'We have to bear in mind that unfortunate formula which the King of the Hijaz was induced to agree to at the meeting between him and Mark and Picot,' Clayton reflected nearly a year later. 'That embarrassing formula . . . places us in an awkward position.'[25]

After the meeting Feisal grasped Sykes by the hand and took him to one side. 'We are ready to cooperate with France in Syria to the fullest extent and with Great Britain in Mesopotamia', he said quietly, 'but we do ask that Great Britain will help us with Ibn Saud and the Idrisi, without in any way infringing on their independence, rights, or liberties – we beg that Great Britain will endeavour to induce them to recognise the King's position as leader of the Arab movement.'[26] The following day Sykes sent a telegram to Percy Cox, the political officer with British forces in Baghdad, to ask whether he could persuade Ibn Saud to tell the Sharif 'that he regarded him as a titular leader of the Arab cause without in any way committing his independence or local position'.[27] Not wanting to annoy Ibn Saud, Cox refused to act.

Over 600 miles north of Jeddah, early in the evening of 19 May, Sharif Nasir, Lawrence and Auda abu Tayi crossed the railway. Lawrence paused briefly for twenty minutes to blow the track with guncotton and cut the telegraph wire, which he then tied to the saddles of the camels, before shooing them on, to pull down the telegraph poles behind them. Then the party headed east, crossing the watershed between the Hijaz and Wadi Sirhan, still 150 miles away to the north-east, early the following morning. They now faced the worst part of their journey to Wadi Sirhan, where they hoped to find the Huwaytat. Between the Hijaz Railway and wadi lies an enormous empty plain, scored by the sand and devoid of life, then known to the Bedu as Al Houl – 'the Terror'. 'This is a grey country, utterly without trees or shrubs, or any grazing – whence its name,' Lawrence observed.[28] The only noise was the 'hollow tapping and cracking of rock slabs' as the camels trod on them, and the sound of the sand 'creeping round the ridges and along between the rocks'.[29] Hot gusts blasted them with sand. 'This wind is killing me,' Lawrence jotted.[30] He was carrying a sheaf of blank army telegraph forms, writing

copious notes on the plain reverse side. The other, boxed, side was a
testing ground for odd phrases he might use in his book: '*Harra* drinks
starlight' was one musing on the blackness of the weathered lava flows
they had to cross; 'deadness of this open country without wind', 'the
incredible slowness of the moon', 'Auda's wonderful echoed singing',
others.

To pass the time, Auda began to describe the complex politics of the
fractured Huwaytat tribe, telling Lawrence for the first time that he had
seized the leadership of the tribe from his rival Ibn Jazi, who had in turn
killed his own son, Annab. Auda had killed seventy-five men since 1899
when, Lawrence noted, 'he began to keep tally'.[31] It was a relief when
they finally reached Fajr well, halfway to Wadi Sirhan, on 21 May. There
they watered the camels before camping half a mile away to avoid raiders
who might pass by the well in the night for, as Lawrence later wrote, 'in
the hours of darkness there were no friends in Arabia'.[32]

Continuing north-eastwards, the following day's route took them
across vast mudflats. These pans of dazzling white mud were 'purgatory.
Sun reflects from them like mirrors.'[33] The answer seemed to be 'Ride
eyes shut', but the light was blinding even then. The heat pumped off the
blazing ground and Lawrence found himself occasionally blacking out – a
brief release before more torture.

The twenty-fourth of May was Empire Day. While, in the neat,
verdant gardens of the Residency in Cairo, Wingate held a tea-party for a
thousand convalescing soldiers wounded in the two attempts to capture
Gaza, Lawrence hoped to escape the endless mudflats and reach Wadi
Sirhan, where he expected to find the Huwaytat and sufficient meat and
grazing to meet the needs of Feisal's force. At Auda's insistence they
started in the middle of the night. Dawn revealed a level plain of stones
sunburned to the colour of congealed blood over which the mirage
shimmered into a dirty, pale blue sky. 'Hijaz sun does not scorch but
slowly blackens and consumes anything – men or stones – subject to it,'[34]
Lawrence observed. Suddenly, however, they scared two ostriches and
stopped to cook the two enormous eggs the birds abandoned over a fire of
shredded blasting gelatine. One of the two was rotten.

Straining to see further signs of life ahead, Lawrence suddenly realised that he had lost Gasim, the outlaw from Maan. 'This was a dreadful business,' he recalled.[35] There was no chance that Gasim would catch up: the mirage made it impossible to see more than two miles and the stony ground was trackless. By desert law, Lawrence was responsible for his servant: he would have to turn around and find him. He had been carefully tracking the party's course since they left Wajh, so now he twisted his compass through 180 degrees, turned his camel, and began to retrace his steps. The only signs of human habitation were strange threshing pits scraped in the ground six years earlier, when there had last been a good harvest of *semn*, a red seed which could be milled into flour. Filled with drifting sand, the pits looked like 'grey eyes in the black stony surface'.[36]

After an hour and a half's riding, through the wobbling mirage Lawrence saw a black blob. It was Gasim, nearly blinded and mad from the sun. He was 'standing there with his arms held out to me, and his black mouth gaping open'.[37] Lawrence gave him some water, hoisted him on to his camel behind him and turned to hurry back towards the caravan. Another hour's riding passed. Then, in front of them another black bubble appeared, 'lunging and swaying in the mirage ahead'. Auda emerged. He had turned back in search of Lawrence and was angry that Lawrence had gone back for Gasim, whom Nasir and he deemed worthless. 'Wasted two hours and a half looking for Gasim,' Lawrence recorded that night,[38] wishing perhaps that Auda had seemed slightly more impressed by his decision to impose the Bedu code upon himself. Had he shirked the duty, he later wrote, Auda and Nasir would have understood, 'because I was a foreigner: but that was precisely the plea I did not dare set up while I yet presumed to help these Arabs in their own revolt'.[39]

Putting himself through the same dangers as the Bedu seems to have been Lawrence's way of expiating the guilt which his conversation with Sykes had so starkly raised. 'We thought you had been generous to the Arabs,' he later wrote accusingly to Sykes, although the letter was never sent, 'and were told unofficially that the need of bolstering up French courage and determination in the war made it necessary to surrender to her part of our own birthright.' He went on to express his disillusionment at what had followed after the revolt began. 'What had been a generous attempt to revive an Arab state in Syria under the aegis of France and England, became the sphere which the Sharif might obtain if he succeeded. You observe that we gave him no reward for his efforts on our side. He might take – what we had already given,' he said, in a reference to the contradiction between the commitment made by McMahon and the Sykes-Picot agreement's allocation of Syria to the French.[40]

Up to this time, Lawrence had been working on the assumption that British and Arab interests coincided: both wanted to ensure that the French were denied Syria. His discovery, little more than two weeks earlier, that Sykes had already offered Syria to the French knocked him sideways: Sykes had effectively pitted Britain and France together, against the Arabs. As Lawrence turned this apparent *fait accompli* over in his mind, he became only more determined that the Arabs should reach Damascus first. If Husein could reach the regions divided by Sykes and Picot before either the British or the French, his claim to those areas would be much stronger.

That evening, the party reached the edge of Wadi Sirhan. Lawrence slept the night on his stomach to ward off the cramp of hunger. Early the following morning they finally reached water. But there was no sign of any of the Huwaytat. Lawrence instantly disliked the wadi. The abundant tamarisk was too tough for the camels to eat, yet too green to be used as firewood. The wiry *dum* palms yielded only bitter, inedible dates. He summed it up in two words: 'Pretty barren.'[41]

It was also a dangerous place to halt. The brackish water attracted poisonous snakes which would swim in the water after dark and festoon themselves in the bushes by day. The Bedu had a treatment for snakebite: they would bind the affected part 'with a snakeskin plaster, and read chapters of the Koran to the sufferer until he died', Lawrence recalled.[42] The availability of water also attracted other raiding parties, who had no shortage of hiding places in the thicket which grew in the wadi's flint-and-gravel bed. One night, when Lawrence's party were having coffee around the fire, there was a shot. The Ageyl pouring the coffee, who had just stood up from serving Lawrence, fell fatally wounded into the circle 'with a screech'. As one of Auda's tribesmen scuffed sand into the fire to extinguish its flames, the other Bedu rolled down behind the bushes and started firing back in the direction of the dunes from where the shots had come. For a few minutes the darkness bristled with yellow muzzle flashes, before the invisible assailants stopped shooting. Then the silence was only broken by the moans of the dying man.

Persevering northwards down Wadi Sirhan, on 27 May they reached the first Huwaytat tents and relative safety. At lunch and dinner for the next three days Nasir, Auda and Lawrence were invited to feast. Each meal followed an increasingly wearying formula. The diners sat down while, from one end of the tent, 'urgent whispered cooking directions wafted through the dividing curtain, with a powerful smell of boiled fat and drifts of tasty meat-smoke'.[43]

After a lengthy wait, two men staggered out from behind the curtain, carrying a deep copper tray, piled with rice which was topped with pieces of sheep and crowned by the sheep's boiled head, buried in rice to its ears, 'jaws opened to breaking-point and yawning upwards showing the open throat, the tongue sticking to the teeth and the prickly hair of the nostrils'.[44] Heaving the dish into the centre of the diners, the men ladled over it the remains of the cooking juices: intestines, fat, muscle, meat and skin, swimming in grease. The feasters watched intently, 'muttering satisfactions when a very juicy scrap plopped out'.[45] Once the host had reached into the cauldron, found the liver of the sheep and placed it on top of the pile, there was a chorus of 'Bismillah al Rahman al Rahim',* and each man could finally delve into the scalding pile of rice with his right hand to knead a ball of rice, meat and offal, which he then tossed into his mouth.

The experience rapidly paled. 'Have feasted noon and sunset since evening of May 27 and am very tired of it,' Lawrence wrote three days later,[46] depressed by the lack of headway. Auda, in the meantime, had set off to meet Nuri Shaalan, taking with him a further £6,000 in gold to try to win the backing of the powerful old sheikh. On 2 June the party regrouped at Nabk, 120 miles north-west down the snake-infested wadi. There, Auda reported that Nuri had again been sympathetic, but he

---

* A phrase with complex meaning, which might be translated as 'To the Glory of God, the Compassionate, the Creator'.

remained unwilling to back Feisal openly. This was a blow. Further headway north depended on Shaalan's support, which Feisal had hoped to secure by approaching the old sheikh overland – addressing Shaalan's fears that if he backed the Arabs the Turks would cut his food supply off.

Nesib al Bakri, the Damascene who had accompanied the party, advocated going on to Damascus to incite revolt among the urban nationalists there, regardless of the setback. In the cultivated settlements of Syria, however, Lawrence suspected that the nomadic tribesmen, whose reputation for violence went before them, would encounter fear rather than friendship. Nor did he see Syrians reacting *en masse* to a call to arms. In an article published in the *Arab Bulletin* earlier that year, he had warned that

> Syria and Syrian are foreign words. Unless he has learnt English or French, the inhabitant of these parts has no word to describe all his country. Syria in Turkish (the word exists not in Arabic) is the province of Damascus. Sham in Arabic is the town of Damascus. An Aleppine always calls himself an Aleppine, a Beiruti a Beiruti, and so down to the smallest villages. This verbal poverty indicates a political condition. There is no national feeling.[47]

Like Clayton, Lawrence worried that precipitate action of the sort Bakri now suggested would meet with a weak response. The Turks would deal savagely with any troublemakers, terrorising the remaining population into acquiescence. Bakri, however, ignored Lawrence and decided he would set out for Damascus.

Lawrence was utterly dejected. He fully expected Bakri to ruin the revolt in Syria by premature action. His own mission, to find food for Feisal's men, who would be about to set out, was impossible in the disappointing wastes of Wadi Sirhan. And he was disgusted by the concessions Sykes had made to the French, who were now to be rewarded at the end of the war for risks the Arabs had taken. But there was still a glimmer of a chance that, if only he could help the Arabs win Syria, he could frustrate French ambitions. At the full moon on 5 June, he wrote in his diary: 'Can't stand another day here. Will ride N[orth] and chuck it.'[48] On one of the telegram sheets he composed a valedictory note to his boss: 'Clayton: I've decided to go off alone to Damascus hoping to get killed on the way. For all sakes try and clear this show up before it goes further. We are getting them to fight for us on a lie and I can't stand it.'[49]

12

AQABA

(June–July 1917)

Unaware though he was of Lawrence's predicament, Clayton might not have been surprised to know that Lawrence felt as he did. Writing at the end of May Clayton had dismissed Feisal's plan to turn north as 'impracticable' and commented, in a rather detached fashion, that 'The venture is in the nature of a gamble.'[1]

Clayton continued to insist that the existing strategy, of trying to force the surrender of Medina, was more realistic because he believed that starvation was the Arabs' 'only efficient weapon'.[2] He continued to think that, 'The fall of Medina, or even a striking success against the Hijaz railway in the neighbourhood of Al Ula or elsewhere would greatly strengthen his [Feisal's] position . . . and, on the face of it, it would appear the wiser course to delay the northern move until his position is more assured and until the situation has developed further.'[3] While Lawrence, taking his unorthodox views on the qualities of the tribesmen with him, was heading deep into Syria in a bid to save the revolt from starting prematurely and failing, in the Hijaz plans were put in train for a spectacular raid on the line, which would throttle the slender supply line on which Fakhri's army depended.

Support for a large-scale raid reflected the British officers' frustration at the ineffectiveness of their tactics so far. 'Someone in authority had formed the opinion that we possessed more dynamite than the Turks did rails,' Garland afterwards recalled.[4] He believed that 'our efforts were but little worry to the Turks. They had an inexhaustible stock of spare rails.' The Turks also showed an uncanny ability to locate mines the British officers had buried. Hornby and Newcombe toyed with trying to fix explosives under one of the bridges, where they would not be noticed, 'to be let off either by shooting or by the engine cutting a string to drop a weight',[5] but this idea proved as unworkable as it was ingenious. In the end Newcombe resorted to laying mines in broad daylight, after the search parties had passed by.

Garland wondered if more devious methods might drive the Turks to distraction. He advocated cutting the track at the same point two nights running, blowing up alternate rails to maximise the length of line which needed repair, and bashing the heads of the screws holding the rails together with a hammer, to make it harder to remove the damaged sections. He also suggested destroying curved sections of track, which had to be specially manufactured, wherever possible and detonating the charges just before dawn to limit the hours of darkness when the Turks could replace the broken rails most safely.[6]

It was not just that the Hijaz Railway and its timetable were proving unexpectedly resilient. Newcombe, Hornby and Garland were discovering that the Bedu were remarkably intractable. On 17 May – the same day that he bumped into Lawrence – Henry Hornby reported 'a pretty strenuous and exasperating seven days' to Newcombe, in which his Ageyli dynamiters had managed to waste most of their explosive: 'How you stuck it for so long, beats me!' Garland was more philosophical: 'I am not sure that the taking of Bedouin parties is a white man's job. They always leave you in the lurch.'[7] Newcombe moaned about his inability as an adviser to enforce any discipline: 'A man has but to refuse to do a thing and he is petted and patted and given bakhshish. I am not allowed to punish anyone and cannot send a man back or take away his rifle. Everyone knows this; hence the trouble.'[8]

Problems with the Bedu made the British officers sympathetic to Sykes's plans to create an Arab Legion. This unit, dreamed up by Sykes on his way out to Egypt earlier that spring, would consist of trained Arab troops who would stiffen the existing small army of ex-Ottoman Arab soldiers already fighting in the Hijaz. In Cairo, Clayton already had an idea of the officer who might lead this force to strike the railway.

Jafar Pasha al Askari was a former Ottoman Army officer who had fought one irregular conflict during the war already. Early in 1915 he had been sent to assist the Senussi, a fanatical sect who lived in the Libyan desert, in an uprising against the British. Captured by the British in February 1916, he was sent to Cairo as a prisoner of war. A burly Iraqi who 'closely resembled the statues of the human-headed bulls that are found in the ruined palaces of ancient Assyria',[9] Jafar had tried to break out of the Citadel in Cairo, where he was being held, to rejoin the Senussi's campaign. Having filed his way through the bars of a window, he had begun to descend the prison's fifty-foot curtain wall when his 'rope' of knotted blankets broke under his considerable weight. While his ankle healed from the fall, Jafar was shown a copy of a newspaper which described the hangings in Beirut and Damascus that May. One of his friends was among those executed. 'I made up my mind there and then to seek revenge, and to make every effort to join the Sharif of Mecca at the earliest possible opportunity,' he explained in his memoirs.[10] His interest in doing so quickly came to the notice of Bertie Clayton. Clayton had summoned him early in the summer of 1917, explained that Feisal needed a commander for his regular troops, and sent him to the Hijaz.

Early in June, refreshed by a short break in Cairo, Newcombe began to make detailed plans for an ambitious raid in which he hoped to destroy 10,000 rails – or nearly sixty miles of railway if Garland's maxim of destroying every other rail was followed. He intended to isolate the major Turkish depot at Al Ula, a mud-brick town in a dramatic, red sandstone valley 180 miles north of Medina, and then occupy the line for a fortnight, stopping trains running in either direction and so forcing the smaller stations to surrender through lack of food and water.

The base for these operations would be at Jaydah, a wadi high in the mountains halfway between Wajh and Al Ula. Aerial reconnaissance on 30 May had established Jaydah's exact location, and days later, RFC pilots set out by car to take a closer look. They returned to Wajh having discovered a possible landing ground in the 3,000-foot-high valley and, as one of them put it, 'water in abundance (for the Hijaz)'.[11] Plentiful water made Jaydah an attractive location to spend the summer, but a risky place from which to launch bombing raids, since the heat and the

altitude made it harder for the heavily laden biplanes to take off. Detailed
aerial photographs of Al Ula for Newcombe's raid were finally taken on
17 June.

By this time, Lawrence was nearly 300 miles further north, having
completed a reconnaissance of Syria which ranks among the most daring
behind-the-lines missions ever made. On 5 June, having decided to
'chuck it', he later told Clayton that he had ridden northwards out of
Wadi Sirhan. Three days later he reached Ayn al Barida, 130 miles north-
east of Damascus. According to his report, his hope – in complete
contrast to the suicidal ambition he expressed in his diary and in the
message which Clayton never saw – was to resolve a feud between the
Huwaytat and the Wuld Ali, a far-ranging tribe whose tolerance, if not
support, Feisal's force would need to operate out of the desert east of the
Hijaz Railway in future. This he failed to do. But at Ayn al Barida he met
a sheikh from a branch of the Aniza tribe named Dhami. Dhami proved
friendly and led Lawrence westward, round the head of the Anti-Lebanon
mountains in a 100-mile journey which enabled him to demolish a small
railway bridge at Ras Baalbek – sixty miles north-east of Beirut in the
Bekaa valley in modern Lebanon – on 10 June. The impact of this action,
which seems to have spurred the local Metowila* tribesmen into open
revolt, excited Lawrence: 'The noise of dynamite explosions we find
everywhere the most effective propagandist measure possible.'[12]

From Ras Baalbek Lawrence rode southwards, passing tantalisingly
close to Damascus. Nearby he met Ali Riza al Rikabi, an Arab nationalist
who had kept his true leanings so secret that he had been entrusted with
the defence of the city by the Turks. Rikabi, however, was not
encouraging. He told Lawrence that without outside assistance he was
in no position to help Feisal. Departing south-east, Lawrence then passed
by Salkhad, a castle built on an old volcano in the Jabal Druse, where he
met the Druse leader Hussein al Atrash. Atrash seemed willing to revolt,
as long as Feisal met a number of conditions, which, though Lawrence
did not specify them, would seem likely to have included the

---

* The Metowila were likely rebels. According to Gertrude Bell, they were 'an unorthodox sect of Islam' which
had 'a very special reputation for fanaticism and ignorance'; *The Desert and the Sown*, New York 1907, p.160.

provision of food and arms. From the Jabal Druse Lawrence headed south to the tumbledown castle at Azraq, where he finally met Nuri Shaalan, the intimidating warlord on whose approval the Arabs' northern plans would rest. An old man with a bitter smile, who dyed his hair and beard 'a dead black' and whose eyes seemed to glint red in the sunlight, Shaalan, however, remained wary.[13] He would not revolt unless the Druses did, he told Lawrence, although he admitted that 'he would certainly be involved sooner or later' and was determined to back Feisal ultimately. 'He is willing now to compromise himself to any extent, short of open hostilities pending the collection of his year's food supply' from the Turks, Lawrence wrote in his notes.[14] Lawrence arrived back in Nabk, at the mouth of Wadi Sirhan, on 18 June.

In Lawrence's absence, the young leader of the Arab expedition, Sharif Nasir, had mustered a force of just 560 Huwaytat tribesmen, but he felt he was now ready to head west towards Maan, where his aim was to frighten the local Turkish forces enough to achieve the recall of their small garrison in Aqaba at the head of the Red Sea. With Lawrence, Nasir, Auda and the Huwaytat left for Bair, a remote well sixty miles south-west of Nabk, on 19 June. But when they reached Bair they discovered that three out of the four wells had been recently dynamited; the fourth would not supply enough water daily for the 500 camels in the party. The sabotage was not entirely unexpected for, as Lawrence later admitted, he had encouraged Nuri Shaalan to tell the Turks of the Arabs' whereabouts. As the explosives expert Lawrence was obliged to climb down into the least damaged of the wells, where, having extracted some unexploded charges, he was able to establish that the well was not completely blocked at the bottom. It was a 'nasty job for all well lining was loose', he wrote.[15] Realising the Turks had worked out where he was, Nasir decided to stop while the next wells, forty miles further south-west at Jafr, were cautiously reconnoitred. While the remaining tribesmen waited, buoyed by the effect he had had at Ras Baalbek, Lawrence apparently again turned his attention northwards.

He later told Clayton that he went north with Auda's young nephew, Zaal, and one hundred Huwaytat to Jizah, just south of the modern

Jordanian capital, Amman. There he met another Arab dissident, Fawaz ibn Faiz, a leading sheikh of the Bani Sakhr tribe,* before crossing the Hijaz Railway and heading north-west to Um Keis, a village in the strategically important Yarmuk valley, just south-east of Lake Tiberias. Down this valley ran the railway from Syria into Palestine: the main supply route for all the Turkish troops in Palestine. Lawrence had travelled up the valley by train in 1911 and, having refreshed his memory, he returned to Mafraq on the main line halfway between Dara and Amman. Near there, at Minifir, he spent some time observing the railway, before demolishing a curved section of the track and leaving a Garland mine, which apparently wrecked the train that later came down to repair the damage.

From there Lawrence's raiders followed the railway southwards back towards Bair. On 27 June they reached Atwi station. While Lawrence watched from a rise to the east, some of the Huwaytat, led by Zaal, crept up a valley to within eighty yards of the two station buildings. Zaal stopped and – Lawrence remembered – carefully took aim at the easiest target among the group of officials sitting in the shade outside the ticket office. When he squeezed the trigger, 'the fattest man bowed slowly in his chair and sank to the ground under the frozen stare of his fellows.'[16] Zaal's men rushed from their hiding place and charged forwards, but they were too slow. The survivors raced inside the station, slamming its heavy metal door behind them. The Arabs now found themselves under fire. While they were taking cover behind the other station building, a trolley party arrived back from its morning patrol of the line. They shot dead all four men aboard and drove the station's herd of sheep away before butchering them and feasting lavishly. Then they rode through the night back to Bair.

While Nasir, at Bair, was now preparing to take action to deliver Aqaba into the Arabs' hands, far to the south at Jaydah Newcombe was making final preparations for a spectacular attack on Al Ula. He and Hornby had driven up to the remote wadi at the end of June, followed by a

---

* The Bani Sakhr were the dominant tribe in the upland region immediately east of the Dead Sea. Lawrence had identified Fawaz ibn Faiz as the 'biggest man' of the tribe by October 1915.

detachment of Indian machine-gunners, and camel-mounted Egyptian soldiers, and Arab volunteers. Joyce and Feisal arrived at the end of June, but by then, however, Newcombe had received copies of the aerial photographs taken a fortnight earlier. Having called the officers together, Newcombe explained that the photographs showed that both Al Ula and the next station south, Badai, were too heavily defended to risk a direct assault. Besides which, the Arabs were also reluctant to fight because Ramadan had begun. Instead, 'all energies have to be concentrated on line smashing', Joyce reported.[17]

A week later Newcombe launched two attacks on the railway north and south of Al Ula. After dark on 6 July, a mixed party of Egyptians and Harith tribesmen – Lawrence's 'robbers for generations' – scouted the area south of Al Ula between Badai and Zumrud stations before picking Sahl al Matran, a honey-pink fort on a grey plain fenced by jagged mountains, as their target. 'We crept up to the tracks at the dead of a very dark night,' recalled Jafar Pasha, who was also there.[18] Near the station the party laid over 500 charges – one to each rail – which they detonated at two in the morning. 'The noise of the dynamite going was something grand and it is always satisfactory finding one is breaking things,' reported an excited Joyce, who was more usually burdened with administrative chores like that, a few weeks earlier, which had required him to guess the average shoe-size of arriving Arab volunteers, so that a selection of appropriately sized boots could be dispatched from Suez to Wajh.[19]

From inside Sahl al Matran, three signal rockets shot into the warm night sky to warn the stations either side that they were under attack. 'When the dynamite went off in a series of terrifying explosions I could see the silhouettes of a horde of Turkish soldiers coming towards us,' Jafar remembered.[20] This counterattack caused some panic among the Arabs; Newcombe and Joyce decided to depart rapidly. Only at dawn did Newcombe realise that several of his Egyptian soldiers were missing, but there was no time to go back. 'It was a great pity we could not stop on the line and see what happened but we were thirty miles from water and dared not stay,' Joyce explained to Wilson.[21] A few miles north of Al Ula, the same night Hornby supervised the destruction of 300 more rails. On

8 and 10 July, he continued to destroy rails nightly, even after a guncotton charge exploded in his face, rupturing his inner ear and leaving him permanently slightly deaf.[22]

On 11 July three British biplanes left Jaydah to bomb Al Ula. One clipped a bush while taking off and crash-landed, but the other two successfully reached the target. The raid was repeated the following day. A further sortie on 16 July hit the water tower at the station. 'Unfortunately we now found ourselves short of petrol,' explained one of the pilots, Thomas Henderson, 'as many tins had been lost or damaged in transport and several had burst with the heat of the sun, which was intense.'[23] Alternately roasted in the sun and drenched by dew at night, the biplanes also suffered from the sand-devils which scoured Jaydah daily. At first sight of these whirling dust-spouts 'Everyone would stand to and hang on to the machines,' Henderson remembered. 'The tents went down every time. Sometimes they went up. Afterwards all was chaos and the noise of the sandstorm was only equalled by the expressions of discontent by the RFC personnel and the wailings of the Arabs.'[24]

Following the attack on Sahl al Matran, Newcombe and Joyce went south to see Abdullah, who was still based in Wadi Ais. Newcombe, finally reconciled to the fact that finishing the campaign through a single, large-scale raid was unachievable, now told Abdullah that 'the easiest and best way to cut the railway was in small lots, but frequently; that this achieved better results than all going in one day and doing 6,000 rails at a time'.[25] It was, he said, 'much better to do what we can at once and cut line now, when it will be much easier to make big operations on a line already cut'.

No sooner had Lawrence returned to Bair than Sharif Nasir and Auda wanted to set out for Aqaba, which was now their goal. Aqaba was attractive for a simple reason: without immediate support in Syria for a revolt, the port would provide a natural base closer to Suez and Syria than Wajh, to which British explosives, ammunition and gold could be shipped to foment unrest further north. Although impregnable from the seashore, on the landward side the little port could be reached from

Maan most directly through Wadi Itm, a shattered chasm of red and black rock, and it was down here that Auda now intended to go.

The Arabs started south-west from Bair, reaching the shining mudflats of the Jafr plain on 30 June. They stopped at Jafr, a clump of dirty-green palms flickering in the silty mirage, while the Huwaytat launched two diversionary attacks: on the railway near Unayzah, a lonely caravanserai north of Maan, and at Fuweilah, at the foot of the Jabal al Batra ridge, which divided Aqaba from Maan. The tribesmen's attack on Fuweilah was initially disastrous. The Turks fought back and massacred the tribesmen's families in their tents. Outraged, the tribesmen attacked again, storming the fort in Fuweilah and taking no prisoners. Alarmed by the outbreak of violence, the Turks sent troops to reinforce their post on the pass over the Batra ridge, at Abu al Assal.

Once Nasir had heard that the Arabs had attacked Fuweilah he decided to cross the railway twenty miles south of Maan and ascend the Jabal al Batra ridge to attack the Turks stationed on the road between Maan and Aqaba. He, Auda, Lawrence and the remaining tribesmen, mounted on a mixture of camels and horses, headed south across the flat grey plain towards the Hijaz Railway. Two miles beyond the station of Ghadir al Hajj, they found one of the stocky bridges which had so far defied the demolition teams in the Hijaz. It was the first time Lawrence had seen one of these bridges close up, but the drainage hole which emerged from the spandrel between each arch invited an idea. Lawrence plugged this fist-sized outlet with several pounds of explosive which, when fired, 'brought down the arch, shattered the pier and stripped the side walls, in no more than six minutes' work'.[26] Hoping that the explosions would draw the Turks' attention southwards, the Arab party now hurried away west towards Jabal al Batra, climbing the ridge in the dark. To the south the Quwayrah plain glowed green and gold in the dawn light, and angular mountains in the distance marked the head of Wadi Itm, the gorge leading down to Aqaba.

The Arabs found the Turks' reinforcements clustered at Abu al Assal, a fold in the Jabal al Batra ridge which, though offering plentiful water, gave the Turks little chance to defend themselves. Having surrounded the Turkish outpost early on 2 July, Auda's men began to snipe at the soldiers below. 'Our rifles grew so hot with the sun and the shooting that they seared our hands,' Lawrence would later remember: 'It was terribly hot – hotter than ever before I had felt it in Arabia and the anxiety and constant moving made it hard for us.'[27]

Although the Turks were trapped, the Huwaytat attack stalled in the withering heat. In the safety of a hollow behind the ridge Lawrence paused for a rest where he was joined by Nasir and then Auda. When Auda accused him of slacking, Lawrence angrily replied that his tribesmen were no use: 'they shoot a lot and hit a little'.[28] This accusation enraged Auda, who turned and ran back up the hill, shouting at his men to gather round him. Lawrence, who had followed Auda back to the crest of the ridge, wondered whether he had done the wrong thing. Suddenly there were yells: Lawrence crawled forward to the edge of the ridge, to see, led by Auda, 'our fifty horsemen coming down the last slope into the main valley like a run-away, at full gallop, shooting from the saddle'.[29]

With the Turks transfixed by Auda's charge, Sharif Nasir saw an opportunity. 'Come on,' he shouted at Lawrence, and they mounted their camels and led the remaining tribesmen in a headlong dash down the hill into Abu al Assal. The Turks did not see them until it was too late. They 'fired a few shots, but mostly only shrieked and turned to run', recalled Lawrence who, bouncing along on his galloping camel, was shooting back with his pistol.[30] Suddenly, his camel tripped and fell. 'I was torn completely from the saddle, and went sailing grandly through the air for a great distance, and landed with a crash which seemed to drive all the power and feeling out of me.'[31] When he came round, Lawrence found that he had shot the beast in the back of its head.

Auda appeared. His horse had been killed under him, his binoculars were shattered, and his holster and scabbard holed. Six bullets had hit his equipment in total, but none had touched him, an escape that he attributed to his purchase years earlier of a miniature Quran, for which Lawrence privately thought he had vastly overpaid. In all the Arabs had suffered two deaths and one man was seriously wounded. About 300 dead and dying Turks lay in the scorching hollow around the well.

From a prisoner Lawrence learned that it would probably have been easy to capture Maan, but to do so at this point would have been a diversion from the opportunity which now existed to secure the surrender of Aqaba. In his diary Lawrence recorded that he slept after the battle, which had lasted throughout the afternoon. But in *Seven Pillars of Wisdom*, he described spending much of the night neatly arranging the naked bodies of the dead in line – the tribesmen always stripped their victims and wore their clothes as trophies – under the light of the waxing moon, before helping Auda to write letters to the Turkish outposts down to Aqaba, threatening them with a similar fate unless they capitulated quickly.

The letters had some effect. Down on the plain below, Quwayrah itself, a tiny telegraph station, fell without a shot being fired. The tribesmen pushed onwards, into the deep cleft of Wadi Itm. On the following day, 4 July, they surrounded the next Turkish outpost, halfway down the narrowing wadi. An attack that night, coinciding with the lunar eclipse, which gave the moon a copper colour, terrified the Turks there into surrender as well. Finally the Arabs reached the Turks entrenched at Wadi Itm's mouth. Though their defences pointed out towards the sea, the Turks proved reluctant to give in but, Lawrence recollected, when 'we explained the situation on the road behind us; our growing forces; and our short control over their tempers', the Turkish officer the Arabs had summoned agreed to surrender at dawn the following day.[32] 'We mounted our camels,' Lawrence recalled, 'and raced through a driving sand-storm down to Aqaba, only four miles further, and splashed into the sea, on July the sixth, just two months after our setting out from Wajh.'[33]

Lawrence paused only briefly in the port, shattered by frequent offshore bombardment by the British. The dates in the palms were still green and unripe and, short of fishing using dynamite or killing their own camels, there was no other available food. His diary chronicles a rapid turnaround, but also the fact that his arrival was expected: 'Entered Aqaba 10am. Read letter from Newcombe. Left in afternoon.'[34] With a select band of tribesmen, he immediately set out westwards across Sinai for Suez to raise food and help, and to break the news of the Arabs' momentous achievement.

13

THE IMPACT OF AQABA

(July 1917)

In Cairo, Bertie Clayton spent the morning of 10 July putting the finishing touches to a memorandum which summarised the difficulty of supporting Feisal's imminent move northwards. He remained concerned about how Feisal would be supplied with food and the stream of money, weapons and ammunition which had fuelled the revolt for over a year. Supply via Aqaba, Clayton said, involved 'insuperable difficulties at present' partly due to the fact that 'the section between Aqaba and Maan is in Turkish hands'.[1]

With the memo despatched, and after a brief lunch, Clayton was back at his desk in the Savoy Hotel when he became aware that an Arab had walked into his office. *'Mush fadi,'* he said, without looking up: telling whoever it was to leave him be.

The Arab replied in Oxford English: Clayton's head shot up.

'I . . . got a very hearty welcome', Lawrence later recalled.[2] He had crossed the Sinai by camel in just over three days. He gave Clayton his report of his journey northwards straightaway and presented him with a long list of supplies that were urgently needed in Aqaba, including a request for 6,000 cigarettes.[3] That afternoon, Clayton withdrew £16,000 in gold to cover the promises Sharif Nasir had made to buy tribal support and dispatched the money by train to Suez for immediate shipment to Aqaba. Then the two men sat down to talk.

The British had kept a close eye on Aqaba after Lawrence set out north. In mid-June a warship off Aqaba reported that the port appeared to have been evacuated following clashes between the Turkish garrison and Arab tribesmen, before being reoccupied by the Turks a fortnight later.[4] Shortly afterwards the British learned that the Huwaytat were in revolt in the Maan area, that a bridge on the railway south of Maan had been blown up, and that Auda had arrived at Azraq. Although, on 5 July, Clayton cautiously reported that 'It is not known what are the present whereabouts of Captain Lawrence',[5] he guessed correctly that Lawrence was behind the bridge attack, since without Lawrence's influence the Huwaytat uprising was hard to explain.[6] Even so, Clayton must have been astounded by Lawrence's unannounced arrival in his office only a day after his report of Huwaytat unrest was published in the *Arab Bulletin*.

Wingate was delighted by Lawrence's sudden appearance. That night he telegraphed the Chief of Imperial General Staff, Sir William Robertson, with the news that 'Captain Lawrence arrived Cairo today by land from Aqaba. Turkish posts between Tafilah, Maan and Aqaba in Arab hands. Total Turkish losses 700 killed, 600 prisoners including 20 officers.'[7] A fortnight later, the *Arab Bulletin* archly reported that the explanation for recent disturbances in the Maan area 'has reached us in the person of Captain Lawrence', but made no mention of the fact that he had reached Aqaba nor that the port was now in Arab hands.[8]

The scale of Lawrence's achievement, claims by some Arabs, including Nesib al Bakri, that Lawrence never set out north on his own, and Lawrence's subsequent coyness about his journeys have raised questions over whether he invented the journey he made far into northern Syria. Lawrence certainly enjoyed the mystery surrounding his journey. In the earliest surviving draft of *Seven Pillars of Wisdom* he would gloss over his first ride as 'long and dangerous, no part of the machinery of the revolt, as barren of consequence as it was unworthy in motive', but could not resist a fleeting reference ten pages later to his 'long trip round Baalbek and Damascus and the Hauran'.[9] Quizzed by his biographer Robert Graves, he described his report to Clayton as 'part of the truth' and suggested some tantalising text which Graves might use, which would encourage Graves's readers to believe that Lawrence had achieved all he claimed.[10] Graves, though slightly sceptical, used Lawrence's suggested words in full.

Whether or not Lawrence went where he claimed is, however, ultimately unimportant. What matters is that his colleagues believed him. When another intelligence officer, who had got wind of the existence of the report Lawrence wrote for Clayton, asked him for a copy that September, Lawrence half-heartedly tried to dampen his interest. The report, he claimed, was 'rather dull, except to one who knew Syrian politics'.[11] In fact there was a good reason for secrecy. As Wingate immediately recognised, and warned London when he heard where Lawrence had been, 'for political reasons it is very important that nothing should be known publicly as to Lawrence's Syrian reconnaissance'.[12] Besides the danger that public knowledge would stimulate a witchhunt in Syria by the Turks for anyone who had helped Lawrence, Ras Baalbek lay inside the zone allocated to the French who, though they knew about the tribal disturbances which followed Lawrence's raid there, had no inkling that Lawrence was involved. For months afterwards they remained under the impression that Lawrence's journey to Aqaba had taken him no further north than Tafilah, in the south of modern Jordan and safely inside the zone allocated to the British.[13] As for the truth of the events, British and French intelligence reports, which refer to trouble in the Ras Baalbek area, separately corroborate the most audacious episode in Lawrence's story.[14] And despite Wingate's efforts, so too, perhaps, does the untimely death of Fawaz ibn Faiz, possibly poisoned by the Turks, within weeks of his meeting Lawrence.[15]

Wingate's sensitivity to French concerns reflected his own determination to revise the Sykes-Picot agreement. At the beginning of July he approached the Foreign Office, arguing that the British zone of influence delineated in the treaty should be extended southwards to encompass the whole of Arabia. 'Anything less than this jeopardises our whole position in the East,' he claimed. This one-sided alteration to the Sykes-Picot agreement was justified, he said, on the grounds that while Britain had helped the Sharif and captured a chunk of Mesopotamia, the French had done next to nothing.[16] Wingate had already dispatched Hogarth to London to help press for the treaty to be re-examined. 'I can't say I feel keen about it,' Hogarth wrote to his wife. 'I hate the lobbying which reporting entails.'[17]

By early July, Hogarth was back in Britain. 'So far I have found no one who both takes the S.P. Agreement seriously and approves it – except M.S. himself,' he wrote to Clayton shortly after arriving in London.[18] Feeling he was pushing at an open door, on 10 July – before he knew of the capture of Aqaba – Hogarth submitted a memorandum calling for the Sykes-Picot agreement to be scrapped because Russia had already 'renounced her claim to a large part of her allotment'.[19] He proposed a commitment either to the Arabs' complete independence, to protection by the British, or decentralised independence under the Ottomans, instead.

Although widespread dislike of the Sykes-Picot agreement favoured Hogarth, events in France, Russia and Turkey all discouraged precipitate action to destroy the treaty. During June, the French Army had been shaken by a serious mutiny. In Russia the Bolsheviks' power was growing but the British remained hopeful that Russia might yet remain in the war. Following rumours that the Turkish high command had fallen out with their German advisers, the British had organised secret talks with the Turkish Minister for War, Enver Pasha, to try to secure the Ottomans' exit from the war in return for a very large bribe. Nevertheless, Hogarth reviewed the options: 'Either the W[estern] Front situation demands encouragement of the French at any cost, in which case this Agreement must stand,' he acknowledged, or – and this was his personal preference – the Sykes-Picot treaty should be torn up and no further attempt to redivide the Ottoman Empire made until the outcomes of the political situation in Russia and the overtures to Enver had become clear.[20]

Little chance though it had of changing government policy, Hogarth's proposal still made Mark Sykes livid. 'Hogarth arrived and played hell by writing an anti-French anti-Agreement memorandum. Pouring cold water on the Arab movement and going in for Gnome-Imperialism and a British Mecca,' Sykes wrote to Clayton.[21] Sykes's violent opposition ensured that there was little appetite for reopening the treaty in London. 'I doubt if my note has effected anything except the embitterment of Mark Sykes,' Hogarth concluded dolefully.[22]

Sykes was beginning to realise that Hogarth was not his only adversary. The most ardent opponent of his cherished agreement was Lawrence. Although he told Clayton through gritted teeth that 'Lawrence's move is splendid and I want him knighted',[23] in a bitter, defensive letter to the Foreign Secretary, Arthur Balfour, he revealed his true opinions: 'I have had to contend . . . with many difficulties: the prejudices of the past both British and French, the mutual suspicions and susceptibilities of out-of-date minds, the anti-British policy of Brémond, the anti-French attitude of Lawrence and Newcombe and', in a reference to the location of a tense stand-off between French and British forces over the ownership of the southern Sudan in 1898, 'the Fashoda memories of the British and French functionaries in Cairo.'[24]

'Tell him to be careful not to justify Mark's idea of him as a Fashoda propagandist,' Hogarth told Clayton to warn Lawrence.[25] But he was confident that the allegation would not stick: 'The W[ar] O[ffice] is optimistic about Arabia and Syria,' Hogarth said, 'and much bucked by TEL's report and scheme.'

The scheme was for the next stage of the Arabs' revolt, which Lawrence had devised on the back of a sheet of telegraph paper, perhaps on the train between Suez and Cairo on 10 July. In the final version, after Clayton had encouraged him to be more cautious about the chances of success, Lawrence envisaged a roughly coordinated attack by up to seven different Arab forces, which he believed could be arranged by the end of August if they were given the necessary assistance.[26] A southern force would seize the fertile, grain-producing upland areas east and south-east of the Dead Sea around Karak and Tafilah as soon as possible. Four other forces, based east of the railway, at Azraq, Bair and Jafr, would stage simultaneous attacks along a 350-mile stretch of the Hijaz Railway between Maan, in the south of modern Jordan, and Hama, a hundred miles north of Damascus in present-day Syria. Then, from the Hauran, 6,000 'not bad' Druses would once again rebel, descending westwards on Dara, the vulnerable ganglion of the Syrian railway network which connected Palestine, southern Syria and the Hijaz to Damascus. At the same time, Lawrence advocated attacking the railway west of Dara, where it descended the Yarmuk valley, to cut the Turks in Palestine off from Syria. He hoped that the Druses might follow up success at Dara with the occupation of Damascus, but his final proposal was less assured than his original draft, in which he anticipated the early occupation of the city. His tactics relied on tribesmen and the Druses, but he hoped that their concerted action would precipitate 'risings of a local character in the hills between the Jordan and the Hijaz Railway, from Dara to opposite Jericho and to similar risings in the hills along the Nazareth–Damascus roads'.[27] If these revolts in the settled, agricultural belt east of the Jordan succeeded, then Turkish rule in Syria would be short-lived.

The consequences if the risings failed, however, were likely to be terrible. The Turks had crushed an uprising in Karak – a hilltop town in southern Jordan – seven years earlier by hanging eight members of the town's two leading families in the market square, and Clayton and Lawrence both knew that local fears of Turkish recrimination stood in the way of their plan succeeding. Clayton began to push for a British invasion of Palestine to keep the Turkish Army busy. A revolt in Syria, he said, was 'entirely contingent on a decision to undertake major operations in Palestine with which the movement of the Arabs must synchronise . . . Unless operations of such magnitude as to occupy the whole of the Turkish Army in Palestine were undertaken the proposed Arab operations must be abandoned.'[28]

On 12 July General Sir Edmund Allenby, the new commander-in-chief of the British forces in Egypt, called Lawrence in to see him. After the second British defeat at Gaza in April, Allenby had been sent out to Egypt to replace Archibald Murray. Allenby's was not an enviable position. Before leaving London he had come under significant pressure from the Prime Minister to take 'Jerusalem by Christmas' but the War Cabinet was split on this strategy. Robertson continued to argue forcefully against any distraction from the Western Front and repeatedly warned Allenby privately that he could not expect to receive further troops to meet his needs. This combination of political pressure and Robertson's opposition had undone Murray, and Allenby realised he needed to tread carefully to avoid falling into the same trap.

A fortnight into his new job, which he saw as a demotion from his previous command in northern France, uncertain of the bewildering array of tribal allegiances, but ready to listen to advice, Allenby sat almost silently as Lawrence took the opportunity to explain his plan. Lawrence was effectively asking Allenby to support the Bedu by committing himself to an invasion of Palestine, an offensive for which so far there was inadequate political support in London. It was perhaps just as well that he did not know that, three days earlier, Allenby had written to his wife with some local colour: 'The Bedouin are not very friendly to strangers, British or Turk; and we don't allow them near us,' he explained. 'Of course, they are Turkish in sympathy as a rule.'[29]

'At the end,' Lawrence later recollected, Allenby 'put up his chin and said quite directly, "Well, I will do for you what I can." '[30]

Allenby's guarded response concealed the fact that the new commander was greatly impressed by what he had just heard. He also realised that the excitement generated in London by Lawrence's journey could reinforce his own request for two more divisions of men, which he transmitted to London the same day, and which was rapidly approved.[31] Allenby wrote to Robertson four days later, warmly reporting Lawrence's ideas. 'Even the partial success of Lawrence's scheme would seriously disorganise Turkish railway communications south of Aleppo, whilst its complete success would destroy effectively his only main artery of communication,' he explained.[32] Besides the possibility of causing havoc behind Turkish lines, Allenby also welcomed the security the Arabs could bring to his eastern flank because he worried that the Turks might counterattack from the Maan area as he advanced northwards. But he did not immediately fully endorse Lawrence's strategy.

Fulsome praise of Lawrence from both Robertson and Wingate for his achievement made it possible for Allenby to go further. With the backing of the High Commissioner for the scheme, and an enthusiastic endorsement from the War Office,[33] Allenby sent another telegram to Robertson on 19 July, this time making his support explicit and tying his own plans to advance to the need to make the most of the situation Lawrence had created. 'The advantages offered by Arab co-operation on lines proposed by Captain Lawrence are, in my opinion, of such importance that no effort should be spared to reap full benefit therefrom.'[34] If the Arabs' operations were successful, he said, 'such a movement, in conjunction with offensive operations in Palestine, may cause a collapse of the Turkish campaigns in the Hijaz and in Syria and produce far-reaching results, both political as well as military'. He warned Robertson, however, that 'the scheme proposed by Captain Lawrence can only be realised in conjunction with the prosecution of offensive operations by me in this theatre'. He intended to be ready to advance northwards into Palestine by mid-September, a date fixed by the fact that action was needed before the tribesmen headed deep into the desert during the winter to graze their livestock. To coordinate the tribesmen to the east of the Jordan valley with the British Army to the west, Allenby proposed bringing Feisal and Lawrence under his command. The consequence of this arrangement was to undermine the Sykes-Picot agreement's attempt to lock the Arabs out by drawing them formally into the British plans to invade Palestine. Now that the Arabs were an ally, as Clayton warned Sykes, 'My own advice to the French would be to encourage and back Feisal and the northern Arab movement as much as possible.'[35]

Expecting Sharif Husein to be suspicious of Allenby's subordination of Feisal, Lawrence volunteered to go to Jeddah to reassure him. On his voyage southwards he stopped at Wajh and was flown inland the same day to meet Feisal, who was up at Jaydah. The situation in the wadi was chaotic. A sandstorm had hit the camp earlier that day, badly damaging two of the aeroplanes and preventing further air-raids. Lawrence spent the night there, describing his two-month-long journey to Feisal and making preparations to move the British and Arab operations at Wajh north to Aqaba. He left for Jeddah the following morning, with letters from Feisal to Husein to allay any fears his father might have about the new command structure set out by Allenby.

Feisal had finally moved inland to provide moral support for New-combe's ambitious plans to attack the railway. But soaring daytime temperatures seemed likely to scotch plans for further raids – big or small – against the line. 'The heat is grilling us all . . . I have experienced nothing to equal it,' Joyce told Wilson: 'the hot wind off the rocks is like the wrath of a furnace.'[36] Jafar Pasha, who had served before the war with the Ottoman Army in central Arabia, accompanied Joyce to Wadi Ais to see Abdullah and described the terrible journey:

One memorable feature of the wadi was its huge, leafless trees, totally desiccated and covered in vicious thorns. Such was the burning heat that the camels were unable to resist sidling up even to these spreading skeletons for shade and the spines would rip our clothing to shreds . . . Never in my life have I experienced a thirst as intense as the one on this journey. The whole world would turn red before my eyes and I would have to lie down in the niggardly shade of one of those prickly, naked trees to be gradually revived by sips of water from a can.[37]

Joyce and Jafar went on to spend 'three utterly wretched days in Wadi Ais, plagued day and night by incessant sand storms'. In his memoirs, Jafar admitted he was 'overwhelmed by anxiety that we would all die if we stayed here much longer'.

Newcombe refused to be beaten. While Joyce headed to the pass south of Mudarraj, where Lawrence had nearly mined the train carrying civilians out of Medina that April, to carry out some final demolitions, Newcombe set out to search for the old Zumrud caravanserai, which was close to the railway about fifty miles south of Al Ula and rumoured to have fresh water. Before dawn on 26 July he found the grim little fortress, standing in a gravel wadi two miles west of the railway. Though in a tumbledown state today, in 1917 it was a perfect base for raiding, but its supply of water made it contested property. Four days later W.A. Davenport, the latest recruit to the campaign, received an anxious message from Newcombe in the caravanserai, saying that he was under attack. When Davenport arrived, Newcombe sent him with his party of Egyptians into the hills immediately north of the caravanserai, while he headed south. It was an uneasy night. The 'Turks were very jumpy and kept up bursts of excited fire at intervals', Davenport reported,[38] but Jafar Pasha arrived the following day with a relief force, attacking Sahl al Matran again, which diverted the Turks and freed Newcombe to return to the railway.

Newcombe's strike on the railway south of Zumrud was almost a disaster. After dynamiting nearly five miles of track with Davenport, he went south to demolish a further section. Having already alerted the Turks to their presence in the area by seizing the only water supply and then attacking the railway, it was hardly surprising when the Turks appeared in force. The two British officers were lucky to escape after a three-hour rearguard action in which Newcombe lost his satchel and, with it, his prized billets-doux. Jafar remembered how Newcombe

> came to me shamefacedly on the following day to explain how deeply he regretted his insistence on staying behind: he had lost the pouch containing most of the maps he had drawn during his tours in the Hijaz, and also the official reports he had written dealing with the situation. After that, when we wanted to pull his leg . . . we would bring up the loss of his beloved and irreplaceable pouch.[39]

Husein came down to Jeddah to meet Lawrence on 28 July, and approved Feisal as his military representative in the north.[40] Most of the meeting he devoted to his concerns about the post-war settlement of Syria. He told Lawrence that he would refuse to accept French annexation of Beirut and Lebanon, but explained how delighted he was to have 'trapped' Picot into admitting that Syria should be governed along similar lines to Mesopotamia. Unsure of how Mesopotamia would be run, Lawrence evidently asked the Sharif to explain. 'That, he says, means a temporary occupation of the country for strategical and political reasons (with probably an annual grant to the Sharif in compensation and recognition) and concessions in the way of public works,' he reported.[41] Husein devoted much of a second meeting the following day to a description of the threat posed to him by Wahabism, the austere version of Islam espoused by Ibn Saud.

Husein's agreement with the command arrangements which Lawrence explained to him meant that Allenby could confirm early that August that he would now control all operations north and west of a line between Aqaba and Maan.[42] The British commander also received a letter from Robertson, who was worrying that the Russian collapse would allow the Germans to concentrate their forces in France and Flanders. 'With Russia practically out of the war we have got to consider the necessity for economising shipping and men and also for being strong on the West front,' he told Allenby, grumbling that 'Extensive operations in distant theatres mean a great strain upon shipping.'[43] But he was also forced to admit that, whatever his own reservations over an advance into Palestine, 'the Prime Minister is very much in favour of it and eventually the Government may decide to do it.' A further sentence in the letter was pregnant with possibility: 'Lawrence's scheme seems to be a good one and I hope we shall be able to take advantage of it.'

14

IMPOLITIC TRUTHS

(August–September 1917)

Allenby received further directions from the War Cabinet on 11 August 1917. He was ordered to take advantage of the capture of Aqaba and attack the Turks, 'since a good success achieved against them will tend to strengthen the morale and staying power of this country during a season when important successes in Europe may not be feasible'.[1] Rightly worried that the Russian collapse would shortly liberate thousands of Ottoman soldiers to fight on the Palestine and Mesopotamian fronts, the War Cabinet's orders revealed a heavy reliance on Lawrence's belief that he could mobilise thousands of tribesmen in Syria to paralyse the Ottoman rail network that September. On this assumption, the War Cabinet advised Allenby to press the Turks soon, to draw them into Palestine rather than Mesopotamia. Lawrence's Arabs would swing into action behind the Turks, bottling them up in Palestine by destroying the slender railway link which connected Palestine with Syria. It was a clever plan, in theory.

Robertson remained sceptical. While he liked Lawrence's scheme because it was so economical, in a letter to a colleague he privately admitted he was 'a bit doubtful' about Allenby's plans, though he thought they were worth trying. To those politicians who were 'dying to go to Jerusalem and Damascus, and other places',[2] however, Robertson remained an implacable opponent, a fact which explains why the Cabinet's orders set Allenby no geographical objective nor, more alarmingly, did they promise him enough troops to continue beyond Jerusalem, or even to maintain his position if he reached the holy city.

In a separate private letter designed to undermine Allenby's faith in his orders, Robertson described the split in the War Cabinet. Lloyd George, he said, thought the instructions did not go far enough; others, that they went too far. He also tried to play down the significance of the War Cabinet's instructions:

> They simply amount to doing the best you can with what you have got; to giving the Turk as hard a knock as you can; and at the same time avoiding going too far forward and getting into a position from which you can neither advance nor go back and which might involve us in commitments which we could not properly meet having regard to other places and to our resources.[3]

At least, Allenby thought, the situation in Aqaba was good. Lawrence had passed through the port on his return from seeing Husein in Jeddah, and told Allenby on his return to Egypt that all was well there and that, contrary to his earlier fears, the tribesmen would not disappear into the desert to graze their camels at the first sign of the winter rains. In fact, Lawrence was simply buying time because the situation was far worse than he made out. Down at Jeddah, he had received intelligence which suggested that Auda had contacted the Turks in Maan, offering his services if the Turks treated him as well as they had done Nuri Shaalan. He raced to Aqaba, riding back up Wadi Itm to Quwayrah, where the Huwaytat were based. There, Lawrence challenged Auda and his deputy, Mohammed al Dheilan, about the letters he revealed he knew they had sent to Maan.

According to Auda, Mohammed had borrowed his seal to write to the Governor of Maan, offering to swap sides. The Ottomans replied enthusiastically, offering a reward if he did. When Auda found out, he robbed the Turkish messenger who had come bearing an advance. Lawrence was clearly unconvinced by this story. Although he wired Wilson to say that the situation was 'satisfactory'[4] and although he then told Allenby all was well, he later admitted that his claim that there was 'no spirit of treachery abroad . . . may have been hardly true, but the deception was mine, and I regularly reduced impolitic truth in my communications'.[5] Believing Lawrence, Allenby told Robertson that Lawrence would 'organise a movement, on a large scale, between Aqaba and the Dead Sea' and that 'now the Arabs are in, he can keep them in, and an early start in September by my troops is not now a necessity'.[6] This was a good excuse for Allenby, because his troops' special training and the supply arrangements needed to sustain them in a rapid advance through waterless country were taking longer than expected to complete.

Arab reinforcements began arriving in Aqaba late in August. On 18 August, Jafar Pasha arrived with 800 men. A further 300 disembarked two days later, and Feisal arrived on 23 August with 500 more. Pierce Joyce also arrived in Aqaba late in the month to take charge of the Arabs' base, assisted by another officer, Raymond Goslett, who had run a plumbing business on the Charing Cross Road in civilian life. Hornby, but not Newcombe, would also shortly join them there. Newcombe was 'in Egypt, ill; (nerves mostly)', Lawrence commented in a letter home.[7] Following Newcombe's narrow escape near Zumrud Lawrence suggested to Wilson that Feisal would not need his services in the northern campaign.

A major port centuries earlier, Aqaba was by 1917 a backwater of about a hundred mud houses screened from the sea by a belt of palm trees, and a square fort which the British had already ruined by naval bombardment. The sandy shoreline ran back from the sea to end at the base of the gigantic cliff wall which separated Aqaba from the hinterland. There was no grazing nor, besides the slowly ripening dates, any local source of food: the port would be entirely dependent on the Royal Navy for supplies from Egypt.

Although Aqaba was protected by a British warship, *HMS Humber*, which was moored offshore like a seaborne goalkeeper, Joyce felt vulnerable. There were two routes from Aqaba to Maan: one – still impassable to motor vehicles – followed Wadi Itm; the other, easier, road went north up Wadi Araba then east over the 3,000-foot-high ridge and down towards Ain Dilagha and Maan. The British urgently needed to build a road up Wadi Itm to supply the tribesmen on the Quwayrah plain. But while Wadi Itm reverberated with the crack of exploding dynamite as British soldiers hurriedly cleared a road up the narrow valley, the Turks were reported to be gathering in numbers at Ain Dilagha to retake Aqaba.[8]

The report of Turkish activity seems to have galvanised Lawrence, who had been taking a few days off in Cairo. With a promise from the Royal Flying Corps of support, he immediately returned to Aqaba and headed north-west to the edge of the Sinai to set up a rudimentary airstrip stocked with fuel and bombs for British aircraft flying from Egypt. The aircraft – new biplanes to replace those damaged at Jaydah – flew to this airstrip on 26 August and flew on to bomb Maan, a station further south, and the advance Turkish camps at Fuweilah and Abu al Assal over the next three days.

Back in Aqaba, Lawrence found that another officer from the Arab Bureau, Macindoe, was planning to write a critical report on the situation there. Having seen the report, he worried that it could erode Allenby's trust in the Arabs' operations. On 26 August – the day before MacIndoe dispatched his conclusions – Lawrence wrote to Clayton to explain that the point of Jafar's force was 'not so much to engage Turkish forces on equal terms, as to stiffen the Beduin resistance, by providing the comfortable spectacle of a trained reserve, and to impress the Turks with the fact that behind the Beduin screen lies an unknown quantity, which must be disposed of before they can conquer Aqaba'.[9] The Turkish commander, he argued, would not dare to attack Aqaba with fewer than 2,000 men, the number under Jafar Pasha's command, whose 'quality, so long as it is not proved bad by premature action, has of necessity to be estimated by the Turks as good'.

Fortunately the Turks did not come, because the Arabs were disorganised. 'Most troublesome were the volunteers from the Hijaz and Yemen,' their commander Jafar Pasha wrote afterwards. 'They were unaccustomed to obeying orders and wearing army uniforms.'[10] In particular, they 'seemed to be allergic' to wearing trousers. 'One day, with his trousers over one shoulder, one of them fell to his knees before the Amir Feisal. Pointing a finger at the offending legwear he cried: "My Lord, I will withstand eternal hellfire but I shall never stand these!"' Feisal burst out laughing and asked Jafar not to insist that the men wore uniform. Jafar came up with an alternative, like a kilt, to keep the volunteers happy.

Amid scenes like these, Lawrence's fears were justified, for Macindoe's report, in which he described Jafar Pasha's men as 'so-called Regular Troops' whose 'one desire . . . is to be left alone to eat and sleep',[11] turned out to be sufficiently damning to encourage Clayton to come to Aqaba to see for himself. Once he had arrived, however, Clayton endorsed Lawrence's opinion. Joyce, as the man who would have to organise the impromptu defence of Aqaba if the Turks broke through, drew no consolation from his own belief that Jafar Pasha's men were divided into Syrian and Iraqi factions and, 'in reality more of a bluff than an effective fighting force'.[12] He wanted reinforcements from the Camel Corps to come to Aqaba. Lawrence disagreed. 'One squabble between a trooper and an Arab, or an incident with Beduin women, would bring on general hostilities,' he wrote, in a robust rebuttal of the idea.[13]

While he was in Aqaba, Clayton showed Lawrence a blustering letter he had received from Sykes, in which the Tory MP vehemently attacked what he described as the 'Foreign Office pro-Turk gang' who had been trying to negotiate a separate peace with the Ottomans over that summer, and told Clayton 'never to yield to Fashoda-ism French or British'. On this subject, Sykes had a blunt message for Lawrence. 'Tell him now that he is a great man he must behave as such and be broad in his views. Ten years' tutelage under the *Entente* and the Arabs will be a nation. Complete independence means Persia, poverty and chaos. Let him consider this, as he hopes for the people he is fighting for.'[14]

Lawrence was not in the mood to take high-minded advice from Sykes and, after Clayton had returned to Egypt, he wrote a long and penetrating reply. Telling Sykes that he had 'a few queries about Near Eastern affairs', he explained, with a thinly veiled threat, that he hoped that Sykes would be able to answer them 'since part of the responsibility of action is inevitably thrown on to me and unless I know more or less what is wanted there might be trouble'.[15] When he was last in Cairo, Lawrence had met Aaron Aaronsohn, a farmer-turned-spy and Zionist who told Lawrence that his plan was for the Jews to buy up the land from Gaza to Haifa and 'have practical autonomy therein'.[16] Lawrence evidently made no effort to conceal his feelings about such an arrangement: after their meeting Aaronsohn wrote in his diary that Lawrence was 'a Prussian anti-Semite talking English'.[17]

Like Clayton, who had also directly asked Sykes for guidance on how to deal with the Zionists, Lawrence wanted Sykes to clarify British policy towards the Zionists. 'Now Feisal wants to know (information had better come to me for him, since I usually like to make up my mind before he does) . . . What have you promised the Zionists and what is their programme?' Was the acquisition of land by the Jews, Lawrence asked, 'to be by fair purchase or by forced sale and appropriation'? And, given that the Jews rarely employed Arabs on their farms, Lawrence wondered whether 'the Jews propose the complete expulsion of the Arab peasantry, or their reduction to a day-labourer class'.[18]

Next, Lawrence turned to the French who, after a year of promising, had finally supplied artillery to assist the Arabs. Feisal, said Lawrence, suspected that the French had suddenly provided the guns to make the Arabs indebted later. But, Lawrence explained, 'You can't buy gratitude by a secretly-conditional gift.' Anticipating Sykes's likely retort that he was a 'Fashodist', Lawrence reminded Sykes that 'Fashoda occurred before my time, and so the gibe is a generation late'. If there was any 'anti-French bias' among the British officers in Cairo, he added, he blamed Sykes 'for not educating us in Egypt officially to the knowledge of how much the French do require to stiffen them to last out the war in the West'. The Sharif would succeed, Lawrence told Sykes, 'he will take by his own efforts . . . the sphere we allotted to our foreign-advised "independent Syria", and will expect to keep it without imposed foreign advisers'. Husein's title to the regions his forces captured, Lawrence argued, 'will be a fairly strong one – that of conquest by the means of the local inhabitants – and what are the two powers going to say about it?' He concluded:

> You know I'm strongly pro-British, and also pro-Arab. France takes third place with me: but I quite recognise that we may have to sell our small friends to pay for our big friends, or sell our future security in the Near East to pay for our present victory in Flanders. If you will tell me once more what we have to give the Jews, and what we have to give the French, I'll do everything I can to make it easy for us . . . We are in rather a hole:

please tell me what, in your opinion, are the actual means by which we will find a way out.[19]

Lawrence finished the letter, and attached it to a covering note to Clayton, asking him to forward the letter to Sykes. In this, he admitted his reasons for writing to Sykes: 'Some of it is really thirst for information, and other is only a wish to stick pins in him.'[20] Then he headed up Wadi Itm. With him went the two instructors drafted in to train the Bedu, Sergeant Yells and Corporal Brook, whom Lawrence christened 'Lewis' and 'Stokes' in line with their respective fields of expertise: the Lewis machine-gun and the Stokes mortar, and the crack Bedu shot Zaal, as well as tribesmen from the Huwaytat and Bani Atiyah tribes, who lived in the area in which Lawrence now planned to operate. His target was Mudawwarah, a remote station about halfway between Maan and Tabuk, which was the only source of water between the two towns. Lawrence's plan was to destroy the well there, creating a waterless stretch of track of almost 150 miles along which the Turks would have great difficulty running any trains. He also took a new electric detonator which he hoped would enable him to mine a train more effectively than the pressure mines devised by Garland. It was, believed Clayton, the first litmus test of Lawrence's plan.

Tribal trouble among the Huwaytat at Quwayrah and a shortage of camels both delayed Lawrence, who finally set out on the fifty-mile journey to Mudawwarah on 16 September. The raiders headed east out of Wadi Ramm, a cluster of mighty sandstone buttresses which tower a thousand feet over boulevards of pink-orange sand, into a landscape of low, decapitated hills rising out of the sand, rendered very desolate in places by a thin layer of stones weathered grey by the sun.

It was again an awkward journey. The sheikh accompanying Lawrence – from the plunder-loving Harith – went blind, and Lawrence was left with the task of trying to unite the disparate elements of the raiding party, which he described as like 'a broken necklace'.[21] Consequently, he complained, he had 'more preoccupation with questions of supply, transport, tribal pay, disputes, division of spoil, feuds, march order, and the like, than with the explosive work'.[22]

Towards evening the following day Lawrence found Mudawwarah well in the hills about three miles west of the station. Its water was a disappointment 'for over its face was a thick mantle of green slime, from which swelled curious bladder-like islands of floating fatty stuff'. The Bedu explained that months earlier the Turks had thrown dead camels into the pool to deny them water. The foul taste these left, they reassured Lawrence, had 'now grown faint'. 'It might have been fainter for my taste,' Lawrence would later recall, 'but it was all the drink we could get in the neighbourhood, unless we took Mudawwarah station, so we . . . filled our water-skins at once.'[23]

When I followed the same route in 2004, I found that the station – two single-storey whitewashed buildings and a wind-pump, but missing the water tower which stood there ninety years ago – is today occupied by the Jordanian police, and as I arrived, a miscreant was being led inside, his arms firmly handcuffed behind his back. After shaking many hands, I was quickly installed on a cushion under an awning outside – decorated with a photograph of Jordan's late king, Hussein, the grandson of Abdullah – with a hot glass of tea in my hand. Lawrence's intelligence was absolutely right. The Jordanians have tapped the water beneath Mudawwarah so that the surrounding area now sprouts circular green fields which, from the air, look like verdant, alien crop circles. All that remains of the railway are its corrugated-iron sleepers, which serve today as simple fencing. From the police station, 300 yards away to the west I could see a dark hill which rises steeply out of the dusty plain. It must have been from there that, on the night of 17 September 1917, Lawrence, Zaal, Yells and Brook looked down on the station behind me, which was blazing yellow light from within. Lawrence thought that the range was too long to use the mortar, and he and Zaal crawled in closer to estimate the Turks' numbers. Deciding that the garrison was perhaps 300-strong and therefore twice the size of the raiding party, which was in any case 'not a happy family',[24] Lawrence ruled out a direct assault that night.

The following day the raiders followed the railway south until they found a perfect site to bury the mine: a bridge on a bend overlooked by a hill close by. This hill, from which the track and the bridge looked like a toothy smile, was a near-perfect site for the mortar and the two machine-guns. Leaving Yells and Brook on this spur behind him, Lawrence descended to the bridge, where he excavated some ballast and buried a sandbag packed with fifty pounds of gelatine under the rails. It was an enormous mine, three times the size of the one placed by Garland that February on the first successful British raid.

Lawrence worked alone. This part of the line is sandy and he wanted to keep the number of footprints near the track to a minimum. Inserting an electric detonator into the now-hidden bag of sun-warmed explosive, Lawrence attached the wires and ran out the coil away from the track. It had already taken him two hours to lay the mine, and would require nearly four more to bury the wires under sand which Lawrence tried to sculpt convincingly with a sandbag and wafts of his cloak.

No amount of artistry, however, would keep the tribesmen quiet and out of sight for such a long period of time, and early the following morning shooting broke out from the station immediately to the south, from where the Turks had spotted the Bedu on the horizon. Some Turkish soldiers emerged from the station but Lawrence managed to divert them by sending some tribesmen to shoot at them before disappearing into the hills. The greater danger was a second party of one hundred Turks coming from Mudawwarah. Lawrence was on the point of calling for a retreat when from the south a train was spotted. When he saw that there were two locomotives tugging ten wagons slowly up the line towards him, Lawrence decided to wait and detonate the mine under the second engine, hoping that the explosion would also pitch the front locomotive off the track and over the side of the bridge into the wadi below. Just after the front locomotive reached the bridge, Lawrence gave the order to press the plunger.

There followed a terrific roar and the line vanished from sight behind a spouting column of black dust and smoke a hundred feet high and wide. Out of the darkness came shattering crashes and long, loud metallic clangings of ripped steel, with many lumps of iron and plate; while one entire wheel of a locomotive whirled up suddenly black out of the cloud against the sky, and sailed musically over our heads to fall slowly and heavily into the desert behind.[25]

For a moment there was silence, and a grey haze bearing the metallic tang of burned explosive drifted towards the Arabs.

As fire from Yells's machine-gun erupted overhead, Lawrence went back up the hill to join him and Brook. 'In the midst of the affray, with a complete disregard of flying bullets, he strolled over to see how we were faring: his bearing made us feel that the whole thing was a picnic,' Brook would remember years later.[26] The Turks who had survived the explosion took cover on the far side of the railway embankment and were shooting back from between the wheels of the wagons at the Arabs who, seemingly oblivious to the gun battle, and united in pursuit of loot, were running towards the train. Brook fired two mortar bombs, which dropped in the area beyond the track, killing twelve Turks and forcing the rest to flee. No longer hidden behind the railway wagons, the Turks were exposed to further devastating machine-gun fire.

Within ten minutes it was all over. 'All but 20' of the Turks were dead, according to Lawrence, who ran forward to inspect the dreadful wreckage. The first arch of the bridge had vanished, and into the void had fallen the first wagon of the train. Lawrence peered inside. It had been 'filled with sick. The smash had killed all but three or four, and had rolled dead and dying into a bleeding heap against the splintered end. One of those yet alive half-deliriously called out to me something which contained the word typhus. So I wedged shut the door, and left them there, alone.'[27] Nothing but 'a blanched pile of smoking iron' remained of the second engine under which the mine had exploded. Seeing that the first locomotive, still teetering on the bridge, was not beyond repair, Lawrence tried to break its boiler with a slab of guncotton. He had almost forgotten the Turks who were closing on them from each station either side. Surrounded by hysterical women who had been travelling at the rear of the train, the Arabs piled their camels high with loot from the train, and set off westwards back towards Wadi Ramm. Having set the charge, Lawrence grabbed a blood-red Afghan prayer rug and hurried after them.

Back in Aqaba after the raid, Lawrence wrote two letters describing what had happened. In the first, to his friend Edward Leeds, a shy archaeologist who worked in Oxford, he briefly explained how, during 'the last stunt', he had 'potted a train with two engines (oh the gods were kind) and killed superior numbers'. But doubts had set in: 'I'm not going to last out this game much longer,' he confided to Leeds, describing his 'nerves going and temper wearing thin, and one wants an unlimited account of both'.[28] And beneath the bravado, he was shocked by the devastation he had caused.

> I hope that when the nightmare ends I will wake up and become alive again. This killing and killing of Turks is horrible. When you charge in at the finish and find them all over the place in bits, and still alive many of them, and know that you have done hundreds in the same way before and must do hundreds more if you can.

A day later, he wrote to Frank Stirling in Cairo. His tone, to a fellow intelligence officer, was rather less soul-searching. Branding the ambush as 'the hold up of a train', he explained how the mine had 'gutted' the locomotive and 'rather jumbled up the trucks', and Turkish resistance had been crushed by 'two beautiful shots' from the mortar. 'I hope this sounds the fun it is . . . It's the most amateurishly Buffalo-Billy sort of performance, and the only people who do it well are the Beduin. Only you will think it heaven, because there aren't any returns, or orders, or superiors, or inferiors; no doctors, no accounts, no meals, and no drinks.'[29]

Undoubtedly each letter was tailored to its recipient: an admission of the horror of war for the tweedy academic, the *Boy's Own* abridgement for Stirling, who would later entitle his own memoirs *Safety Last*. Yet it was possible to feel both: the intoxicating elation of simply surviving these ambushes, glimpsed in both letters, was a short-lived elixir. The long-term psychological impact of what he had seen would remain with him for the rest of his life. In a later letter to another friend, Lawrence shed some light on the contradiction: 'We ride like lunatics,' he wrote, 'and with our Beduins pounce on unsuspecting Turks and destroy them in heaps: and it is all very gory and nasty after we close grip. I love the preparation and the journey, and loathe the physical fighting.'[30]

When Hogarth met Lawrence a fortnight after the raid, for the first time since February, he noticed a distinct change in his former student. Lawrence was, he wrote to his wife, 'rather run down but very hard and his reputation has become overpowering'.[31] It was not simply Lawrence's exploits which contributed to his renown. Following the rushed retreat from the Mudawwarah attack, in which Yells and Brook both lost pieces of their kit, Lawrence wrote to Clayton, requesting that the items lost be replaced without charge to either man. 'He was ever thoughtful of us,' Brook remembered afterwards.[32]

Joyce believed that the great weakness of the British was having no one else with nearly the same expertise as Lawrence: 'We can all perhaps help a bit having gained some knowledge, but it is his intimate and extensive knowledge of the history and the tribes and the language that really counts.'[33] From Cairo, George Lloyd observed how Lawrence had 'done wonderfully good work and will some day be able to write a unique book. Generally the kind of men capable of these adventures lack the pen and the wit to record them adequately. Luckily Lawrence is specially gifted in both.'[34] Lawrence knew it too. Responding to a generous letter of congratulation from Wilson, who was sore that his own involvement in the revolt had not been recognised at all, Lawrence promised he would recognise Wilson's contribution, 'if ever I get my book on it out'.[35]

15

DIFFICULT TIMES

(September–October 1917)

Clayton read Lawrence's barbed letter to Sykes and decided not to forward it. 'I am somewhat apprehensive lest your letter to Mark may raise him to activity,'[1] he explained in a reply to Lawrence dated 20 September. The Sykes-Picot agreement, he said, was 'in considerable disfavour in most quarters' and 'wounded . . . severely' by the ongoing collapse of the Russian war effort and pressure on both Britain and France from America to renounce their imperialist war aims. Though he acknowledged a need, in deference to French sensitivities, not to kill off the treaty, it was 'moribund', he believed. 'It was never a very workable instrument and it is now almost a lifeless monument.'

True, opposition to Sykes's agreement was growing in Whitehall and Lloyd George himself was keen to see the treaty amended to cede Britain Palestine, but the treaty was perhaps not as defunct as Clayton suggested. Sykes was making efforts to adapt to changing public opinion, if only to save his own reputation. Over that summer in response to mounting criticism of annexation as a policy he had worked on an amendment to his treaty that would enshrine the Hijaz as an independent sovereign state. 'I am going to slam into Paris to make the French play up to the Arab cause as their only hope,' he told Clayton in July: 'Colonialism is madness and I believe Picot and I can prove it to them.'[2] But the sense in London that the Sykes-Picot agreement was an outdated embarrassment was not shared in Paris and the French resisted pressure to reopen the treaty. The real reason why Clayton did not want to pass the letter on had nothing to do with the potential life-span of the treaty. It was because he did not want to make a powerful enemy.

Believing Sykes was suspicious of him, Clayton had already tried to reassure him in August that he was stamping on Francophobia among his staff. He knew that this claim would inevitably be called into question if Sykes read Lawrence's letter. Sykes's stock was far from worthless — later that year the *Observer* newspaper would describe him as 'a world-famous authority on all Eastern questions'[3] — and Clayton may have decided to prevent Lawrence, whom Sykes had already identified as hostile, from stirring the temper of an MP who might easily ruin them both. Besides which, Clayton placed increasing faith in the ability of the British advance into Palestine to destroy the Sykes-Picot agreement. With that offensive still over a month away, at the end of September he tried to persuade Lawrence not to take precipitate action: 'I want to ensure that . . . nothing is done which will bring down upon Syria a storm which we cannot avert and for which we shall inevitably have to bear the blame,' he warned Lawrence.[4]

Lawrence must have received Clayton's response after he had returned to Aqaba from the Mudawwarah raid. The situation he found on his return to the port was bleak. German aircraft based at Maan had begun bombing the port and although Joyce laughed off the danger — 'Fritz comes over most mornings but he is a dam[n] bad shot so far thank God!'[5] — the Arabs had suffered casualties. Feisal, who was suffering from an ear infection, was 'rather despondent and thinks he is being let down by the British Government', Joyce reported. Chief among the problems for which Feisal blamed the British was a shortage of food and money, which had already caused some of his tribesmen defending the plain above Aqaba to surrender to the Turks.

Problems with supplies would have come as no surprise to Lawrence, who had warned Clayton a month earlier that paying and feeding all the Arabs who had come to Aqaba to join Feisal would be very difficult. 'It seems . . . as if we had underrated the local requirements,' he wrote, as hundreds of men began to appear daily to pledge their allegiance.[6] The local Bedu's commitment to Feisal's cause was probably only a secondary reason for their arrival: news of free food travelled fast at a time when famine was afflicting much of Syria. 'The Huwaytat swear they are starving,' Lawrence commented, though he believed that the tribesmen were perfectly able to pay for food, if it was made available on sale in the port. The arrival of so many tribesmen also strained financial resources. On 18 September Joyce advised Clayton that the anticipated expenditure of £50,000 a month for buying the tribesmen's support was inadequate; he calculated that a sum of up to £80,000 was needed.[7]

Part of the problem was that previously free-flowing supplies of British gold had not encouraged Feisal to be thrifty. When a further shipment of gold arrived days later Joyce decided to ration it out in an effort to slow down Feisal's spending. 'Lawrence and I did a dreadful thing and only gave him £10,000 instead of £50,000,' Joyce confessed to Clayton:

> The other £40,000 remains on the *Humber* to be given to him as occasion arises. We have now been through so many of these critical moments when we have been told success or failure depends on a few thousands that we know the absolute necessity of a certain amount at short call and therefore dared to keep back the above amount. We hope you won't give us away to the police![8]

High demand was not the only problem, however. Wemyss, the admiral who had done so much to help the revolt in its early stages, was recalled in July to London and his replacement, in Lawrence's words, 'did all he could to be obstructive'.[9] Three of the ships which had previously run supplies to Wajh were withdrawn for other duties. As a result, British supplies to Aqaba, Feisal believed, were 'completely disorganised'[10] and shortages persisted through September. By 1 October, the captain of the *Humber* reported that, due to the absence of animal fodder, the horses, mules, and camels at Aqaba had had no food for four days. An attempt, he said, was being made 'to get them to eat rice, but they are all looking very poor'.[11]

Feisal was badly affected by the problems. He was frightened that the Turks might attack at any time, in which case 'he would not have a single transport animal fit to carry supplies and ammunition to his troops' and he was frustrated by the lack of progress since the capture of Aqaba.[12] 'He says that if things had been otherwise he would now have been on the *offensive* and not the *defensive* and . . . the whole of the Arab tribes of the interior would be on his side,' the *Humber's* captain reported. Feisal even threatened suicide.

'I had a very difficult time with Feisal for a few days. He is not a strong character and much swayed by his surroundings,' Joyce reported to Clayton. 'However your messages and information did much to reassure him and we got him over the bad days.'[13] Clayton had tried to defuse the situation by telling Joyce that he did not expect the Turks to attack because they were too busy safeguarding their own supplies of food and timber to the north from an expected Arab attack.

Feisal was also depressed by the attitudes of his father, Husein, and his elder brothers, Abdullah and Ali, whom, he told Joyce, were 'taking no interest in the Syrian movement'. He was also under pressure from his father, who was reluctant to let the revolt slip out of his grasp and had made it clear to Feisal that he did not support his move north to Aqaba. When the French paid almost a million francs to Husein that summer he refused to pass any of it to Feisal.[14]

One reason for Husein's frugality was that he was becoming increasingly worried about the challenge to his authority east of Mecca posed by his rival Ibn Saud. The annual pilgrimage to Mecca, the Hajj, fell in September that year. The most notable visitor was Ibn Saud's brother, Mohammed, who brought 7,000 armed tribesmen to Mecca with him. While the British necessarily reported that the encounter between the followers of Husein and Ibn Saud – both British allies – went smoothly, Brémond witnessed friction between the Saudi tribesmen and the cosmopolitan populations of Mecca and Jeddah. Ibn Saud's men were 'real savages, taking everything they saw if needs be by violence; some even said: monkeys', he claimed.[15]

Abdullah shared his father's concerns about the Saudis. Although, after the war, Abdullah put his own inability to capture Medina down to the fact that his resources were too thinly spread along the line, and the quality of his troops and guns inferior to those of Feisal, Feisal believed that Abdullah's unwillingness to capture the city stemmed from a fear that if he did so, the monthly British payments to his father would cease.

There seems to have been some truth in this. The British heard that November that Husein had turned down an offer from Fakhri to leave Medina and withdraw to Syria.[16] Earlier that summer, Abdullah's elder brother, Ali, angrily vetoed a letter one of his Iraqi officers, Ali Jawdat, wanted to send to Fakhri in Medina, demanding that the Turks surrender. The incident caused a breakdown in relations between Husein's sons and their Iraqi soldiers, and the Iraqis' leader, Nuri Said, took advantage of a bout of pneumonia that summer to be transferred to work with Jafar Pasha in Aqaba. Other officers, including Ali Jawdat, followed Nuri Said and the campaign against the railway in the Hijaz lost momentum. No sooner had Jafar and Feisal gone than, from Abdullah's camp, Davenport reported that 'practically all interest in the war' had 'ceased'.[17]

On 26 September, Allenby informed Robertson in London that he expected to be ready to launch his offensive one month later, on 27 October. He planned to open the attack by bombarding Gaza. The move was designed to make the Turks believe that, again, the main British assault would focus on the town. This time, in fact, action against Gaza would be a diversionary ruse. Three nights later, at the full moon, Allenby's main force would strike the town of Beersheba, thirty miles inland, to the south-east.

Excited by the imminent prospect of Allenby's attack, the War Cabinet discussed the situation in Turkey in its meeting on 5 October. At its conclusion, Robertson – as ever, opposed to action in Palestine – was instructed to contact Allenby to explain that the War Cabinet believed that a push to Jerusalem would, 'if followed by suitable diplomatic measures, induce her to break with her Allies'.[18] Asked for his opinion, Allenby disagreed. Having explained that the security of his right flank now depended on the Arabs in the hills east of Wadi Araba, the fault which forms the modern border between southern Jordan and Israel, he told the politicians bluntly that ongoing help from the Arabs 'depends on continued belief by them that we shall keep our promises not to conclude any peace which would leave the Arab territories under Turkish domination. Any idea in their minds that we intend separate peace with Turkey with possibility of their being left under Turkish rule would bring them against us and endanger my communication.'[19]

Other factors also ruled out further attempts to secure peace with the Ottomans. At the time the German Kaiser was visiting Constantinople, and the British feared that he might encourage the Turks to offer the Arabs autonomy and to bribe them into quiescence. This possibility alarmed British officials in Egypt, where the political situation was increasingly unstable, since any deal the Turks did with Arabs would inevitably increase the pressure on the British to offer similar concessions in Egypt. While Clayton dismissed Egyptian calls for self-government as 'rot', the fact was that nationalist sentiment was rising.[20] A secret note circulated that summer warned that 'From the immediate entourage of the Sultan down through all the educated classes runs an almost unanimous wish that we may be compelled to withdraw at the end of the war.'[21] Then the Sultan himself – whom the British regarded as a compliant puppet – died in early October and the British were forced to appoint his brother, who was regarded as less loyal, as his successor. When, a few days after the Kaiser's arrival in Turkey, an intelligence report received from Switzerland seemed to confirm that autonomy was about to be offered to the Arabs, the Foreign Office abruptly shelved its plans to approach the Turks once Jerusalem was in Allenby's hands, because it would 'discourage our friends in the East in general and the Arabs in particular'.[22]

On 26 September too, Lawrence set out again for the railway. He was accompanied this time by an Algerian French officer, Captain Rosario Pisani. Pisani, who was described by another British officer as a 'brigand disguised unconvincingly as a French officer' who claimed that he 'had a wide variety of lovers anxiously awaiting his appearances on leave',[23] had arrived in Aqaba as the French military mission's representative. Brémond had warned him that Lawrence was a 'focused character', who dreamed of 'an English Syria and has some difficulty in giving up this idea' and encouraged Pisani to follow Lawrence around.[24]

Besides Pisani, Lawrence took three Syrian nationalists who had escaped Turkish custody, and a handful of Haurani peasants, whose unruly credentials he was hoping to assess. As well as another electric mine, he took a pressure mine because he did not expect to be able to bury the wire on the stony plain south of Maan where he planned to operate. Pausing under the cliffs at Ramm to explain to the tribesmen how both types of device worked, Lawrence recruited almost a hundred Bedu and headed towards the railway.

Disagreements between the Huwaytat who followed Lawrence made it a difficult journey yet again. 'During the six days' trip I had to adjudicate in twelve cases of assault with weapons, four camel thefts, one marriage-settlement, fourteen feuds, two evil eyes and a bewitchment,' Lawrence reported in the *Arab Bulletin*.[25] On 3 October he buried the pressure mine south of Shedia station, over a culvert, the most southerly of three which pierced an embankment across a wadi. But no train appeared on the following day, nor the day after that.

When, early on 5 October, a water train arrived from the north and passed over the mine, there was no explosion. At midday, when he hoped the Turkish guards were taking a siesta, Lawrence crept forward again and laid an electric mine beside the pressure mine. Then he sent everyone forward towards the culverts. Having laid the mines over the most southerly, Lawrence left a party under the middle bridge with the detonator and positioned the machine-guns under the northern bridge, from where they could cut down anyone escaping from a disabled train.[26]

'I asked Major Lawrence for the honour of positioning myself beneath the bridge so that I could blow up the train,' Pisani reported afterwards.[27] Lawrence, however, refused. Though he told Pisani that he was worried that, in the chaos of an attack, the Bedu might mistake him for a Turk because of his uniform, and shoot him, it seems equally likely that he did not want Pisani to play too central a role in the ambush.

At eight o'clock the following morning a train arrived from the north. From off to one side, Lawrence signalled to the men with the detonator when the locomotive was over the bridge. The explosion was devastating. It 'shattered the fire-box of the locomotive (No. 153, Hijaz), burst many of the tubes, threw the l.c. [locomotive] cylinder into the air, cleaned out the cab, warped the frame, bent the two near driving wheels and broke their axles. I consider it past repair,' Lawrence dryly reported, like some sort of malevolent train-spotter.[28] Twenty passengers travelling in the first wagon were killed by the blast, the force of which decoupled the rear carriages, which began to roll back down the hill. The Bedu snatched some booty, but with the Turks approaching from blockhouses to the north and south, they did not delay for long, hurrying away westwards to safety and Wadi Ramm.

These two devastating ambushes had a profound effect, Lawrence believed after the war. The locomotives' drivers went on strike and, for those brave enough still to travel, seats at the rear of the train could be purchased at a premium.[29]

On his return to Aqaba on 9 October Lawrence found a summons to go to Egypt to see Allenby. Allenby wanted to brief Lawrence on his offensive at the end of the month, but he also wanted Lawrence to clarify his own tactics. Clayton had already warned Lawrence of the danger that, if both Lawrence and Allenby each succeeded in pushing the Turks northwards, they would actually make their enemy more compact, more easily supplied, and therefore stronger.[30] When Lawrence met Allenby, he argued that his attacks – against the trains rather than the track – were designed to attenuate Turkish resources along the railway without doing so much damage that the Turks took the decision to abandon Medina and consolidate at Maan, where they would present a serious threat to the rear of Allenby's army as it advanced into Palestine. Allenby was satisfied: 'Lawrence is doing good work on the Hijaz Railway,' he told Robertson on 17 October.[31]

Allenby had also been dealing with a request by the French to attach Pisani to all Lawrence's missions north from Aqaba. French diplomats appear to have learned details of the true extent of Lawrence's Syrian journey by the beginning of October and, alarmed by the political ramifications, they approached Allenby. Allenby, however, batted them away. The French 'were not pleased', he reported, 'but I was quite polite and firm'.[32] Allenby did not trust the French not to leak details of Lawrence's trip to frustrate the Arabs' Syrian ambitions. 'Details of Lawrence's reconnaissance into Syria north of Maan area,' he explained afterwards, 'were kept very secret in order to avoid enemy obtaining information which might handicap Lawrence's future movements and jeopardise safety of those with whom he had been in touch.'[33]

Allenby told Robertson he intended to continue to withhold information from the French, on the grounds that 'so far there has been no action by Lawrence in French zone', but this was wrong since Ras Baalbek fell inside the region earmarked for future direct French rule in the Sykes-Picot agreement. If Lawrence did enter the French zone, Allenby said that he would inform the French 'as fully as military exigencies permit'. There was a particular reason for this caveat. Information Allenby had received led him to believe that the number of enemy divisions facing him had more than doubled. He urgently wanted to stop further Ottoman reinforcements from arriving in Palestine and decided that the best way to do this was to disrupt the railway running down the Yarmuk valley, which Lawrence had suggested in the plan he had put to Allenby that July. The valley, however, was not only the vulnerable artery from Syria into Palestine on which the Turks depended for supplies but also the border of the zone which – under Sykes-Picot – would come under French influence. Allenby did not want inevitable French objections to obstruct his plans to attack the railway there.

Lawrence had seen the valley both in 1911 as a railway passenger, and on his second reconnaissance trip early that summer and believed that the railway, which crossed and recrossed the valley over a series of bridges to achieve the gentlest gradient, was very vulnerable. When Allenby asked him if he could attack one of the Yarmuk bridges on 5 November, six days after his offensive was due to begin, Lawrence said he could. He was despondent at the time. The timetable of his optimistic summer plan was in tatters, and any chance the Arabs had of reaching Damascus, he felt, now rested on the successful demolition of the railway at Yarmuk, which would box the Ottomans in Palestine and leave the way to Damascus clear.

Hogarth briefly saw Lawrence during his visit to Allenby's headquarters. Lawrence was 'not well', he told a colleague, 'and talks rather hopelessly about the Arab future he once believed in'. He was also pessimistic about Lawrence's chances of success. 'I doubt if he will manage to get North again. Recent successes have drawn rather too many troops down on to the Maan section of the Railway. Medina probably cannot be starved out, and nothing short of a local mutiny will reduce Fakhri.'[34]

Clayton, on the other hand, was altogether more confident. He was delighted that Allenby had vetoed any attempt by the French to follow Lawrence around, and with the Palestine offensive days away he wrote again to Sykes:

> As the situation develops, it becomes more and more evident that the French will never make good their aspirations in Syria unless they take some more active military part in this theatre. It cannot be disguised that they are unpopular with both Arabs and Syrians as a whole – their colonial and financial methods are disliked, and they have never been able to live down the seizure of Picot's papers by the Turks and the consequent execution or ruin of various notables.

A British victory in Palestine and east of the Jordan for the Arabs would, Clayton crowed, 'still further weaken the French political position'.[35] He could barely hide the note of triumph in his voice.

16

GAZA AND YARMUK

(October–November 1917)

'You want to buy gun?'

'No, thank you,' I replied, anticipating the reception I might meet at the airport if I tried to export the particular memento of Jordan I was holding. Then I put the rifle back where I had found it.

Few castles offer the departing visitor quite the range of antique firearms that the souvenir seller below the ramparts of Shawbak castle, in southern Jordan, can boast. It was here, midway through October 1917, that Pierce Joyce arrived during a brief raid. On 12 October, he had set out north from Aqaba into the hills west of Maan on a foray with Mawlud Mukhlis, another of the Iraqi officers who had joined the Arabs' army. Just as they had been for the Crusaders hundreds of years earlier, the hills were a vital source of grain and wood, which the Arabs had been anxious to seize from the Turks as soon as they arrived in Aqaba. They captured the mighty Crusader castle at Shawbak without difficulty, and from there, went on to destroy part of the light railway which linked the area with the Hijaz Railway to the east. They had also tried to persuade the Arab and Armenian woodcutters who worked there to join them, but without success. As Joyce commented afterwards, the raid

demonstrated that the 'tip and run' operations to which they have been accustomed in the Hijaz, will not suffice in Syria. The people of Shawbak, I firmly believe, are entirely with the Sharif, but they have had sad experience of the heavy hand of the Turk, and until they see a reasonable chance of protection for their own people, can scarcely be blamed for being somewhat cautious about arousing the anger of their oppressors.[1]

In fact, not wanting to aggravate the population by a heavy-handed approach, the Turks decided there should be no retribution in Shawbak.[2] Their shortage of fuel forced them instead to concentrate on trying to expel the Arabs from the villages they had occupied in the hills. On 21 October, they attacked Wadi Musa, the valley of the ancient city of Petra, in strength. Initial reports suggested that the Arabs had been beaten. In fact, the reverse had happened: the Turks were routed. 'Even though their strength was about double our own,' recalled Jafar Pasha, 'we managed to inflict such a severe defeat on them that we were unable either to bury their dead or move the injured from the battlefield.'[3]

The Arabs' victory, however, increased the pressure on the British to speed up the deployment of the Arab Legion to hold their gains in the hills, but it was still being trained in Egypt. 'There is an awful lot to do,' reported the officer in charge of the Legion at the beginning of October: 'pay sheets are taking a tremendous lot of doing. Nearly everybody is passing himself off at least a grade higher than that he had in the Turkish Army.'[4] He worried constantly that one of his trainees might raise the question 'as to what was intended with regard to Syria and Baghdad. In anything I have said I have been most awfully careful to steer clear of such things, but I cannot help feeling that we are not absolutely straight with these people.'

Having agreed with Allenby that he would attack a bridge in the Yarmuk valley, Lawrence arrived back in Aqaba on 15 October. He thought he had good news for Feisal because Allenby had promised to increase the flow of supplies to Feisal's army. However, cholera had been diagnosed in the Arab camp al Aqaba the day before and the medical officers in Egypt instantly vetoed all traffic to and from the port.

'You can have no idea how this cholera business has upset everything here,' Clayton told Joyce:

The very name terrifies the Quarantine and Medical people and it is not really to be surprised at when one considers what an awful thing it would be to get into the country just now, with a huge army and enormous quantities of transport passing to and fro . . . It is most annoying that this should have happened at this particular time when your operations were coming on and Lawrence was just moving out, and we particularly wanted plenty of intercommunication.[5]

The interruption in supplies annoyed Lawrence, who was on the point of starting north for the Yarmuk valley. Feisal was 'touchy at the moment',[6] he said and he did not want the British to fuel Feisal's uncertainty about the future of Syria by appearing reluctant to help the Arabs. In a letter to Clayton on 24 October, he asked for the immediate dispatch of the Arab Legion and some armoured cars, regardless of concerns about cholera. Even if the Arab Legion's training was unfinished and the armoured cars required further work, he said, 'something should come down in the *Hardinge*; They will be a great comfort here.'[7] On 2 November Clayton wired the Foreign Office, asking it to approve the dispatch of the Legion to Aqaba immediately.

Apprehensive about attacking Yarmuk, Lawrence complained to Clayton that the equipment he had requested had not arrived. 'I asked for nine exploders. Only four have been sent . . . Also about the cable. I received at first 400 yards thick single cable (doubled this makes 200 yards of line) and after using it wired for 1000 yards light twin cable. You sent 500 yards of the old thick single in reply.'[8] The shortage of cable would mean that Lawrence would need to be dangerously nearby to trigger an electric mine under a train. But he could not afford to wait any longer. Having let off steam to Clayton, that afternoon he left Aqaba for the north.

Lawrence was under no illusion about how dangerous the task ahead was. In case he was killed, he also took a Royal Engineer named C.E. Wood, an explosives expert who was recovering from being shot in the head in France. To lead the raid, he picked Ali, a sharif from the Harith tribe. Ali was a headstrong, conceited man with luxuriant black hair, whom Lawrence chose because he had 'out-newcombed Newcombe about

Al Ula'.[9] Finally, he added a handful of Indian machine-gunners to his party. There were also two last-minute additions: George Lloyd, from the Arab Bureau, and another escapee from Turkish incarceration, Abdul Qadir al Jazairi, who had lived in Damascus, and who told Lawrence that he could command the support of the Algerian community clustered on the north side of the Yarmuk valley. It was Abdul Qadir's eponymous grandfather who had led resistance to the French in Algeria in the 1840s. Attracted perhaps by this promising ancestry, Lawrence ignored Brémond's warning that the young Abdul Qadir was a traitor.

Lloyd's sudden interest in joining Lawrence seems to have stemmed from rising concerns about Lawrence's health among his colleagues. 'I am very anxious about Lawrence,' Clayton wrote. 'He has taken on a really colossal job and I can see that it is well-nigh weighing him down.'[10] He had wanted to pull Lawrence out, but recognised that 'the time is not yet, as he is wanted just now'. Instead, Clayton sent Lloyd to Aqaba to offer Lawrence some company. He also wanted Lloyd to calm Lawrence down over the Sykes-Picot agreement. Lloyd was an obvious man for this task because, an unashamed imperialist, he too was vehemently opposed to French ambitions in the region.[11]

Lloyd was amazed by the scenery as he and Lawrence set out from Aqaba late on 24 October. The view up Wadi Itm, he recalled, 'was magnificent, 400 feet of jagged towering basalt and granite rock on either side of us, and the moon shining in our faces adding to the impression. Sharif Ali rode ahead of us with two or three . . . slaves and looked like some modern Saladin out to meet a crusade.'[12]

Lloyd quickly raised Clayton's concerns with Lawrence. He explained 'the necessity of tying down the Arab movement to its military purpose, its original aim and objective, and to risk no breach of faith with the Arabs by raising hopes beyond it'. But from there, the conversation ranged much further. Lloyd mentioned his own hopes of encouraging a revolt in the town of Karak if Lawrence's attack at Yarmuk succeeded, and they both discussed the position of the French depending on how the revolt, and the Palestine offensive, developed.[13]

Deep in conversation, Lawrence and Lloyd only realised when they stopped at midnight that they had lost Wood. After spending much of the next morning hunting for him, Lawrence sent a man on to Quwayrah to continue the search, while they followed a shortcut into Wadi Ramm. It was 'a stupendous scene', remembered an awed Lloyd, who then described how he and Lawrence had ridden down the middle of the sandy avenue between the red cliffs, 'feeling like gnats in size'.[14] They found the missing sapper had already been delivered to the Arab camp in Ramm by the time that they arrived. 'He was completely broken down, grousing and refusing to eat and doubting if he could go on. This was rather an eye-opener to L and myself. We had all had some 20 hours in the saddle out of 24 and were tired but there seemed no excuse for such a pother,' noted Lloyd, rather unkindly, given the trauma from which Wood was still recovering.

The following morning Wood seemed better. Lloyd was also pleased: 'I had a conspicuous success in making Lawrence eat a real European breakfast, tea, bully beef, and biscuits. He is only too glad to behave like a Christian – gastronomically at all events – if he is taken the right way.'[15] As the day passed, Lawrence increasingly opened up to Lloyd. He showed Lloyd the *Times* cutting in his notebook about his dead brother Will, and told him about his family and upbringing, his time at Oxford, archaeology in Syria before the war, and about Hogarth, with whom Lloyd worked in Cairo. Finally, their conversation soared towards escapism. 'Lawrence and I made great plans for a peace tour in Arabia after the war,' Lloyd also reported. 'We would defy Victorian sentiment and have a retinue of slaves and would have one camel to carry books only . . . and we would talk desert politics all day.'[16]

'He was the one fully-taught man with us in Arabia,' Lawrence later said of Lloyd, 'and in these few days together our minds had ranged abroad.'[17] From the rough notes Lloyd made at the time it is clear that they had talked extensively about what might happen if Feisal succeeded, and it is these that provide the best contemporary record of the thinking behind Lawrence's strategy. 'Situation resultant:– Sharif's flag flies along coast from Acre northwards; French protests? Our attitude? Feisal's attitude will be non-negotiatory – "What I have I will keep",' Lloyd scribbled. Lawrence's view was that as the Sharif was never a party to the Sykes-Picot agreement – indeed he said, Husein had never even seen it –

'Agreement at best one between France and England for partition of a country in armed occupation of forces of Sharif of Mecca'.[18]

That evening they reached a point a few miles west of the railway, where they stopped to wait until it was dark and they could cross in safety. Lawrence and Lloyd went on ahead, and narrowly avoided walking straight into Ghadir al Hajj station. Turning back to prevent the other members of their party from making the same mistake, when they turned towards the railway again, they became lost. Lawrence, according to Lloyd, was 'for some reason or other . . . convinced that if we marched faithfully with our eyes fixed firmly on Orion we should find the railway again'. Lloyd – in Lawrence's words – 'began to speak bitterly of reaching Baghdad in the morning'.[19] Lloyd eventually snapped: 'An hour's pursuit of Orion shook Lawrence's faith, and I insisted on a compass, and at midnight we struck the railway.' They crossed the track without incident and, after a full day's riding next day, they reached Auda at Jafr, the wells marked by a thicket of palms at the edge of an enormous plain of baked white mud. Though worried about the defection of two tribes previously allied to him, Auda seemed to have overcome the earlier wobble in his loyalty. His looks, Lloyd reported, 'are much enhanced, as his allegiance to us is much fortified – by the timely gift of a set of false teeth from Cairo made some weeks ago by Lawrence', which finally replaced the set he had smashed in disgust at Wajh, that May.[20]

Sharif Ali and Abdul Qadir arrived in Jafr later the same evening. Although Lloyd wanted to accompany Lawrence further, Lawrence would not let him. According to Lloyd, Lawrence said that 'although he did not pretend he would not like me to come he felt that any additional individual who was not an expert at the actual demolition only added to his own risk'.[21] As one of the most strident critics of the Sykes-Picot agreement, Lloyd was more useful to Lawrence back in Britain. 'He felt that there was a risk that all his work would be ruined in Whitehall and he thought I could save this,' Lloyd remembered.

Later that evening, Auda suddenly called for silence. A hush descended as each man strained to hear the threat Auda seemed to have heard. 'After a while', Lawrence recalled, he had distinguished 'a creeping reverberation, a cadence of blows too dull, too wide, too slowly easily to find response in our ears. It was like the mutter of a distant, very lowly thunderstorm.' Auda turned to look westward, and said: 'The English guns.'[22] One hundred and thirty miles to the north-west, the British bombardment of Gaza had begun.[23] Knowing that Allenby would now be trying to move his attacking force secretly east in preparation for the main attack on Beersheba, on 30 October Lawrence started north. Before he did so, he discussed the timing of his raid with Lloyd. 'I said I thought Nov 5th was traditionally auspicious,' Lloyd, the Member of Parliament, recalled, 'and he decided to do it that night if in any way possible.'[24]

Following several days' bombardment of Gaza – believed to be the most intensive shelling in the war outside Europe – the British attacked Beersheba in the early hours of 31 October, a misty, moonlit night. The attack caught the Turks completely by surprise. During this attack Newcombe outflanked Turkish lines with a small force of about a hundred soldiers and Bedu. He succeeded in generating the impression that a much larger British encircling movement was under way, but the perhaps inevitable consequence of this achievement was that he was captured on 2 November by the large Turkish force which had been sent to deal with him. Hogarth was not surprised. 'It was mainly his own fault,' he wrote to his wife, describing Newcombe as 'a wild bird who will beat against the bars'.[25] He was on edge. Newcombe's capture only reminded him of Lawrence's equally dangerous mission.

Hogarth was up at the front to watch the secondary attack on Gaza, which began on 1 November. 'It was rather terrible both to hear and see,' he wrote to his son Billy the following day: 'From 11pm to 4am was a continuous roar with the horizon lit up as by summer lightning.'[26] The attack was a success. By dawn, British forces had captured a crucial position overlooking Gaza's harbour. Gaza itself was evacuated by the Turks overnight on 5 November. In the Beersheba area to the east, however, British forces were faced with serious water shortages and a violent sandstorm which engulfed much of the front: 'We could not see the road for a yard ahead and once ran right into a mule column,' Hogarth told his son.[27] Given time to regroup, the Turks avoided the

British pincer movement from Gaza and Beersheba and withdrew with most of their force intact. The British restored the momentum of their offensive with a cavalry advance. On 13 November, they captured Junction Station, which linked the Gaza and Jerusalem lines to the railway north towards Dara, and three days later, British troops entered Jaffa. At a cost of over 6,000 casualties, they were now within striking distance of Jerusalem.

'Lawrence by now must be very near his objective,' Joyce had written to Clayton on 4 November: 'I hope he is lucky. Fortunately he has got brains as well as dash and the two I trust will pull him through, but one cannot help feeling anxious.'[28] Lawrence, in fact, was still over fifty miles from the Yarmuk valley. He had experienced problems at Azraq, the rundown castle east of Amman where he had hoped to enlist the support of the Serahin, the local tribesmen from Wadi Sirhan. But the tribesmen proved reluctant to accompany him as far as the westernmost bridge in the gorge, which had been his original target. They feared being discovered by the Turkish forces now cutting down trees in the area because of the shortage of fuel throughout Syria. Lawrence had accordingly changed his plan, deciding to approach the valley from the north, through the villages where Abdul Qadir's presence would win local support. But the Serahin proved equally suspicious of Abdul Qadir and the villagers, who would be hostile. Then on 4 November, Abdul Qadir disappeared, suggesting that Brémond's advice had been correct.

'We were now in deep trouble,' Lawrence later wrote. 'The Serahin were our last resource, and if they refused to come with us we would be unable to carry out Allenby's project by the appointed time.'[29] That night, beside the dying fire, Lawrence made a last-ditch effort to make the tribesmen follow him. It was only after he had offered to attack the nearest bridge in the Yarmuk valley, at Tell al Shehab, and appealed to their honour that the Serahin agreed to join him.

After a long night-march with the Serahin, a few Bani Sakhr who had joined him at Bair, Wood, and the Indian machine-gunners, Lawrence reached the eastern end of the Yarmuk gorge early in the night of 7 November. Across the valley the dim glimmer of a fire identified the location of the Turkish guard tent. Having left the Indians at the top of the scarp to machine-gun the tent if the lone sentry on the bridge raised the alarm, Lawrence crept forward with Sharif Ali and the Serahin, who were carrying the bags of explosive, down towards the metal bridge which spanned the black chasm. Discovering that he could not reach its vulnerable lower girders, Lawrence had just turned to tell the Serahin to follow him on when, far above, there was an unmistakable clatter as someone dropped a rifle.

Sixty yards away across the void, the Turkish sentry twitched, looked up and spotted the Indians, who were in the process of moving to a more shadowy position because the moon had risen. He shouted a challenge and began shooting, yelling at the same time for help. 'Instantly all was confusion,' Lawrence later recollected.[30] The Bani Sakhr behind him, who had been invisible, immediately returned fire, giving their position away in the process. Before the Indians had had time to riddle the guard tent with bullets, the Turkish guards rushed out and began shooting back at the Bani Sakhr. The Serahin carrying the dynamite panicked because they had been warned that, if hit by a bullet, their burdens would explode, blowing them to smithereens. Awoken by the gunfire, the villagers turned out. With volleys of shots blasting into the night sky, the raiders beat a hasty retreat. The raid was a complete failure. 'Tell al Shehab is a splendid bridge to destroy, but those Serahin threw away all my explosive when the firing began and so I can do nothing,' Lawrence wrote to Joyce: 'I am very sick at losing it so stupidly.'[31]

The loss of almost all his blasting gelatine left Lawrence with some mines and an inadequate length of electric cable with which to detonate them. He had intended to head north after the Yarmuk raid to attack the railway where it crossed the River Orontes at Hama, a hundred miles north of Damascus, to encourage as widespread a revolt as possible in Syria if the British breakout from Gaza succeeded. With little explosive and no news of what had happened in southern Palestine, Lawrence was unsure what to do next.

'Let's blow up a train,' the Harith sheikh Sharif Ali suggested.[32] Lawrence reluctantly agreed. He would have preferred to carry out an ambush with the Indian machine-gunners in support, but they were exhausted from the cold and hunger. He was forced to send them back to Azraq with Wood to recover, before riding with Ali and the remaining Bani Sakhr on to Minifir, midway between Amman and Dara, where he had mined the track earlier that year. Then, he had been gently baked by the June sunshine; now, shards of icy rain soaked his clothing as he excavated a space for an electric mine under the rails where the track crossed a culvert. A train had passed just as they arrived at the railway. Another passed before there was time to set up the exploder. The wires would only stretch sixty yards from the track, and Lawrence had no choice but to huddle behind a small bush with the plunger. Now another train, groaning with the weight of its open carriages full of soldiers, appeared, struggling up the hill from the south. As it passed, he pressed the trigger; but nothing happened. The rain or the ride had broken the exploder, and Lawrence found himself sitting in his white robes in full view of the troop-train as it crawled past. 'The bush, which had seemed a foot high, shrank smaller than a fig-leaf; and I felt myself the most distinct object in the country-side,' he would remember.[33] Though the troops ignored him, the officers stared at Lawrence and pointed. Lawrence waved back, waited for the train to inch by, and then ran.

The following day, the Arab watchman Lawrence had posted to the north signalled that a two-engined train was rapidly approaching. Having mended the exploder, Lawrence raced back towards the line and fired the mine as the train passed over it. Too close to the track, 'The explosion was terrific,' he recalled afterwards:

> The ground spouted blackly into my face, and I was sent spinning, to sit up with the shirt torn to my shoulder and the blood dripping from long, ragged scratches on my left arm. Between my knees lay the exploder, crushed under a twisted sheet of sooty iron. When I peered through the dust and steam of the explosion, the whole boiler of the first engine seemed missing. Just in front of me was the scalded and smoking upper half of a man.[34]

Both locomotives and the first two coaches plunged through the hole in the bridge, and behind them, the remaining carriages were concertinaed down the track. A flag flew from one of the rear coaches, which was carrying Mehmed Jemal Pasha, the commander of the Eighth Corps of the Ottomans' Army.

Reeling from the impact, and lacking the support which the Indian machine-gunners could have provided, Lawrence came under fire from the surviving Turks. He was rescued by Ali and the Bani Sakhr, but not before seven of the tribesmen had been killed by Turkish fire. Lawrence discovered that a piece of shrapnel had broken his toe and said he had been grazed by five bullets. The Arabs hurried Lawrence, limping, up the wadi, and turned only to fire delaying pot shots at the Turks. It was a narrow escape.

The following day Ali and Lawrence arrived back at Azraq. Jackals, hyenas, even leopards prowled through the undergrowth. The lakes, which gave the place its name – Azraq means blue in Arabic – resounded with the liquid croaking of thousands of frogs. Overhead, black kites swirled.

Almost none of this survives today. The lakes have shrunk, the wild boar hunted, the trees cut up for firewood, the thickets grazed into dust. Azraq is a grimy truckspot on the road to western Iraq. But among the grubby flat-roofed houses supporting large and rusty satellite dishes, the castle survives.

It was here that November 1917 that Lawrence installed himself in the dark, vaulted room over the southern gate. His first task was to let his colleagues know that he had failed to demolish the Yarmuk bridge, but had survived. The following day, 14 November, he wrote to Joyce, mentioning that Abdul Qadir had gone missing – 'Tell Feisal I think he was afraid,' Lawrence commented – and suggesting that the British report the Arab success at Minifir to the press. Lawrence had realised quickly that press coverage of the Arabs' northernmost achievements would bolster their claim against the French after the war, and would write, a month later, how 'we must try and enlist on our side a favourable press'.[35] Knowing that Hogarth would be worrying about him, Lawrence also wrote to his old tutor the same day. Finally he wrote to his mother, telling her his plans to stay at Azraq for a few days, before heading back to the railway, and asking her if she could send a new pair of brown shoes.

Wood was suffering badly with dysentery, so Lawrence sent him with the letters back to Aqaba.

Wood arrived in Aqaba on 24 November, bringing the first news of Lawrence. The following day, Joyce paraphrased Wood's muddled report and transmitted it to Cairo. Wood, he said, had 'Returned last night. L[awrence] left at Azraq. Found original objective impossible. On Nov 7th L[awrence] destroyed 1 train with 2 engines. Reported considerable casualties to Turks.'[36]

Hogarth was relieved to hear that Lawrence was safe. 'I have been on tenterhooks', he told his wife, 'as he was on a very dangerous venture, which failed as I feared it must, but without involving him in the worst fate.'[37] Three days later he added: 'Tell his mother I have news of him up to about the 20th and know where he is now, what doing, whither about to go. So far as I can judge he will be safe; but he won't return to our Ark just yet.'[38] Hogarth knew that Lawrence next planned to go north to attack the railway beyond Damascus. The implication in Hogarth's letter is that Lawrence had told him he had not planned to start north until about 20 November. His full report on the destruction of the train near Minifir confirms the reason why. In it, he concluded that 'sixty yards of cable is too little for firing heavy charges under locomotives. I had first to survive the rain of boiler plates, and then to run up a steep hill for 400 yards under fire. By good chance it was impossible to carry off the wire, so the performance cannot be repeated till more comes from Aqaba.'[39] During this time, he was waiting for supplies.

Yet Lawrence was not one to sit and kick his heels during enforced periods of inaction. On the way to Tell al Shehab he had seen the lights of Dara in the distance. According to his later account in *Seven Pillars of Wisdom*, Lawrence now decided it was time to have a closer look at this nerve centre of the Turks' railway network in Syria. While Wood carried his request for more supplies southwards, Lawrence apparently decided to go north to reconnoitre Dara, which was the target of the next stage of the grand plan he had concocted earlier that year. He said he spent a 'few days' march' circumnavigating the town with a sheikh, Talal, another outlaw who hailed from the village of Tafas a short way to the north, before setting out on an expedition of his own.

Accompanied by a Haurani peasant, Lawrence said he entered Dara late on 20 November. In his account in *Seven Pillars*, he described how, while looking around the town, he was apprehended by a Turkish soldier who seemingly suspected him of being a deserter. 'The Bey wants you,' the soldier reportedly said, and Lawrence followed him. 'There were too many witnesses for either fight or flight,' he later explained.[40]

17

DARA OR AZRAK?

(15–21 November 1917)

Lawrence reappeared, unexpectedly perhaps, in Aqaba on 26 November, having ridden non-stop for three days from Azraq. Almost immediately, he wrote up in his diary where he had been on his return journey. There are some crossings-out – the previous days were evidently a blur – but the writing itself is firm and breezy: quite different from the tiny scrawl of the desperate moments that summer when he was utterly exhausted.[1] There is other evidence to suggest that he was in rude good health. When Hogarth saw Lawrence on 9 December, he described him as 'looking fitter and better than when I saw him last.'[2] His view is corroborated by some of the only footage of Lawrence from the campaign, taken two days later during Allenby's formal entry into Jerusalem, which shows him grinning broadly.

From the report Lawrence had sent on ahead with Wood, by the time he arrived in Aqaba his colleagues already had a good idea of what had happened in the Yarmuk valley and how lucky he had been to escape more serious injury when he detonated the mine under the train near Minifir. None of them had any inkling of the ordeal Lawrence would say he underwent in Dara, until eighteen months later. It was only midway through 1919 while he was writing *Seven Pillars of Wisdom*, that Lawrence abruptly told Stirling how

I went into Dara in disguise to spy out the defences, was caught, and identified by Hajim Bey, the governor, by virtue of Abdul Qadir's descriptions of me. (I learned all about his treachery from Hajim's conversation, and from my guards.) Hajim was an ardent paederast and took a fancy to me. So he kept me under guard till night, and then tried to have me. I was unwilling, and prevailed after some difficulty. Hajim sent me to the hospital, and I escaped before dawn, being not as hurt as he thought.[3]

The reason why Lawrence decided to describe what he had undergone in Dara at the end of 1917 lies in the context of the events which took place immediately after the war. In Damascus, Feisal came under pressure from the French to accept the crown of Syria in return for achieving a settlement with the militant Arab nationalists in the city, who included Mohammed Said al Jazairi, the brother of Abdul Qadir. Abdul Qadir himself had been shot dead in Damascus shortly after the end of the war; his brother continued to nurse ambitions to replace Feisal, which Lawrence deeply opposed: not just out of loyalty to his wartime Arab comrade but because he believed that Mohammed Said was completely untrustworthy. This revelation of what had happened to him at Dara was the most graphic, personal illustration he could offer Stirling, by then the deputy chief Political Officer in Cairo, to warn the British not to press Feisal to accept the French proposal, which would give Mohammed Said al Jazairi greater power.[4]

Lawrence, however, then changed the key detail of this story in *Seven Pillars of Wisdom*. In the book he said that Hajim did not recognise him, suggesting that Abdul Qadir had not betrayed him. But he expanded on the bones of the story he had given to Stirling. His friends, among whom he circulated the first printed draft of *Seven Pillars* in 1922, must have found the lengthy account very disturbing. According to Lawrence, the Bey – a great, stubble-haired bully – grabbed him and tried to drag him on to his bed. 'When I saw what he wanted,' Lawrence wrote, 'I twisted round and up again, glad to find myself equal to him in wrestling.'[5] The Bey tried a new tack, promising that he could make Lawrence his orderly, relieving him from parades and duties, if only he would acquiesce. Lawrence refused. When the Bey came close, he said that he had kneed the Turk so hard that he 'staggered back to his bed, and sat there, squeezing himself together and groaning with pain'.[6]

Gasping for the guards, the Bey had Lawrence whipped. According to Lawrence, one soldier began 'to lash me across and across with all his might, while I locked my teeth to endure this thing which wrapped itself like flaming wire about my body. At the instant of each stroke a hard white mark like a railway, darkening slowly into crimson, leaped over my skin, and a bead of blood welled up wherever two ridges crossed.'[7] Finishing by slashing the whip across Lawrence's groin, two guards pushed him to the floor and prised his legs apart, while the third 'astride my back rode me like a horse'.[8]

Repelled by the sight of his potential 'bedfellow streaming with blood and water, striped and fouled from face to heel', Hajim then ordered the soldiers to carry Lawrence away. After they had dressed his wounds, the soldiers locked Lawrence in an outhouse. There he lay until dawn, when, having recovered a little, he discovered his makeshift prison was insecure. He found some tatty clothes, clambered out through a window and hobbled away towards Azraq. It was early on 21 November. Five days later he would be back in Aqaba.

Suspicion over whether he could have completed his return journey so quickly had he sustained the injuries in Dara he described raises the question of whether what he claimed happened at Dara is true. There is no corroboration of Lawrence's story. After the war, Hajim's relatives strenuously denied Lawrence's allegations, even producing contemporary evidence which suggested Hajim was an inveterate womaniser. The relevant page of Lawrence's pocket diary, covering the period 15–21 November, when these events allegedly took place, is missing. It was probably torn out by Lawrence himself and is the only missing page in either of his diaries for 1917 and 1918, both of which he gave in 1926 to his confidante, Charlotte Shaw, to whom he had also described his Dara story. Perhaps he removed the page to obliterate the episode. There was no need to hide the matter from Shaw, who had read the draft of *Seven Pillars of Wisdom* in which there was an account of the assault – unless of course it never occurred.

Charlotte Shaw gave both diaries to the British Library, where it is possible to read them today. On the previous page, before the missing leaf, the three previous entries are all, as Lawrence spelt them, for 'Kasr

Azrak'.* Under the last of these three, on 14 November, there is an additional vague note: 'To Hauran', a reference to the fertile region east of Dara, but it is written differently and possibly rather later. The first entry following the missing page, for 22 November, is also for 'Azrak', the writing is slightly more pinched, but at the same angle as the entries over a week earlier, suggesting that Lawrence may have written all the entries up in one go afterwards.

What was written on the diary's missing page? Forensic scientists have developed a technique – Electrostatic Data Analysis, or ESDA – to disclose words written on a missing sheet of paper, using static electricity and fine carbon powder to reveal any indentations made by a pen or pencil through that absent page on a surviving sheet of paper below. At the beginning of 2005, the British Library gave permission for Lawrence's diary to be analysed by ESDA in an attempt to establish what he may have written on the absent page.[9]

A ninety-year-old piece of paper, exposed to extreme heat and humidity, did not make firm results likely, and the three speckled grey transparent films produced by the process looked, unsurprisingly, disappointing. But a close look later revealed that in the space for 18 November – four days after Lawrence suggests he left for the Hauran – there are the faintest signs of a short word beginning with Lawrence's characteristic capitalised lowercase 'a', a word that is almost certainly 'Azrak'. There are other tantalising signs of handwriting, but none of it is legible. This discovery suggests that Lawrence did not leave Azraq for the Hauran as soon as he claimed. It reinforces the impression that he spent more time in the castle, lent by his extensive description of the 'slow nights' at Azraq in *Seven Pillars of Wisdom*, and comments in letters to his mother that he was 'staying here a few days', on 14 November,[10] and to his parents in December, that 'I stayed for ten days or so there', which might otherwise be dismissed as white lies.[11] The suggestion from the ESDA film that he was still at Azraq on the night of the 18th dramatically shortens the time he had left to do both the reconnaissance with Talal – which he said lasted a few days – and visit Dara, where he

---

* Kasr: a palace.

said he was arrested on the 20th, since he cannot have left Azraq before 19 November. If he did undertake this reconnaissance with Talal, it must have happened during the time that he claimed to have been a prisoner of the Bey in Dara. It also raises the question of why he added 'To Hauran' in his diary. If he tore the page from the diary out of disgust, he cannot have needed to remind himself of where he had gone. The only other person he can have been trying to deceive was Charlotte Shaw, whom he had told about his treatment in Dara, and whom he asked to burn the diaries once she had read them. Was it that his diary, as the ESDA analysis suggests, did not match his subsequent version of what happened during 15–21 November?

Why Lawrence included so much detail about his experience at Dara, including the description of the effects of the whip on his back which he could not possibly have seen, can be explained, like his letter to Stirling, in light of what happened after the war. From early in the 1920s Lawrence revealed a masochistic urge to be whipped. One man, John Bruce, whom he paid to administer beatings to the backdrop of Beethoven on the gramophone, Lawrence described to Charlotte Shaw as making him feel like 'a squashed door-mat of fossilised bones, between two layers. Good, perhaps, to feel like a prehistoric animal, extinct, and dead and useless: but wounding also.'[12]

Writing *Seven Pillars of Wisdom* gave Lawrence an opportunity to indulge his secret predilection but also left him with a dilemma, as he explained to Shaw. Referring to the section on Dara, he wrote: 'Working on it always makes me sick. The two impulses fight so upon it. Self-respect would close it: self-expression seeks to open it. It's a case in which you can't let yourself write as well as you could.'[13]

At first Lawrence gave self-expression free rein, describing how 'a delicious warmth, probably sexual'[14] swelled through him after the whipping was over. Though this sentence survived his editing, a second admission that the incident had left him with 'a fascination and terror and morbid desire, lascivious and vicious perhaps, but like the striving of a moth towards its flame', he eventually excised.[15]

Whether something did happen in Dara to kindle this desire, or whether Lawrence, having initially concocted the story to smear a hated opponent, decided to elaborate on it to express his proclivities in a way which would avoid censorship and inspire pity, not condemnation, from his former colleagues, cannot currently be proven. But it now seems likely that Lawrence removed the page from his diary because its contents did not correlate with the tale he would subsequently tell the world.

18

THE JEWS AND JERUSALEM

(November–December 1917)

Clayton's hope that the government would develop a formal policy towards the Zionists was answered rather more publicly than he might have anticipated. On 7 November *The Times* published a letter from the Foreign Secretary, Arthur Balfour, to Lord Rothschild, a Member of Parliament and prominent British supporter of Zionism, the twenty-year-old campaign to obtain the Jews a state in Palestine. 'I have much pleasure in conveying to you,' Balfour theatrically announced to Rothschild, 'the following declaration of sympathy with Jewish Zionist aspirations which has been submitted to, and approved by, the Cabinet.' It ran:

> His Majesty's Government view with favour the establishment in Palestine of a national home for the Jewish people, and will use their best endeavours to facilitate the achievement of this object, it being clearly understood that nothing shall be done which may prejudice the civil and religious rights of existing non-Jewish communities in Palestine, or the rights and political status enjoyed by Jews in any other country.[1]

The Balfour Declaration was, paradoxically, not really about the government of Palestine. It was a plea for support to the Jews worldwide.

At the turn of the twentieth century, the belief that the Jews wielded considerable political influence around the world was widespread. Driven by repression from eastern Europe, Jews had migrated westwards in large numbers in the years before the war. The Jewish population in Britain quadrupled to just over 250,000 in the thirty years to 1911. A lobby in New York, meanwhile, bolstered by significant Jewish migration to the United States before the war, managed to block the Tsarist government's attempts to raise loans on Wall Street.[2] The Jews were increasingly seen as a cohesive political entity capable of exerting their weight collectively and independently.[3] When Clayton, for example, returned from a visit to Britain in the summer of 1916, he told Wingate:

> One impression I gained which confirmed what I have always thought, and which I know you take an interest in, was the widespread influence of the Jews. It is everywhere and always on the 'moderation' tack. The Jews do not want to see anyone 'downed'. There are English Jews, French Jews, American Jews, German Jews, Austrian Jews and Salonica Jews – but all are JEWS, and moreover practically all are anti-Russian. You hear peace talk and generally somewhere behind is the Jew. You hear pro-Turk talk and desires for a separate peace with Turkey – again the Jew (the mainspring of the CUP). I do not mean that the Jews are disloyal in any way, but it seems to me that the ties which bind the Jew to his fellow-Jews all over the world must induce in him an attitude of sort of semi-neutrality. On the other hand of course they are an increasing power as the war becomes more and more a question of who has the deepest pocket and the longest credit.[4]

Clayton's view was not extraordinary.

Just as Faruqi had persuaded Clayton two years earlier that the Arabs were a powerful latent force with undecided allegiance, so the Zionists in London similarly depicted the Jewish diaspora as an influential constituency which had to be won over if the Allies were to win the war. One man to whom they spoke frequently was Sykes.

Sykes had been infuriated by the overtures for peace with the Ottomans which had emerged from within the Foreign Office during the summer of 1917. Though no particular supporter of Zionism, he too began to believe that the Zionists were key to sabotaging these peace initiatives. By persuading British Zionists that peace talks threatened their hopes of colonising Palestine because they would leave the Ottoman

Empire intact, he managed to derail one peace mission to Turkey by the former American ambassador to Constantinople, Henry Morgenthau. Sykes also began to see the Jews as part of an 'Arab-Jewish-Armenian barrier between Persia-Egypt-India and the Turco-German combine', which would stop the Germans marching eastwards.[5] He felt that the Zionists should be encouraged to create 'a self-supporting Jewish community which . . . should be a proof to the non-Jewish peoples of the world of the capacity of the Jews to produce a virtuous and simple agrarian population'.[6] In Sykes's flyaway imagination, Jews across eastern Europe would flock to Palestine to become its milkmaids and apiarists. Sykes, Wingate warned, had become 'carried away by the exuberance of his own verbosity'.[7]

So much for Sykes's romantic vision. By the summer of 1917, there were other, harder-edged incentives for the British government to reach a settlement with the Zionists. The Foreign Office believed that the enormous Jewish population in Russia, which had been denied equal rights by its own, Tsarist, government, was mostly Zionist in outlook. As the situation in Russia deteriorated during the course of 1917, British officials hoped that, if they offered the Jews Palestine, Russian Zionists might, behind the scenes, arrest their country's descent into revolution and probable exit from the war – an outcome that would allow Germany to concentrate her forces on the Western Front. Sykes liked the idea. Until now, in the face of Tsarist oppression, Jews had tended to turn towards socialism and communism for alternatives. He thought that offering the Zionists Palestine might undermine 'the extreme Socialist Jews of the underworld who regard Karl Marx as the only prophet of Israel'.[8] But time was running out. The same day that *The Times* published the Balfour Declaration, it also reported news of Lenin's Bolshevik coup in Petrograd.

Even if Russia collapsed, there was another good reason for supporting Zionist aspirations. At Russian insistence, under the Sykes-Picot agreement the 'Brown zone' of Palestine was to be internationally administered. Anticipating the British offensive into Palestine, Lloyd George realised that supporting Zionism was a useful tool to deflect criticism of British imperialism and camouflage his real ambition to turn Palestine into a British possession after the war. When the United States had joined the war, President Wilson had promised that the Americans would fight 'for the ultimate peace of the world and for the liberation of its peoples . . . for the rights of nations great and small and the privilege of men everywhere to choose their way of life and of obedience'.[9] By helping the Zionists, so apparently would Britain.

Vague and half-hearted though the Balfour Declaration was, its significance was immediately grasped in Cairo. Sykes wrote enthusiastically to Clayton, telling him that the Declaration emphasised the need for the Arabs to ally themselves with the Zionists. Clayton replied to Sykes that the 'prospect of seeing Palestine and even eventually Syria in hands of Jews whose superior intelligence and commercial abilities are feared by all alike' meant that the announcement was received with 'little short of dismay'.[10] He was even more caustic about Sykes in private to Gertrude Bell, the Arab Bureau's correspondent in Baghdad. 'The Arab of Syria and Palestine sees the Jew with a free hand and the backing of HMG and interprets it as meaning the eventual loss of his heritage. Jacob and Esau once more. The Arab is right and no amount of specious oratory will humbug him in a matter which affects him so vitally,' he told Bell.[11] 'Experience such as I have gained in this war, impels me to deprecate strongly incautious declarations and visionary agreements. We are like men walking through an unknown country in a fog and it behoves to feel our way and take care of each step we take.'

Bell agreed. 'I hate Mr Balfour's Zionist pronouncement,' she later told her mother:

> It's my belief that it can't be carried out; the country is wholly unsuited to the ends the Jews have in view; it is a poor land, incapable of great development and with a solid two thirds of its population Mohammadan Arabs who look on Jews with contempt . . . it's a wholly artificial scheme divorced from all relation to facts and I wish it the ill-success it deserves – and will get, I fancy.[12]

In the Balfour Declaration, Clayton saw just one glimmer of light. 'It may perhaps result in consolidating the Arabs, however,' he suggested to

The declaration of jihad on 14 November 1914 in Constantinople.
The summons sparked British fears that widespread Muslim unrest might follow.

The Holy Mosque in Mecca. The city's importance to the Muslim world encouraged the
British to foment a revolt there designed to blunt the jihad.

The Hijaz Railway under construction, near Amman. The steam engine abruptly ended the Bedu's monopoly on transport of pilgrims and grain through the desolate landscape of southern Syria and north-west Arabia.

Two Bedu. 'The term "fighting man" in the Hijaz meant anyone between twelve and sixty, sane enough to shoot,' wrote Lawrence.

Sharif Husein ibn Ali in December 1916, at the height of the Rabigh crisis.
He was 'the most obstinate old diplomat on earth', Hogarth felt.

Three men, three pledges. *Top left:* Sir Henry McMahon offered a vaguely defined empire to Husein, assuming that the commitment would never have to be honoured. *Left:* Sir Mark Sykes secretly promised the Lebanon and Syria to the French. *Top right:* Named after Arthur Balfour, the Balfour Declaration expressed support for Zionist ambitions to win Jewish backing for British control of Palestine.

Council of war at Jeddah, October 1916. Behind Sharif Abdullah are (*from left to right*) Cyril Wilson, Aziz Ali al Masri and Ronald Storrs. Wilson and Storrs had to tell Abdullah that the British would not send troops or aeroplanes to help the Arabs.

A more jovial Abdullah. In his youth, he and his brothers had been sent to live with the Bedu in the desert by Husein, in order to maintain strong links with the tribesmen, which would become invaluable once the revolt began.

Sharif Feisal ibn Husein at the Paris peace conference. Feisal refused to
concede to the French and returned to Syria in April 1919.

T. E. Lawrence, David Hogarth and Alan Dawnay in Egypt, 1918. Dawnay's textbook professionalism contrasted with the unorthodox approach relished by Hogarth and his former student, Lawrence.

Dark Days. Lawrence was nevertheless very pleased with this photograph he took of the Arabs' camp in the mouth of Wadi Yanbu at dawn, December 1916.

Jeddah, October 1916. Despite renewed trade, Jeddah's merchants were wary of Sharif Husein and the Bedu. Feisal never won widespread support in the towns and villages in Syria.

'Not an army but a world'. Feisal, here leading the Arabs towards Wajh in January 1917, conceived the march in order to win over further adherents with a show of strength.

Bedu dancing at Abdullah's camp. Impromptu celebrations and spur-of-the-moment songs were regular features of nomadic life.

A 'tulip' exploding on the railway near Dara, September 1918. The explosion beneath the metal sleepers warped long sections of track beyond repair.

Wrecked train, south of Wayban in the Hijaz, in March 2005. Damage to the footplate and firebox (*right*) was probably caused by a mine.

Turkish repairs to the line. Despite the frequent demolitions, Turkish repair gangs were able to keep the railway working until April 1918.

A peacetime metallurgist, Herbert
Garland successfully mined the
first locomotive in February 1917.

Stewart Newcombe in the Hijaz in 1917. He
had a reputation as a wild man, and was
eventually captured by the Turks during the
battle for Beersheba that November.

Auda abu Tayi. The arrival of
the fearsome outlaw in Wajh
in April 1917 enabled Feisal
and Lawrence to realise their
hopes of moving northwards
into Syria.

Wadi Itm, 5 July 1917. The tribesmen surprised Aqaba's small garrison by approaching from inland down this narrow, red valley.

A Bedu inspects the machine gun of a British biplane. The Arabs were fascinated and heartened by the military technology that Britain supplied.

Armoured Rolls Royce and Talbot cars and their crews at Quwayrah, 1918. The cars were used in a major raid in April 1918 which cut the railway south of Maan permanently.

The bridge over the Yarmuk at Tell al Shehab. With a party of Indian soldiers and tribesmen Lawrence tried and failed to destroy this bridge after dark on 7 November 1917.

The British enter Jerusalem, 11 December 1917. Allenby's advance into Palestine
brought the city into Christian hands for the first time since 1187.

Going their separate ways. Victorious Bedu fighters and Turkish prisoners pass in the street, Damascus, 1918. After the war, however, the French would replace both as rulers of the city.

Feisal leaves the Victoria Hotel in Damascus, 3 October 1918. As some of the expressions on faces in the crowd suggest, the arrival of Feisal and his tribesmen in the city was regarded with trepidation.

An exhausted Lawrence, on 3 October 1918 in Damascus.
The following day he left for London to continue his efforts to keep the French out of Syria.

Bell. 'Up to date the Syrian Arab has shown the utmost distaste for any idea of a Government in which Meccan patriarchalism has any influence. Hence a lack of real sympathy with the Sharif. Fear of the Jew may cause a rapprochement.'[13]

Clayton's belief reflected the fact that it was slowly dawning on the British that Sharif Husein was very unpopular in Syria. Increasing contact between the Syrians and the man they had approached to be their advocate in 1915 only revealed the width of the cultural gulf between them. Clayton sensed 'a very real fear' among the Syrians: 'They realise that reactionary principles from which Sharif of Mecca cannot break loose are incompatible with progress on modern lines.'[14]

The contrast was clear to anyone who could visit Mecca. After seizing power in 1916, Husein replaced the Turkish legal code with Sharia law. Cafés were now forced to shut at prayer-times and, among other things, alcohol and gramophones were banned.[15] From Jeddah, Wilson tried to persuade Husein to ban the practices of beating Turkish prisoners and forcing them to work chained together in iron collars, but, according to Brémond, 'les managements du colonel Wilson étaient vains'.[16] Wilson continued to raise his concerns about Sharia punishments, including the amputation of offenders' hands and feet, into 1918. 'It is not an easy subject to talk to the King about as he is most impatient of any criticism,' he admitted, though he hoped that to avoid aggravating the cosmopolitan inhabitants of Jeddah, 'in future such mutilations will only be carried out in the interior'.[17]

Husein's style of rule in the Hijaz was all the more awkward for the British because he showed no signs of giving up his claim to Syria. When Wilson gingerly asked Husein about his attachment to Syria, the Sharif had replied that any attempt to confine his jurisdiction to the Hijaz 'would drive him either to abdicate . . . or to repudiate his connection with us and make the best possible terms with the Turks'.[18] Wingate decided that the best way to disguise the growing problem was with money.

Even before the Balfour Declaration was published, Wingate had been planning to counter any Turkish plans to buy the Arabs off with a timely injection of cash. When Husein began to ask for more money that autumn to soothe the increasingly fractious tribesmen of the Hijaz, Wingate was inclined to support him. 'Old standing feuds are showing signs of reasserting themselves,' he warned London on 2 November, explaining that Husein was 'fully alive to this' and had repeatedly suggested 'an increase in subsidy which will enable him to placate discontented elements'.[19] Aware, too, of the strategic importance of Feisal's forces to the security of the British front line in Palestine, Husein believed that the British government should foot most of the bill for Feisal's army and wanted an increase over and above any extra money allocated to Feisal. Wingate agreed. 'It is desirable for political reasons that King Husein should not bear the whole brunt of operations in Maan area and North and thus secure a preponderating voice in regard to future settlement of Syrian problem,' he argued, with the concerns of the Syrians and the French in mind.[20]

Extracting more money from London was always difficult. Although the sums involved were relatively trivial – the £1.5 million paid to the Sharif in the first year of the revolt was equivalent to 'the cost of the war for about 7 hours', one civil servant calculated[21] – the subsidy was payable entirely in gold. The Foreign Office even hoped that the money might ultimately be repaid: 'Are these subsidies to be regarded as loans eventually repayable from funds of new Arab kingdom?' one official asked brightly early in 1917.[22] Optimistic though he was, the hope that the payments to Husein might be recoverable never quite disappeared: a Treasury minute of August 1918 noted that a total of £4,520,000 had been 'advanced' to the Sharif.[23] That raised the thorny question of how Husein would repay the money after the war was over. As an article in the *Arab Bulletin* admitted, 'We have changed the political status of Hijaz, but neither we, nor any others, have changed its economic status. Someone outside must still pay for its government and provide its food.'[24] Without Syria or another fertile province, the Hijaz alone would never be a viable state. And so, as the British came to appreciate the strength of Syrian opposition to Husein, the Sharif's future prospects looked increasingly downbeat.

It was Allenby who broke the impasse over funding. Concerned possibly, too, by the impact of the Balfour Declaration on the Arabs, on 15 November he contacted Robertson to add his support to Wingate's request for more money for Feisal. Allenby was nervous of the consequences if the Arabs went unpaid: 'any slacking on their part will render my position insecure,' he warned London.[25] Allenby's endorsement was valuable because he was riding high. By capturing Junction Station the previous day, the Turks could no longer supply Jerusalem, fifteen miles to the east, directly by rail. Allenby now planned to cut the road north out of Jerusalem to the nearest railhead still in Turkish hands, at Nablus, forty miles to the north, to isolate the holy city altogether and starve its Turkish defenders out: it was vital that the city should not be damaged by fighting. The War Cabinet's only worry was that he was advancing so fast that he might overstretch his lines of communication. The following day Robertson wrote to congratulate him, and to apologise if his previous telegrams seemed reluctant to advise a strong push forward. On 17 November the Foreign Office approved Wingate's request to raise the authorised amount which could be spent on Arab operations from £200,000 to £500,000, 'provided it does not entail further despatch of gold from here'.[26] At the same time, payment of the fee promised to Husein if he captured Medina was brought forward, regardless of the lack of success: from January 1918 onwards Husein received £225,000 a month from the British. Though the Foreign Office's caveat would provoke financial crisis in Egypt early the following year, for the time being more money for the Arabs had been arranged.

Early on 9 December – a bright, sunny Sunday – two British soldiers were out looking for eggs in a valley three miles north of Jerusalem. They were surprised when they met a rag-tag crowd carrying a large white flag. At its head, Jerusalem's mayor explained that the Turks had left the holy city northwards for Jericho and Nablus, and offered both men his surrender. But neither private was willing to return to their officers' mess with the keys to Jerusalem but no breakfast, and so the mayor was forced to trudge onwards. It was only later that day that he finally found a British officer willing to accept his surrender.

Whitehall had been waiting for this moment. Almost three weeks earlier, Robertson had contacted Allenby, advising him that 'in the event of Jerusalem being occupied, it would be of considerable political importance if you, on officially entering the city, dismount at the city gate and enter on foot. German Emperor rode in and the saying went round "a better man than he walked".'[27] Robertson now hoped Allenby would offer a humble contrast.

On 11 December, Allenby entered Jerusalem. It was 'a brilliant day; hoar frost here . . . and then iced sunshine, with no wind', he told his wife.[28] 'The procession was all on foot,' he reassured London in a telegram later that day. Behind, in the multinational force which followed him, walked Clayton and Lawrence, who had come over from Aqaba by aeroplane to discuss the next stage of the campaign and swapped his Arab robes for a uniform. 'The indescribable smell of Jerusalem rose to meet us,' wrote another British officer, 'a mixture of spices and sweet herbs, strange eastern cooking and dried fruits, camels and native garments and open drains.'[29] Large crowds turned out to greet the British and, to the sound of distant artillery and rifle fire beyond the city walls, hear Allenby's pledge that he would uphold religious freedom in the holy city. 'Great enthusiasm – real or feigned – was shown,' Allenby recorded.

Picot was also present. At a buffet lunch following the formal declaration in Jerusalem, he raised the future government of Jerusalem.

'Tomorrow, my dear General, I will take the necessary steps to set up civil government in this town,' he said, according to Lawrence. Instantly there was silence. 'Salad and chicken mayonnaise and *foie gras* sandwiches hung in our mouths unmunched,' Lawrence remembered, 'while we turned our round eyes on Allenby and waited.'

Allenby went red.

'In the military zone the only authority is that of the Commander-in-Chief, myself.'

'But Sir Edward Grey –'

'Sir Edward Grey referred to the civil government which will be established when I judge that the military situation permits.'[30]

Even though Allenby had been warned by Robertson that Picot would press for Palestine to be jointly administered, the British were evidently taken aback by the boldness of his request. On 27 December, Ronald

Storrs, newly commissioned as an army officer, was hurriedly installed as military governor of Jerusalem. 'He has had little administrative experience and in this respect may prove a disappointment,' remarked Wingate the same day, 'but he is well worth a trial and may at any rate serve as a useful stopgap.'[31]

The capture of Jerusalem was a remarkable propaganda coup for Lloyd George. The news was announced to the House of Commons on 10 December, and the following day's newspapers were enthusiastic. The *Glasgow Herald*'s editorial suggested that 'the taking of Jerusalem marks the end of an epoch of darkness, decay and despair, and the beginning of an era of light and hope such as was dreamed of by prophets long ago'.[32] *The Times* anticipated 'a new order' in the Holy Land, 'founded on the ideals of righteousness and justice'.[33] Across Britain, church bells pealed the victory. But in the background, another problem was already brewing. In Russia, within days of taking power, the Bolsheviks released details of the secret treaties to which Russia was a party. Among them was the Sykes-Picot agreement.

Jemal Pasha knew the details of the Sykes-Picot agreement within a week and decided to exploit them as best he could. 'We were completely informed as to the internal differences and tensions . . . in King Husein's household,' claimed Franz von Papen, a German staff officer with the Turkish Fourth Army in Syria, and later Chancellor of Germany. Feisal had kept in touch with Jemal, he said, 'and we had very much the impression that his basic intention was not to find himself on the losing side'.[34] On 13 November Jemal wrote directly to Feisal. Pointing at the British advance deep into Palestine, he asked him: 'How could you imagine establishing an Arab Government which would be responsible for the administration of the Moslem world independently and with dignity when the Allies have declared that Palestine will be an international religious settlement, Syria will be annexed to France and Iraq to the British Government?'[35] Then he offered Feisal an amnesty: 'The time to remedy mistakes . . . has not yet passed . . . Let us discuss the matter.'[36] Not waiting for Feisal's reply, he announced a month-long amnesty the following day.[37]

On 5 December Jemal spoke at a meeting in Beirut. Saying nothing about the provision in the Sykes-Picot treaty that gave France Syria, possibly because this might be welcomed by some in his Lebanese audience, he focused instead on the behaviour of Sharif Husein. It was a contradictory speech, which played on his audience's fears of being ruled from Mecca and suggested that all Husein had done was to make himself the unwitting puppet of British interests.

'I had been astounded at the revolt,' Jemal suggested to his audience, 'and it was not till recently that I learnt from one of the Sharif's men the true cause: namely that there was an agreement between England, France and Russia to establish an Arab kingdom comprising the Hijaz, Iraq and Syria, of which the Sharif was to be King.'[38] Like the British, Jemal knew that the Hijaz was unsustainable on its own. In his speech he claimed the British, having suffered heavy losses in their campaigns in Palestine and Mesopotamia, now planned to pare Husein's kingdom down to 'Mecca and Medina, towns without those things necessary for independence, namely gold, agriculture and commerce'. Britain's aim was to turn the Hijaz into a protectorate, in which 'the Sharif, because of his ignorance, will be nothing better than England's slave'. Again, Jemal offered to initiate talks:

> I believe that the Sharif began to repent, when he found out the real intention of the British, and I have therefore sent him a letter, pointing out that his dignity, his sincerity and his conscience cannot approve of his conduct towards his country, and asking how he could allow himself to become the slave of England if he has any self-respect.

This approach would come to nothing. Jemal was recalled to Constantinople later the same month and, it transpired, his letter to Husein was intercepted along the way.

Husein first indicated that he was aware that 'some secret understanding' existed between Britain and France on 26 November, by which time Feisal had passed on the letter he had received from Jemal.[39] But it was not until just before Christmas that Husein forwarded the letter on to Wingate. This letter and Jemal's speech in Beirut, a copy of which

Wingate appears to have received about now, explained another discovery earlier that month, when the Arabs had ambushed a train one hundred miles north of Al Ula, travelling south. They killed the senior officers aboard and an Arab sheikh, Suleiman Rifada, who was always suspected of colluding with the Turks. On Rifada they also found the letter from Jemal to Husein that Jemal had mentioned in Beirut. The train contained £24,000 in gold. With evidence suggesting that the Turks were trying to buy the Arabs, Wingate rapidly dispatched Lawrence back to Aqaba to talk to Feisal.

Lawrence arrived in Aqaba on Christmas Day. Just how worried he looked is suggested by Edward Robinson, an Arabic-speaking signaller who was based at Aqaba and remembered Lawrence appearing at the Christmas party thrown by the captain of the *Humber*: 'Sight of him was quite enough to put the celebrations in their place.'[40]

Joyce and Lawrence worked on a denial of Jemal's interpretation of the Sykes-Picot agreement. Jemal, they told Husein, 'either from ignorance or malice' had 'distorted its original purpose . . . omitted its stipulations regarding consent of native populations and safeguarding their interest and . . . ignored fact that subsequent outbreak and success of Arab Revolt and withdrawal from Russia had for a long time past created a wholly different situation'.[41]

Awareness of the Sykes-Picot agreement caused ripples around the world. In London, Lloyd George also moved to counteract the damage caused by the revelation. Addressing the Trades Union Congress – a group of people more likely than most to be sympathetic to the revolutionaries in Russia – at the beginning of January 1918, he said that 'Arabia, Armenia, Mesopotamia, Syria and Palestine' were entitled 'to a recognition of their separate national conditions' though, not surprisingly, he glossed over what form the recognition would take. He did say, however, that it would be 'impossible to restore' any of these territories to the Turks.

In Washington, in his celebrated Fourteen Points days later, President Wilson went rather further. His twelfth point covered the Ottoman Empire. 'The Turkish portions of the present Ottoman Empire should be assured a secure sovereignty,' he advocated, 'but the other nationalities, which are now under Turkish rule, should be assured an undoubted security of life and an absolutely unmolested opportunity of autonomous development.' It was a clear warning to both Britain and France. It also raised Arab expectations.

19

FIGHTING DE LUXE

(January–February 1918)

The capture of Jerusalem provoked an enthusiastic reaction in Britain that ignited War Office interest in the Palestine campaign. In London, the strategists pored over their maps and realised how important control of the country east of the River Jordan was to the security of Allenby's front.

After some thought, on 10 January, the official in charge of railway transport at the War Office in London dispatched a telegram to Egypt. The Director of Railways and Roads, he said, 'writing demi-officially, asks me to draw attention to the fact that some of the bridges etc. on the Hijaz Railway may now be within distance for bombing by aeroplane. I imagine that this is already known, but write as the War Office suggest it.' The Egyptian Expeditionary Force's Quarter-Master General, Walter Campbell, forwarded the advice on to the Arab Bureau. 'I think this may interest you,' he added in a covering note. 'I daresay the D of R and R at W.O. thinks that we are not perhaps aware of the fact that there *is* a Hijaz Railway.'[1]

'I hope to operate against Hijaz railway during wet season, and while waiting for my railway to overtake me, as there are still 20,000 Turks south of Amman,' Allenby had already explained in a telegram to Robertson on 14 December 1917. He was also clearly concerned that the Turks might outflank him to the east by using the railway because, shortly afterwards, he repeated that he felt it was 'advisable before advancing much further north to clear Turkish forces on Medina railway'.[2] He might have left the task of cutting the railway to the Arabs, but Lawrence's failure at Tell al Shehab had revealed their limitations. By the beginning of December, he was already mulling over the possibility of raiding the railway in the Amman area using his own forces, once he had captured Jericho.[3]

Like Allenby, Lawrence had also lost confidence in the Arabs. Documents recently seized from the Turks suggested that the Turkish commander in Maan had obtained 'considerable, and not altogether inaccurate, information' on the Arabs' plans and whereabouts.[4] With the likelihood that there was a spy among the Arabs, and having discovered that the price on his head had dramatically risen following his devastating raid on Mehmed Jemal's train at Minifir, Lawrence recruited a bodyguard of Ageyli whom, well-paid and detached from the internecine tribal structure of western Arabia, he felt he could trust not to betray him. Joyce decided that on their next raid they would take no tribesmen at all, but test the armoured cars instead. At the beginning of December, Joyce and Lawrence had taken a car and driven up Wadi Itm. Having proved that the vehicles would cope with the new, rough road up the narrow valley, Joyce ordered the Rolls-Royce armoured cars and the Talbots, which carried light field guns, to move to Quwayrah, twenty-five miles north-east of Aqaba. He and Joyce then took three lighter Rolls-Royce cars and, leaving the Christmas sports on the beach at Aqaba, set out on 26 December up Wadi Itm and east across the velvety mudflats north of Wadi Ramm to reconnoitre Mudawwarah. After the bone-shaking ride up Wadi Itm, this was ideal territory for the cars, which trailed long streams of yellowy grey dust as they raced across the plain. '30–40–50–60–70,' wrote one driver, Sam Rolls, remembering his speedometer's clockwise ascent as he tried to satisfy Lawrence's 'craze for speed'.[5] Following months of waiting in Aqaba, Lawrence recalled, 'It cheered up everybody, this twisting in and out among the flats, at top speed, skirting clumps of tamarisk, and roaring along under the great sandstone crags.'[6]

After a night of 'bully-beef and tea and biscuit, with English talk and laughter round the fire',[7] Joyce and Lawrence established the following day that it was possible to reach Mudawwarah by car, and returned to Quwayrah to collect the other vehicles. On further reconnaissance on the last day of 1917 the two officers discovered that the low, flat-topped hills through which they had driven the day before now petered out. Ahead lay the railway, in a vast plain of brown stone and drifting sharp yellow sand bounded by pinkish hills in the distance. It was too open to dare to mine a train, but open enough for the cars. After more investigation on foot on 1 January 1918, Joyce decided they should attack the small posts defending the railway north of Mudawwarah, using the light artillery mounted on the Talbot cars.

'Armoured car work was fighting de luxe,' Lawrence decided, 'for all our troops were steel-covered, and could come to no hurt.'[8] He and Joyce sat on top of a nearby hill and watched the battle develop through their binoculars. However, the flatness of the plain made it hard to judge distance, and the Talbots ventured too close to the Turkish position and came under what Joyce later described as 'a very hot rifle fire'.[9] With bullets shrieking off their armour-plating, the cars withdrew southwards, stopping to bombard Tell Shahm station, where they destroyed a number of wagons, before driving away. Summing up the raid, Joyce noted with satisfaction that the appearance of the armoured cars on the railway for the first time had evidently caught the Turks by surprise, but he realised that the raiders had also been lucky. As Lawrence later admitted, he and Joyce had been so preoccupied by whether the cars could reach the railway that they had given little thought to the tactics they would employ when they got there. And although excellent on the flat, the cars could not cross the shallow wadis which criss-crossed the plain, and Joyce observed that further careful reconnaissance was needed to avoid the danger of being cornered in future.

Good news followed Joyce back to Aqaba. On 3 January, a force of about 1,000 Bani Sakhr tribesmen and 150 well-armed Arab regulars, led by Sharif Nasir and Nuri Said, had recaptured Abu al Assal, the well on the pass through the Jabal al Batra ridge between Aqaba and Maan. Joyce headed there immediately. Further news followed four days later. In a move like an enormous question mark, the Arabs had then crossed the railway and, having skirted the east side of Maan, returned towards the railway and attacked the station at Jurf ad Darawish, thirty-five miles north of Maan.

Jurf, a sleepy, mellow stone halt, with graffiti carved in its parapets by bored guards, gives the impression today of a station which was wholly unprepared for the violent attack that overwhelmed it that grey January day.[10] To the east, the station is overlooked by a line of purplish hills.

Having occupied this ridge overnight, at dawn Nasir's Bani Sakhr charged down into the valley on their camels, terrifying the garrison. Nuri's men followed and turned the station's only, abandoned, field gun on the railway buildings with devastating effect. In the ensuing battle, eighty Turkish soldiers were killed, and over 200 more were captured. The Arabs, just two of whom were wounded, held the station for three days until a shortage in supplies forced them to move on.

Storrs had originally been planning to visit to reassure Husein about the Balfour Declaration, but his unexpected promotion to Jerusalem meant that he had no time to return to the Hijaz. The task instead fell to Hogarth, whose visit had been accelerated by the sudden arrival in Jeddah of another British diplomat, Harry Philby. An envoy of the Government of India, the 32-year-old Philby had come overland from Riyadh, and Husein was deeply suspicious of his sudden appearance, fearing, correctly, that he was being pressured to come to an agreement with Ibn Saud.

Hogarth sailed to Jeddah early in January to see Sharif Husein. It was his first visit to the Red Sea port, which he had described years earlier as 'before and since notorious for hatred of Christians'.[11] With this perhaps in mind, he walked self-consciously though the city's 'little dark earthen alleys blocked with Bedouins and camels and watersellers and beggars and hawkers and pilgrims'.[12]

It was the first time Hogarth had met Husein. The Sharif was, as ever, the perfect host and their meetings were accompanied by a constant stream of cups of cardamom-flavoured coffee and glasses of sweet sherbet. But 'for all his benignity and hand-patting and endearments', Husein, it quickly dawned on Hogarth, was 'the most obstinate old diplomat on earth and knows to an inch where he has you!'[13] He had already been trying hard to poison Britain's relationship with Ibn Saud. He argued that Fakhri was holding out so well in Medina because he was receiving surreptitious support from Ibn Saud. Philby, however, had anticipated this and brought with him letters Fakhri had written to Ibn Saud, in which the beleaguered general asked why Ibn Saud never replied. Husein refused to read the letters, and Hogarth concluded that a *rapprochement* between him and Ibn Saud was, for the time being at least, impossible, as the Sharif explained 'once more how he loves us all but can't do what we want, and won't!'[14]

Philby's behaviour annoyed Hogarth, because it emphasised the continuing divide in British policy on the Middle East. Hogarth told Wingate how Philby had refused to attend any meetings at the British residency in Jeddah or aboard the *Hardinge*. As a consequence, Hogarth felt, Philby had little idea of the magnetic, 'Imam-like' personality of the Sharif. He was, said Hogarth, 'deeply imbued with the idea that Ibn Saud, as his man, is to be championed against a "Cairo Champion"'.[15]

Hogarth came with confirmation that the Arabs would be 'given full opportunity of once again forming a nation in the world',[16] and that Britain supported Jewish settlement in Palestine provided it did not affect the freedom of the existing population. Husein elegantly parried the Declaration. He 'seemed quite prepared for formula', Hogarth reported back to Cairo, and had replied enthusiastically that 'he welcomed Jews to all Arab lands'.[17]

Hogarth was left with a lasting impression that Husein was vulnerable. 'His manner to me was most cordial throughout . . . With Mr Philby he comported himself, even when most contradictory and impracticable, less in anger than sorrow, and ended two of the most heated discussions not only with apologies to us all but an impulsive kiss to Mr Philby.' Hogarth suspected that Husein hoped to force France's hand on the future of Syria at the post-war peace conference, and was anxious to maintain good relations with the British, expecting them to back him. 'He is quite firm in his friendship to us,' Hogarth concluded, 'but none too firm on his throne.'[18] This frailty was a theme to which Hogarth would return in a further report on Husein for the *Arab Bulletin*. 'He is born to rule, but, probably, not to rule much farther than his eyes can see.'[19]

*   *   *

High in the mountains at Abu al Assal, the Arabs were badly prepared for the atrocious weather that winter in southern Syria. Joyce had warned almost three months earlier that the Meccan troops still fighting with Feisal already looked miserable with the cold. 'They hadn't enough blankets and tents to ward off the weather,'[20] recalled another British soldier, although Jafar Pasha blamed this on the troops, who 'stubbornly kept to their flimsy attire' and refused to wear more clothing.[21] It was an attitude that was to cost some their lives. On 10 January Joyce reported that, overnight at Abu al Assal, ten men had died from exposure. Many others over that winter suffered a similar fate, being found frozen rigid the following morning by their comrades. Though Lawrence did not yet know it, among the casualties was his servant Ali who, with Othman, had accompanied him all the way to Aqaba the previous year.

Despite the heavy snowfall, Nasir's force made good progress west from Jurf ad Darawish. In the hills south-east of the Dead Sea, his tribesmen attacked the branch line of the railway to Hishe, where the Turks cut down wood to fuel their locomotives, then Shawbak and finally, on 15 January, captured Tafilah, a quiet town forty-five miles north of Maan, surrounded by rolling, stony fields. Tafilah not only lay in the heart of the grain-producing uplands east of Wadi Araba but was also the southernmost of the hill towns that the Arabs needed to control to secure Allenby's right flank. Unfortunately, however, it had taken the arrival of Auda abu Tayi and his confrontational demand: 'Dogs, do you not know Auda?',[22] to convince the villagers to surrender and, as Lawrence discovered when he arrived shortly afterwards, the situation there was far from stable.

'There is shooting up and down the streets every night, and general tension,' Lawrence reported to Clayton from Tafilah, seven days after the Arabs arrived.[23] The people of Tafilah were split into two factions, who opposed each other and the appearance of the tribesmen. As a consequence, Lawrence's hope that the Arabs would find food to boost their own supplies proved overly optimistic. Harvested in March and April respectively, by wintertime barley and wheat were scarce and expensive, and the prospect of imminent fighting between the tribesmen and the Turks led the townspeople to hoard what stocks they had. There was little chance that their attitude would change, Lawrence thought, until the tribesmen had taken the towns of Karak and Madaba to the north as well.

The chance of taking either town was unlikely, Lawrence admitted to Clayton in his letter, because he was acutely short of money. Feisal's younger brother Zeid had just arrived to take charge of operations, and had paid the Bani Sakhr tribesmen a total of £22,000 – nearly four times more than they were owed. 'We are going to be out of funds perhaps before we take Karak, even,' Lawrence confessed. He asked Clayton for a special grant of £30,000 to be sent overland from Palestine for speed. Then he dispatched the letter with a local tribesman from the Wadi Araba, and waited.

On 24 January, the British intercepted an important message from Mehmed Jemal, commander of the Turkish Eighth Corps in Damascus, to one of his officers on the Hijaz Railway south of Amman. In it, Jemal explained that the Turkish troops from Karak were heading for Tafilah to recapture the town, on which the Turks would depend for food later in the year, and that he should send troops in the same direction. It transpired to be an expensive demand.

The same day, Turkish forces clashed with Arab patrols in Wadi al Hasa, a dramatic canyon a few miles north of Tafilah, which separated the town from Karak to the north. Lawrence decided he would have to stand and fight the pitched battle he had always advised the tribesmen to avoid. Yet there were good reasons to seek a decisive battle. Days earlier, the Arabs had sent messengers north to Karak, but there, as in Tafilah, the political situation was complicated. Two families, the Majali and the Tarawna, controlled the medieval town and its surrounding lands, but the violent way in which the Turks had crushed the uprising there in 1910 had left its scar. Moreover the ringleader of that revolt, Qadar Majali, had mysteriously died on a recent visit to Damascus as the Ottoman government's guest.[24] The Majali were consequently reluctant to act. The other family, the Tarawna, offered Lawrence higher hopes. They were 'secretly pro-Sharif', he believed, 'and may call up enough courage to take a visible plunge'.[25] Lawrence hoped that an Arab victory against the Turks at Tafilah would encourage the Tarawna to declare themselves in favour of the Sharif, taking the people of Karak with them. Another factor may also have been weighing on Lawrence's mind: to relinquish Tafilah without a fight was hardly likely to bolster Allenby's dwindling confidence in his handling of operations east of Wadi Araba. Besides which, to turn and run would only confirm the townspeople's fears that the nomads would leave them to face Turkish retribution on their own.

Overnight, following the first skirmish, the Arabs took up a defensive position on the edge of an abrupt valley on the north side of Tafilah. When he returned to the town shortly before dawn, Lawrence found its inhabitants in a state of panic and preparing to flee: 'Mounted Arabs were galloping up and down, firing wildly into the air, and the flashes of Turkish rifles were outlining the further cliffs of the Tafilah gorge.'[26]

Exactly what happened during 26 January remains unclear. At dawn, after Turkish bullets began to snap through the olive grove where the Arabs were trying to hide, Lawrence sent some lightly armed Arab troops to support the Tafilah peasants who were still holding a low ridge on the north side of the valley. When he himself made his way down into the valley and up to the ridge, the peasants counterattacked and drove the Turkish cavalry – the advance guard of the main 600-strong force – back towards Wadi al Hasa. Here they ran into the main Turkish force. Even from a distance Lawrence realised that the fighting had become 'very hot': the clatter of machine-gun fire and scream and blast of shells were audible from the town.

On his way towards the battle Lawrence met Abdullah, the leader of the small local force which had beaten off the Turkish cavalry, who was going in the opposite direction. Five of his men were dead, Abdullah said, and he had run out of ammunition. While Abdullah hurried back to fetch reinforcements, Lawrence headed for the small mound, defended by a few Huwaytat and the remaining locals, and realised that they were about to be outflanked on both sides. Shells from the Turkish field guns were also beginning to fall closer and closer to the Arabs. Leaving a few of the Huwaytat to cover their retreat, Lawrence took the locals back to the ridge just north of the Tafilah valley where they had started the day. Here he found the reinforcements Abdullah had mustered, more machine-guns, and an Egyptian Army mountain gun.

As he had run back from the exposed mound, Lawrence counted his paces and so, when the Huwaytat finally retired and the Turks occupied the same mound they had just left behind, Lawrence knew they were just over 3,000 yards away. Meanwhile, one of the Arab officers, Rasim Sardust, led some soldiers around to the right, and attacked the Turks from behind. At about the same time, local villagers from Aymah, just north-west of Tafilah, also joined the fighting. Either through luck or judgement, they were in the right place to attack the Turks from behind, from the other side. Caught in a three-pronged, simultaneous attack on gently undulating, stony ground, which offered no protection from shells or ricocheting bullets, the Turks suffered terrible casualties. By nightfall 200 had been killed, and a further 250 were captured including the commander, Hamid Fakhri Bey, who later died of his wounds. Many of the wounded froze to death on the battlefield overnight. The Arabs lost 25 men and a further 40 wounded. With Tafilah now secure, Lawrence sent some tribesmen down northwards to the Dead Sea to destroy the small Turkish fleet there, which Allenby believed was ferrying supplies across to Jericho, where the Turks were still holding out.

Lawrence won a medal for his role in directing the action. But he later admitted that his report, the sole basis for the decoration, was 'a nearly proof parody of regulation use',[27] in which he portrayed himself as a tyro who had directed the battle with the thumb of one hand marking the relevant page in a copy of Clausewitz's manual, *On War*. Headquarters missed the joke. 'We should have more bright breasts in the Army,' Lawrence laughed, 'if each man was able, without witnesses, to write out his own despatch.'[28] Nevertheless, the award reflected the importance Allenby's headquarters staff now attached to operations east of the Jordan. Further proof came with the arrival in Tafilah during February of the gold that Lawrence had requested. Its escort was a young, tall and ruthless officer who had grown up in Alexandria, Alec Kirkbride.

Lawrence, whom Kirkbride remembered as 'a small bedraggled figure',[29] was clearly impressed by the six-foot-three Kirkbride, because he quickly offered him a job as 'Intelligence-cum-Demolition officer'.[30]

After Clayton's concern about his health, Lawrence had been looking for other British officers to share his work and Kirkbride, though only twenty years old, spoke fluent Arabic and had made the journey back across Wadi Araba with an Arab guide and £30,000 in gold without incident. This, together with the further money Lawrence had gone to beg from Joyce in Quwayrah, would replenish Arab funds, he thought. He set out southwards with Kirkbride, accompanying him down through the wild Dana gorge into Wadi Araba. There they parted, Kirkbride for Aqaba to the south, Lawrence to the shore of the Dead Sea, northwards.

When, on his return to Tafilah, Lawrence told Zeid of his plans to head north towards Karak and Madaba, Zeid interrupted him.

'But that will need a lot of money,' Zeid said.

Lawrence reminded him of the £30,000 Kirkbride had brought, saying the sum would more than cover further operations.

Zeid looked embarrassed. He had spent it all, he said.

'I was aghast; for this meant the complete ruin of my plans and hopes,' recalled Lawrence afterwards.[31] He was unimpressed by Zeid's failure to do anything while he had been away to see Joyce and described the Arabs as 'the most ghastly material to build into a design' in a letter to Clayton.[32] He could not believe that Zeid had managed to spend so much in the short time he had been away, which meant that Zeid could only be lying. When Zeid refused to offer any better reason, Lawrence replied that he had no choice but to leave. On 19 February he hurried away towards Beersheba and the British Army's headquarters. 'I was going across to Allenby to explain,' he told a startled Joyce, who had just arrived in Tafilah, 'and to put my further employment in his hands.'[33]

20

NEW CONDITIONS

(February–April 1918)

'Can you identify the individual, sir?' the corporal asked. He directed his question at the officer who had just unexpectedly greeted the short and unusually ruddy 'Arab' he had arrested wandering through the tents of British headquarters at Bir Salem, ten miles inland from Jaffa on the Jerusalem road.

'Yes,' the officer replied, recognising the white-robed 'Arab' from his time working for Colonel Wilson in Jeddah.

'What name?'

'Lawrence. A British officer.'

'Very good, sir,' said the corporal, lowering his rifle and turning on his heel.

'It often happens,' sighed Lawrence. It was the second time that day he had been stopped.[1] 'You see I have ridden over from Karak and am staying with the Chief. I am coming now to see Clayton. Thanks so much for giving me my release. Shall we go in to lunch?'[2]

'Like a bolt from the blue,' wrote Alan Dawnay of Lawrence's sudden appearance in Palestine. Dawnay was the new staff officer responsible for 'Hijaz Operations', a precise and conscientious man with an 'Oxford drawl',[3] who had met Lawrence only a fortnight earlier, while he was at Quwayrah, drawing up plans for an attack on Maan with Joyce.[4] He had only just been trying, without success, to fly a message to Lawrence in Tafilah, asking him to come to headquarters. Recent developments meant that there was no question that Lawrence would not be needed in the operations that were now being planned.

'I told Clayton a little how I felt,' Lawrence would recollect, 'but he said that in the new conditions there could be no question of letting me off. In his opinion the East was only now going to begin.'[5]

There was much for Clayton and Lawrence to discuss. The 'new conditions' were those Lloyd George had deftly shaped from the euphoria following the capture of Jerusalem. Bypassing his chief military adviser, Sir William Robertson, Lloyd George persuaded the Allies' Supreme War Council – the body comprising the heads of government and senior generals of all the Allies – that the British should unleash another offensive against the Ottomans during 1918. Then he dispatched a member of his War Cabinet, Jan Smuts, to Egypt to assess whether this strike should come from Palestine or Mesopotamia. In the meantime in London, Lloyd George finally managed to sideline Robertson. Over breakfast on Monday, 18 February, Robertson read in the newspaper that he had resigned.[6] Three days later, British forces captured Jericho just as Smuts was completing his tour of the Palestine front. On his return to Britain, Smuts endorsed action in Palestine.

The capture of Jericho not only solidified political support for a further advance; by giving Allenby direct access to the River Jordan, it also made possible another scheme he had been plotting for same time. 'If I could destroy 10 or 15 miles of rail and some bridges; and get touch with the Arabs under Feisal – even temporarily – the effect would be great,' Allenby had told Robertson late in January, of his hope of raiding the Hijaz Railway.[7] News that Zeid had either misspent or stolen the money only just dispatched to him may have further encouraged Allenby to take matters east of the Jordan into his own hands. In a valedictory letter to Robertson, he commented that 'The Arabs, led by Lawrence, have been doing pretty well; but they are an unstable lot.'[8] Although he had been reassured by Lawrence that the Arabs would make further headway, given continuing British encouragement and money, Allenby believed that 'they cannot run alone, and must have British leaders they know and trust', dismissing at a stroke Lawrence's offer to resign.

Increasingly, Allenby favoured an attack on Amman. The beauty of such a scheme was that a break in the railway at that point would not only prevent troops from Medina reaching the Turkish front line north of

Amman, but also stop troops from Damascus launching a surprise attack from Maan behind his lines. Moreover, such an attack would work just as effectively as Arab action further south[9]. The appearance of British troops east of the Jordan might force the Turks to give up plans to retake Tafilah, and finally convince the farming communities in the hills east of the Jordan to trust the tribesmen.

Nevertheless, the threat posed to Allenby's supply lines by the sizeable Turkish garrison at Maan, possibly reinforced by troops from Medina, remained and was to become an increasingly pressing concern as Allenby prepared to advance northwards. Lawrence was optimistic that the Arabs could capture the town if their own supplies could be improved. Allenby agreed to provide two Egyptian camel transport units to help, but on the condition that they came under Joyce's, and not Arab, command. Then, at a conference at headquarters on 26 February, it was decided that the Arabs should attack Maan at the same time as the British occupied Salt, a picturesque town with a large Christian population thirty-five miles north-east of Jerusalem, high in the hills just east of the Jordan. Salt would be the springboard for a British attack on the railway at Amman, fifteen miles to the east.

Lawrence advised Allenby against involving Arab forces in the British raid, but said he would follow up the British incursion by raising a force to occupy the fertile hills around Madaba and Salt immediately afterwards. He also seeded an idea – born out of his growing disillusionment with the Arabs – that the Imperial Camel Corps, a 300-strong unit of camel-mounted troops, might be used to attack Dara when Allenby restarted his advance into northern Palestine. Then he left, via Jerusalem, for Cairo and Aqaba.

There was one more task for Lawrence before he could return to Aqaba to prepare for operations. Clayton's concern about his health, the importance of having a replacement ready should he be killed, and the need for someone to manage the Arabs' supplies between Aqaba and Quwayrah meant that Lawrence was looking for a recruit to the campaign. Back in Cairo, he went straight to the Savoy Hotel to meet the man he had recommended.

'I had heard vaguely of Lawrence's capture of Aqaba, and of his success with the Sharifian forces, but I did not know for certain that it was he who had sent for me,' Hubert Young later recalled. 'It was not until . . . the door opened to admit the familiar little figure, that I was enlightened.'[10]

'They asked me to suggest someone who could take my place in case anything happened to me,' Lawrence said, smiling mischievously, 'and I told them I thought no one could. As they pressed me, I said I could only think of Gertrude Bell and yourself, and they seemed to think you would be better for this participatory job than she would. It is quite amusing, and there is plenty of honour and glory to be picked up without any great difficulty.'[11]

Three years older than Lawrence, Young had been meandering home to India through the Middle East before the war when he first met Lawrence, who was working on an archaeological dig at Carchemish, on the Euphrates in eastern Syria. 'I have seldom enjoyed a week more than that week of Carchemish,'[12] Young declared in his memoirs, remembering drinking coffee from recently excavated Hittite cups and practising shooting at a matchbox from thirty yards.

Lawrence hoped that Young would be 'the right sort of man', he wrote to his mother: 'the work is curious and demands a sort of twisted tact, which many people do not seem to possess. We are very short-handed, and it will make things much easier if he fits in well.'[13] This was to prove a strange misjudgement. During the voyage to Aqaba Young and Lawrence 'clashed incessantly' according to Kirkbride, who was aboard the same ship.[14] It may even have been that the wrong Young was sent to Cairo. Lawrence had originally approached Cyril Wilson's assistant, J.W.A. Young, midway through 1917, asking him to join the campaign.[15]

From Aqaba, Dawnay, Lawrence and Young drove up Wadi Itm, through Quwayrah and, occasionally having to get out and push the car, up the steep hill to Abu al Assal on the Arabs' bitterly cold front line. It was raining hard when they arrived, so the three British officers and the Arab commander, Jafar Pasha, ducked into Feisal's tent to discuss the next stage of the campaign. Feisal was already there, twiddling a set of amber worry beads. He looked like 'some beautiful thoroughbred quivering at the starting-gate', thought Young.[16] The middle of the tent was uncarpeted and littered with cigarette ends – evidence of the argumentative discussions that often lasted late into the night.

Sitting in a hollow circle on mud-encrusted rugs, with rain pattering on the canvas of the tent, Feisal, the British and Arab officers reviewed the situation. Lawrence soothed Feisal's fears that the Turks were advancing towards Tafilah once more. He explained that, with the British about to attack Amman, and the Arabs Maan, the Turks would quickly be forced to withdraw from Tafilah. But the assault on Maan was easier said than done: 'We lacked the means for an immediate frontal attack on the town as we were threatened on both flanks,' Jafar Pasha remembered.[17] So, inside the tent, the officers agreed that the Arabs would first cut the railway twenty miles north and south of Maan. To create a further diversion, the British also decided to launch a further raid, south of Mudawwarah, using the armoured cars. Only then would the main Arab force assault Maan. Satisfied with this arrangement, Dawnay headed back to Aqaba.

Joyce, who was going down with pneumonia, suggested to Young that he should take the Indian machine-gunners and reconnoitre the railway south of Mudawwarah to ensure that the route was suitable for the heavy armoured cars. The reconnaissance, however, only proved that the plan conceived at Abu al Assal was impossible. Having driven seventy miles to Dhat al Hajj station, twenty miles south of Mudawwarah, Young described how

> We had only to look across from the top of the hill to see that our armoured car plan was out of the question. All the way from our look-out post to the line were wind-swept billows of bright yellow sand, through which no armoured car could go, and there was nothing for it but to go back and report failure.[18]

The British did not launch their armoured-car attack, and the Arab assault on Maan did not happen either. Jafar Pasha vividly remembered how, as he was descending towards the railway south of Maan, 'A torrential downpour soaked us to the skin and further progress became impossible. Camels and pack animals were floundering in mud, and our men were so beset that during the night some of them died of exposure to the bitter cold and rain.'[19] He had no choice but to turn back. On 20 March, Feisal was forced to admit defeat. Although he was 'quite ready to attack', he told his father, he had been thwarted by the 'worst weather'.[20] Further snow made a renewed attempt impossible.

The British attack on Amman, which set out on 21 March, also rapidly degenerated into a fiasco. The Turks often successfully decoded British radio traffic and appear to have established that a raid on Amman was about to begin; under no pressure from the Arabs at Maan, they were able to move 900 men northwards to reinforce the town three days before the British began to cross the Jordan. With any element of surprise already lost, the British then took two days to cross the swollen river, giving the Turks more time to prepare to defend Amman.

By the time the British reached the top of the precarious climb to Salt, the German general, Liman von Sanders, who had been given command of all the Ottoman and German forces in Palestine at the end of February, had established through a second intercept that the British camels were slipping in the mud.[21] 'Many of them did the splits with their legs splaying out in either direction,' remembered one British soldier on the raid. Others went over the side of the mountain path. The conditions were so treacherous that camels which slipped off the mountain path had to be shot where they lay even if not fatally injured by the fall.[22] The attack on Amman finally began on 27 March, a day late due to the troops' exhaustion. Having completed some insignificant railway demolitions south of Amman, the British withdrew after dark on 30 March, spurred in their retreat by misleading intelligence they had received that 15,000 Turkish troops were converging on their position. They abandoned their plans to hold Salt and re-crossed the Jordan on 2 April, followed by a gaggle of about 5,000, mostly Christian, refugees who feared Turkish reprisals. More than 1,200 British soldiers were killed or wounded in the operation, the impact of which was then clearly inflated. The *Arab Bulletin* reported that over ten miles of track had been destroyed, more than twice the distance which was actually damaged, and Allenby claimed in a letter to the War Office that his forces had withdrawn simply because the capture of Amman station would 'involve considerable loss'.[23]

Other disturbing news also curtailed Allenby's operations. The same day that he launched the abortive Amman attack, the Germans began their Spring Offensive on the Western Front: the gains they made were devastating. After two days, Lloyd George telegraphed the British ambassador in Washington, telling him to inform President Wilson that 'the situation is undoubtedly critical and if America delays now she may be too late'.[24] Within two more days, the Germans had taken over 45,000 British and French soldiers prisoner. On 27 March, the War Office contacted Allenby to tell him that its plans to send him troops from Mesopotamia were cancelled and that British troops and heavy artillery would be taken from him for France as soon as shipping became available. 'You will adopt a policy of active defence in Palestine as soon as the operations you are now undertaking are completed,'[25] Allenby was told.

Dawnay returned to Aqaba to replace Joyce, whose pneumonia required treatment in Cairo. Since 'everything was done on the most approved Staff College lines' by Dawnay, recalled Young[26] – in the strange circumstances of the Arab revolt into which he had been suddenly plunged it was not long before Dawnay blundered. After arriving at Abu al Assal on 7 April, he told Feisal that the British had pulled back from Amman. Realising too late that Feisal was 'clearly concerned by this apparent reverse',[27] he rapidly tried to claim the attack was a raid, not an attempt at a permanent advance. It was a weak excuse: unknown to Dawnay, Lawrence had already given Feisal a written promise from Allenby that he would permanently establish a base at Salt.[28]

No amount of Staff College training equipped Dawnay for life with the Arabs, which was rarely dull. The officers liked Scotch whisky and playing poker for gold sovereigns. There were 'incidents when faces got slapped, with those involved reaching for their pistols', Kirkbride remembered, 'but they went for their guns slowly enough for bystanders to be able to intervene and induce the combatants to embrace and make friends again'.[29] Many of the officers had been associated with the secret

Arab societies formed before the war and now felt the dream they had 'of recreating the wide empire of their forefathers was capable of realisation', Kirkbride recalled.[30] They 'were not soldiers, but pilgrims, intent always to go a little farther', Lawrence wrote afterwards, borrowing a phrase from his late friend, the poet James Elroy Flecker.[31] Joyce was not so sympathetic. Before departing to Cairo, he warned Dawnay about the 'hopelessly incompetent, ignorant and conceited'[32] Syrians. This uncompromising view probably informed the *Arab Bulletin*'s judgement shortly afterwards that the Syrians were 'worst in respect of political intriguing' and behind growing 'anti-European chauvinism' believed to result from 'suspicions about secret agreements among the Allies'.[33]

When Dawnay discovered that the plan to attack the railway each side of Maan had been abandoned, he put it down to 'the influence of Nuri [Said] and the anti-British element among the Arab leaders', who were now calling for a direct and immediate attack on Maan.[34] Lacking the guidance of Lawrence, who advised his colleagues never to disagree openly with the Arab leaders,[35] he now threw himself into an argument over the plan to capture Maan. On 7 April he bluntly asked Feisal how he expected to take on a well-armed and defended garrison and, if he succeeded, hold the town without cutting the rails north and south to prevent the arrival of Turkish reinforcements. After a heated discussion lasting over two hours, 'Feisal appeared evidently disconcerted and worried', Dawnay observed, believing him to be 'more than half convinced of the error of his decision', but as yet 'unwilling to recede, fearing the opposition which such a course might provoke among his Arab advisers'.[36] At a further meeting the following day, a compromise was eventually agreed: Jafar and Nuri would attack north and south of the railway respectively, before turning in and jointly attacking the town.

Both raiding parties set out on 11 April, when there was no moon. That night Nuri attacked Ghadir al Hajj, the first station south of Maan, destroying five bridges and about 900 yards of track. Forty miles north of Maan, Jafar's attack on the small station at Abu el Jurdhan as dawn broke the following morning quickly lost momentum as a hail of Turkish machine-gun fire swept the open plain around. Renowned for his violent temper, Jafar, Young recalled years later, 'used to burst out into torrents of bilingual abuse at the smallest provocation'.[37] He now decided that the time had come to harangue his men. 'This exhortation had the desired effect,' Jafar wrote in his memoirs.[38] His men rushed forward to take the station. It was 'a dashing attack culminating in a bomb and bayonet charge', Dawnay reported, which forced the wounded Turkish commander to surrender.[39]

Some way to the north, Lawrence could see bright flashes in the distance as Jafar's men started their attack on Abu el Jurdhan. He had spent the previous week escorting an enormous caravan of camels carrying rifles to the area south-east of Amman, to arm the Bani Sakhr tribesmen so that they could assist the British attack on Amman. Though he met the Bani Sakhr, when it eventually became clear that the British attack on Amman had failed – an outcome he criticised as 'deplorable' – he turned south again. The return journey should have been straightforward but the party ran into a Turkish patrol. Lawrence was reluctant to fight, but the tribesmen insisted, and in the gun battle that followed, his remaining servant, Othman, was fatally shot.

'We tore his clothes away and looked uselessly at the wound,' Lawrence recollected. 'The bullet had smashed right through him, and his spine seemed injured.'[40] It was clear that Othman had only hours to live.

Even a few hours was too many. Lawrence knew full well the vengeance the Turks would wreak on Othman if they found him alive – 'we had seen them mutilate or burn alive our hapless men'[41] – and he knew he had to escape. But before he could, he would have to kill Othman. Kneeling down beside the wounded man, Lawrence kept his pistol out of Othman's eyeshot near the ground, rather as a dentist hides his pliers, and looked into his eyes.

It was Othman who spoke first.

'Ali will be angry with you.'

'Salute him from me,' Lawrence replied.

'God give you peace,' Lawrence remembered Othman saying before he closed his eyes 'to make my work easier'.[42]

On 13 April, the Arabs combined in an attack on Simna, a knoll west of Maan. Even though their Iraqi commander, Mawlud Mukhlis, was seriously wounded when a bullet shattered his leg, the ease with which they captured this outpost encouraged the Arab officers to press on. Two days later, they launched an attack on Maan station, slightly east of the town, a drab and dusty outpost at the edge of the encroaching desert. The station – a cluster of cream stone offices, workshops and train sheds with terracotta pantile roofs – was strongly fortified with concrete machine-gun emplacements. Amid fierce fighting on 17 April, Nuri Said reached the station outbuildings, but the French artillery fire on which he was relying for support suddenly petered out. Even years later, Nuri felt let down: 'I still remember quite vividly that this battery did not do its job and that it fired a few shells only, to determine distance and direction,' he complained.[43] In fact, up on the ridge overlooking Maan, Pisani had simply run out of ammunition. Lawrence, who had returned to watch the battle, found him 'wringing his hands in despair'. The French officer told Lawrence that he had begged Nuri not to attack given he was almost out of shells.[44]

At nightfall the Arabs were forced to withdraw. Over 90 had been killed and a further 200 wounded. Lawrence would not forget how 'The eyes of the wounded men, gone all rich with pain, stared accusingly at us as they were carried past. The human control had gone from their broken bodies, and their torn flesh took free play with its own nerves, and shook them helplessly.'[45] Of the officers, whose arguments and intrigue had enlivened the wintry camp at Abu al Assal, Jafar estimated that over half had been either killed or wounded.[46] Mawlud Mukhlis was left permanently crippled.

Now that the attack on Maan had started, Dawnay revived the plan to attack the railway near Tell Shahm, south of Maan, using the armoured cars, the Egyptian Camel Corps, which Allenby had sent over, and some tribesmen. His crisp organisation for the attack came as a shock to the other officers. 'Gun sites, times for aeroplane co-operation, lines of approach for armoured cars, successive positions for the ECC,* even the general direction of the Bani Atiyah† camel charge were planned out

* The Egyptian Camel Corps.
† The Bani Atiyah tribe ranged over an area from Maan south to Dar al Hamra, fifty miles north of Al Ula.

in the utmost detail,' remembered Young, who had accompanied Dawnay on the reconnaissance beforehand. Looking down at the oblivious little garrison of the station, he 'could not help feeling that it was really not quite fair of Dawnay to make such up-to-date and elaborate plans for their destruction'.[47]

Dawnay's plan also worried Lawrence for more serious reasons. He was wary of mixing the Bedu with the Egyptians because, as experience at Rabigh had shown, each hated the other. The Egyptians looked down on the Bedu, but the superiority they felt was not reflected in their salaries. 'The most embarrassing thing,' the Egyptian Camel Corps' commander, Frederick Peake, recalled, 'was to see Lawrence pouring golden sovereigns into the hands of the Bedouin while the Egyptians only had a few piastres added to their meagre pay.'[48] On 18 April Lawrence decided to accompany the party to try to ease the consequences of the mistake he feared Dawnay was making. 'I drove into his camp above Tell Shahm after midnight,' he recalled, 'and offered myself, delicately, as an interpreter.'[49]

Dawnay was pleased to see Lawrence. By torchlight, he unfolded a piece of paper and explained his detailed plans — 'orthodox-sounding things', Lawrence remembered, 'with zero timings and a sequence of movements'.[50] The armoured cars would attack the first Turkish outpost at dawn the following morning, and a second post while the railway was demolished. After further demolitions 'while the force lunched', the combined force would attack a third outpost, before a massed assault on the station, which Dawnay calculated would be taken eleven and a half hours after the dawn attack began.[51]

'It was like picking a ripe peach,'[52] Lawrence wrote of the operation afterwards. In the lull after the capture of the first outpost, to stop reinforcements arriving from Mudawwarah to the south by train, he and Hornby raced down the line, fastening bricks of guncotton to each length of rail and stuffing the drains of the bridges with explosive. Tom Beaumont was a young machine-gunner standing in the turret of one of the Rolls-Royce armoured cars. He remembered how Lawrence 'lit the fuses and ran like a hare down the slope and jumped into the seat of the car. Suddenly there was a hell of a bang, then another, another, another, until hundreds of yards of rails were twisted and bent like cheap hairpins. The great span bridge crashed with a terrific roar onto the ground below.'[53] From behind the steering wheel, Rolls vividly remembered 'the screaming of ripped iron, as great pieces of the rails were torn clean out and sent flying and whizzing over the desert'.[54] Lawrence made light of the fact that he had narrowly missed being hit by one of these whirling fragments: 'Only once was there a great hit, when a twenty-pound lump of flint dropped, with a sounding clang, plumb on a turret head and made a harmless dint.' He summed up the day as 'fighting de luxe, and demolition de luxe: we enjoyed ourselves'.[55] Later that afternoon, the Turks at Tell Shahm surrendered, ten minutes ahead of Dawnay's meticulous schedule, and the force rushed towards the station.

It was only when Peake's Egyptian cameleers tried to stop the Bedu from looting that trouble erupted. 'A somewhat dangerous situation arose between the Arabs and the Egyptians; serious consequences were, however, averted by skilful handling of the Bedouin by Colonel Lawrence,' Dawnay diplomatically reported afterwards.[56] Years later, Lawrence put it rather more frankly: 'We were all within a hair's breadth of getting scragged,' he told his biographer, Robert Graves.[57]

The raiders then turned south. The Turks had already abandoned the next station south and so, the following morning, the British armoured cars took a wide loop to approach Mudawwarah from the east from out of the rising sun. But the Turks spotted them and began to fire their howitzers, so the cars swerved southwards, completing a demolition on the track about four miles further down the line towards Medina, before turning around and roaring northwards up the stony plain, past Tell Shahm, to the next station, Wadi Rethem. Relying on the invincibility of the cars again – to small-arms fire at least – Dawnay ordered one car forward to the station, which was then demolished with explosive. Its battered remains can still be seen today among the sands – the colour of old mustard – in the very south of Jordan.

Very few people knew about the extent of British involvement, and those who did, did not learn it from the newspapers: 'Hijaz Railway Cut: Arabs occupy 53 mile section', read the headline in *The Times* of 29 April, before reporting an extract of a communiqué from the War Office: 'As a result of operations conducted by the Arab troops of the King of Hijaz against the Hijaz Railway during the week ended April 24 a section of the line extending over some 53 miles to the south of Maan has been occupied effectively.'

The horizon north of Wadi Rethem is dominated by the dark Batn al Ghul escarpment which the French agent, Antonin Jaussen, had recommended as a target almost two years earlier. Taking advantage of the chaos caused by the armoured-car raid, it was to Batn al Ghul that Peake and Hornby returned days later, to destroy the narrow cutting down which the railway descended from Syria into Arabia. On 9 May the raiders reached the scarp. Concentrating on the curved rails on the steepest sections of the descent, which would be hardest to repair, they also blew in a thirty-foot-deep cutting and completely demolished the stations at Batn al Ghul, on the top of the escarpment, and at Aqabat al Hijazia, one stop north. Sitting in an ancient watchtower that night Hornby treated the party to some of his favourite songs.[58] Suddenly, the situation appeared to be improving, but that impression would not last.

21

A COMPLETE MUCK-UP

(April–May 1918)

'In the last three days nothing has happened to break the monotony,' Hubert Young wrote gloomily on 21 April.[1] Promised honour and glory by Lawrence, he had not expected to be relegated to the role of sentry at one of the important wells between Quwayrah and the railway for the Tell Shahm attack, for which he had helped prepare. By the time Dawnay launched his attack on the railway, Young was bored and furious. 'It seemed to me,' he later wrote, 'that I was falling between two stools, and I was clearly not wanted to understudy Lawrence.'[2]

When Dawnay returned from the Tell Shahm raid he was confronted by Young, who was never a man to suppress his views. Young told him how bored he was, referring to a time when he had sat for two and a half hours with Lawrence and Feisal, without once being brought into their conversation. And he attacked Dawnay for arriving from Cairo to take over an operation for which he thought he should have been given responsibility. It was only later that he admitted how 'The fact was that Dawnay was getting tired of only doing staff work at Cairo and wanted a little fun for himself, and who shall blame him?'[3]

Dawnay agreed that Young should do more. Both he and Lawrence had just been called to see Allenby in Palestine and, while they were away, he suggested, Young might act as a liaison officer between Nuri Said and some Bani Sakhr tribesmen in an attack on Jurf ad Darawish station designed to maintain the pressure on the Turkish garrison at Maan, thirty-five miles south.

Cramming his pockets with tins of Maconachie – the British Army's staple meat-and-vegetable ration – Young set out immediately north-wards with the band of colourful Ageyli bodyguards whom Lawrence had lent him. Young met Nuri, who revealed that he planned initially to attack a Turkish *karakul* – one of the intermediate camps between stations which the Turks had established along the line – south of Abu el Jurdhan, and complete the destruction of two bridges damaged in the raid on the station led by Jafar Pasha a fortnight earlier.

Nuri Said set off at four the following morning, following a delay when his guides failed to arrive. Discovering that all but one of the soldiers had already fled to Abu el Jurdhan, the Arabs set fire to the pile of wooden sleepers being used to support the track over one of the missing bridge arches, and dynamited the other bridge. Young recom-mended Lawrence's technique of plugging the drainage duct with explosive: an Arab sapper tamped the charge home and lit the fuse. There was a loud crack and the arch, cut 'as clean as a rasher of bacon', slid into the wadi below.[4]

Nuri Said's plans then went awry when the waterhole east of the railway on which he was relying turned out to be dry. Young headed east to Jafr to seek help from Auda abu Tayi. But the great raider who had led Lawrence to Aqaba had fallen out with Feisal and, after a brief and unfruitful meeting, Young returned north-west to Wadi Mushayyish, to gather the Bani Sakhr. There, one of the tribe's chief sheikhs, Mirzuq, explained that a few days earlier he had sent envoys directly to Allenby's headquarters to request help in attacking the Turks. Mirzuq was surprised when these messengers returned with a letter from Allenby saying that he proposed to cooperate, and a verbal message that, in fact, he intended to cross the Jordan and attack Salt again the following day. Young, who knew nothing of this plan, was surprised. Mirzuq looked frightened by the scale of the reaction his impromptu appeal had generated. Rather than take action, he decided to send a messenger to Abu al Assal to seek confirmation of Allenby's plans.

The message from Allenby to the Bani Sakhr turned out to be completely accurate. At 4.30 in the morning on 30 April, Allenby launched a hurried second attack across the Jordan. Political pressure, dwindling time, new intelligence and a hint of desperation had forced him into action. After the initial panic following the beginning of the German offensive, the War Office had wired him to ask whether there was the 'possibility of further raids on Hijaz Railway through Madaba or south of Dead Sea' to relieve the pressure on 'the Arab situation, which does not appear to be wholly satisfactory', a reference to the Arabs' failure to capture Maan and British concerns that German gains might cause the Arabs to swap sides.[5]

Two other factors added to the pressure on Allenby. As he explained to Sir Henry Wilson, who replaced Robertson as Chief of Imperial General Staff, an important reason for launching the raid was to 'deny to the Turks the grain harvest of the Salt-Madaba area'.[6] By the time he wrote, on 20 April, the barley and wheat harvests were imminent; both were expected to be good. It was also Allenby's last chance to use some of his best troops, who had been earmarked by the War Office to return to fight in France.

During the course of April Allenby had to send two divisions – well over 30,000 men – back to France; further units were recalled to the Western Front in May. The smaller Allenby's force became, the greater his reliance on the Arabs to capture Maan and secure his eastern flank. The Arabs' failure to do so caused escalating concern at British head-quarters. In theory, the safest solution to the problem was to withdraw to a position that would eliminate the possibility of being outflanked by the Turks from the Maan area – but, since this would mean relinquishing Jerusalem, in practice it was unthinkable. Allenby, in any case, believed that it was more secure to advance than retire, because his line north of Jerusalem between the Jordan and the Mediterranean would be narrower, and because 'any retirement would alienate the Arabs and result in disaster'.[7] Knowing that he would soon have even fewer troops to defend his position, Allenby's only way was forward.

These were the circumstances in which the approach from the Bani Sakhr appeared. The dominant tribe in the region east of the Jordan, the Bani Sakhr had raided the Hijaz Railway during the first British assault on Amman and now seemed to be volunteering to cut off the Turkish supply route between Amman and their front line on the Jordan during a further British attack on Salt. The tribesmen's willingness to act corroborated other promising intelligence Allenby had received that the people of Salt were now 'prepared to lay down their lives for the Sharif'.[8] Convinced that there was a groundswell of support that would help him retake Salt, Allenby decided to act, but could not tell Lawrence because he knew that his wireless communications with Aqaba could be intercepted by the Turks. Lawrence had been anticipating a further attack, but not so soon. He did not appreciate the time constraint because, at this stage, he had little, if any, news about the German onslaught in France. He later portrayed the raid as an overhasty gambit conceived by Allenby's short and eager chief of staff, Louis Bols, in a 'Eureka' moment in the bath.[9]

The Turks had reinforced their front line on the east bank of the Jordan in anticipation of a further British attack, and although the British force — of mainly Australian and New Zealander troops — successfully re-occupied Salt on 1 May, they soon found themselves the target of a ferocious Turkish counterattack. By the 3rd, Liman von Sanders decided that it was time to make an all-out effort to recapture Salt. 'In the evening I issued an order to HQ Fourth Army and to the Third Cavalry Division to penetrate into the town from the north by means of a night attack,' he recounted afterwards.[10]

At the time, Liman von Sanders was rather less composed, remembered Franz von Papen, who had narrowly escaped being captured in the British advance. He took Liman von Sanders's call that night in Jarash, twenty miles north-east of Salt. 'By this time my nerves were at breaking point,' von Papen later recalled: 'and all I got was the shouted order over the telephone, "If you have not retaken Salt by tomorrow I will have you court-martialled!"'[11] Liman von Sanders had chosen his angle of attack carefully. Worried that if he boxed the British in he would provoke a fight to the death in which his own troops would be defeated, he deliberately allowed his enemy the opportunity to escape southwards towards the Jordan. As Mirzuq was waiting for confirmation of Allenby's intentions from Abu al Assal, support from the Bani Sakhr, which might have stopped the Turks from counterattacking, never materialised. Having suffered over 1,500 casualties, the British force re-crossed the Jordan late on 4 May; in the words of one British soldier, 'the second . . . Salt stunt was a complete muck-up'.[12]

Not that either the Arabs or Husein heard as much. The 'Raid [was] completely successful', the British hurriedly told them, explaining that the objective all along had been to retain 'enemy troops on [the] Jordan front so as to arrest movement of Turkish reinforcements to Maan area'.[13] Yet now that the British had withdrawn, the Turks were once again free to reinforce Maan, and news of heavy reprisals in Salt, where over 700 townspeople were killed by the returning Turkish forces, undermined what willingness there may have been to support the Sharif. In truth, the operation – a military failure – was more significant as a political disaster.[14]

Miles to the south, Hubert Young was oblivious to what had happened in Salt, though he spent the following days desperately trying to establish when the planned attack on Jurf ad Darawish would now take place. After further to-ing and fro-ing he established that the Arabs would congregate at Towana, just west of Jurf, five days later. Following a disagreement between the Arab soldiers and the tribesmen, however, Nuri Said abandoned his plans to capture Jurf, deciding instead to concentrate on a further attack on Abu el Jurdhan, which was planned for the first day of the new Muslim month – a decision which left the timing dependent on the appearance of the new moon. A dispute over when the new month began led to a day's delay and it was not until 12 May that the assault was launched. Nevertheless, the attack was, in Young's words, a 'brilliant success'. Not only did the Arabs take 150 Turkish prisoners, but they also managed to destroy the crucial reservoirs at the station.

Young spent the next few days on an unsuccessful quest to track down guns for the Arabs, during which his car broke down, and he was forced to hitch a ride in one of the British armoured cars operating with the Arab forces. The commander of the car refused to let Young take his valise with him, and deprived of the padding it contained, which he used as a saddle, he then suffered what he delicately termed 'internal damage' from riding a camel over the following days. He was forced to watch another attack on Abu el Jurdhan on 17 May from a distance. The Turks rapidly emerged with their hands in the air. Young was lucky to have been incapacitated. The surrender turned out to be a trap: when the Arabs approached the station, they came under heavy machine-gun fire.

Almost all of them were killed or wounded, including their Baghdadi commander, Rashid Ali, and the Turks secured the station itself with reinforcements from the north.[15]

The failure of the Bani Sakhr to support his forces during the second Salt attack undoubtedly strengthened Allenby's existing doubts about the Arabs. Nor was he the only one to wonder about their loyalty. 'I'm afraid the Arabs can't be relied upon to any great extent until they are quite certain our side is going to win,' Wingate wrote to Allenby in the aftermath of the Salt débâcle.[16] Another officer in the Arab Bureau warned that the Arabs' support for the British was waning: German gains on the Western Front, he suggested, were 'causing them furiously to think'.[17]

In the circumstances the Turkish commander Mehmed Jemal felt confident that he might yet win the Arabs over simply by offering Husein autonomy in the Hijaz.[18] On 3 May, he wrote – from Salt – to Feisal, offering to open talks in four days' time. 'I feel sure we shall be able to fulfil the wishes of all Arabs,' he added as a postscript.[19]

When Ahmed Jemal Pasha had contacted Feisal late in 1917, Lawrence claimed afterwards that he had secretly encouraged Feisal to reply with exorbitant demands. Jemal's objections to these, he calculated, would cause infighting between the Turkish nationalist and pan-Islamic factions within the 'Young Turk' party because the nationalists were willing to countenance an agreement with the Arabs whereas Jemal – an old-fashioned pan-Islamist – was not. This time, on 10 May, without consulting Lawrence, who spent much of May at Allenby's headquarters and in Cairo, Feisal replied to Mehmed Jemal with a number of demands.[20] The Ottomans should withdraw all their forces deployed down the Hijaz Railway and in Medina, to Amman. Arab officers serving in the Ottoman Army should be freed to serve in the Arab army, which might in the future fight side by side with the Turks, but under Arab command. Syria's future relations with Turkey, he said, should be along the same lines as the close alliance between Prussia and Austro-Hungary. Finally, food in Syria should be placed under the control of the Arab army.

It is difficult to assess how seriously Feisal made these demands, which were certainly steep. But Mehmed Jemal's overture came at a point when British relations with his father, Sharif Husein, were under strain. The situation was not helped by the fact that Cyril Wilson had been absent from Jeddah for almost half of 1918. He had been struck down by a bad attack of dysentery the previous December, and would spend nearly six months recuperating in Cairo. Husein missed Wilson. 'He evidently likes Wilson very much and trusts him,' reported another British officer, who believed that Wilson's 'transparent honesty and shall we whisper stupidity avail where another man's cleverness would fail'.[21]

Wilson's replacement, J.R. Bassett, was a rather different quantity. By May 1918, he was engaged in a dispute with Husein after the British asked the Sharif's family to use British cyphers in their communications with one another. Husein was suspicious. 'Believe me, my dear lord,' Bassett wrote to him, 'this suggestion was made only to facilitate matters because messages can be put into our cypher in very much fewer groups of figures than is the case in Your Highness's own cypher.'[22] British faith in the security of their own communications had been dented earlier that year by the discovery that the Turks in Maan possessed a foreknowledge of Arab movements verging on the clairvoyant. But besides wanting the Sharif to swap to more sophisticated British codes, the British also wanted easy access to the traffic between the Sharif and his sons, because relations between them were increasingly uneasy. Bassett had already managed to spike a tetchy telegram from Husein to Feisal late in April but the floral language used by the Sharif and the unwieldy Arab cypher created a lot of extra work.

Some bad-tempered telegrams got through. Early in May Feisal was stung by an accusation made by his father that he was wasting money on the Bakri family, prominent Damascus nationalists. The source of this information had in fact been Hogarth, who had remarked to Husein during his January visit to Jeddah – no doubt as a result of Lawrence's own suspicions about Nesib al Bakri – that he thought that spending money on the Bakris was unwise. When Feisal met Joyce and Wilson, who were now both well enough to return to duty, at Abu al Assal on 13 May, he raised his father's complaint and said that he had wanted to travel south to the Hijaz to clear the matter up. Husein, however, refused. In a shrill message Bassett forwarded to Aqaba on 8 May, he told Feisal to 'die at Maan or capture it', before he would countenance seeing him.[23] With relations between the Sharif and Feisal at a new low, Wilson hurried on to Jeddah, promising Feisal he would do his best to persuade the Sharif to change his mind.

The British attitude towards Husein had evolved noticeably during Wilson's absence. British officials in Cairo were increasingly critical of Husein. His determination to rule using Sharia law alienated the more liberal Syrians while his reliance on a few Hijazi officials, which stemmed from his reluctance to confer power to either Iraqi or Syrian Arabs, led to bad government and further eroded support for him in and beyond the Hijaz. Poor government – which Husein's son Abdullah acknowledged was partly due to the incompatibility of the Sharia with modern life – was an ominous advertisement for the Arab state Husein wanted to rule.

On 27 May Wilson met Husein for the first time that year, in Jeddah. He was touched when, to save him climbing the stairs, the Sharif met him halfway down the house where he was staying, rather than in the airy rooftop chamber where he would usually conduct meetings. 'For the most part of the interview the King had an arm round my shoulders, which attitude though affectionate made one rather warm,' reported Wilson.[24]

Meetings with Husein, according to Hogarth, involved 'inevitable endless preambles and recapitulations before we could get to business',[25] and it was only when Wilson met Husein again the following day that he raised the question of whether the Sharif would meet Feisal. When Husein replied that it was an inevitable consequence of war that fathers did not see their sons, Wilson interrupted and asked Husein bluntly why he would not see Feisal. Husein admitted that his real concern was that his son's return to the Hijaz might be interpreted as a sign that he had been defeated. Wilson explained that Feisal wanted to return home to tell his father about his plans and how Ottoman territory would be ruled after the war, and begged Husein to reconsider his decision. Husein relented. Feisal could come home, he said, so long as he returned before the beginning of Ramadan, on 7 June. That afternoon Wilson sent a telegram to Joyce, telling him that Feisal needed to return to Jeddah within the next ten days.

What Wilson did not know was that the British had just agreed a meeting between Feisal and Chaim Weizmann. Weizmann had arrived in Cairo early in April at the head of a Zionist Commission paving the way for Jewish immigration after the war. With his insistence that he wanted not a Jewish government, but simply 'to provide a home for the Jews in the Holy Land',[26] he greatly impressed the British officers. Even Clayton was positive. 'I feel convinced,' he wrote to Sykes after meeting Weizmann, 'that many of the difficulties which we have encountered owing to the mutual distrust and suspicion between Arabs and Jews will now disappear.'[27]

Syrian representatives whom Clayton had met days earlier also seemed amenable to the British government's line that, to realise their own ambitions, the Arabs should support Zionist aspirations too. Though he was adamant that he could not 'conscientiously carry out any line of policy which will go against our pledges to the Arabs', Clayton now felt that a *rapprochement* was possible, 'provided we go very easy and don't scare the Arabs'.[28] That was the hope behind the British decision to introduce Weizmann to Feisal. 'From what I gathered of the Zionist aims, in rather a short conversation, I think there should be no difficulty in establishing a friendly and sympathetic relation between them,' Dawnay told Joyce, explaining that Weizmann would soon be on his way.[29]

Wilson was furious when he belatedly found out that Feisal was meeting Weizmann. He had only just persuaded the Sharif to write to Feisal to explain that he had never accused him of wasting money and he now feared that Husein would explode when he found out that Feisal appeared to be negotiating with the Zionists without his prior approval. The matter was so sensitive that the Arab Bureau asked Wilson simply not to tell Husein about what was going on. When he met Husein again on 31 May, two days later, Wilson told Husein that there was no possibility that Feisal could come before the start of Ramadan, because of military plans.

By now, something else was bothering Husein. 'The King then

suddenly began to talk about his title of "King of the Hijaz" and about his Government being called the Hijaz Government in official correspondence,' Wilson reported.

'Why could not it be called the Arab Government?' Husein asked.

The question startled Wilson. 'I have no idea what made King Husein suddenly open this subject which he has never before discussed at any great length with me,' he wrote to Wingate afterwards.[30] He told Husein that the British government could not recognise an Arab government with Husein at its head, unless he was supported by the other Arab chiefs.

It was only when Wilson met Husein again, on 1 June, that slowly the causes of Husein's anxiety began to emerge. In a three-hour meeting that evening, Husein rehearsed the story of his correspondence with Kitchener and McMahon, claiming that, from Kitchener's first tentative communication in October 1914, he had understood the British to be in favour of restoring an Arab caliphate. Yet his title, King of the Hijaz, was meaningless, he complained, before threatening to resign. 'I have never deceived you or His Majesty's Government and never will,' Husein said, predicting that if no single ruler of Arabia emerged, the consequences would be 'very bad indeed'.[31] When Wilson asked what he would do if the other Arab chiefs did not recognise him, Husein said that he would force them to join a united Arabia. It was a veiled hint that he was prepared to fight Ibn Saud.

British officials had already noticed that Husein was diverting an increasing proportion of the British subsidy towards staving off the threat of Ibn Saud, but Husein's suggestion that he was willing to risk armed conflict with his eastern rival was a deeply worrying development, as it raised the possibility that Feisal might go home to help his father, leaving Allenby's eastern flank exposed.[32] The most likely flashpoint which would turn the tension into war was Khurma, an oasis 120 miles east of Mecca. Ibn Saud had accepted Husein's overlordship of this contested part of inner Arabia eight years earlier, but Husein had now heard that Ibn Saud had begun to tax the Utaybah tribesmen in the area, and the sheikh of the village had just announced that he had converted to Ibn Saud's Wahabi creed. He raised the status of the village with Wilson on 28 May. Faced with a clear challenge to his authority, Husein was blunt.

He now wanted a definite answer as to whether the British government still wanted him 'to maintain his present non-committal and friendly attitude towards Ibn Saud'.[33]

On 5 June Wilson wrote to Wingate. He reminded him how, six months earlier, Hogarth had told Husein that Britain and France were 'determined that the Arab Race shall be given full opportunity of once again forming a nation in the world'. The time was drawing near, he felt, when Britain would have to decide whether to back Husein or Ibn Saud. It seems he was under no illusions that Ibn Saud was the stronger of the two: 'If our policy is now to aim at the formation of an Arab Confederation under King Husein's Suzerainty,' he said, 'we must be prepared for the possibility of a situation developing which would probably prove to be a serious embarrassment to his Majesty's Government.'[34]

Feisal had met Weizmann the previous day, at Waheida, just north of Abu al Assal. When Weizmann explained that he had been sent by the British government to discuss the development of the Jewish interests in Palestine, Feisal, though polite, was stubborn. He was, he explained, acting as his father's agent and so unable to discuss the settlement of Palestine in detail and not, in any case, until Arab affairs were 'more consolidated'. Weizmann went on to say that the creation of a 'Jewish Palestine would be helpful to the development of an Arab Kingdom', which the Jews would support.[35] He reiterated that the Jews did not want their own government, but rather to work under British protection. The *Arab Bulletin* put an optimistic gloss on the 45-minute encounter. 'Some mutual esteem' had been produced, its correspondent claimed, which might help 'when the time for bargaining comes'.[36]

22

PREPARING FOR THE PUSH

(May–June 1918)

On 28 May 1918, a junior German officer named Lieutenant Thalacker took charge of the Hijaz Railway station at Amman. When he arrived, the station was the target of frequent British air-raids. From British records we know that the station was bombed three days after Thalacker arrived, and again on the morning of 11 June. Thirteen aeroplanes took part in that raid, dropping 2,100 pounds of bombs. The pilots claimed twelve direct hits.[1] 'The bombs possessed highly sensitive percussion fuses,' Thalacker reported, 'and, with their splintering effect, almost always led to the loss of lives.'[2] The raids on the station, the nearest major depot to the town of Salt, convinced the local Turkish commander that the British were planning to launch another attack across the Jordan shortly. Thalacker's orders were to ensure that, amid the mounting chaos, the trains on the railway ran on time.

What Lieutenant Thalacker discovered on his arrival disturbed his orderly Teutonic mind. While, north of Amman, the trains ran on schedule, the situation south of Amman could not have been more different. An acute shortage of fuel meant that fewer trains ran, more slowly. Coal stocks were largely exhausted and enormous quantities of timber were needed to run the steam engines: a shunting locomotive burned fifteen tons a day. Wood needed to be brought in from further and further afield, partly as local supplies were felled, partly because the woodcutters were deserting, terrified by the British bombing raids. By the end of the war, olive groves and vineyards were being cut down to keep the trains running. Between May and August that year, the amount of freight carried by rail fell by two-thirds.[3]

Water shortages were also a problem. On the 160-mile stretch from Dara south to Al Hasa, there was only abundant water at Amman. South of Amman, Arab attacks and drought meant that the available water was not enough to meet the needs of the troops stationed along the line, let alone the locomotives. By the time Thalacker arrived at the end of May, only a shuttle service operated between Amman and Al Hasa, seventy-five miles away. The frequency of attacks on the railway beyond Al Hasa had made it impossible to travel any further south by train. Twenty-five bridges were destroyed in Arab raids, orchestrated by Young, Peake and Hornby, during 1–19 May. 'The continued blowing up of bridges and rails was sensibly felt,' the German general Liman von Sanders remarked after the war, 'because repair material was becoming scarce.'[4]

Inadequate supplies of fuel and water were not the only obstacles to a punctual timetable. 'Never have I seen such a loathsome crew of debauched, brutalised scoundrels as the permanent staff of the Hijaz railway,' Mark Sykes had written following his visit to the region before the war.[5] At a halt on his way down to Madain Salih at around the same time, the archaeologist Antonin Jaussen watched the driver and mechanic of his train polish off a bottle of the fiery aniseed spirit arak in a little over three-quarters of an hour.[6] In Syria, the local governor punished miscreants by setting them to work on the track south of Dara. The legacy of this draconian sentencing policy, Thalacker observed, was that the further south one went, the more unreliable the railway staff became. Trains travelling south would become progressively more delayed because, following the need for tighter security after the increase in Arab attacks, each station telegraphed the next station down the line to let it know a train was on its way. No train was allowed to depart until an answer from that station was received, sometimes hours later, confirming that the line ahead was safe. Dependent on staff whose main characteristic, according to Thalacker, was their 'lack of punctuality and interest', this safeguard meant that idling locomotives frequently ran out of steam while they waited for clearance to continue on their way.

Battling Turkish resistance, Thalacker managed to make some changes. 'Delays which were up to 10 hours could now be reduced to 1–2 hours,' he reported proudly. He successfully supervised the delivery

of enough water down the line that July to supply a force of 3,000
Turkish troops and their pack animals at Qatranah, fifty miles south of
Amman, which was being prepared to deal with the Arabs.

Lawrence, who had spent much of May in Cairo and at Allenby's
headquarters in Palestine, knew that the continuing Turkish presence at
Qatranah threatened the Arabs further south and Allenby's eastern flank.
Allenby shared his fear. Having failed to capture the farming uplands
east of the Jordan in time for that year's harvest, he now warned the new
Chief of Imperial General Staff, Sir Henry Wilson, that, with replenished
supplies, the Turks might now advance southwards from Amman. If they
recaptured the Dead Sea area, Allenby warned, they would recapture the
Hijaz because the Arabs would sue for peace. He feared the reverberations
that this would cause in an increasingly unstable Egypt: 'Whatever
strategical purists may say about side shows, you are committed deeply
here,' he warned Wilson in mid-June: 'and if you lose Egypt, you lose the
Empire which hinges thereon.'[7]

The reason for this dire warning was that Allenby was deeply
concerned about the political situation in Egypt and, in particular,
about the enemy propaganda that was circulating. 'It is fairly believed, by
the majority in Egypt, that the English and French are beaten in Europe;
and that those of our troops who are not removed from Egypt in time,
will be made prisoners here at the end of the war,' he reported that June.[8]
Britain's Indian troops, according to the rumours, would be left behind,
sacrificed to cover the retreat.

There was disconcerting confirmation that Turkish propaganda was
working when a handful of Muslim Indian soldiers crossed to Turkish
lines, early in June. Allenby immediately withdrew the other members of
their unit to work behind the front line, but he remained disturbed by
the fact that his Muslim troops were often within earshot of the Ottoman
Army's muezzins, who would proclaim the call to prayer loudly across no
man's land. He knew that in future he would depend increasingly on
Indian troops, more than a quarter of whom were Muslims. During
Lawrence's stay, Allenby had been digesting news that he would have to
send back a total of 60,000 British troops to fight in France. Just one
trained, 'all white' division would be untouched. Nine out of twelve

battalions in each of the other six were recalled to France. The War Office
promised that these would be replaced, but with Indian troops whose
training and battlefield experience Allenby felt was considerably weaker
and who, he feared, were vulnerable to Turkish subversion. Deeply
opposed to the changeover, Allenby pleaded to Sir Henry Wilson: 'I
cannot urge you too strongly; not to carry out this project, in this
country, at this time.'[9] He was ignored.

Indeed, Allenby was under relentless political pressure to make further
territorial gains. As had long been anticipated, the Russians had made
peace with the Germans in March that year. Shortly afterwards Sir Henry
Wilson's predecessor Robertson had raised the need 'to establish a barrier
to German progress eastwards' through a combination of Japanese
intervention in Siberia, continued pressure on the Palestine and Mesopotamia fronts and support for anti-Bolshevik forces in the Caucasus.[10]
Wilson's ambitions were grander still: 'I want to see Aleppo joined to
Mosul joined to Baku joined to the Urals joined to the Japanese army;
and from that base an advance against the Boches,' he proposed to
Allenby late in May, desperate for pressure on the Germans' eastern front
that would curb their seemingly relentless westward advance.[11] There
was no chance of an advance during high summer but, to meet the
demand for rapid headway northwards as soon as the hot season had
passed, Allenby reorganised his forces, disbanding the Imperial Camel
Corps but increasing the number of mounted divisions from three to
four.[12]

Having heard about the reorganisation, at headquarters one evening
over dinner Lawrence asked Allenby for 2,000 camels.

'What do you want them for?' asked Allenby.

'To put a thousand men into Dara any day you please,' Lawrence
boldly told 'The Bull', who rapidly agreed.[13]

In *Seven Pillars of Wisdom*, Lawrence outlined the plan he had conceived
and put to Allenby. By attacking Dara, he hoped to force the Turks to
pull one or even two divisions back from Palestine to secure their line of
communications and attack the Arabs at Azraq. This would enable
Allenby to press forward and capture Nablus, thirty miles north of
Jerusalem. The possession of Nablus, Lawrence believed, would make

Salt 'a dangerous salient' which Mehmed Jemal, the Turkish commander in charge of troops east of the Jordan, would be reluctant to defend. He would be forced to retire to Amman where his forces would be cut off from Damascus by Arab demolitions on the railway around Dara.

Allenby liked the idea of an Arab raid on Dara, which he thought would help deceive Liman von Sanders into thinking he would attack across the Jordan again. He 'quite realises now that the proposition must be regarded in the light of a gamble', Dawnay explained to Joyce, 'and, as a gamble, he is prepared to take it on, so that we can now set to work, and do what we can, with easy consciences.'[14]

The problem with the plan was time. It would take about a month to ferry the camels to Aqaba, and a further two to change their diet. In Palestine, the camels were fed on barley, and Lawrence knew that to survive on the steppe in Syria, they would have to learn to graze on thorny scrub. While they did so, the Arabs would need to keep the Turks at bay by maintaining operations against the railway.

At dawn on 23 May Sharif Nasir's tribesmen, with Peake and Hornby, attacked Al Hasa station, forty-five miles north of Maan, and destroyed four miles of track, the points and the station's well and water tower, which provided the only year-round water supply between Amman and Maan stations, 150 miles apart.[15] The following day Nasir moved on and attacked Faraifra, a halt on the line a few miles to the north. While Lawrence ventured into the Madaba area to gauge local support for his planned September advance northwards, early in June Hornby attacked the bridges north of Faraifra. By now both Hornby and Peake were desperately short of food and explosives. 'I am sick with those blasted Bedouin pinching all your rations,' Joyce wrote to Hornby on 2 June, in a letter accompanying three tins of Nestlé milk and a packet of tea, in which he urged Hornby to keep going for just a little longer. 'If we keep the line cut North I think we must get Maan,' he added, promising Hornby a 'liberal ration of rum' as soon as he could send it.[16] He had, he admitted, already sent Peake all the cigarettes he could lay his hands on. Peake probably needed them more: on one occasion he had only escaped being captured by the Turks by hanging on to the tail of the horse of one of his Arab helpers, and being pulled for half a mile.[17]

With the railway south of Amman now effectively wrecked as a result of Hornby's and Peake's exploits, the Arabs now turned their attention to inflicting a decisive blow against Jurf ad Darawish station, where 400 Turks continued to hold out.[18] Dawnay wrote to Joyce on 12 June, willing the Jurf raid to be a success. The removal of the Turks there, he said, would 'very usefully extend our elbow room for future dirty work north of Maan, and it will also add greatly to our own security by compelling the Turk to make his own base, for any operations he may undertake for the relief of Maan, at a respectable distance'.[19]

Dawnay had also spent some time reconsidering the question of which British officers should be attached to the Arab forces. Following his run-in with Young, he decided that Young's 'present nominal position as understudy to Lawrence has never . . . really panned out entirely satisfactorily, and I am not sure, taking the personal factor into account, that it is ever likely to'.[20] Instead he proposed making Young responsible for the logistics that would now be critical to the Arabs' push north to Dara. At the same time he advocated swapping Maynard, an officer who had been working on demolitions south of Maan, for Frank Stirling. Stirling, a bon vivant on the pre-war Cairo social circuit, who spoke Arabic and had since worked in intelligence, 'would be just the fellow to send off stunting with the circus', Dawnay believed, freeing Joyce to concentrate on running 'the whole show' and Lawrence to run 'his peculiar brand of Lawrentian stunt and carrying on as usual'.[21] Joyce was reluctant to lose Maynard, but agreed with Dawnay's suggestion for Young, who, he said, had 'put everyone's back up in Aqaba'.[22]

Lawrence's clandestine tour through the settled communities in the hills east of the Jordan was not encouraging. Seemingly drawing on his impressions, on 11 June the *Arab Bulletin* reported that, discouraged by the failure of the two raids east of the Jordan, 'Most of the tribesmen, who own lands, have been compelled to patch up a peace with the Turks and hold their hand till better times.'[23] In Karak, the Majali, that family of infamous troublemakers who had previously courted Feisal, were 'pro-Turk' and 'now supreme'. Not only that, they had raised a force of 400 locals to defend the town against attack by Feisal's men. Feisal's failure to attract the townspeople to join the revolt reflected the ongoing, essential divide between the nomadic and settled ways of life – the desert and the sown. It was a difference mirrored within his army: Nuri Said's attack on Jurf ad Darawish, which took place on 10 June, was again handicapped by rivalry between the regular forces, comprising Arab volunteers from the settled lands, and the Bedu tribesmen on the raid, and degenerated into an inconclusive artillery duel with the Turks, from which Nuri was forced to withdraw.

After further reflection, from Cairo – where he went after his journey through the Jordan uplands – Lawrence wrote a gloomy, longer account. The two Abu Tayi sheikhs, Auda and Mohammed al Dheilan, he reported, had fallen out. Their Huwaytat tribesmen were tired of fighting and rich enough from British gold to be averse to taking further risks.[24] Auda himself had decided that he too was a sharif, and had begun building a mud-brick palace at Jafr, roofed with telegraph poles from the railway line. The Huwaytat's rivals the Bani Atiyah from the south of Maan were similarly exhausted, and would shortly be retired. To the north, the Bani Sakhr, who had let down the British in the second attack on Salt, though not sympathetic to the Turks, were still taking payment from them. They were demanding £30,000 a month from Feisal in return for that year's barley crop, a sum that Feisal simply could not afford. The Rwala sheikh Nuri Shaalan appeared to be profiting from illicit trade between Kuwait and Damascus and showed no signs of warming more to Feisal. There were also unwelcome signs of sectarianism. In the largely Christian town of Madaba twenty miles south-west of Amman, Lawrence discovered there had been celebrations at the news that the inhabitants of Salt had been violently punished by the Turks following the British withdrawal. The only way to raise the agricultural communities east of the Jordan, he decided, was to send a force of several thousand Arabs to help them, once Allenby's advance began.

Further work was also needed to reassure several influential Syrians who had approached the Arab Bureau in Cairo with concerns about the future status of their country. 'Nothing hampers so greatly our local relations with the existing non-Jewish inhabitants of Palestine, as the vagueness of our declaration in favour of Zionism,' an article in the *Arab*

Bulletin, probably written by Hogarth, had stated three months earlier.[25]

Following several days of secretive discussions, on 16 June Lawrence, Hogarth and Wingate offered the Syrians a commitment from the British government, which they hoped would address their apprehensions. The 'Declaration to the Seven Arabs', as the document became known, recognised four types of territory in the region and explained British policy on each. The Declaration committed the British government to recognise the 'complete and sovereign independence' of territories that had either been in Arab hands before the war or had been liberated by the Arabs since. Territory liberated by the Allied armies would be governed according to the 'principle of the consent of the governed'. This policy, the document declared unequivocally, 'will always be that of His Majesty's Government'. Finally, in territory still under Turkish control, the British desired that 'the oppressed peoples . . . should obtain their freedom and independence', before paying tribute to those engaged in the struggle to liberate those regions and offering them 'every support' in their efforts.[26]

On 21 June, Lawrence left for Jeddah in the hope of meeting Sharif Husein. He wanted the Sharif's permission to divert some of the Arabs fighting with Abdullah and Ali to the force he envisaged operating in the settled agricultural belt east of the Jordan. But Husein proved unwilling. Using Ramadan as his excuse, he refused to leave Mecca to meet Lawrence. All Lawrence could do was write a letter praising Husein's achievements, but obliquely pointing out that Feisal would need three times the number of men he had if he was to achieve Husein's demand to capture Maan, which was defended by 4,000 well-entrenched Turks. Explaining that the railway south of Maan had now been permanently cut, he tried to encourage Husein to release troops from the Hijaz for service further north. Worried by the rise of Ibn Saud, Husein ignored the hint.

Days earlier Wilson had received a letter from Husein. In it the Sharif, who had been ruminating over the implications of his previous discussion with Wilson, wondered whether Wilson laughed at him for signing letters 'King of the Arab countries', while Wilson addressed him as 'King of Hijaz'.[27] Wilson replied quickly the following day to say that he certainly did not. Husein knew why he styled himself as he did, Wilson wrote, just as he knew why Wilson had to refer to him as King of Hijaz. 'I personally believe that after this war the world will see some new titles appear and some old titles disappear,' Wilson added encouragingly, 'but we must entirely defeat our enemies before such matters can be usefully discussed.'[28]

Husein was unmoved. On 26 June he announced that he intended to resign. 'If Your Highness resigns,' Wilson hurriedly replied two days later, 'I personally think the effect on the Arab Cause would be very bad indeed – "*Without the key stone the arch falls*" – and I can only assure you that as far as HM's Government is concerned there is nothing they have done or intend to do to justify your resignation.'[29]

While Lawrence was in Jeddah, unexpected good news of a sort arrived from Joyce at Abu al Assal. On 18 June Turkish aeroplanes had bombed Nuri Shaalan's camp at Azraq, causing several casualties. 'Situation in North developing rapidly,' Joyce's message read, explaining that both Nuri Shaalan and his son had written to Feisal offering their services.[30] Could Lawrence urgently go to Aqaba, Joyce asked, to discuss plans which might require a 'large increase in foodstuff and ammunition'?

Lawrence seems to have been strangely ambivalent. He replied that he planned to return to Suez on 6 July and that his plan thereafter was 'probably to operate [in] Bani Sakhr country', if Husein continued to block his attempt to draw reinforcements from the Hijaz and the Turks dispatched a relief force to Maan from Qatranah. Even then, he said, he was prepared for a couple of months' delay. In a letter to an old friend shortly afterwards he shed light on his mood, suggesting that his increasingly equivocal attitude stemmed from his feeling that what was going on around him was unreal:

It's a kind of foreign stage on which one plays day and night, in fancy dress, in a strange language, with the price of failure on one's head if the part is not well filled . . . Whether we are going to win or lose, when we do strike, I cannot ever persuade myself. The whole thing is such a play, and one cannot put conviction into one's day dreams . . . Achievement, if it comes, will be a great disillusionment, but not great enough to wake one up.[31]

He also described the intense feeling of listlessness that inclined him to be awkward:

> I change my abode every day, and my job every two days, and my language every three days, and still remain always unsatisfied. I hate being in front, and I hate being back and I don't like responsibility, and I don't obey orders. Altogether no good just now. A long quiet like a purge, and then a contemplation and decision of future roads, that is what to look forward to.

Knowing that Hornby and Peake were also exhausted, Joyce was starting to worry that operations against the railway north of Maan were flagging. He was annoyed by Lawrence's languid reply to his urgent call to return to Aqaba and let off steam to Dawnay. He was, he said, annoyed that Dawnay and Lawrence had conceived the Dara raid without involving him at all – even though he was supposedly in charge of British operations with the Arabs. He was also uncertain whether he would be able to meet the demands of the plan they had concocted with the resources he had to hand.

Jafar Pasha was also becoming restive. He asked the British to supply gas shells in an attempt to end Turkish resistance at Maan more quickly. Dawnay – who had been wounded on the Western Front – instantly voiced his opposition to the scheme. 'Personally, I am very much opposed to the idea of introducing western frightfulness into our very gentle-manly little war,' he said, predicting that the Turks would only retaliate in kind: 'one cylinder let loose on the Arab army unprotected would finish off the whole show for good in half an hour.'[32]

Dawnay also belatedly tried to smooth over the situation with Joyce. 'You may now feel absolutely assured,' he wrote to Joyce, 'that in future no scheme or plan will receive official sanction and approval unless and until examined and recommended by yourself.'[33] But unexpected events would force him to break this promise within two weeks.

23

HOLDING OPERATIONS

(July–August 1918)

On 13 July, using a mainly German force, Liman von Sanders launched a surprise counterattack on Allenby's bridgehead on the east bank of the Jordan, just to the north-east of Jericho. The German general later admitted that the assault, which was beaten off the following day by Australian troops, revealed the decline in the quality of his Turkish forces. But his belligerent move unsettled Dawnay, who feared that if Liman von Sanders were to press an attack of similar strength against the Arabs east of the Jordan, he would annihilate Feisal's force, leaving Allenby's flank exposed and ruining Allenby's plans for an autumn offensive.[1] He began to think urgently about a scheme that would discourage Liman von Sanders from attacking again.

Five days after the German attack was repelled, Frank Stirling landed at Aqaba to join the Arabs' operations. He arrived with a letter for Joyce from Dawnay. 'Frankly I am nervous about the next four weeks,' Dawnay explained, before gingerly revealing plans for a 'stunt' using the Imperial Camel Corps to attack Mudawwarah and demolish the railway viaduct at Kissir, just south of Amman.[2] Having promised only a fortnight earlier that he would involve Joyce in any future military planning, Dawnay admitted that the scheme, which he had hurriedly drawn up with Lawrence without consulting Joyce at all, was 'simply to keep the Turks occupied on the line and to bridge over the dangerous period till we are ready to set the tribes in motion'. The surprise appearance of the ICC east of the Jordan was designed to force the Turks on the defensive, while the 175-mile distance between the two proposed targets would reinforce the impression that more than one British force was scouting the area in advance of an autumn offensive across the Jordan. Interestingly, to ensure that there was no chance that the Turks would receive any prior warning of the attacks, Dawnay asked Joyce not to mention the plans to Feisal.

This raid ran roughshod over the arrangements for the Dara raid which Hubert Young, now fully recovered from the intimate injury he had acquired from camel-riding, had spent the previous fortnight devising. Dawnay tried to soften the impact of the change of plan by advising Joyce to take no action until headquarters had officially approved the scheme, but the telegram from headquarters giving the go-ahead arrived in Aqaba the same day as his letter. 'Joyce and I discussed this telegram with some grinding of teeth,'[3] Young recalled. It must have been particularly galling to both men. Joyce had only just been told, in a throwaway line from Dawnay, that 'only the man on the spot can really judge of what the actual situation demands. In that, more power to you – and all good luck.'[4] Young had spent the previous fortnight working on a meticulous plan to supply a raiding force of more than 650 men for thirty-five days in the desert, only to watch it abruptly discarded by Dawnay before it had even been considered at headquarters.

It was up to Lawrence, who flew in to Abu al Assal on 29 July, to give Young's idea the *coup de grâce*. 'Young and Joyce were not best pleased when I returned to say that the great schedule had been torn up,' he recalled afterwards.[5] Lawrence, however, was able to add the important news that could not be revealed in the telegram: Allenby had just decided to bring forward his offensive into September, ruining the timescale on which Young's carefully thought-out schedule was based.[6] 'This put a different complexion on the matter,' Young admitted, 'though it did not explain why Joyce had been saddled with the ICC without having been consulted.'[7] Joyce opposed the appearance of so many white troops in the Arabs' camp at Aqaba. Although Lawrence would later snidely remark that Joyce's view was 'an untimely victory of my principles so preached from Yanbu',[8] he had himself vetoed Joyce's call for the ICC a year earlier, and there were good reasons for Joyce's concern. That April a young British soldier had been fatally wounded in Wadi Itm after a dispute with a tribesman over water, and more recently an intelligence officer who had stopped to urinate along the road to Abu al Assal had been stabbed and robbed by a Bedu. Joyce feared that the arrival of the ICC might lead to further casualties. The argument, however, was academic because the ICC had already set out from Suez across the Sinai four days earlier. The following day the 314 men rode into Aqaba on their swift, white Sudanese camels. 'As we emerged into the flat Wadi Araba we heard the firing of rifles and wondered if Aqaba was being attacked,' one of the ICC's officers recalled. 'To our amazement some mounted Arabs galloped towards us on their rough looking ponies, their clothes flying in all directions, greeting us with cries and rifle shots.'[9]

Lawrence came to Aqaba from Abu al Assal to meet the men of the ICC and their leader, Robin Buxton. A former county cricketer, Buxton likened the raid to 'an attempt on the part of the Huns to blow up Waterloo Bridge', in terms of the distance the ICC would have to cover to reach the viaduct at Kissir and its proximity to the Turkish headquarters in Amman.[10] By the time that Lawrence arrived, tension within the camp among the seashore palm groves was already rising – just as Joyce feared it would. Unused to the 'rattle of musketry'[11] constant in the Arabs' camp, the soldiers thought they had been shot at while bathing in the sea that afternoon and, after further gunfire that night, several soldiers had been about to go and deal with the Arabs with some hand grenades when Lawrence suddenly appeared. 'He stood in the middle of the square, flung back his *aba*,* showing his white undergarment, and, illumined by the countless fires, raised his hand,' one soldier remembered. 'Immediately the firing ceased, the hubbub died down and we had a peaceful night.'[12]

The following evening, 'after supper Lawrence gathered the men around the fire and gave them the straightest talk I have ever heard,' remembered Frank Stirling, who was accompanying the expedition.[13] To soldiers used to the formal hierarchy of conventional operations, his speech was 'a most unusual experience' because only rarely would an officer take his men into his confidence. The ICC left for Mudawwarah early the following morning.

* *Aba*: cloak.

By 7 August, a scorching day at the height of summer, the ICC were within forty miles of Mudawwarah. During the day, some of the officers set out in two cars to reconnoitre the station, crawling up a wadi for the last few hundred yards until they reached a point offering a good view of the Turkish defences. 'We . . . even caught a glimpse of the fat garrison commander as he ambled about on his mule,' recalled Stirling.[14] Returning to the ICC camp late that night, the officers briefed the soldiers, and the force set out straightaway. The moon was new, and the ICC were able to approach the station unobserved.

The Camel Corps' attack began with a noisy diversion west of Mudawwarah in the small hours the following morning that drew Turkish troops away from the station, which was then rapidly captured along with the southernmost of the three redoubts guarding the line. By dawn the Turks only held out in the most northerly redoubt. They were better defended with artillery and machine-guns, and would not be successfully assaulted by the lightly armed raiders alone. The British had allowed for this in their plans, however, and once it was light, aircraft from the Royal Flying Corps appeared from the west to bomb the remaining redoubt. 'I had the job of controlling what must have been one of the first ground-to-air controlled bombardments,' claimed Laurence Moore, a signaller with the Camel Corps. The planes communicated with Moore by klaxon in Morse code; Moore replied with letter signals on the ground in an arranged code. The biplanes each dropped a couple of bombs in the redoubt; 'the Turks came streaming out, waving any dirty rag that could serve as a white flag, and I gave the planes the signal "Cease Fire",' Moore recalled.[15] The ICC captured the station and its fortifications at a loss of six men dead, and a further seven wounded, including one of the officers, Joe Lyall, who lost the tip of one thumb to a Turkish bullet which also broke his arm.[16] More than twenty Turks were killed; the remainder, 130 in all, were taken prisoner. Finally, the vital water tower at Mudawwarah was blown up. A copy of a photograph taken in the aftermath, which shows its diced masonry scattered across the desolate valley floor, can be found today among Lawrence's photographs in the Bodleian Library in Oxford, together with his dry caption: 'Showing as much of the water tower as could be got into the finder of the camera after Scott-Higgins had finished it.'[17] Without this crucial water supply, a railway journey from Maan to Medina was now impossible.

Lawrence, however, had not witnessed the Mudawwarah attack himself. The day before Buxton's men attacked the station, he had flown from Quwayrah to the shimmering mudflat at Jafr for a meeting with Nuri Shaalan to pave the way for the Dara raid the following month. Tested to its limits by the hot summer air, the biplane that was carrying him only narrowly scraped over the Abu al Assal ridge, and for a moment Lawrence wondered whether he might die. He was not looking forward to the encounter, because he faced questioning from Nuri Shaalan on the Sykes-Picot and Balfour agreements, news of both of which had emerged since they had last met at Azraq in June the previous year.

When Lawrence arrived, Nuri asked the question he had been anticipating. 'Old Nuri Shaalan, wrinkling his wise nose, returned to me with his file of documents, asking in puzzlement which of them all he might believe.'[18]

'The last in date,' Lawrence replied, pointing to the Declaration to the Seven Arabs, made in Cairo seven weeks before, which committed the British government to respecting the independence of Arab-liberated territory and self-determination.[19]

Nuri Shaalan's 'sense of the honour of his word made him see the humour', Lawrence later wrote. 'Ever after he did his best for us, only warning me, whenever he failed in a promise, that he had superseded it by a later intention.'[20] The following day, Nuri announced his intent to back the Arabs.[21]

'We wanted no rice-converts. Persistently we did refuse to let our abundant and famous gold bring over those not spiritually convinced,'[22] Lawrence later claimed. But the economic grounds for backing the Arab movement were now compelling to Nuri, because the Turks had lost control of trade in the region. The railway raids in May and June disrupted Turkish influence and British gold was making Aqaba a magnet for trade to, and from, the Hauran. By mid-August, a German diplomat in Damascus observed that 'For about two months an organised caravan traffic has existed from Aqaba across the Hauran . . . Sugar, coffee and cotton goods are imported, and apricot paste is exported, together with great quantities of grain.'[23] The British would buy cereals with gold, and could offer goods which had been scarce in Syria for moderate prices. Among the beneficiaries of this trade was Nuri Shaalan. 'Things have got to such a pass,' the German noted despairingly, 'that it is almost impossible for the Turks to get grain from the Hauran. Only the places on the Western outskirts towards Dara still deliver supplies to us.'[24]

Nuri Shaalan's pledge of support contrasted with the increasingly fraught situation in the Hijaz. Three weeks earlier, Husein's dispute with Ibn Saud over the Khurma oasis had looked set to boil over into open warfare, just as the British had feared it would. Husein had arrived in Jeddah on 18 July, demanding to know whether Britain supported his leadership of Arabia. 'I told the King,' Wilson wrote afterwards, 'that, so far as I knew, His Majesty's Government, whilst expressing a strong hope and desire for eventual Arab Union, had never guaranteed the formation of an Arab Kingdom under the Kingship or Suzerainty of himself or any other individual.'[25] The British, he went on, had approached Husein because he was 'accessible' and 'renowned' and 'well fitted to act as spokesman for the Arabs generally'.[26]

This answer was hardly reassuring to Husein, who then again threatened to resign. This situation, already serious, became worse when Wilson discovered that the Sharif had dispatched Shakir, the Bedu sharif who had accompanied Lawrence on his first trip to the railway the year before, with a force armed with machine-guns, to reimpose his authority over the contested oasis. Worrying that the Khurma dispute might undermine the Arabs' plans in Syria, on 20 July Wilson was forced to confront Husein about the purpose of Shakir's mission and Husein's willingness to use force.

Husein reacted angrily. According to Wilson, he 'said he was sick of the subject, was obstinate in refusing to understand my point and finally lost his temper'.[27]

'Am I a fool?' Husein demanded: 'I am not a child in politics, and the last thing I want is a state of open hostilities between Ibn Saud and myself.' Yet when Wilson suggested he write to Ibn Saud to calm the situation, Husein refused, on the grounds that such an approach would only reduce his own authority in the eyes of his rival, and again offered to resign.[28] Wilson refused to accept his offer and, following the meeting, on 24 July the British government sent a message to Husein confirming what Wilson had said.[29] Realising that he could not call on British support to see him recognised as the ruler of all Arabia, four days later Husein gave his resignation in writing, announcing that he would not do any work not related to his own private affairs.[30]

Wilson's colleague Bassett suspected that the 'increasingly nervous and highly-strung' Husein was trying to bluff Britain into backing him, because he knew that the British could not afford to let the Arab movement collapse at such a critical moment.[31] Yet both Bassett and Wilson were well aware that infighting between Husein and Ibn Saud would shatter the illusion of Arab unity which was so vital to the campaign further north. An urgent gesture was needed to mollify Husein, who was threatening to withdraw Arab troops from Syria to deal with the situation in Khurma, after Shakir's force was routed by the local tribesmen. Bassett felt that a 'definite assurance' from the government that Britain wanted to see a 'United Arabia under one supreme Head' would be enough to postpone the friction over Khurma until after the British offensive was under way.

Whitehall rapidly obliged. At the beginning of August Bassett wrote to Husein, enclosing the text of a declaration which, as he explained, accepted Husein's assurances to Wilson that he simply wanted to restore the situation in Khurma, before warning him that 'Your Highness knows that there are mischievous people who, for their own ends would be glad to see trouble between Your Highness and Ibn Saud, and that Turkish influence is probably behind them'.[32] Finally, he added, the government could not 'regard seriously a decision of abdication taken by your Highness under a mistaken impression that Your Highness had lost the confidence of HMG', when in fact, 'HMG regard your leadership of the Arab movement in the war as vitally necessary'.

'You know, as well as I do, that my operations depend entirely on the cooperation of the Hijaz Arabs,' Allenby wrote to Sir Henry Wilson in

London on 12 August, commenting on the potential for a shortage of gold to upset his plans. He was just as sensitive to the danger posed by Husein's increasingly beligerent attitude towards Ibn Saud. Warning Wilson on 14 August that, if further violence flared in Khurma, Ibn Saud would probably give Husein 'a hammering' which 'might, conceivably, draw Feisal away South; to support his father',[33] Allenby argued that Britain must openly back Husein and bully Ibn Saud into withdrawing his supporters from the oasis immediately, until the question of the boundary between the men's lands could be settled.[34] The Cabinet agreed, accepting that Husein had sent the force 'to suppress a rebellious subject', and proposed to arbitrate a frontier between Husein and Ibn Saud after the war was over.[35] Tensions in central Arabia were temporarily suppressed.

By this time, Lawrence had returned to Jafr to join Buxton's Camel Corps, who had marched northwards after raiding Mudawwarah. Buxton confirmed his plan to continue onwards to Kissir and arranged for Lawrence to accompany the ICC northwards into tribal territory. He was already convinced by Lawrence's expertise, writing in his diary: 'One has that feeling that things can not go wrong while he is there.'[36] Nevertheless, he arrived at Bair to find that half of the rations which Young had arranged had already been pilfered. 'Plans had to be quickly revised,' wrote Buxton. 'I have had to send back one officer and fifty men and a hundred camels as I can't feed them . . . with the remainder we shall make a dash for it.'[37] After a second day at Bair – Lawrence's thirtieth birthday – the ICC left for the Kissir viaduct.

Over the next four days, the men of the Camel Corps rode towards Amman. They would start at about three or four in the morning, ride until six, stop for two hours, and ride until ten, when they would stop for a long halt during the hottest part of the day, before setting out again at three. During one midday stop Moore, who was sitting under a shelter made from an army blanket, trying to shield himself from the sun, noticed that an armed Arab appeared to be stalking Lawrence, who was sitting under a similar shelter, reading.

The Arab flattened out to take aim and I grabbed for a gun but he beat me to it and fired. The bullet sent up a flurry of sand and feathers about a yard from where Lawrence lay, and the Arab calmly walked forward and picked up the shattered remnants of a small sandgrouse, which he had blown to bits, and carried them away. Lawrence merely raised his head for a moment and then resumed his reading.[38]

On 20 August, as the ICC reached a ruined palace at Muwaqqar, fifteen miles south-east of Amman, they were overflown by two Turkish aeroplanes. On arrival at the ruins, Buxton, Lawrence and the other officers discussed their options. It seemed likely that the pilots would have identified the soldiers, and that the Turks would reinforce Kissir bridge. Arabs who had scouted ahead brought more bad news: Turkish soldiers had arrived in force in the villages between Muwaqqar and the railway to enforce the collection of taxes, which followed each year's harvest. There were also Bedu encamped in the area, and Lawrence was concerned that, if the raid went ahead, the tribesmen and their families might become the Turks' target for recriminations, with political consequences which would outweigh the benefits of blowing up the bridge.

Buxton worried that they might be attacked by a large force of cavalry from Amman.[39] The ICC had only been lent to help the Arabs on the understanding that, in Lawrence's opinion, the casualties would be 'infinitesimal',[40] and Lawrence knew that during a night attack it was inevitable that the force would suffer some, possibly considerable, losses. Reluctantly, they decided to pull back to Azraq.

There was one last task. 'We were to make the Turks aware of our presence and give them the impression that we were a much larger force than in fact we were,' recalled Moore.[41] Each man was ordered to open three or four tins of bully beef, eat or burn the contents and litter the ground with the empty tins. Meanwhile, the cars that accompanied the force drove furiously around the area to leave a muddle of criss-crossing tracks. The cameleers also dropped the animals' dung that they conserved for fuel, to suggest that there had been many more camels in the vicinity. Then the ICC headed through the darkness east towards Azraq, stopping *en route* at Qasr Amrah, where the officers slept under its domed ceilings' frescoes of cavorting, naked women, painted to arouse the Umayyad caliphs thirteen hundred years before.

The following day, 22 August, the ICC arrived at Azraq, but the oasis in midsummer was not as hospitable as Lawrence remembered it. Grey, green-eyed flies with a bite 'like the sharp end of a drawing pin'[42] plagued men and camels alike. 'Our stay was poisoned by the grey flies, and then ruined by a tragic accident,' remembered Lawrence, referring to the moment when Robert Rowan, a young Scottish intelligence officer attached to the ICC, was shot dead.[43] Although his death was reported as an accident which happened when an Arab dropped his loaded rifle while shooting fish, Moore did not agree. 'I was close to Rowan at the time and saw and heard him raise his sjambok and curse them [the Bedu] in what we used to call Cairo Arabic. The Arabs muttered and slunk away and a little later there was a shot from the rim of the crowd which killed him instantly,' Moore claimed later, believing that the real circumstances were covered up for reasons of political expediency.[44]

Accident or not, the ICC left the following morning southwards towards Bair. By the end of August they had returned to Beersheba. Allenby's great deception plan, of which they were a part, was working. At the end of August, a German Army officer attached to the Ottoman Eighth Army, which covered the coastal section of the front, concluded that 'The general situation leads one to expect that in the event of not being too pre-occupied on the Western Front, the English will carry out this autumn, like last year, a well-prepared attack, whose strategic objective would be primarily Dara and its political objective Damascus.'[45] If its officers thought that the brunt of Allenby's attack would be directed east of its lines, the Eighth Army was in for a terrible surprise. While Allenby made final preparations for his attack, all that was needed was for the Arabs in southern Syria to hold their positions. But even that ambition, simple as it was, was about to be tested, almost to breaking point.

24

THE DARA RAID

(August–September 1918)

Far to the south in Mecca, on 19 August the *Qibla* newspaper, which was controlled by Husein, published an unexpected announcement about Jafar Pasha. Jafar, the *Qibla* stated, had never been the commander-in-chief of Husein's Northern Army. He was 'undertaking the supervision of a section of that army and no more'.[1]

News of the *Qibla*'s announcement nearly caused the complete collapse of Feisal's army when it became known at Abu al Assal. Though, years later, Jafar airily claimed that 'Ranks, titles and appointments had never featured among my ambitions',[2] Alec Kirkbride remembered that at the time Jafar 'took deep offence . . . refused to do any work, and spent most of his time in his tent smoking a *nargileh*'.[3]

Joyce, who saw translations of every telegram, was 'seriously alarmed', according to Kirkbride.[4] The same day that the *Qibla* had been published, he had received a message that the date of Allenby's offensive had been brought forward and that the Arab raids must take place no later than 16 September. Precise timing for the raid on Dara was crucial. Allenby wanted the Arabs to attack the railway junction three days before the beginning of his own offensive. He hoped that the raid on the railway junction would confirm that the British attack would take place across the Jordan, drawing the Turks in that direction, and away from the Mediterranean coast, where in fact he planned to strike.

The news of the change of plan was 'another fearful shock' to Young because it left his transport arrangements in turmoil.[5] To strike Dara on 16 September, he calculated, the two convoys of baggage camels which were needed would have to leave Aqaba on 26 and 28 August.[6] Allenby's change of plan meant that there were only seven days left in which to make these columns ready, and, in the meantime, the political problem created by Husein's announcement in the *Qibla* still had to be addressed.

While Lawrence and Joyce worked feverishly to undo the damage that Husein had caused, in Aqaba Young hurriedly prepared the supply convoys for their departure to Azraq: 'The place was one seething, snarling, sweating mass of camels and Arabs, each as difficult as the other to control,' he said, remembering how on the morning of their departure the appearance of two swooping German aeroplanes temporarily caused chaos.[7]

Young 'would have no man hinder him', recalled Lawrence.[8] 'I am afraid that my eagerness to get things done occasionally offended some of the more sensitive Arab officers,' Young acknowledged, before recalling how Nuri Said had once soothed his own officers after they were upset by Young's abrupt treatment of them.[9] 'Why worry my dears?' Nuri had asked, before pointing at Joyce and Kirkbride: 'he talks to them as he does to us.'[10]

On 27 August, while preparing the second convoy, Young realised that he needed ten more camels.

'We know thee not,' retorted a tall, black Meccan standing at the head of a small knot of Arabs on the beach in Aqaba, when Young arrived and bluntly explained what he wanted. Young later admitted how

> for the first and I think the last time, I lost control. Having told them all at the top of my voice what I thought of them in the most abusive Arabic I knew, I finished up by spitting almost in the Meccan's face. Funnily enough, this did the trick. The others roared with laughter, hustled the discomfited black man away, and loaded up the camels without more ado.[11]

On 28 August, as planned, a solemn Feisal arrived at Abu al Assal in his new green Vauxhall to review his troops before they set out for Azraq. 'This advance north is a rather risky venture,' he confided to Jafar: 'I sincerely hope we may succeed.'[12] Past him trooped 450 camel-mounted soldiers, hand-picked and led by Nuri Said, a French battery of mountain guns commanded by Pisani, three British armoured cars towing tenders full of petrol cans and other supplies, Peake's Egyptian Camel Corps, a section of camel-mounted Gurkhas, and Lawrence's and Sharif Nasir's private bodyguards. 'They picked their way daintily past him two by two among the limestone boulders which studded the broad grass track over the downs,' remembered Young. 'As each section saluted Feisal I even felt an absurd lump in my bearded throat at the greatness of the sight.'[13]

Behind the scenes, however, there was uncertainty over whether the raid would happen at all. When he heard about the report in the *Qibla*, Jafar immediately resigned, taking his commanders with him. Lawrence intervened: 'I begged them to pay no heed to the humours of an old man of seventy, out of the world in Mecca, whose greatness they themselves had made,' he wrote later, though his appeal had no effect.[14] Pushed by both Iraqi and Syrian factions in his army, who both resented Husein, Feisal – who had appointed Jafar himself – took umbrage at his father's intervention and resigned as well on 29 August. It became clear that Feisal would only be satisfied with an apology from his father. In a telegram to Cairo the following day, Lawrence estimated he had just four days to save the situation.[15]

The trouble was that – as Lawrence afterwards acknowledged – it might take weeks to engineer Husein's climb-down, and in 'three days, if at all, our expedition to Dara must start'.[16] But the likelihood that a man as patriarchally minded as Husein would relent was small, and growing smaller. Husein dispatched a telegram to Zeid, describing Feisal as 'rebellious and dishonest' and encouraging him to take command of the army.[17] With Frank Stirling, Lawrence managed to buy some time by persuading Nuri Said, who had resigned his commission at the same time, to set out for Azraq anyway, on the understanding that he could turn back if there was no apology from Husein. Nuri Said's force left on 3 September, a day later than planned.

One drastic option remained. Using their knowledge of the Arab cyphers, Joyce and Lawrence could doctor the angry telegrams travelling back and forwards between Husein and Feisal. Lawrence secretly decoded the incoming messages, and then scrambled the offending passages and re-encrypted them, before taking them to Feisal. Unable to understand the full text, Feisal would then reply to his father, asking him to resend the telegram.

The result, Lawrence observed, was a gradual *détente*, as each 'fresh version [was] toned down a little from the original harshness'.[18] Eventually, 'there came a long odd message, whose first half comprised a withdrawal and lame apology of the mischievous proclamation, which the second half repeated in a new and glaring form.' Lawrence took the first half, marked it 'Very Urgent' and took it into Feisal's tent. Feisal's secretary deciphered the bowdlerised telegram and passed it to his master. Having read it to himself, Feisal glanced suspiciously up at Lawrence, before reading the apology aloud, and announcing that honour had been satisfied. On 5 September Lawrence left for Azraq by armoured car.[19] With him was Lord Winterton, an officer of the Imperial Camel Corps who had stayed on after Buxton returned to Palestine. Tall and thin, with a skeletal face, Winterton was 'perhaps the most genuine-looking brigand' of them all.[20]

'The sort of antic cut by King Husein over Jafar ruined any chances he ever had of achieving his ambition to be accepted as King of the Arabs,' Kirkbride later wrote.[21] Lawrence himself was incandescent. 'It was intolerable,' he exploded, 'to be at the mercy of so crass a person.'[22] The damage was compounded by a letter to Fakhri in Medina which Husein wrote the same day that the *Qibla* article was published. In it he mocked Fakhri for having to feed his men on *hibnah*, a herb more usually eaten by goats. As the *Arab Bulletin* commented, this attack on Fakhri was unjustified, and only likely to stiffen his will to hold out in Medina. 'As all reports show that the prolonged resistance of the garrison is in no small measure due to this man's proud and resourceful spirit, it is, perhaps, a pity that he was not spared these pinpricks.'[23] Fakhri, who earlier that summer had circulated recipes for cooking locusts among his men, defiantly replied to Husein a fortnight later, telling him about a dream in which the Prophet Muhammad had appeared before him. 'As I am now under the protection of the Prophet,' he wrote to Husein, 'I am busying myself with strengthening the defences and building roads and squares in Medina. Trouble me not with useless requests.'[24]

Under a dusty, pale blue sky, Lawrence's Rolls-Royce burned across the dazzling Jafr plain through the streaming mirage to reach Azraq in time for the attack. Rapidly, he began to overtake the Arabs who had set out earlier, passing a stream of men and tribesmen, slowly trekking northwards to Azraq.[25]

Thanks to tarmac, the 180-mile drive to Azraq takes little more than three hours today. Jockeying, hooting petrol tankers joust along the road, which is scarred black in places where, in head-on collisions, their drivers have met premature, fiery ends. After the flat grey Jafr plain, where, in George Lloyd's words, the 'going is as good as the Bath road',[26] the road crosses some low hills separating the Jafr basin from Bair, and then climbs gradually towards the three distinct peaks known as the Jabal Thlaithukhwat, before sloping downwards, across redder, undulating soil into the bubbling mirage of the Azraq plain.

Lawrence was the first to arrive at Azraq, reaching the ruined castle on 7 September 1918. Three days later two British aeroplanes, guided by his directions to the mile-long lagoon, landed on a prepared strip at the remote hideout. Then Joyce, with Stirling, Young and the other armoured cars arrived, followed by Peake and his cameleers. The tribesmen – Auda's indigo-cloaked Huwaytat and Nuri Shaalan's Rwala – converged on Azraq from out of the desert. Finally, on the 12th, the final elements of the Arabs' raiding force arrived. There was no spare time, because of the delays resulting from the uncertainty caused by Husein. The following day the party set out north for Dara.

Peake split off to the west, taking his Egyptian Camel Corps and the Gurkhas to attack the railway south of Mafraq, but his raid was not a success. His own men were tired, and the Gurkhas found camel-riding difficult to master and were grumpy for a reason Peake admitted he could not understand. When he arrived at the railway, on the night of the 15th, some Bani Sakhr tribesmen who were camped near by objected to the raid. They had come to an agreement with the Turks not to attack the railway in exchange for water, and did not want to bear the brunt of any Turkish reprisal. Peake was forced to head back towards the main column, which he found at Umtaiye, ten miles north-east of Mafraq. Winterton had arrived earlier with the armoured cars. 'We . . . put the cars in a semicircle for defence with the orders "no lights",' he remembered.[27] He was unsettled by the Arabs' refusal to follow basic safety drills, though even he was enchanted when Lawrence's Arab escort arrived and lit their fires. A maverick Member of Parliament who had flitted around the glittering salons of Edwardian London, Winterton drew on his knowledge of the ballet to describe the Rwala tribesmen who appeared the following morning. 'Their blue, brown and saffron cloaks,' he believed, 'would delight Bakst', a famous set designer of the era.[28]

Peake's failure was a setback. Lawrence knew that he needed to break the railway between Amman and Dara which would otherwise be used to shuttle Turkish reinforcements rapidly northwards to attack the Arabs later. That afternoon – the 16th – he took Winterton and Joyce and headed for a stretch of railway north of Mafraq, in the armoured cars and tenders packed with guncotton, lurching over the rough ground until they reached a low ridge overlooking the track. While Winterton and Joyce stayed with the tenders on the ridge, Lawrence approached the bridge in one of the armoured cars and 'took a post of open-mouthed Turks too suddenly for them to realise that we were hostile'.[29] He then wrecked the four-arched bridge beside the outpost. It was a perfect demolition which left the bridge intact but so unsafe that the Turks would have to pull it down before they could start rebuilding.

While the other armoured car straddled the track to provide cover should the Turks attempt to counterattack, Winterton and Joyce rushed northwards up the line to try a devious new demolition technique, which they had christened the 'tulip'. Each man scraped a hole under the hollow metal sleeper midway along each pair of rails, placed two fifteen-ounce slabs of guncotton in the space under the sleeper, ensuring that the charge did not touch the metal, and replaced the ballast before lighting a twelve-inch fuse. The explosion punched each sleeper about eighteen inches into the air, bending it double into a shape like a tulip bud, and dragging the rails attached to it up, towards each other, and twisting them in opposite directions simultaneously. The three-dimensional distortion, Lawrence noted with satisfaction, was 'impossible to straighten'; the affected lengths of rail had to be cut away and scrapped.[30] Winterton thoroughly enjoyed himself. 'We could indulge in a love of destruction which had lain latent in us since we were small boys,' he later reminisced. 'We were in fact outside the rules, which is always exhilarating.'[31]

Fifteen miles further south in Amman, at 3.50 p.m. that afternoon Lieutenant Thalacker received the first news of Lawrence's attack. 'We were taken by surprise,' he later admitted. The bridge had been 'blown up in broad daylight' and the troops in the camps each side, who were supposed to be guarding the bridge, had 'simply observed the activity without lifting a finger: only when the explosion had taken place, once the enemy was retreating in [an] easterly direction, did they commence firing'.[32]

Nuri Said, meanwhile, was hurrying northwards towards Dara. That morning he had agreed with Nasir, Joyce and Lawrence that he would bypass the town to the east, crossing the embankment of the old railway line to the Roman city of Busra, originally built to collect the grain harvest from the Hauran, and then cross the northern, main line to Damascus and take control of Tell Arar, just to the north of Dara. The tell – one of the area's many distinctive, man-made hills formed by ancient settlements – commanded good views south towards the railway junction. It offered a good base from which Nuri could organise the first attack on the railway running north from Dara, cutting the town off from Damascus, as well as further operations around the railway junction. Nuri was light-hearted and confident, said Young, who rode with him. 'His great joke was to offer us what he and his brother officers of the Arab army called "calories". These were draughts of a yellow liquid which, to the infidel, smelt and tasted like whisky, but which was by courtesy referred to only as a food value.'[33]

By now, the Turks were aware of the Arabs' arrival. When Young and Nuri drank a further 'festal calorie' astride the railway line at dawn on 17 September, their celebrations were rudely interrupted by gunfire from the Turkish position on Tell Arar and they were forced to take cover. After some confusion, the Arabs launched a headlong attack against the Turks, capturing the hill with the loss of only one man. Following the Arabs up to the summit, Kirkbride found six dead Turkish soldiers, all of whom had been shot through the head.

Demolitions on the railway below should have begun immediately, but Peake's Egyptians refused to work hungry and sat down to eat in a field of maize beside the railway. Peake's batman prepared a sumptuous meal for his boss, but his breakfast was about to be rudely interrupted.

'I had hardly sat down to my bacon and eggs,' Peake recalled, 'when Lawrence supercharged with zeal dashed up in his car, and was heard to be asking for the officer in charge.' Lawrence had driven overnight from Umtaiye to catch the Arabs up, and arrived at Tell Arar that morning. 'I wanted the whole line destroyed in a moment: but things seemed to have stopped,' he remembered afterwards.[34] Wondering why there were no demolitions going on, he set off to find Peake.

'A moment later', Peake recalled, Lawrence was led through the maize to where he was sitting. 'When he saw the table with the white cloth, a certain amount of shiny plate on it and a box of Corona cigars, and all around the Egyptians and Gurkhas eating peacefully, his surprise was such that I shall never forget it.'[35]

'It was like Drake's game of bowls,' Lawrence commented, acidly.[36]

Once Peake and the Egyptians had set to work planting the 'tulips', Lawrence climbed the tell to survey Dara. Before him the town was clearly visible, with the railway radiating from it like the points of a compass. From the north to his left was the line from Damascus, now being methodically uprooted by Peake. Out of Dara to the east spiked the short branch-line to Busra which he had negotiated in the night. From off this branch, southwards, the Hijaz Railway disappeared south towards Mafraq, where they had destroyed the bridge the day before. And west ran the line through Mezerib, which continued down through the Yarmuk valley towards Palestine, where Lawrence had tried and failed to destroy the bridge at Tell al Shehab the previous November.

So far the Arabs' advance had been almost unopposed. Liman von Sanders only heard about the attacks on the railway during 17 September. 'I realised at once that these attacks on our only line of communications were the beginning of serious fighting,'[37] he wrote in his memoirs, describing how he had sent a small number of troops to reinforce Dara.

Frantic activity in the town caught Lawrence's eye. Through his binoculars he could see that the aerodrome 'was alive with gangs pulling machine after machine into the open. I could count eight or nine lined up.'[38] The first aeroplane appeared over Tell Arar minutes later, just as Peake's first demolitions began. More aeroplanes, eight in all, followed quickly, bombing and machine-gunning the hill. From among the rocks on the south side of the tell, Nuri's machine-gunners fired back at them, while Pisani upended his antique mountain guns and blasted the air with shrapnel.

Of the two British biplanes sent to cover the Arab advance to Dara, the better, a Bristol, had already been badly damaged in a dogfight near Umtaiye. The other, an obsolete BE 12 piloted by Hugh Junor, now lumbered into view, initially causing the enemy aircraft to scatter. Too late, Junor realised he was heavily outnumbered and twisted away, followed by a swarm of hostile aircraft. But he was running low on fuel, and minutes later he turned back towards Tell Arar, dropping a message to the British officers below to say he had to land. The officers rushed down the hill towards the railway, to clear a landing ground. 'Junor made straight for the white T which we had put down to mark the beginning of the landing strip, and . . . touched down in what looked like a cloud of tracer bullets,' Kirkbride recalled.[39] As he did so, there was a gust of wind, flipping the biplane on to its back. Astonishingly, Junor climbed out unhurt, apart from a cut on the chin. He barely had time to remove his two machine-guns from the aircraft before a German plane returned and dropped a bomb on the wreck, which caught fire.

Lawrence turned his attention to the western spoke of the railway lines radiating from Dara, which connected the junction to the Turkish positions in Palestine that Allenby planned to assault the following day. Leaving Joyce behind on top of the tell, he took his bodyguard and headed south-west towards Mezerib, a major depot for rolling stock filled with supplies bound for the Palestine front. Despite being bombed again, Lawrence reached the first of the two stations in the village early in the afternoon, capturing it without loss. A few point-blank shots from Pisani's artillery secured the other station.

While the Arabs ransacked the station and the sidings in what Young described as 'an orgy of looting', Lawrence and Young clambered on to the station roof to sever the telegraph link between Palestine and Syria. 'Reaching out for the thick wires we cut them one by one,' Young wrote.[40] 'It was odd to stand looking out over the peaceful landscape . . . and to think of the consternation which the closing of those nippers must have caused in distant Nablus.'* Liman von Sanders immediately lost contact with Damascus and Constantinople, but the extent of the breakdown of communications was only revealed several days later when he finally received a message from the capital. 'The telegram,' he recalled afterwards, 'inquired whether I was willing to offer a prize for a sack race in a competition in Constantinople on October 8th.'[41]

West of Dara, Lawrence and Young split up to continue their devastation. While Lawrence set out to destroy the points, Young went a little east towards Dara to lay a series of 'tulips' under the track. 'I had planted half a dozen when something made me look along the line towards Dara,' recalled Young: 'my heart stood still, for a train was crawling slowly out of the town towards Mezerib'.[42] His first thought was to warn Lawrence, who was oblivious to the incoming threat. Rushing along the railway line, Young shouted that a train was coming.

'A plane?' asked Lawrence, mishearing, and dismissing the threat.

'Not a plane, you damned fool,' Young bellowed, 'a train.'[43]

Young raced back to light the fuse of the nearest of the charges he had already laid beneath the railway sleepers. Panicking, he could not find the taper he needed and was forced to resort to other means. 'One last dab with the glowing cigarette, and I rushed to my camel,' he wrote in his memoirs: 'It . . . was hardly up before it stumbled and nearly fell, and I realised to my horror that I had forgotten to unhobble it.'[44] Luckily for Young, the explosion of the first 'tulip', though uncomfortably close, was enough to force the engine to withdraw to safety. Under cover of darkness, he returned to complete his demolitions.

For almost a year Lawrence had smarted from his failure to destroy the railway in the Yarmuk valley, and now that he was again within miles of Tell al Shehab, the opportunity to destroy the bridge arose again that night. Leaving the burning sidings of Mezerib, Lawrence, his body-

---

* The headquarters of the Ottoman Seventh Army.

guards, Nasir and some Arabs headed down into the valley. But again they were unsuccessful. Below them, a train carrying the German reinforcements Liman had dispatched to protect Dara had just arrived. 'Nuri was of course quite ready to try it; Lawrence was doubtful; and I was quite definitely against it,' Young said afterwards.[45]

On top of Tell Arar, Stirling and Peake were meanwhile recounting the story of their day's destruction on the railway near Ghazala, the first station north of Dara. Stirling had spread out his blanket, gathered the officers around and produced a half bottle of vintage brandy which, he said, he had been keeping for a special occasion. 'I enjoyed the drink immensely,' Kirkbride recollected, 'and I could not help wishing that there had been more brandy and fewer men to drink it'.[46] In the darkness, Lawrence and Young's work to the west of Dara was easily identifiable. The sky above Mezerib glowed red with flames, and there were intermittent flashes and bangs as Young's 'tulips' exploded.

From Mezerib, Sharif Nasir, Nuri Said, Lawrence and Young set out the following morning, the 18th, south-east towards Nesib, a stop on the Hijaz Railway between Dara and Amman, today on the border of modern Syria and Jordan. They sent a message back to Joyce, explaining their plan to continue their anti-clockwise circuit of Dara, and told him to return to Umtaiye, where they would meet that night to wait for news of Allenby's offensive, which would begin early on the 19th.

The nearness of Dara and its 1,500-strong garrison frightened Young. Behind them, as he had seen the previous night, were German reinforcements and he feared that ahead they would find the bridge Lawrence had destroyed thirty-six hours earlier strongly defended. 'I have never known camels march so slowly, or my own heart beat so fast, as on that sixteen mile ride from Mezerib to Nesib.'[47]

To the south, Thalacker was struggling to restore the line between Amman and Dara. Under the supervision of his colleague, Lieutenant Stuetz, by the evening of the 18th a working party had built piers of wooden sleepers, with girders made of rails laid on top of them to replace the bridge north of Mafraq demolished by Lawrence two days earlier. That night a first repair train passed over the temporary bridge north towards Dara. 'Thanks to the indefatigable work of the German railway troops,' said Liman von Sanders, 'traffic was promptly resumed.'[48]

Normal service was to be short-lived. Lawrence's force materialised on the railway near Nesib, ten miles north of Stuetz's working party, late in the afternoon on the 18th. The Turks, entrenched around the station and a nearby bridge, did not surrender easily this time and a violent firefight ensued. It was only 'after considerable resistance and artillery work', Lawrence reported afterwards, that 'we were able to carry the post on the big bridge north of the station, and to blow up the bridge'.[49]

Knowing Lawrence's tendency to use 'unnecessarily large quantities of explosive', Kirkbride, who had caught up with Lawrence's party and was now setting about destroying the track, asked Lawrence to give him plenty of notice before he destroyed the bridge.

'All right, all right, don't fuss!' Lawrence – shattered – snapped.

Kirkbride was still busy laying charges, he recounted afterwards, 'when there was a terrific detonation and chunks of the bridge showered down around us from the sky. It was only by the grace of God that none of us was hurt.' He went off to protest to Lawrence: 'I was tired, hungry and boiling with rage.'[50] He was angrier still at Lawrence, who simply 'sat on a rock and roared with laughter'.[51] Only afterwards did Lawrence justify using so much explosive. The bridge was 'strategically most critical', he argued, 'since we were going to live opposite it at Umtaiye . . . I was determined to leave not a stone of it in place.'[52] Forced to move on the following morning by Turkish shelling from a train-mounted gun, the Arab raiders and their British advisers were forced to proceed to Umtaiye, just as Allenby's offensive began.

At 4.30 a.m. on 19 September the British launched their offensive. Convinced that the Arabs' activity around Dara revealed Allenby's true intentions, the German general Liman von Sanders dismissed information received from an Indian deserter just before the attack that the thrust would be on the coast as a clever attempt to deceive him. When the British advanced at the far left of their front line between the Mediterranean Sea and the Turkish Eighth Army's headquarters at Tulkarm, after a short, brutal bombardment, the Ottoman Army was taken completely by surprise and collapsed. 'I made only one mistake in my calculations,' Liman von Sanders insisted after the war. 'I hoped that individual units would only be pressed back step by step: I did not expect the complete failure of whole divisions.'[53] Later the same day Allenby wrote to his wife. By now he knew that the Arabs had cut the railway north, south and west of Dara. 'I am beginning to think that we may have a very great success,' he ventured.[54]

The situation at Umtaiye was less promising. Joyce reported that as he and his men withdrew from Tell Arar the previous day they had been shot at by locals enraged by their presence. When they had stopped at Umtaiye while heading north, the Arabs had the advantage of surprise. Now that the Turks knew exactly where they were, Umtaiye was unsafe and all the more vulnerable considering that neither British aeroplane was airworthy. Lawrence had seen three German aeroplanes land nearby and was now worried about the threat they presented. Later that day he and Junor each took an armoured car to try to catch the German aircraft on the ground. Though he managed to shoot up one aeroplane in the valley where it had landed, the other two took to the air. The cars could only travel slowly through the stony ground and arrived back at Umtaiye followed uncomfortably closely by the enemy aeroplanes. 'We crept on defencelessly, slowly . . . feeling like sardines in a doomed tin, as the bombs fell closer,' Lawrence wrote.[55] Back, unscathed, in Umtaiye, he decided that the priority was to borrow new aeroplanes from Allenby to protect the Arabs from further aerial attack.

A British aeroplane was expected to land at Azraq on 21 September, bringing news from Palestine of Allenby's advance. Lawrence now decided to return to Azraq himself to meet the aircraft and fly to Palestine, where he hoped to persuade Allenby to lend him more planes. It was agreed that day that Joyce should return to Abu al Assal to restore communications with Allenby's headquarters. The Arabs, meanwhile, would retreat further into the hills south-east of Dara, where it was hoped they would be more difficult to find.

Lawrence and his Ageyli bodyguards reached Azraq on 20 September. On the 21st, as planned, an aeroplane landed with news from Dawnay of Allenby's early achievements. 'On this side,' Dawnay had written the day before, 'things have gone without the faintest hitch . . . the whole Turkish army is in the net, and every bolt-hole closed, except, possibly, that east of Jordan by way of the Yarmuk valley. If the Arabs can close this, too – and close it in time – then not a man, or gun or waggon ought to escape – *some* victory!'[56] The aircraft also brought an effusive letter from Allenby for Feisal, praising him for the 'great achievement' of his 'gallant troops'. In his covering note, Dawnay asked Lawrence to 'deliver this in suitably flowery language to Feisal'.[57] Finally, Dawnay communicated three other orders for Joyce from Allenby:

(1) He wants the railway *south* of Dara smashed, *as completely as you are able* to smash it, in order to eliminate that flank once and for all; (2) he wants the tribes to close the gap across the Yarmuk valley between Lake Tiberias and Dara, which may be used by parts of the 8th A[rmy] C[orps] from the Amman area and by remnants of other troops who succeed in making their way across from west of Jordan. (3) Above all, he does NOT wish Feisal to dash off, on his own, to Damascus or elsewhere – we shall soon be able to put him there as part of our own operations, and if he darts off prematurely without Gen A's knowledge and consent, to guarantee his action, there will be the very devil to pay later on, which might upset the whole apple cart. So use all your restraining influence, and get Lawrence to do the same, to prevent F from any act of rashness in the north, which might force our hand, and force it in the wrong direction.[58]

That afternoon Lawrence climbed into the observer's seat, and the aircraft raced down the desert airstrip and climbed westwards towards Allenby's headquarters at Bir Salem in southern Palestine. There, Allenby explained his next steps. There would now be three separate thrusts: one, by the New Zealanders, led by General Chaytor, across the Jordan to Amman; a second, by the Indians under General Barrow, against Dara; in the third, General Chauvel's Australians would cross the northern Jordan valley, towards Qunaytira on the Golan Heights. While Chaytor secured the right flank, Barrow and Chauvel would then turn northwards for Damascus. 'We were to assist them,' Lawrence would write in *Seven Pillars of Wisdom*, 'but I was not to carry out my saucy threat to take Damascus, till we did it all together.'[59]

25

THE ROAD TO DAMASCUS

(September 1918) *

Otto Liman von Sanders only narrowly escaped being captured when British troops entered Nazareth on 21 September. Later that day he reached Dara, where he briefly tried to marshal his dwindling forces before leaving for Damascus. He sent an order to the Fourth Army at Amman, to come north to reinforce the Seventh and Eighth Armies on the Palestine front. But, as Thalacker bitterly observed, 'due to the destruction of the track around Dara, the railway line . . . was completely paralysed.'[1] The Fourth Army had no choice but to go by road. When he set out north for Damascus on 22 September, Liman von Sanders himself had to walk one stretch of the line north of Dara which had still not been repaired since Peake's demolitions six days earlier.

The same morning, at Um Surab in the hills fifteen miles south-east of Dara, Young and Kirkbride were frying sausages together when they heard three aeroplanes. Having spent two days taking cover every time they heard an aircraft, both men were relieved to see that the planes had British markings. One by one, all three landed, and out of one jumped Lawrence.

Lawrence had good news. Two of the aircraft – advanced Bristol fighters from an Australian squadron – had arrived to stay, and Allenby's only Handley Page bomber would follow that afternoon with a payload of food, fuel and spare parts for the aircraft and the cars. When, shortly afterwards, German biplanes appeared from Dara, the Australians scrambled for their aeroplanes. This time, 'The contest was brief and one-sided,' Kirkbride remarked.[2] The sausages and tea were still hot,

Lawrence claimed, when both Australian pilots returned. A few hundred yards away, flames and billowing black smoke marked the point where each German biplane had dived into the ground.

In Amman, the atmosphere, Thalacker noted, was 'becoming increasingly hostile and violent' as thirsty troops arriving from the south fought over the station's limited supply of water.[3] With the 'Turkish troops . . . getting totally out of hand' and panic rising, Thalacker was forced to keep order by waving his pistol at the mob. Having heard that the line north to Dara had finally been repaired, on 23 September he dispatched a hospital train to evacuate the wounded northwards out of Amman, which was now being bombed daily. But his plans were to be ruined by the Arabs' determination to smash the railway. That morning, in a sortie in broad daylight, a mixed force of regular Arab soldiers, Rwala tribesmen, armoured cars and tenders returned to Mafraq. There they destroyed the makeshift bridge which had only just been put up to replace the stone bridge that Lawrence had wrecked on 16 September. The hospital train was forced to turn back. To the south, the garrison in Maan surrendered. To the west, Chaytor occupied Salt, unopposed. Thalacker left Amman on the last available trolley after dark on 24 September, six hours before British troops arrived. When he reached Mafraq in the early hours of 25 September he found the station ablaze. Unable to pass through the inferno, he and his colleagues were forced to dynamite their trolley and finish the twenty-mile journey to Dara on foot.

News of the Arabs' exploits was spreading rapidly. Four days earlier Antonin Jaussen had passed on 'another very important piece of news' to his superiors in Cairo. 'Colonel Lawrence,' he reported, 'with a band of Bedouin, has destroyed the bridges of the railway west of Dara . . . not far from Tell al Shehab. What's more, he has cut the track south of Dara, between Dara and Amman.'[4]

The speed of the British advance through northern Palestine, and the Arabs' significant role in the Ottoman Army's collapse, raised French suspicions. On 23 September the French ambassador in London, Paul Cambon, went to see the Foreign Secretary, Arthur Balfour, to remind him that Syria fell within the French sphere of influence determined by the Sykes-Picot agreement. 'It was extremely important,' Cambon explained, 'that this fact should not be lost sight of in any arrangements that General Allenby . . . might make for the administration of the country he was presumably about to occupy.'[5]

The following day an intriguing report on the progress of the Palestine campaign appeared in a French newspaper, the *Echo de Paris*. Having acknowledged Allenby's role in the triumph, the newspaper added that 'we must mention Colonel Lawrence as having played a part of the greatest importance in the Palestine victory'. With his 'experience of the country and his talent for organisation', Lawrence would become a household name in Britain, the newspaper predicted – a self-fulfilling prophecy – and added how, 'At the head of the cavalry force, which he had formed with Bedouins and Druses, he cut the railway at Dara, thus severing the enemy communications between Damascus and Haifa and the eastern side of the Jordan.'[6]

It was the first time Lawrence's – and indeed any British – involvement in the Arabs' northward advance had been acknowledged in public, and it is hard not to detect an ulterior motive behind this apparently magnanimous tribute, which was reprinted the following day in the London press. Until then, as reports in *The Times* show, care had been taken to disguise British involvement in the Arab campaign. This sudden revelation that it was a British officer who was the driving force behind the Arabs' success was designed to discredit the Arabs' hopes of independent rule in Syria after the war.

The British remained determined not to give the French more influence in Syria than they had to. The same day that Lawrence's work was reported in the *Evening Standard*, the Director of Military Intelligence at the War Office contacted Allenby to say that although the government adhered to the Sykes-Picot agreement, Allenby's interpretation of its rules would be final while the country was under military occupation. As to the treaty's stipulation for French officers to be employed for any civilian duties, the DMI, who had never liked the Sykes-Picot agreement, reminded Allenby that 'discretion rests with you re definition of civilian duties'.[7]

Delighted by the havoc that the Arabs had wreaked behind Turkish lines, Allenby made preparations to give them the best possible chance to establish a hold in Damascus. On the 25th, a member of his staff contacted the British officers with the Arabs to tell Feisal – who had followed the raiders as far as Azraq – that there was 'no objection to Your Highness entering Damascus as soon as you consider that you can do so with safety'.[8] Allenby ordered his own forces to avoid entering the city 'unless forced to do so for tactical reasons'.[9]

Lawrence too was determined to press home the Arabs' advantage. Realising on 24 September that the Turks had given up trying to repair the railway between Dara and Amman, he now proposed going north again and stopping just beyond Dara, on the Damascus road. His motive was not only strategic but political. Not only did he hope that the Arabs' presence north of Dara would unsettle the Turks enough to make them leave the town, where they were busy entrenching to fend off a new British attack, but it would also put the Arabs in a position to reach Damascus rapidly. Besides which, 'if we withdrew to Jabal Druse, we ended our active service before the game was won, leaving the last brunt on Allenby', he would explain afterwards.[10] He also wanted the Arabs to be in possession of Dara before British troops arrived, as the town fell just inside the area allocated to France under the Sykes-Picot treaty.

Young, who had ridden with the exhausted Arab regulars and knew how slowly they travelled, was horrified when Lawrence explained his plan. 'Our tiny force would be in the position of the hunter who stands in the only line of escape of the driven lion, instead of waiting on a flank to shoot him as he dashes by,' he feared.[11] He preferred to remain in the Hauran, from where escape would still be possible, were the Turks to regain the upper hand. Like the other officers, he was also fully aware that the war in Europe was drawing to a close, and he thought that Lawrence's behaviour verged on the reckless.

Lawrence disagreed, but was forced to temper his initial proposal, offering the village of Sheikh Saad, rather more north-west of Dara, as a compromise. He also contacted Allenby's headquarters to ask if there were large numbers of enemy forces waiting in the Sheikh Saad area and for Dara to be bombed to reduce the danger that the Arabs would be attacked while they were making the northward move. Young reluctantly agreed. Only after the war, having seen President Wilson's public commitment to the principle of self-determination, did he understand that Lawrence's motive for pressing northwards was to establish the Arabs in the French zone before the war was over.

Headquarters obliged and, covered by a British bombing raid on Dara, the Arabs headed north on 26 September, crossing the railway at Ghazale, ten miles north of Dara between the late afternoon and midnight. 'We saw no one, and if anyone saw us, they did nothing about it,' remembered a relieved Kirkbride.[12] Then, between the railway and the Dara–Damascus road, the Arabs paused to rest.

Young was too anxious to sleep. 'I . . . kept pacing restlessly about with my watch in my hand, torturing myself with visions of the confusion that would be caused by a night attack on our tired force,' he remembered afterwards.[13] When the moon eventually rose, Young went round waking the party. They crossed the Damascus road at three in the morning and stopped again, only a little further west, shortly before dawn. 'But there was no rest,' Lawrence recalled, 'for lost men went about the army calling their friends in that sharp full-throated wail of the Arab villager. The moon had gone down, and the world was black and very cold.'[14] Dawn on 27 September brought warmth, an unexpected encounter with a straggling column of Turkish, Austrian and German machine-gunners, who were quickly captured, and declarations of support from the villagers of the surrounding country who, sensing an opportunity to avenge years of oppressive Ottoman rule, flocked to join the Arabs.

Young's fears were realised when, later in the day, a British aeroplane overflew the Arabs' camp and dropped a message warning them that two Turkish columns, of 4,000 and 2,000 men, were approaching from Dara and Mezerib. Lawrence wisely decided to let the larger column pass, and concentrate the Arab forces on the others, who were approaching the village of Tafas, about halfway between Dara and Sheikh Saad. But, as Young had warned they might be, the Arabs were too slow. By the time they reached the village, the Turks – a regiment of lancers – were there already. Smoke was rising from the village and there was the ominous sound of gunshots. Outnumbered by the Turks, all Lawrence could do was wait until the Turks had ridden off before he could investigate what had happened. As he walked closer, he began to gain an inkling of what had happened minutes earlier. 'Some grey heaps seemed to hide in the long grass, embracing the ground in the close way of corpses. We looked away from these, knowing they were dead; but from one a little figure tottered off, as though to escape from us.'[15] It was a little girl, no more than four years old, whose dirty dress was stained bright red with blood. It looked as though she had been speared by a lance.

'Don't hit me, Baba,' she shrieked. When one of the Arabs, himself a local villager, leapt from his saddle to try to comfort the girl, Lawrence wrote how 'she threw up her arms and tried to scream; but, instead, dropped in a little heap, while the blood rushed out again over her clothes; then, I think, she died.'[16]

There was worse to come. As Lawrence entered the village he saw 'something red and white' sagging over one of the mud walls of the village sheepfolds. 'I looked close and saw the body of a woman folded across it, bottom upwards, nailed there by a saw bayonet whose haft stuck hideously into the air from between her naked legs. She had been pregnant, and about her lay others, perhaps twenty in all, variously killed, but set out in accord with an obscene taste.'[17]

Talal, the village headman, who had accompanied Lawrence on his ride around Dara the previous November, had ridden into Tafas at the same time. 'He gave one moan like a hurt animal,' Lawrence remembered, before pulling his headcloth across his face and galloping after the retreating Turks.[18] Lawrence looked on, transfixed. 'We sat there like stone while he rushed forward, the drumming of the hoofs sounding unnaturally loud in our ears, for we had stopped shooting and the Turks had stopped shooting,' he recalled. As he reached the Turkish rearguard, Talal stiffened in his saddle and shouted his war-cry, 'Talal, Talal.' The Turks turned, there was a rattle of machine-gun fire and Talal fell dead among their lances.

Auda abu Tayi demanded vengeance and the tribesmen chased after the disappearing column of Turkish soldiers. Outraged by the cruelty they had witnessed, and fired by the need for revenge, the tribesmen, Lawrence recalled, fought 'like devils, the sweat blurring their eyes, dust parching their throats'. After the war, he would write how 'In a madness born of the horror of Tafas we killed and killed, even blowing in the heads of the fallen and of the animals; as though their death and running blood could slake our agony.'[19] Neither Lawrence, nor anyone else, seemed to retain any control over the swelling Arab army. Liman von Sanders described how, during their retreat, his soldiers discovered that 'The inhabitants were armed throughout . . . Many were killed and mutilated by the Arabs.'[20] At the end of the battle in Tafas, the 250 Turkish and German prisoners who had been captured were machine-gunned in cold blood. Lawrence immediately tried to cover up the fact that the tribesmen had run amok, by taking responsibility for what had happened. He claimed that, from the outset, 'We ordered "no prisoners" and the men obeyed'[21] and that the shooting of the prisoners who had not already been killed was triggered by the discovery of one Bedu pinned to the ground by German bayonets 'like a collected insect'. Other witnesses suggest otherwise. One of the Iraqi officers, Ali Jawdat – a future Prime Minister of Iraq – described how he and Lawrence had 'tried vainly to save a batch of prisoners from being massacred by the Bedouin, whose latent savagery had been aroused by the sight of butchered women and children'.[22] Frederick Peake also believed that Lawrence did not give any order to kill the survivors, though he did not arrive in the village until after the killings had ended. 'I am certain,' he told Lawrence's younger brother, Arnold, in 1965, 'that Lawrence did all he could to stop the massacre but was quite unable to do anything as any human mob that has lost its head is beyond control.'[23]

An extremely tense evening followed. Young, who was appalled by what had happened, said that the evening was punctuated by 'a series of false alarms' that the tribesmen were about to massacre the prisoners.[24] Both he and Winterton addressed the Bedu, appealing for the killing to stop. Winterton – who as a Member of Parliament perhaps had most to lose if he was subsequently implicated in the killing of prisoners of war – seems to have been particularly effective at defusing the situation. Explaining that, as an MP, he would have an election to fight after the war was over, he provoked immediate laughter among the Arabs. Lawrence, who was translating the speech, turned to Winterton and explained that the MPs who had visited the region before the war were regarded by the Arabs as 'comic creatures' – a none-too-subtle dig at Sykes. Winterton agreed, adding that they were bores as well. More laughter. Winterton then returned to his serious concerns: 'The good people of Horsham and Worthing in England whose votes I shall be seeking . . . might think I connived at the shooting and vote against me. In fact,' he summed up, 'precipitate action . . . might lose me the election.'[25] The Bedu killed a sheep rather than their prisoners.

Nuri Shaalan's Rwala tribesmen entered Dara overnight. Lawrence raced after them the following morning with Kirkbride. The sky over Dara was black with acrid smoke from storehouses burning in the town. Lawrence was anxious to beat Barrow and his Indian cavalry to the railway station and raise the Arab flag there, since Dara sat on the border of the French zone agreed by Sykes and Picot. 'I felt that politics were starting to complicate a war which had hitherto been fairly straightfor-ward,' Kirkbride wrote in his memoirs.[26] After intense bombing and then ravage by the Rwala overnight, the atmosphere in Dara was apocalyptic. 'There was a stench of fire, death and excreta everywhere, with clouds of flies,' Kirkbride vividly remembered years later. 'It was not easy for us to find a clean place in which to squat . . . We had to leave our first choice in a hurry when I sat down on a mound of earth which produced a nauseating smell as a purple and swollen hand popped out above the ground.'[27]

Kirkbride watched a strapping Arab woman walk past, balancing a looted table on her head. A tribesman chased a Turkish cavalryman round and round in circles, whipping him as he went. A Turkish major, the paymaster of his unit, sat in the dirt weeping, stripped of everything but his vest. A little girl, in a grimy, once-pretty dress, told Kirkbride that she had been coming home from visiting her aunt in Damascus when the trains stopped running and she lost her uncle. Kirkbride sat her down on his valise and gave her a cup of tea before finding a doctor who was willing to accompany her onwards to Amman.

Barrow arrived soon afterwards. He had advanced slowly, uncertain of who controlled the town and scared of being bombed by his own side. On his way into Dara, he had found some Bedu looting a hospital train, 'tearing off the clothing of the groaning and stricken Turks, regardless of gaping wounds and broken limbs, and cutting their victims' throats'.[28] 'This place is in a bloody awful mess,' he told Lawrence when he met him. 'My head was working full speed in these minutes', Lawrence remembered, 'since now or never was the moment to put the Arabs in control.'[29] Greeting Barrow as if he were a guest, Lawrence tried to persuade the general to withdraw his men. Appalled by what he had seen, Barrow, however, refused. Lawrence would later claim that, nevertheless, the general had smartly saluted Sharif Nasir's small silk pennant in the station square – implicitly endorsing the Arabs' control over this contested patch of territory.

The following morning, Barrow's Indian cavalry set out for Damascus, with the Arabs on their right, pressing the rearguard of the retreating Fourth Army. The Turks, Stirling said, were 'now in a pitiful state'. He watched as one of their men crawled to a well. 'Half an hour later I came back and found him dead. He had died of starvation and exhaustion.'[30] Another British officer was moved to verse after the war:

> About them in the fields lay endless wreckage strown
> The jetsam of an army, by ebb of battle dropped
> Disdainfully, packs, arms, a driverless car forlorn
> And here a bloated corpse lay miserably alone[31]

Arab attacks eroded the retreating Fourth Army throughout the next two days. Six-thousand-strong when it left Dara, the column had dwindled to 5,000 by the time it reached Sheikh Miskin, fifteen miles north, 3,000 by Mesmiye, thirty miles further on, and 2,000 by Kiswe, ten miles outside Damascus, where the Turks were overtaken by Nasir and Nuri Shaalan, and trapped between their tribesmen and the advancing British. 'In all we killed nearly five thousand of them, captured about eight thousand . . . and counted spoils of about one hundred and fifty machine guns and from twenty-five to thirty guns,' Lawrence reported in the *Arab Bulletin* without emotion weeks later.[32]

On 30 September, Allenby confirmed the administrative arrangements for Damascus in a telegram to the War Office. 'I shall recognise the local Arab administration which I expect to find in existence, and shall appoint French liaison officer as required,' he added, without enthusiasm.[33] He was expecting the Arabs to head into Damascus early the following morning, paving the way for the entrance of his own troops.

Just as Allenby was preparing his entry into Damascus, Liman von Sanders was hurrying to leave. Armed Arabs, shooting into the air, had been arriving throughout the day and the atmosphere was becoming menacing. 'The four coloured flag of the Sharif was displayed from many houses,' Liman von Sanders observed, sensing that the peaceful attitude of the city's inhabitants was on the verge of turning.[34] The situation rapidly deteriorated as the first Arabs – fresh from dispatching the remnants of the Fourth Army – appeared in the city after dark. Fires broke out across the city: the Germans' depots, and both railway stations in the city – at Cadem in the south-west suburbs and the Hijaz Railway terminus itself in the centre – were in flames. By the time the Germans left Cadem that night, they found the main street running north through the city blocked with telegraph poles and Arabs shooting at them 'from all directions'.[35]

Thirty miles further north-west, a frightened nine-year-old girl was standing on the platform at Reyak station. Musbah Haidar's father Sharif Ali Haidar had returned to live in the Lebanese hills since failing to oust Sharif Husein eighteen months earlier, and his family had come to join him. Now they were being evacuated northwards. Reyak station, which had been bombed the night before, was in complete darkness when Musbah and her father arrived. 'On the platform a crowd seethed, fought, prayed and pushed,' she remembered years later.[36] A few German soldiers tried to maintain control, but they were losing. With fixed bayonets, her father's bodyguards poked their way through the scrum of soldiers and wailing refugees, enabling Musbah and her father to board the waiting train to go north.

Lawrence spent the night at Kiswe, on the south side of Damascus. To the north, white flashes instantaneously illuminated the night sky, as the Turks in the city dynamited their remaining ammunition, blasting shells into the night air in lazy yellow parabolas.

'Ever since we took Dara, the end has been inevitable,' Lawrence observed to Stirling, as the two tried to rest beside their Rolls-Royce car, which they had dubbed 'Blue Mist'. 'Now the zest has gone, and the interest.'[37] It was too noisy to sleep. At dawn, he and Stirling climbed into their car and drove forward to the edge of the hills beyond which lay Damascus. Despite a few palls of black smoke hanging in the still dawn air, below them the ovum of minarets and spires of the old city was visible through a slight dawn mist, gleaming in the morning sunlight, and surrounded to east and west by livid green orchards of orange, almond and walnut trees.

Delayed slightly by an altercation with some Indian soldiers, at about nine in the morning on Tuesday, 1 October, Lawrence and Stirling drove into Damascus. Nuri Shaalan and Nasir had already entered the city, and Australian troops had briefly passed through during the night in their pursuit of the Turks northwards. As a result, the streets were already 'aflame with joy and enthusiasm', reminisced Stirling in his memoirs.[38] 'Dervishes danced around us. The horses of the Bedouin, curvetting and prancing, gradually cleared a way for us through the dense crowds, while from the balconies and rooftops veiled women pelted us with flowers and – far worse – with attar of roses. It was weeks before I could get the smell of the essence out of my clothing.'

26

A HOUSE WITH NO DOOR

(October 1918–1922)

Lawrence went straight into the centre of Damascus intending to establish an Arab government in the city. At the headquarters of the Ottoman government, the *Serail*, he forced his way through the scrum which had gathered around the building, only to find that he had been beaten to it. Inside, he discovered not only Sharif Nasir and Nuri Shaalan but also the Algerian brothers Abdul Qadir and Mohammed Said al Jazairi. The Jazairis sprang forward, announcing that they had taken control of the city, with another Arab nationalist, Shukri al Ayyubi. 'I was dumb with amazement,' Lawrence later wrote.[1] He was suspicious of Abdul Qadir, who had suddenly disappeared before his failed Yarmuk valley expedition eleven months earlier. Afterwards he would claim that they were 'both insane, as well as pro-Turkish and religious fanatics of the most unpleasant sort'.[2]

The man whom Lawrence was planning to install as governor of Damascus was Ali Riza al Rikabi, whom he had met during his secret tour of Syria in June 1917. Rikabi was a sensible choice, who would simultaneously provide both continuity and change: not only had he been a key figure in the Ottoman government of the city, but he was also secretly an Arab nationalist. The problem was that Rikabi was so discreet about his true political opinions that he was still nominally in command of Ottoman troops who were now hurriedly retreating towards Aleppo, and there was no sign of him.

Time was short, because there were already signs that the fragile Arab coalition was splintering. Lawrence's attention was briefly diverted by a fight that had broken out between Auda abu Tayi and Sultan al Atrash, the Druse leader, which had begun after the Druse had hit Auda across the face with a stick. Forcing the two men apart, Lawrence pushed Auda into a quiet room, and held him in a chair until he had finally calmed down.

No more than thirty minutes after he had arrived, Lawrence found himself joined by Sir Harry Chauvel, the commander of the Australian forces waiting west of the city. Chauvel had been told by Allenby that, when he arrived in Damascus, he should find the Turkish *vali*, promise him British support and offer assistance with policing the city. If Chauvel had any difficulties with the Arabs, Allenby directed him to Lawrence. When Chauvel went to see Barrow early that morning to finalise the plans for their entry into the city, Barrow had given him the 'disquieting information that Lt-Col Lawrence, who had been with him the night before, had slipped off early that morning without saying anything to him and to the best of his belief had ridden into the city'. Chauvel hurried after him.

Chauvel found Lawrence on the steps of the *Serail* when he arrived at half past nine that morning. 'With him', Chauvel recalled ten years later, was 'an individual whom he introduced as Shukri Pasha'.[3]

Lawrence explained that his early departure that morning was due to his concern to find out what was going on inside Damascus. 'He then proceeded to tell me that Shukri was the Governor of Damascus,' Chauvel recalled. 'Shukri was obviously an Arab so I said I wished to see the Turkish *Vali*.'

Lawrence must have guessed why. Rather than endorse Mohammed Said al Jazairi, on the spur of the moment he replied that the *vali* had fled the previous afternoon with Mehmed Jemal Pasha, and that Shukri had been elected governor by the citizens.[4] In fact Jemal Pasha had appointed Mohammed Said governor just before he left the city, and Lawrence's second claim was an outright lie: there had been no time, let alone any attempt, to consult the citizens of Damascus about their future government. Chauvel agreed to Lawrence's request to keep his men out of the city and to allow the Arabs time to consolidate the new administration. His uncertainty over the exact whereabouts of the

Turks meant that he was happy not to become embroiled in the running of Damascus.

Having fended off Chauvel, Lawrence returned inside the *Serail* and summoned the Jazairi brothers. 'Feisal had begged me to get rid of them,' he later told Frank Stirling, 'so I told them to go, and that Shukri al Ayyubi would be military governor until Ali Riza returned.'[5] Not surprisingly, neither Abdul Qadir nor his brother were enthusiastic at this news. According to Lawrence, Abdul Qadir tried to stab him, but was stopped when Auda abu Tayi punched him to the floor. Both brothers left, threatening revenge.

Thinking that he had seen off the Jazairis, Lawrence was in an ebullient mood and an appropriately symbolic act occurred to him. Walking through the main Hamidiye souk into the heart of the old city, he passed behind the ancient mosque, and went into Saladin's tomb. There, he prised away the gilt wreath presented to the Sultan by the Kaiser twenty years before. He would give it shortly afterwards to the Imperial War Museum in London, where it is displayed today. On an accompanying chit, kept by the museum, he recorded that the wreath was 'removed by me, as Saladin no longer required it'.[6]

In the evening Lawrence turned his attention to the administration of the city. 'My reading of history,' he would later write, 'told me that the steps were humdrum:– appointments, organisation, departmental routine.'[7] The city's electricity had failed; prices stood at ten times pre-war levels, and diseases, including typhus, dysentery and influenza, were scything through the malnourished inhabitants. 'It was a busy evening,' Lawrence commented afterwards with some understatement, admitting that it was only by 'sweeping delegation of office (too often, in our haste, to hands unworthy)'[8] that a frail façade of local government was erected. As the evening call to prayer sounded across the city, and Lawrence prepared to hand power over to the Arabs, he realised that his role in Damascus was coming to an end.

Frank Stirling's first thought the following morning was that he needed a bath – his first in six weeks. With Sharif Nasir he headed to one of Damascus's Turkish baths. 'We sweated and were rubbed and soaped and pummelled until for my part I felt I was being flayed alive,' he remembered. Finally cleansed of desert grime, they lay drinking coffee and smoking cigarettes.[9]

It was only when they left the *hammam* three hours later to find fresh corpses in the streets that Stirling and Nasir discovered what had happened. 'The Jazairis had 'tried to stage a counter-revolution to put themselves in power. Lawrence had been obliged to turn the machine-guns on them,' Stirling later wrote.[10]

Lawrence had been told during the night that the Jazairis had called on the Druses to back them in an armed uprising against the Sharif, whom they described as a British puppet. Suddenly Lawrence feared that he would be the target of the very Druse revolt he had envisaged helping the Arabs' cause, from the safety of Cairo in July the year before. Early that morning, while Nasir and Stirling were sweating in the *hammam*, Lawrence contacted Chauvel to ask for support before he and Kirkbride toured the streets. The shops were shut, and there was looting going on. 'We must have looked an ill-assorted couple, he short and in Arab robes with no arms but an ornamental dagger, and myself long and lanky in khaki, wearing a large Service revolver,' Kirkbride reflected afterwards.[11] 'When we found anyone butchering Turks he went up and asked them in a gentle voice to stop, while I stood by and brandished my firearm. Occasionally, someone turned nasty and I shot them at once before the trouble could spread.' But you can still gain a sense of just how wild the unrest was, if you look up from the spicy fug of the Hamidiye souk today into its arched, iron roof, and see the bullet holes that puncture it.

It was during this tour that Lawrence also gained a truer sense of the terrible condition of the city. Entering one hospital, 'We were met in the corridor by the most appalling stench which set me retching,' Kirkbride remembered.[12] The dead and the living were lying side by side. Some of the dead were so decomposed that the only way to bury them 'was to pick them up in the sheets on which they lay and dump the bundle in the long trench which had been dug by Turkish prisoners in the garden'. The regular army doctors who followed were appalled. 'Indescribably hideous and inhuman' was the verdict of an Australian medical officer the following day.[13]

Order was restored when Chauvel marched his troops through the city centre. Reluctant to admit that order depended on the occupying British force, Lawrence asked Chauvel first to salute the Arab flag at the *Serail*, and then, when he refused, to allow a body of Arabs to lead the British troops. It was 'quite a reasonable request', Chauvel thought, until he saw the size of the flags with which the Arab contingent arrived to join the march.[14] Nevertheless, the demonstration went ahead, and the violence appears to have been short-lived. A photograph taken shortly afterwards depicts a decidedly more subdued crowd contemplating the two makeshift gallows which had been erected in front of the *Serail*.[15] Neither, according to Kirkbride, had to be used. By nightfall electric light and a semblance of calm had both been restored across the city. Blaming the proximity of the hotel accommodating the campaign's war correspondents to the scene of the shooting for the livid press reports that followed, Lawrence would claim afterwards that there had been only five killed and a further ten wounded, of whom Kirkbride accounted for three.

Allenby arrived in Damascus the following day, 3 October. Two days earlier he had been told in a telegram from London that he should recognise the authority of 'the friendly and allied Arabs' in the areas over which the British and French were to have influence, according to the Sykes-Picot agreement. 'The regions so liberated,' the telegram explained, 'should properly be treated as Allied territory enjoying the status of an independent State, or confederation of States, of friendly Arabs', which had through military success and the organisation of government 'established its independence of Turkey and not as enemy provinces in temporary military occupation'. Wherever possible, the War Office advised, Allenby should encourage Arab administration and work through local Arab officials. The reason for this the telegram then made explicit: it was 'important that the military administration should be restricted to such functions as can properly be described as military, so as to give rise to no inconvenient claim to the employment where unnecessary of French civilians'.[16]

Allenby, however, seems to have felt more comfortable relying on the military hierarchy by which he had absorbed the Arab forces under his command after the capture of Aqaba. Presumably he deemed this the easiest way to give practical authority to the Arabs without surrendering the powers he had as the senior military commander on the spot, which enabled him to limit French influence. When he met Feisal the same day for the first time at the Hotel Victoria, he made it clear that he remained in charge. Feisal had wanted a triumphal entry into Damascus; Allenby refused to wait and sent Hubert Young, in a bright red Mercedes left behind by the Germans, to fetch the Arab sharif. Feisal, though, refused to be driven into town. On hearing that Allenby would not wait, he spurred his horse on and galloped into the city.

'I had a long and satisfactory talk with Feisal,' Allenby wrote to his wife that evening. 'He will take over the administration of Damascus; in the same way as Money does Palestine; or rather, will put in a military administration.'[17]

Chauvel's recollection of the meeting was that it was rather less comfortable.[18] Feisal had reacted badly when Allenby informed him that 'France was to be the Protecting Power over Syria' and that Feisal would administer Syria – excluding Palestine and the Lebanon – with French guidance and financial backing. Feisal said that he knew nothing about France's right to be involved in Syria, claimed that Lawrence had told him that the Arabs were to have all of Syria, and flatly rejected French assistance.[19] A month later, Allenby seemed to acknowledge that the meeting had resulted in deadlock. 'The future, when martial law no longer prevails, is not so cloudless,' he told Sir Henry Wilson.[20]

Chauvel said that Lawrence stalked off after the meeting, after denying any knowledge of the terms of the Sykes-Picot agreement. By contrast Lawrence later said that he had parted with Allenby amicably. What seems certain is that the exhausted Lawrence believed he could do more for the Arabs elsewhere. He left for Cairo the following day, 4 October. In his campaign notebook there is a peculiar and resonant phrase which seems to articulate his feelings two days earlier, as he hurriedly sketched out the arrangements through which the Arabs would govern the city. 'In Damascus when prayer silence came, I knew I was worn tool lying in darkness under bench, rejected for ever by the master.'[21]

The men Lawrence left behind were forced to grapple with an impossible situation caused by the contradictory promises Britain had made to the French and to the Arabs. In Beirut, always the strongest centre of Arab nationalist support, the Arabs announced their independence and raised the Arab flag before British troops arrived in the port. Anticipating French opposition, Allenby quickly warned the War Office. With the war not yet over he too was uncomfortable about the development, which might threaten his own supply arrangements. He told London he intended to overturn the Arabs' decision. The Arabs quoted back at Allenby the Declaration to the Seven Arabs made to them that summer, in which the British government had accepted that the Arabs should govern what they conquered, and that, in areas under Allied occupation, the 'future government of these regions would be based principally on consent of those governed'.[22] Allenby was furious: 'I was not consulted before this assurance was given; further, Arab leaders have never been officially notified of terms of Anglo-French Agreement.'

As the contradictions of the various promises the British had made became apparent, Stirling described the atmosphere: 'My office was now thronged with frenzied and almost despairing Arabs who could not believe that we had signed an agreement which would hand them over to the French.'[23] Early in November he wrote to his sister:

The situation here bristles with difficulties. As you know we have fanned the flames of the Arab Revolt and sympathised with money and men in the Sharif's attempt to form a free Arab nation. Up to now the Arabs have a blind confidence in all the Englishmen who have been in contact with them. They almost literally eat out of our hands. The Arab cause has been successful beyond the wildest dreams of anybody. That is just the trouble. Mark Sykes MP never probably believing that the Arab Revolt would ever really reach further north than Aqaba, formed a compact with the French, known as the Sykes-Picot Agreement, whereby Beirut and the entire littoral northward of there should be under French administration and that Damascus, Homs, Hama and Aleppo should be allowed to fall to the Arabs (if they can get there) but should be under French influence . . . But in this present temper the Arab won't have the French at any price. Already the Americans in Beirut are saying that we have sold the Arabs to the French. The results will be as follows – If we keep our part with the

French the Arabs will rightly say we have sold them, that we have raised them up only to cast them down . . . News of this will spread through the Mohammedan World and do us unutterable harm. Also it will entail certain interior chaos and probably war between the French and the Arabs. If we don't keep our pact with France the world will say 'Oh Yes! England land grabbing again'. We don't in the least want any of this country but we simply cannot let the Arabs down. If only we could buy French interests out by the session of land say in the Cameroons it would save so much. Otherwise our name will be mud.[24]

Feisal's relationship with Allenby rapidly deteriorated. While he promised Bertie Clayton that he would not issue any proclamations before consulting Allenby, he announced that the independent government formed in the name of his father 'embraced all Syrian towns'. When he refused to withdraw Shukri al Ayyubi, whom he had sent as his governor to Beirut after Ali Riza had taken over in Damascus, Allenby tried another trick to encourage him to toe the line, by suggesting that all the arrangements were temporary, and would undoubtedly be discussed at the forthcoming peace conference. He warned Feisal that any attempt he made to take control of the coastal 'Blue' area allotted to France under the Sykes-Picot agreement would prejudice his case at the conference, to which he would be invited as a belligerent.[25]

Allenby did not allay Feisal's concerns successfully. 'What he feels most is that all access to the sea is barred,' Allenby reported to Wilson in London. 'I am in a house with no door,' Feisal had reputedly complained.[26] Feisal also told Allenby that he did not trust the French, and feared that their military governors would 'take advantage of their official positions to carry on propaganda' to manipulate any settlement supposedly founded on 'self-determination'. Allenby in turn promised Feisal that he would remove any military governor he found dabbling in politics. Bertie Clayton proposed a more active approach. 'We should now relax local censorship to enable those holding opposite views to French, whose press and other propagandist activity is increasingly active, to state them in moderation,' he advised three days later.[27] Clayton had a point. On his tour around the region following the

Armistice, Antonin Jaussen carefully catalogued towns and Christian communities where he found opposition to British or Arab rule.[28] Shortly afterwards the French would begin a campaign to win support from the Syrian diaspora for their claim to Syria.

In Cairo, Lawrence was trying a little propaganda of his own. Before leaving for Britain, he wrote an article on the capture of Damascus, which was published in *The Times* on 17 October. In it he seeded a revised version of the final days of the campaign, claiming that 'the Arab Camel Corps formed the extreme right of the Allied advance upon Damascus, which was entered on the night of the 30th, Arabs being the first troops in'.[29] Privately, he told the Cabinet on his return to London that Allenby's 'Arab alliance enabled him to throw his cavalry, without lines of communication or the usual precautions, from Jaffa to Aleppo in pursuit of the Turks'.[30]

A·week after the *Times* article appeared, the Director of Military Intelligence in London, Macdonogh, contacted Allenby with news that Sykes and Picot were being sent to Syria to assess the need for political officers to ease the tension between the British, French and Arabs. 'Don't take Mark at his own valuation,' Hogarth – now himself back in Britain – whispered to Clayton days later. 'His shares are unsaleable here and he has been sent out (at his own request) to get him away. He is the last man in the world in my own opinion, to organise or run any Pol[itical] Service: and you can take what line you like about him without fear of being let down.'[31] Hogarth also brought news of the effect of Lawrence's return to Britain:

> Our whole attitude towards the French is hardening here. TEL has put the wind up everybody and done much good . . . He is trying to get the principle accepted that Arabs and Zionists are to be called in to any such 'Conversations' on the S.P. business as Cambon admits must take place eventually. Meanwhile S.P. is considered scrapped here, but not so by Paris.

The British government had considerable bargaining power with the French, who needed British support for their campaign to claim Alsace and Lorraine back from the Germans. Britain now tried to dilute the

Sykes-Picot agreement. On 7 November at British insistence the British and French governments issued a joint declaration committing both to 'the complete and definite emancipation of the peoples so long oppressed by the Turks and the establishment of national governments and administrations deriving their authority from the initiative and free choice of the indigenous populations'.[32] In Damascus the Arabs greeted news of the statement enthusiastically. 'Roughly 200,000 rounds of ball ammunition [were] fired into the air,' Young remembered afterwards.[33] The British were also quietly satisfied with their diplomatic manoeuvre. 'When we are counting up the various weapons we have in our hands for dealing with the Sykes-Picot Agreement later on, I think we shall find ourselves laying very great stress upon the general spirit, if not upon the actual terms, of the declaration,' Lord Curzon asserted in London.[34]

Feisal left Beirut for Europe to join the peace conference late that November. After he had boarded the ship, his chauffeur was stopped by the French and arrested and the Arab flag removed from his car.[35] Although the French military governor, Colonel Piépape, expressed his regret at the incident, it was a sign of what was to come.

Colonel Brémond was assigned to look after Feisal during his stay in France. His instructions were to treat Feisal as 'a person of distinction, but not to recognise in him any diplomatic status'[36] and he took him on a tour of the French battlefields to keep him away from Paris. Finally, on 3 December, Feisal took Brémond to one side. He pleaded:

> We fought the war together, we were brothers in arms. I'm trusting your feelings of friendship and loyalty: tell me frankly what is going on. If the French Government doesn't want me to go to Paris, tell me point blank. I left my brother Zeid, who is young and inexperienced, to replace me in Damascus. The situation there is difficult and I am uneasy. If I am wasting my time here, it would be better for me to return to Damascus.

This, of course, was not what the French wanted: Feisal rapidly secured an interview with the French President, Poincaré, which took place four days later.

Feisal travelled on to London in December. There, at the beginning of 1919, he signed an agreement with Chaim Weizmann, in which both agreed to set a definite boundary between the Hijaz and Palestine, after the peace conference was over. Arabs in Palestine would be 'protected in their property and rights, and shall be assisted in forwarding their economic development' and the 'Mohammedan Holy Places' would come 'under Mohammedan control'.[37] The agreement is often seen as a freely given acknowledgement of the legitimate existence of a Jewish state, but Feisal – who not only still depended on the British for a subsidy of £150,000 a month, but also believed he could still rely on British help to counterbalance French influence in the Middle East – signed reluctantly under British pressure, adding the caveat that he would only honour the deal 'provided the Arabs obtain their independence', defined by conditions set out in a memorandum he had just completed. This statement, drafted with Lawrence's help, maintained that, although the Arabs needed outside assistance, 'we cannot sacrifice for it any part of the freedom we have just won for ourselves by force of arms'.[38] But the memorandum also yielded to British ambitions in the region. 'The world wishes to exploit Mesopotamia rapidly,' it acknowledged, arguing that there was a need for local government, which it advocated should be 'Arab, in principle and spirit' to be 'buttressed by the men and material resources of a great foreign Power'.

Despite opposition from Cairo, the India Office had never abandoned its hope of colonising Mesopotamia. But, in the climate of self-determination created by American criticism of British and French war aims, it was careful to argue its case elliptically, by focusing on the future of Syria. At the India Office, Sir Arthur Hirtzel argued that the idea that France would renounce her claim to Syria was incredible:

If we support the Arabs in this matter, we incur the ill-will of France; and we have to live and work with France all over the world. We have no interests of our own in Syria at all commensurate with those in Mesopotamia; and if we had, and could eliminate the French in our own favour, could we possibly undertake the control of Syrian politics and administration in addition to our responsibilities in Mesopotamia and the Arabian peninsula?[39]

The interest in Mesopotamia to which Hirtzel alluded was oil. Although oil had not been the motive for British interference in the Middle East at the end of 1915, it was certainly a major factor in Britain's determination to remain there after the war was over. By the middle of 1918, the British government had secretly acknowledged that the country was over-dependent on the United States for oil. 'Fuel oil is now essential to the maintenance of British sea power,' a British intelligence report concluded early in 1919: 'Our power to control the world's shipping in time of war is likely in the future to be measured largely by the proportion of the world's oil supply that we shall command.'[40] The question of where this oil could be obtained independently had already been answered by Maurice Hankey, the Secretary to the War Cabinet, who had bluntly told Balfour before the war was over that 'The only big potential supply that we can get under British control is the Persian and Mesopotamian supply.'[41] By the beginning of 1919, it was not just the India Office that recognised what a vital addition Mesopotamia would be to the British Empire. This, Feisal and Lawrence were forced to accept. Lloyd George rapidly demanded Mosul, in modern Iraq, with its rich oilfields, from Clemenceau. Clemenceau agreed that February.

On 10 January 1919, Fakhri, who had defiantly held out in Medina for over ten weeks after the Ottoman armistice, emerged from the city to surrender. The garrison had been seriously depleted by the influenza outbreak which crossed the world at the end of the war, his men were deserting, and finally he had been overthrown by his junior officers. Three days later, Husein's son Abdullah entered Medina for the first time since the outbreak of the revolt. He went straight to the mosque containing the tomb of Muhammad, to pray. He had entered the city first to try to preserve order, but the city was ransacked by occupying Arab forces.

On 18 January, the long-anticipated peace conference finally opened in Paris. Feisal was there as a representative from the Hijaz, but found his name omitted from the official list of delegates. The French told Feisal he should blame the British for failing to explain that he had no formal standing at the conference. The British hit back, arguing that France should accept the two Hijazi delegates because the Arabs had been allies, and had been recognised as independent by the French late in 1916. Middle Eastern matters were peripheral, however, and it was only on 6 February, towards the end of the plenary session, that Feisal finally had the chance to speak, with Lawrence interpreting. It was 'one of the most interesting and statesmanlike speeches', one British observer noted. When the French Foreign Minister, Stéphen Pichon, interrupted Feisal, asking what France had done to help him, Feisal had politely begun by praising the French Government for its support before mentioning that the French had sent 'a small contingent with four antiquated guns and two new ones to join his forces . . . Pichon was sorry he had spoken and looked a fool.'[42]

Although Clemenceau seems to have been largely unbothered about whether or not France colonised Syria, others in France were much more exercised. In Syria, the French military attaché told Stirling that 'though Clemenceau and many thinking Frenchmen are dead against him taking Syria yet the temper of the French People is such that any govt. which gave up Syria would inevitably fall – more particularly if it were given to Britain. There is a strong Anglophobe campaign being waged in France at present.'[43] Under increasing domestic pressure not to give ground to Lloyd George, Clemenceau hardened his views; having got what he wanted in northern Iraq, and believing that there was nothing of great strategic value in northern Syria, Lloyd George was willing to concede. The outbreak of nationalist unrest in Egypt – stoked by public awareness of the promises Britain had made to Syria and Husein, as well as Feisal's invitation to the peace conference – and a collapse in British army morale in Egypt due to the slow pace of demobilisation forced the British to consider pulling out of Syria. That September, Lloyd George took the decision to withdraw. Balfour reputedly told Lloyd George that it was 'preferable to quarrel with the Arab rather than the French'.[44] Thus the Sykes-Picot agreement outlived its rumbustious British negotiator, who had died from influenza at the peace conference. The French would force Feisal into exile in July the following year. The French general responsible is reputed to have gone to Saladin's tomb in Damascus afterwards and announced: 'Nous revoilà, Saladin' – Saladin, we're back.[45]

To compensate their wartime allies, Britain made Feisal King of Iraq, and his brother Abdullah, King of Transjordan. Still closely connected to the west, Jordan today, ruled by Abdullah's great-grandson, Abdullah, is so far the least unstable of the Middle East's regimes. Iraq, of course, is another story.

Britain clung on to Palestine for strategic and sentimental reasons. But the major strategic justification, to secure the Suez Canal, was fast diminishing. In 1922, Egypt was given independence following three years of intermittent violence. In India, a wiry, persistent lawyer, Mohandas Gandhi, began his campaign to end British rule, drawing on widespread outrage at the draconian laws the British enacted after the war, in response to the wartime conspiracies including the Silk Letters. The eastern empire Britain had backed Sharif Husein to save was, slowly but surely, beginning to unravel. And in its place, a new legacy, of increasingly bitter relations between the British and the Arabs, was only just beginning.

EPILOGUE

(1921–2001)

Britain was awarded the mandate for Iraq in April 1920 and was forced to deal with an uprising that summer which persisted for much of the rest of the year. Among those killed during the disturbances was Muhammad al Faruqi, whose desertion to the British five years earlier had formed a significant catalyst for McMahon's overtures to Sharif Husein. The uprising infuriated Lawrence. In an article for the *Sunday Times* that August, in which he was described in his byline as the leader of 'one of the outstanding romances of the war', he publicly blamed the uprising on the Government of India officials who had run the country since the capture of Baghdad: 'Things have been far worse than we have been told, our administration more bloody and inefficient than the public knows. It is a disgrace to our imperial record, and may soon be too inflamed for any ordinary cure. We are to-day not far from a disaster.'[1]

The decision to make Feisal King of Iraq, which was taken at a conference in Cairo convened by the Colonial Secretary, Winston Churchill, in March the following year, changed the nature of the government, although Britain remained the financial and military power behind Feisal's throne. The choice of Feisal was to lead to a close association between many of those involved in the Arab revolt and the new country. The pressure on Churchill to save money led him to reduce the British military presence in Iraq to the Royal Air Force alone, and in 1921 Pierce Joyce was posted to Baghdad to advise the Iraqis on the creation of an army – continuing much the same role that he had done at Aqaba.

Lawrence was immensely proud of his role at Cairo in setting up the
Iraqi state. 'I had repaired, so far as it lay in English power to repair it, the
damage done to the Arab Movement by the signing of the Armistice in
November 1918,' he explained to Charlotte Shaw in 1927.[2] When,
almost exactly a year later, Clayton was appointed British High Commissioner in Baghdad, Lawrence wrote to him to offer his congratulations, and asked his former chief to pass on his regards to Feisal: 'Tell him
that I thought a great deal of him during the war: and that I think far
more of him now. He has lasted splendidly.'[3] Clayton was to die less than
a year later, from a heart-attack while playing polo in Baghdad.

Many of the Iraqis who had joined the Arab revolt also returned to
Baghdad. Jafar Pasha was appointed Minister of Defence before being
appointed Iraq's diplomatic representative in London in 1922. In
November the following year Feisal recalled him to serve, for the first
of two occasions, as Prime Minister. Jafar was murdered in 1936, trying
to use his popularity within the armed forces to forestall a military coup.
Jafar's brother-in-law, and former chief of staff, Nuri Said, followed him
to the Ministry of Defence in 1921, and became Prime Minister for the
first time in 1930. In a statistical testimony to the region's volatility, he
served as Prime Minister a further thirteen times, up until 1958 when he
too was murdered in a coup. Feisal would not have been surprised. After
twelve years as King, in March 1933 he reflected on his unruly subjects:

> There is still – and I say this with a heart of sorrow – no Iraqi people but
> unimaginable masses of human beings, devoid of any patriotic idea,
> imbued with religious traditions and absurdities connected by no com-
> mon tie, giving ear to evil, prone to anarchy and perpetually ready to rise
> against any government whatever.[4]

That September he died.

The crash that would kill Lawrence occurred late in the morning on 13
May 1935. Recently retired from the RAF, in which he had enlisted
under a pseudonym, Lawrence was returning from the post office to his
tiny Dorset cottage on his motorcycle, when he was forced to swerve to
avoid two young cyclists in a lane. He lost control, flew over his

handlebars and hit the road headfirst. Six days later he died, having never regained consciousness. By the time of his death, 'Lawrence of Arabia' had already assumed near-legendary status for his central role in directing the Arab uprising of almost twenty years before. Reacting to the news of his death, Winston Churchill described Lawrence as 'one of the greatest beings of our time'.[5]

Lawrence's death cleared the way for the general publication of *Seven Pillars of Wisdom*. Only 200 copies of the lavishly illustrated first edition had originally been printed, for subscribers who each paid thirty guineas for the book. A general edition was published two months later, that July. It is a pleasingly substantial book, more family bible than war memoir, bound in tan canvas with golden lettering on its face and spine. 'SEVEN PILLARS OF WISDOM' reads the title page inside; below, the simple assertion: 'a triumph'.

'A triumph' aptly summarised the British view of the revolt, from which Lawrence was inseparable. The involvement of his colleagues was largely overlooked, although sporadic newspaper obituaries of old soldiers for many years would identify their wartime association with T.E. Lawrence. Lawrence was the perfect British hero: an eccentric amateur whose unorthodox methods brought victory with an economy and fluidity which had been absent from the Western Front. 'Our duty,' he had written, 'was to attain our end with the greatest economy of life, since life was more precious to us than money or time.'[6] It was his aim – to infuriate the enemy, and not to kill them, and its success – achieved with such economy – that resonated around a land now studded with bright new war memorials.

The success of Lawrence's strategy caused a complete change in the perception of guerrilla warfare, which, up until that point and with the notable exception of the Boers, tended to be seen as the desperate resort of an enemy too weak or disorganised to risk an open confrontation. Lawrence's achievement, together with the advent of motorised warfare, was about to change that. 'Military history cannot dismiss him as merely a successful leader of irregulars,' the outspoken military thinker, Basil Liddell Hart argued. 'He is . . . a strategist of genius who had the vision to anticipate the guerrilla trend of civilised warfare that arises from the growing dependence of nations on industrial resources.'[7] A mobile army could advance faster, but its supply lines were longer, and so more vulnerable to the deadly hit-and-run tactics Lawrence had popularised. The strategy described in detail in *Seven Pillars of Wisdom* would inspire the generation of men who fought in the following war. One of them, the future leader of the Long Range Desert Group, which operated behind enemy lines in the North African campaign, would afterwards recall how 'Lawrence had lit the flame which fans the passion of those who lead guerrilla warfare and I wanted more than anything to experience it.'[8]

The irony was that it was precisely because of the unorthodox origins of the revolt, and its subsequent success, that it raises completely different emotions for the Arabs.

When the idea that the British could support Sharif Husein in a revolt against the Turks was first conceived, no one expected the revolt to break out of the Hijaz. As Ronald Storrs admitted years later, the attempt to wrest the Caliphate from the Ottoman sultan and transfer it to the Sharif was attractive precisely because, in 'uniting the strongest religious with the weakest material power, it would be greatly to our interest'.[9] His attitude, that the Sharif, though a powerful religious influence around the Islamic world, was a political dwarf, encouraged McMahon to take a cavalier approach in the letters that he wrote to him. 'I had necessarily to be vague as on the one hand HMG disliked being committed to definite future action, and on the other any detailed definition of our demands would have frightened off the Arab,'[10] McMahon explained at the end of 1915:

> I do not for one moment go to the length of imagining that the present negotiations will go far to shape the future form of Arabia or to either establish our rights or bind our hands in that country. What we have to arrive at now is to tempt the Arab people onto the right path, detach them from the enemy and bring them on to our side.

Wingate saw the revolt in similar terms. At the end of the war he admitted

> to having been sufficiently opportunist to take the fullest advantage of the situation to treat the Sharif's revolt rather as a really useful war measure

than as a means to an end for the renaissance of a great united Arab Empire
. . . There are others who may still retain such beliefs and hopes and I
admire their enthusiasm, but, personally . . . as long as the movement
served its purpose in knocking out one or two stones of the arch of the
Central Powers, I am satisfied that its object (as far as my intervention is
concerned) has been achieved.[11]

Had the revolt never reached Syria, the cynicism of these calculations
would never have become so clear. Had his forces never reached
Damascus in October 1918, Husein would have found it hard to have
made a strong claim for Syria, which the British then had to deny. It was
precisely because the revolt was so successful – greatly thanks to Lawrence
– that the extent of British bad faith would inevitably be revealed.

Not that the British had no premonition of what would follow.
Throughout the war, when Husein had repeatedly told them that he
trusted Britain to honour the commitments made by McMahon before
the revolt, he caused discomfort. They knew that Husein was – either
deliberately or not – misinterpreting the strength of the assurances they
had given him; but they were frightened to confront the problem in case
it caused a collapse in Arab support, which would first have initially
exposed them to the nebulous threat of jihad and, later and more
materially, greatly affected the security of Allenby's operations in
Palestine. Husein 'has read into the terms of that "pledge" very wide
territorial boundaries, and professes the most implicit trust in the
intention and ability of Great Britain to redeem the "pledge" as he
reads it', Cyril Wilson's colleague, Colonel Bassett, warned early in 1918.
'Anything that would mean for him a "rude awakening", I dread.'[12]

The further northwards Allenby pushed into Palestine, the stronger
the argument for inertia became. Nothing should be done to disabuse
Husein, in case the Sharif reacted by breaking off his support and
leaving Allenby exposed to a Turkish attack from the Maan area.
Allenby, who had originally justified his campaign for its value in
supporting the Arab movement, also recognised that the British alliance
with the Sharif was a powerful piece of propaganda. In the autumn of
1917, he wrote to his wife, enclosing a copy of a leaflet dropped by the

British over Palestine. 'The enclosed photograph of the Sharif of Mecca – and the proclamation by him – is one of the means we have of inducing the Arabs to desert the Turks. We drop these papers – and packets of cigarettes – over the Turkish lines, from aeroplanes,' he explained. The proclamation encouraged the Arabs to desert and join the war 'for the freedom and independence of Arabia . . . A good many come in, as a result of our propaganda.'[13] The use of this sort of tactic only fuelled later Arab claims that they had been misled by Britain. Other leaflets – presumably of British origin – depicted Husein embodying the entire Arab peninsula: a commitment rapidly dropped in the 1920s as the British lost faith in Husein and turned to Ibn Saud, who conquered the Hijaz in 1925.[14]

Debate over the meaning of the correspondence between Husein and McMahon intensified after Lawrence's death. During the 1920s, the Arabs had taken a relaxed attitude to Jewish immigration to Palestine. They were 'annoyed and insulted by Zionist immigration, but not alarmed by it', Sharif Husein's son Abdullah later stated.[15] 'It was steady, but fairly small, as even the Zionist founders thought it would remain. Indeed for some years, more Jews left Palestine than entered it – in 1927 almost twice as many.' Two, linked, events upset this equilibrium. The first was the economic depression triggered by the stock-market crash of 1929; the second, the rise to power of Hitler. Both caused thousands of mostly reluctant Jews to leave Eastern Europe in search of work and safety. They might have gone to the United States or western Europe, had not immigration controls been tightened there. Some went instead to Palestine. The growth in the Jewish population during the 1930s startled the Arabs. 'In 1932,' Abdullah told an audience in 1947, 'only 9,500 Jews came to Palestine. We did not welcome them, but we were not afraid that, at any rate, our solid Arab majority would ever be in danger. But the next year – the year of Hitler – it jumped to 30,000! In 1934 it was 42,000! In 1935 it reached 61,000!'

In 1936, the Arabs in Palestine reacted violently. When Italy invaded Abyssinia the year before, Britain's threat of sanctions raised fears of war. The concerns prompted a collapse in economic confidence in Palestine, where a rather precarious reliance on credit had previously sustained

growth. The Arabs were acutely affected and Jewish immigration began
to aggravate them. Strikes called in the spring of 1936 evolved into
widespread insurgency, which only died away at harvest-time. Two years
of sporadic violence followed.

Looking for ways to undermine the basis for the Jewish influx into
Palestine, the Arabs began to focus their attention on the correspondence
between Husein and McMahon before the outbreak of the revolt in
Mecca, because it seemed to undermine the basis of the Balfour
Declaration. The British government refused repeated requests to publish
the letters. There were 'valid reasons, entirely unconnected with the
question of Palestine, which render it in the highest degree undesirable
in the public interest to publish the correspondence', a junior minister
informed Parliament in August 1930.[16] This was rather disingenuous.
Behind the scenes civil servants worried that, if printed in their entirety,
the letters would reveal an uncomfortable degree of British meddling in
the issue of the Caliphate – still then a sensitive issue in India – and do
nothing to clarify whether or not Palestine was excluded from the area
offered to the Arabs by McMahon. But this position was untenable.
Versions of the letters in Arabic were already circulating, and in 1937,
the government granted the Royal Commission it had appointed to seek
a solution to the situation in Palestine permission to quote from the
Husein–McMahon correspondence in their report. 'It was in the highest
degree unfortunate that, in the exigencies of war, the British Government
were unable to make their intention clear to the Sharif', was the Royal
Commission's verdict.[17]

Exactly what McMahon promised in his letters to Husein has never
satisfactorily been made clear, just as McMahon intended. But his studied
ambiguity, which seemed so suitable at the time, was counter-productive
in the long run. British officials went to enormous lengths to interpret
what McMahon had said, to try to exclude Palestine from the area the
Arabs claimed was theirs. The problems mounted when, after being
missing for nearly fifteen years, copies of the Arabic versions of the two
most significant letters were found in a clear-out of Ronald Storrs's office
in Cairo.[18] Their discovery only increased British discomfort. In his letter
to Husein of 24 October, McMahon had tried to qualify his commitment

with the proviso that he could give assurances in places 'in which Britain is free to act without detriment to the interests of her ally France'. Designed to be ambiguous, the phrase as it was then translated into Arabic read as a confirmation that, except in the areas he had vaguely defined, Britain *was* able to confirm Husein's demands, without affecting French interests. 'This careless translation completely changes the meaning of the reservation, or at any rate makes the meaning exceedingly ambiguous,' the Lord Chancellor admitted, in a secret legal opinion on the strength of the Arab claim.[19] Storrs later admitted that the way in which the letters had been translated, by his secret agent Ruhi, was imperfect. Ruhi was, he said, 'a better agent than scholar'.[20]

The refusal to admit that McMahon's true purpose was to string Sharif Husein along drew the controversy out, into what *The Times* wonderfully described, in McMahon's obituary, as 'a disagreeable aftermath'.[21] By the late 1930s, with war looming yet again, the British needed to maintain the Arabs' support. In 1939, on the sidelines of a London conference on Palestine, the British agreed to a full examination of the correspondence by a committee comprising British and Arab representatives. A single sentence in their report summed up the story: 'Both the Arab and the United Kingdom representatives have tried (as they hope with success) to understand the point of view of the other party, but they have been unable to reach agreement upon an interpretation of the Correspondence.'[22] By then the British, recognising that basing their case on McMahon's words was fruitless, had resorted to defending their argument that Palestine had not been included through a description of the context. This was a stronger argument, because it probably explained McMahon's reluctance to go into detail in the first place, but it ultimately depended on the assertion that it was the French interest in Palestine which meant that Britain could not have ceded the region to the Arabs: an astonishing argument given that the thrust of British policy throughout the war had been to contain and undermine French influence.

The two sides of the revolt – the triumph personified by Lawrence and the betrayal felt by the Arabs – are inextricably intertwined. Without the correspondence, there would have been no British involvement in the revolt, and without the triumph, the insincerity of the letters to Husein would never have been so starkly revealed. Both sides of this legacy – of triumph and betrayal – survive today. A new generation of military advisers in Iraq pore over Lawrence in search of inspiration,[23] while, in the Arab mind, Britain's failure to honour its initial promise has created a reservoir of deep resentment on which opponents of the West continue regularly to draw. In his first public statement after the terrorist attacks of 11 September 2001, Osama bin Laden – who was born in Riyadh and educated in Jeddah – reminded the world that 'our nation has been tasting humiliation and contempt for more than eighty years'.[24] To the Arabs today, the British role behind their uprising ninety years ago remains unforgotten, and largely unforgiven.

ABBREVIATIONS USED IN THE NOTES

BL	=	British Library
CCC	=	Churchill College, Cambridge
IOR	=	India Office Records
IWM	=	Imperial War Museum
LHCMA	=	Liddell Hart Centre for Military Archives
MAE	=	Ministère des Affaires étrangères
MEC	=	Middle East Centre
PCC	=	Pembroke College, Cambridge
SAD	=	Sudan Archive, Durham
TNA	=	The National Archive
Vincennes	=	Château de Vincennes

NOTES

PROLOGUE

1 Photographs taken in 1964 show that the locomotive has in fact been righted and turned round since its derailment, possibly during one of the abortive attempts to rebuild the railway since its destruction during the First World War. *The Times*, 'Tracking the Train that Lawrence Wrecked', 4 December 1964, and Phillip Knightley and Colin Simpson, *The Secret Lives of Lawrence of Arabia*, London 1969, photograph pp.94–5.

2 Valentine Chirol, *Pan-Islamism*, London 1906, p.2.

3 IOR, L/PS/10/12, piece 2181; G.B. Jathar and S.G. Beri, *Indian Economics*, London 1933, p.120. William Ochsenwald (*The Hijaz Railroad*, Charlottesville 1980), however, believes that Western governments overestimated the amounts their Muslim subjects gave.

4 Valentine Chirol, *Pan-Islamism*, London 1906, p.9.

5 Geoffrey Lewis, 'The Ottoman Proclamation of Jihad in 1914', in *Arabic and Islamic Garland: Historical, Educational and Literary Papers presented to Abdul Latif Tibawi*, London 1977.

1 A PARTING OF THE WAYS

1 TNA, FO 882/25, *Arab Bulletin* 29, 8 November 1916.
2 TNA, FO 882/25, *Arab Bulletin* 21, 15 September 1916.
3 TNA, FO 882/25, *Arab Bulletin* 21, 15 September 1916.
4 PCC, Storrs Papers, diary entry, 16 October 1916.
5 MEC, Hogarth Papers, Hogarth to 'Billy', 10 January 1918.
6 Victoria Wester Wemyss, *The Life and Letters of Lord Wester Wemyss*, London 1935, p.354 and MEC, J.W.A. Young Papers, 'A Little to the East', 29 December 1945.
7 TNA, FO 882/13, Hogarth, 'Position and Prospects of King Hussein', *Arab Bulletin* Supplementary Papers, No. 2, 1 March 1918.
8 MEC, J.W.A. Young Papers, 'A Little to the East', 29 December 1945.
9 Lord Winterton, *Fifty Tumultuous Years*, London 1955, p.140.
10 IWM, W.F. Stirling Papers, letter, 1 January 1918.
11 Ronald Storrs, *Orientations*, London 1937, p.143.
12 Storrs, *Orientations*, p.98.
13 Quoted in Jacob M. Landau, *The Politics of Pan-Islam*, Oxford 1990, p.47.
14 Thomas W. Arnold, *The Caliphate*, second edition, London 1965, p.47.
15 Storrs's immediate predecessor as Oriental Secretary, Harry Boyle, evidently expressed reservations. MEC, Baring Papers, Cromer to Boyle, 10 October 1914.
16 Storrs Papers, letter to 'φιλτατε' [i.e. 'dearest'], 22 February 1915.
17 Storrs Papers, Storrs to Abdullah, n.d.
18 TNA, FO 882/4, Note on a conference at Ismailia, 12 September 1916.
19 SAD, Wingate Papers, 134/2, Clayton to Wingate, 29 May 1915.
20 TNA, FO 371/2486, piece 77713, McMahon to Grey, 30 June 1915.
21 TNA, FO 371/3054, Wingate to Balfour, enclosing reports from Lawrence, 16 August 1917; FO 882/27, *Arab Bulletin* 76, 13 January 1918.
22 Ramzi Touchan, David Meko and Malcolm K. Hughes, 'A 396-year reconstruction of precipitation in Southern Jordan', *Journal of the American Water Resources Association*, Vol.35 No.1 (Feb. 1999).
23 TNA, FO 882/25, *Arab Bulletin* 33, 4 December 1916.
24 MEC, J.W.A. Young Papers, 'Three Months in Jedda', n.d.
25 TNA FO 882/25, *Arab Bulletin* 33 and Sharif Husein's Proclamation of Independence, 27 June 1916.
26 IOR, L/PS/11/117, piece 353. The proclamation in which this complaint was made was issued before 14 November 1916.
27 Arnold, *The Caliphate*, p.48.
28 IOR, L/PS/11/117, piece 353, dated before 14 November 1916.
29 Sharif Husein's Proclamation of Independence, 27 June 1916.
30 Husein to McMahon, 14 July 1915, in George Antonius, *The Arab Awakening*, p.414.
31 TNA, FO 371/2486, piece 117236, McMahon to Grey, 22 August 1915.
32 Antonius, *The Arab Awakening*, p.167.
33 McMahon to Husein, 30 August 1915; Husein to McMahon 9 September 1915, in Antonius, *The Arab Awakening*, p.417.
34 Eliezer Tauber, *The Arab Movements in World War I*, London 1993, p.76.
35 Storrs, *Orientations*, p.165.
36 John Buchan, *Greenmantle*, London 1916, p.6.
37 Buchan, *Greenmantle*, p.9.
38 TNA, FO 371/2354, piece 127705, *Daily Chronicle*, 30 August 1915.
39 SAD, Wingate Papers, 135/2, Clayton to Wingate, 9 October 1915.
40 TNA, FO 371/3486, piece 150309, Kitchener to Maxwell, 13 October 1915.
41 TNA, FO 371/2486, piece 153045, McMahon to Grey, 18 October 1915.

2 WILL THIS DO?

1 TNA, FO 371/2486, piece 155203, McMahon's draft, 20 October 1915.
2 Ronald Graham, quoted in Elie Kedourie, *In the Anglo-Arab Labyrinth*, Cambridge 1976, p.35.
3 Lord Hardinge, quoted in Kedourie, *In the Anglo-Arab Labyrinth*, p.35.
4 TNA, FO 882/2, Clayton to Tyrrell, 30 October 1915.
5 TNA, FO 371/2486, piece 152729, minute by George Clerk, 19 October 1915.
6 TNA, FO 371/2486, piece 163832, McMahon to Grey, 26 October 1915.
7 TNA, FO 371/2486, piece 163832, McMahon to Grey, 26 October 1915.
8 SAD, Clayton Papers, 469/11, Wingate to Clayton, 15 November 1915.
9 Husein to McMahon, 1 January 1916, in Antonius, *The Arab Awakening*, p.426.
10 Djemal Pasha, *Memories of a Turkish Statesman*, London 1922, p.168.
11 TNA, FO 882/19, Husein to McMahon, 18 February 1916.
12 SAD, Clayton Papers, 693/10, Clayton to Director of Military Intelligence, 3 March 1916.
13 Djemal Pasha, *Memories of a Turkish Statesman*, p.197.
14 Djemal Pasha, *Memories of a Turkish Statesman*, p.197.
15 Djemal Pasha, *Memories of a Turkish Statesman*, p.215.
16 Graves, ed. *Memoirs of King Abdullah*, London 1950, p.137.
17 Djemal Pasha, *Memories of a Turkish Statesman*, p.217.
18 Djemal Pasha, *Memories of a Turkish Statesman*, p. 212.
19 TNA, FO 882/25, *Arab Bulletin* 21, 15 September 1916.
20 Djemal Pasha, *Memories of a Turkish Statesman*, p.224.
21 Djemal Pasha, *Memories of a Turkish Statesman*, p.224.
22 PCC, Storrs Papers, Storrs's report, 14 June 1916.
23 Storrs, *Orientations*, p.185.
24 TNA, FO 882/4, Clayton to Wingate, 9 June 1916, reporting Storrs's account of events.
25 IOR, L/PS/10/598, piece 3040, Storrs's telegram, 6 June.
26 D.G. Hogarth, 'Mecca's Revolt against the Turk', *Century Magazine*, 1920.
27 TNA, FO 882/25, *Arab Bulletin* 22, 19 September 1916.
28 LHCMA, Joyce Papers, 1/43, 1–5 February 1917.
29 T.E. Lawrence, *Seven Pillars of Wisdom*, London 1935, p.94.
30 Graves, ed. *Memoirs of King Abdullah*, p.144.
31 Graves, ed. *Memoirs of King Abdullah*, p.148.
32 Earl of Cork and Orrery, *My Naval Life, 1886–1941*, London 1942, p.94.
33 IWM, F. Hayward Papers, Hayward to Lawrence, 6 September 1936.
34 Earl of Cork and Orrery, *My Naval Life, p.*97.
35 Proclamation of Sharif Husein, 26 June 1916, and TNA, FO 686/149, evidence of Sayyid Mehdi Hasan.
36 Musbah Haidar, *Arabesque*, London 1944, p.82.

3 A STRANGE UNCANNY PLACE

1 BL, Mss Eur E 264/7, Chelmsford to Chamberlain, 13 June 1916.
2 IOR, L/PS/10/599, piece 2506, Chelmsford to Chamberlain, 29 June 1916.
3 IOR, L/PS/10/599, piece 2542, Chelmsford to Chamberlain, 1 July 1916.
4 IOR, L/PS/10/599, piece 3113.
5 IOR, L/PS/10/597, piece 2394, McMahon to FO and response, 19 and 21 June 1916.
6 Malcolm Brown, ed. *T.E. Lawrence: the selected letters*, London 2005, Lawrence to Sarah Lawrence, 1 July 1916, p.87.

7 SAD, Wingate Papers, 137/4, Wingate to Clayton, 15 June 1916.
8 MEC, Hogarth Papers, Hogarth to 'Mary', 19 January 1918.
9 SAD, Wingate Papers, 138/5, Wilson's report, 7 July 1916.
10 TNA, FO 882/4, Cornwallis's report, 8 July 1916.
11 SAD, Wingate Papers, 138/5, Wilson's report, 7 July 1916.
12 PCC, Storrs Papers, note on the Pilgrimage, n.d.
13 SAD, Wingate Papers, 138/5, Wilson's report, 7 July 1916.
14 SAD, Wingate Papers, 147/6, Beryl Wilson to Wingate, 28 December 1917.
15 LHCMA, Joyce Papers, 1/323 and 1/324, Wilson to Wingate, 16 February 1936; Wingate to Wilson, 21 February 1936.
16 N.N.E. Bray, *Shifting Sands*, London 1934, p.75.
17 SAD, Wingate Papers, 139/2, Clayton to Wingate, 7 August 1916.
18 Vincennes, SS Marine Q 85, Arabie Révolte du Chérif, Jaussen's report, 15–31 July 1916.
19 TNA, FO 686/10, note dated 1 August 1916.
20 IOR, L/PS/10/598, piece 2739.
21 BL, Add 52463, Robertson to Murray, 14 July 1916.
22 IWM, F. Hayward Papers, letter to T.E. Lawrence, 6 September 1936.
23 BL, Add 52463, Robertson to Murray, 16 October 1916.
24 BL, Add 52463, Robertson to Murray, 1 August 1916.
25 BL, Add 52463, Robertson to Murray, 29 August 1916.
26 SAD, Wingate Papers, 139/2, Robertson to Wingate, 8 August 1916.
27 IOR, L/PS/10/599 and TNA, FO 686/11, Ali Haidar's proclamation, 9 August 1916.
28 IOR, L/PS/11/113, Chamberlain to Asquith, 16 August 1916.
29 SAD, Clayton Papers, 470/3, Wingate to Clayton, 6 August 1916.
30 SAD, Clayton Papers, 470/3, Wingate to Clayton, 14 September 1916.
31 IOR, L/PS/10/600, piece 3894, Wilson's report, 17 August 1916.
32 TNA, FO 882/4, Ibrahim Dmitri's report, written after 17 August 1916.
33 SAD, Wingate Papers, 139/5, Wilson to Wingate, 23 August 1916.
34 TNA, FO 882/4, Wilson's report, 1 September 1916.
35 TNA, FO 882/4, Note on the Conference at Ismailia, 12 September 1916.
36 SAD, Clayton Papers, 470/4, Wingate to Clayton, 30 November 1916.
37 IOR, L/PS/10/600, piece 3894, Wilson's report, 17 August 1916.
38 IOR, L/PS/10/600, piece 4238, Wilson to McMahon, 24 August 1916.
39 SAD, Clayton Papers, 693/10, Clayton to Hall, 10 September 1916.
40 TNA, FO 882/4, Note on the Conference at Ismailia, 12 September 1916.
41 Wemyss, *The Life and Letters of Lord Wester Wemyss*, p.236.

4 FOREIGN INFLUENCES

1 TNA, FO 686/149.
2 BL, Mss Eur E 264/7, Chelmsford to Chamberlain, 15 September 1916.
3 TNA, FO 686/149.
4 TNA, FO 686/149.
5 TNA, FO 686/149, Cleveland's memorandum, 14 September 1916.
6 Storrs, *Orientations*, p.204.
7 IOR, L/PS/10/615, piece 3768, McMahon to Grey, 13 September 1916.
8 SAD, Clayton Papers, 693/10, Clayton to Hall, 10 September 1916.
9 Bray, *Shifting Sands*, pp.66–7.
10 MEC, Sykes Papers, War Committee Minutes, 16 December 1915.

11 Mark Sykes, *The Caliphs' Last Heritage*, London 1915, p.596.

12 SAD, Wingate Papers, 135/6, Sykes to Director of Military Operations, 21 November 1915.

13 TNA, FO 882/2, minutes of the second meeting of the committee discussing the Arab Question and Syria, 23 November 1915.

14 TNA, FO 882/2, internal note on the second meeting with Picot, 23 November 1915.

15 Quoted in Roger Adelson, *Mark Sykes*, London 1975, p.200.

16 Quoted in Adelson, *Sykes*, p.201.

17 SAD, Clayton Papers, 470/2, Wingate to Clayton, 24 April 1916.

18 SAD, Clayton Papers, 694/4, 'Note on the Arab Question', 5 July 1916.

19 TNA, FO 371/2767, Nicolson's Committee Meeting, 17 January 1916, quoted in Adelson, *Sykes*, p.202.

20 Edouard Brémond, *Le Hedjaz dans la Guerre Mondiale*, Paris 1931, p.35

21 Pierre de Margerie, 'Note to the President of the Council', 19 July 1916, quoted in Christophe Leclerc, 'The French Soldiers in the Arab Revolt', *Journal of the T.E. Lawrence Society*, Vol. IX, No. 1 (Autumn 1999).

22 SAD, Clayton Papers, 694/4, 'Notes on a Conference held at the Commander in Chief's house on 5th September 1916, with regard to the French military mission to the Hedjaz'.

23 BL, Add 52463, Murray to Robertson, 5 September 1916.

24 Storrs, *Orientations*, p.192.

25 Storrs, *Orientations*, p.193.

26 PCC, Storrs Papers, diary entry, 27 September 1916.

27 PCC, Storrs Papers, diary entry, 27 September 1916.

28 Storrs, *Orientations*, p.193.

29 PCC, torrs Papers, diary entry, 27 September 1916.

30 PCC, Storrs Papers, diary entry, 27 September 1916.

31 Brémond, *Le Hedjaz dans la Guerre Mondiale*, p.52.

32 MEC, J.W.A. Young Papers, 'Three Months in Jedda', n.d.

33 Storrs, *Orientations*, p.194.

34 IOR, L/PS/10/600, piece 4160, Parker to McMahon, 3 October 1916.

35 MEC, Sykes Papers, 'Despatch of an Expeditionary Force to Rabigh', 13 November 1916, contained Robertson's early advice to the War Committee dated 20 September 1916.

36 IOR, L/PS/10/600, piece 4054, McMahon to Grey, 29 September 1916.

37 IOR, L/PS/10/600, piece 3977, Wilson to FO, 28 September 1916.

38 SAD, Wingate Papers, 140/8, Wigram to Wingate, 28 September 1916.

39 IOR, L/PS/10/600, piece 4238, War Committee Minutes, 3 October 1916.

40 Quoted in H.V.F. Winstone, ed. *The Diaries of Parker Pasha*, London 1983, p.137.

41 SAD, Wingate Papers, 142/11, McMahon to Wingate, 6 October 1916.

42 IOR, L/PS/10/600, piece 4209, Wingate's telegram, 11 October 1916.

5 ALL CLAWS AND TEETH

1 PCC, Storrs Papers, diary entry, 15 October 1916.

2 IOR, L/PS/10/600, piece 4238, FO to Wingate, PCC, 13 October 1916.

3 PCC, Storrs Papers, 14 November 1916.

4 Baroness Elles, interview, July 2004.

5 Storrs, *Orientations*, p.200.

6 Storrs, *Orientations*, p.220.

7 Egypt, Ministry of Finance, Survey Department, *A short note on the Design and Issue of Postage Stamps Prepared by the Survey of Egypt for His Highness Husein Emir and Sharif of Mecca and King of the Hejaz*, November 1918.

8 David Garnett, ed. *The Letters of T.E. Lawrence*, London 1938, pp.195–6, Lawrence to Hogarth, 22 March 1915.

9   T.E. Lawrence, *Crusader Castles*, Oxford 1988, p.116–22.

10   SAD, Wingate Papers, 135/1, 'The Politics of Mecca', 8 February 1916.

11   SAD, Clayton Papers, 693/10, Clayton to Hall, 2 February 1916.

12   University of Newcastle, Gertrude Bell archive, Bell to Hugh Bell, 16 January 1916.

13   TNA, FO 882/13, Lake to Chamberlain, 30 March 1916.

14   Lawrence, *Seven Pillars of Wisdom*, 1935, p.57.

15   TNA, FO 141/736, Lawrence to Arab Bureau, 9 April 1916.

16   TNA, FO 141/736, Lawrence to Arab Bureau, 9 April 1916, quoting Shakespeare to Cox, 17 January 1915. Shakespeare's letter was reprinted in *Arab Bulletin* 25 on 7 October 1916.

17   SAD, Wingate Papers, 137/7, Lawrence's report, 'Intelligence, IEF D', cover note dated 12 June 1916.

18   W.F. Stirling, *Safety Last*, London 1953, pp.66–7.

19   Lawrence, *Seven Pillars of Wisdom*, p.58.

20   Storrs, *Orientations*, p.220.

21   Lawrence, *Seven Pillars of Wisdom*, p.65.

22   Garnett, ed. *The Letters of T.E. Lawrence*, Lawrence to his parents, 24 January 1911.

23   BL, Add 45914, 'Haud Rediturus', *The Times*, 15 March 1916.

24   Malcolm Brown, ed. *Lawrence of Arabia: the selected letters*, London 2005, p.81, Lawrence to E.T. Leeds, 16 November 1915.

25   SAD, Clayton Papers, 470/5, Wilson to Clayton, 22 November 1916.

26   SAD, Clayton Papers, 693/11, Lawrence to Clayton, 18 October 1916.

27   PCC, Storrs Papers, diary entry, 16 October 1916.

28   PCC, Storrs Papers, letter to 'Colum', 21 December 1916.

29   PCC, Storrs Papers, diary entry, 16 October 1916.

30   Storrs, *Orientations*, p.203.

31   Graves, ed. *Memoirs of King Abdullah*, p.157.

32   Graves, ed. *Memoirs of King Abdullah*, p.158.

33   Storrs, *Orientations*, p.203.

34   SAD, Clayton Papers, 470/5, Wilson to Clayton, 18 October 1916.

35   Lawrence, *Seven Pillars of Wisdom*, p.71.

36   Lawrence, *Seven Pillars of Wisdom*, p.73.

37   Graves, ed. *Memoirs of King Abdullah*, p.158.

38   PCC, Storrs Papers, diary entry, 17 October 1916.

39   IOR, L/PS/10/602, piece 5195, Wilson's report, 20 October 1916.

40   MEC, J.W.A. Young Papers, 'Three Months in Jedda', n.d.

41   T.E. Lawrence, *Seven Pillars of Wisdom*, Oxford 1922, p.57.

42   Storrs, *Orientations*, p.208.

43   BL, Add 45914, f.22.

44   PCC, Storrs Papers, Lawrence to Clayton, 17 October 1916.

45   PCC, Storrs Papers, Lawrence to Clayton, 17 October 1916.

46   SAD, Clayton Papers, 693/11, Lawrence to Clayton, 18 October 1916.

47   SAD, Clayton Papers, 693/11, Lawrence to Clayton, 18 October 1916.

48   TNA, FO 882/25, *Arab Bulletin* 32, 26 November 1916.

49   Lawrence, *Seven Pillars of Wisdom*, 1922, p.75.

50   TNA, FO 882/25, *Arab Bulletin* 32, 26 November 1916.

51   Lawrence, *Seven Pillars of Wisdom*, 1935, p.91.

52   Lawrence, *Seven Pillars of Wisdom*, 1935, p.91.

53   Lawrence, *Seven Pillars of Wisdom*, 1935, p.91.

54   TNA, FO 882/25, *Arab Bulletin* 32, 26 November 1916.

55   TNA, FO 882/25, *Arab Bulletin* 32, 26 November 1916.

56   TNA, FO 882/25, *Arab Bulletin* 32, 26 November 1916.

57   Lawrence, *Seven Pillars of Wisdom*, 1935, p.67.

58   TNA, FO 882/25, *Arab Bulletin* 32, 26 November 1916.

59 Winstone, ed. *The Diaries of Parker Pasha*, p.173, report to Arab Bureau, 8 November 1916.
60 TNA, FO 882/25, *Arab Bulletin* 32, 26 November 1916.
61 Charles Callwell, *Small Wars*, second edition, London 1899, p.3.
62 Callwell, *Small Wars*, p.105.
63 Cork and Orrery, *My Naval Life*, p.99.

6 CRISIS OVER RABIGH

1 IOR, L/PS/10/637, piece 4932, Wilson to McMahon, 31 October 1916.
2 IOR, L/PS/10/637, piece 5321, Wilson to McMahon, 5 November 1916.
3 IOR, L/PS/10/637, McMahon to Grey, 21 November 1916.
4 SAD, Wingate Papers, 143/6, Clayton to Wingate, 23 November 1916.
5 IOR, L/PS/10/637, piece 5235, FO to Wingate, 11 December 1916.
6 IOR, L/PS/10/602, Wingate to FO, 7 November 1916.
7 SAD, Wingate Papers, 143/6, Cornwallis to Wingate, 30 November 1916.
8 MEC, Hogarth Papers, Hogarth to Laura Hogarth, 7 November 1916.
9 MEC, Hogarth Papers, Hogarth to Laura Hogarth, 19 January 1917.
10 SAD, Wingate Papers, 143/6, Cornwallis to Wingate, 30 November 1916.
11 Bray, *Shifting Sands*, p.103.
12 BL, Add 52463, Murray to Robertson, 14 November 1916.
13 SAD, Clayton Papers, 694/4, 'Observations by Lt Lawrence', 18 November 1916.
14 SAD, Clayton Papers, 694/4, 'Observations by Lt Lawrence', 18 November 1916.
15 SAD, Clayton Papers, 694/4, 'Observations by Lt Lawrence', 18 November 1916.
16 Brémond, *Le Hedjaz dans la Guerre Mondiale*, p.98.
17 PCC, Storrs Papers, Storrs to Sybil Graham, 21 November 1916.
18 IOR, L/PS/10/602, Wingate to Grey, 22 November 1916.
19 SAD, Clayton Papers, 470/4, Wingate to Clayton, 20 November 1916.
20 SAD, Wingate Papers, Wingate to Wilson, 23 November 1916.
21 TNA, FO 882/6, Lawrence's diary of his visit to Feisal, 2–5 December 1916.
22 Lawrence, *Seven Pillars of Wisdom*, 1935, p.119.
23 TNA, FO 882/6, Lawrence's diary of his visit to Feisal, 2–5 December 1916.
24 TNA, FO 882/6, Lawrence's diary of his visit to Feisal, 2–5 December 1916.
25 Lawrence presented the rifle to King George V after the war, who in turn gave it to the Imperial War Museum in London, where it is displayed today.
26 TNA, FO 882/6, Lawrence to Hogarth, 5 December 1916.
27 TNA, FO 882/6, Lawrence to Hogarth, 5 December 1916.
28 TNA, FO 882/6, Lawrence to Hogarth, 5 December 1916.
29 BL, Add 45914, entry dated 5 December 1916.
30 TNA, FO 882/6, Lawrence to Hogarth n.d.
31 BL, Add 45914, entry dated 6 January 1917; TNA, WO 158/625, P184A.
32 Lawrence, *Seven Pillars of Wisdom*, 1935, p.129.
33 IWM, H. Garland Papers, lecture n.d. (but before April 1921). Garland's draft lecture notes contain a great deal of criticism about the Bedu, some of which he then crossed out, but which is still legible. I have quoted freely from this material, on the basis that it appears to represent Garland's heartfelt views, even if he did not wish to share them with an audience.
34 IWM, H. Garland Papers, lecture n.d.
35 Lawrence, *Seven Pillars of Wisdom*, 1922, p.121.
36 TNA, FO 882/6, Lawrence to Director, Arab Bureau, n.d.
37 Garnett, ed. *The Letters of T.E. Lawrence*, p213, Lawrence to Wilson, 6 December 1916.

38 LHCMA, Joyce Papers, 1/J/4/2, Lawrence to Ross, 9 December 1916.
39 LHCMA, Joyce Papers, 1/7, Joyce to Wilson, 9 December 1916.
40 LHCMA, Joyce Papers, 1/1, Joyce to Wilson, 15 November 1916.
41 Brémond, *Le Hedjaz dans la Guerre Mondiale*, p.88.
42 LHCMA, Joyce Papers, 1/3, Joyce to Wilson, 26 November 1916.
43 LHCMA, Joyce Papers, 1/11, Joyce to Rees-Mogg, 21 December 1916.
44 TNA, FO 141/736, Joyce to Arab Bureau, 24 January 1917.
45 IWM, T. Henderson, *The Hejaz Expedition, 1916–17 – A Narrative of the Work done by the Arabian detachment of No. 14 Squadron RFC while attached to the Hejaz expedition*, n.d.
46 PCC, Storrs Papers, 'Visit to Grand Sharif', 13 December 1916.
47 LHCMA, Joyce Papers, 2/2, 10 December 1916, Minutes of a Military Council meeting held in Yanbu.

7 TURNING POINT

1 BL, Add 52463, Robertson to Murray, 1 December 1916.
2 IOR, L/PS/10/602, Hirtzel, minute, 8 December 1916.
3 IOR, L/PS/10/602, piece 5213, Chamberlain, note, 11 December 1916.
4 LHCMA, Robertson Papers, 4/4/63, Robertson to Murray, 11 December 1916.
5 IOR, L/PS/10/602, FO to Wingate, 11 December 1916.
6 IOR, L/PS/10/602, piece 5230, Wingate to FO, 11 December 1916; TNA, FO 686/6, George Lloyd's report 22 December 1916.
7 TNA, FO 882/6, Wilson to Arab Bureau, 12 December 1916.
8 IOR, L/PS/10/602, Wingate to Wilson, 11 December 1916.
9 PCC, Storrs, *Orientations*, p.212.
10 PCC, Storrs Papers, 'Visit to Grand Sharif', 13 December 1916.
11 FO 882/6, Wilson to Arab Bureau, 12 December 1916.
12 Storrs, *Orientations*, p.213.
13 TNA, FO 686/6, Report on the Hijaz, 22 December 1916.
14 TNA, FO 882/25, *Arab Bulletin* 29, 8 November 1916.
15 Bray, *Shifting Sands*, pp.79–80.
16 TNA, FO 141/736, Wilson to Arab Bureau, 7 January 1917.
17 Liman von Sanders, *Five Years in Turkey*, Nashville 2000, pp.144–5.
18 Liman von Sanders, *Five Years in Turkey*, p.231; George Stitt, *A Prince of Arabia, The Emir Shereef Ali Haider*, London 1948, pp. 174–5.
19 Stitt, *A Prince of Arabia*, p.171.
20 TNA, FO 882/26, *Arab Bulletin* 39, 19 January 1917.
21 Lawrence, *Seven Pillars of Wisdom*, 1922, p.124.
22 TNA, T 1/12249.
23 Cork and Orrery, *My Naval Life*, p.108.
24 TNA, FO 882/25, *Arab Bulletin* 32, 11 November 1916.
25 TNA, FO 882/26, *Arab Bulletin* 39, 19 January 1917.
26 TNA, FO 882/26, *Arab Bulletin* 37, 4 January 1917.
27 TNA, WO 158/625, piece 171A, 11 December 1916.
28 Stitt, *A Prince of Arabia*, p.171.
29 TNA, FO 882/28, *Arab Bulletin* 110, 30 April 1919.
30 LHCMA, Joyce Papers, 1/15, Joyce to Rees-Mogg, 3 January 1917.
31 Winstone, ed. *The Diaries of Parker Pasha*, Parker's report of 10 October 1916, p.141.
32 Lawrence, *Seven Pillars of Wisdom*, 1922, p.131.
33 TNA, FO 686/6, Lawrence to Wilson, 8 January 1917.

34 TNA, FO 686/6, Lawrence to Wilson, 8 January 1917.
35 IOR, L/PS/11/116, piece 243, Hirtzel's memorandum, 15 January 1917.
36 SAD, Wingate Papers, 145/1, Murray to Wingate, 5 January 1917.
37 SAD, Clayton Papers, 694/5, Draft orders for GOC Rabegh, 7 January 1917.
38 TNA, FO 141/736, Wilson to Arab Bureau, 7 January 1917.
39 IOR, L/PS/11/116, piece 243, Hirtzel's, memorandum, 15 January 1917.
40 SAD, Wingate Papers, 145/1, Wingate to Foreign Office, 12 January 1917.
41 SAD, Wingate Papers, 145/1, Murray to Wingate, 19 January 1917.
42 IOR, L/PS/11/118, piece 585, Wingate to Balfour, 24 January 1917.
43 Brown, ed. *Lawrence of Arabia: the selected letters*, p.106, Lawrence to Sarah Lawrence, 16 January 1917.
44 Cork and Orrery, *My Naval Life*, p.102.
45 Cork and Orrery, *My Naval Life*, p.102.
46 Lawrence, *Seven Pillars of Wisdom*, 1922, p.137.
47 BL, Add 45914, entry for 18 January 1917, f.43.
48 Brémond, *Le Hedjaz dans la Guerre Mondiale*, p.120.
49 MEC, Newcombe Papers, Lawrence to Newcombe, 17 January 1917.
50 TNA, FO 686/6, Lawrence's report to Wilson, 8 January 1917.
51 BL, Add 45914, entry for 22 January 1917, f.49.

8 WAJH AND AFTER

1 Wemyss, *The Life and Letters of Lord Wester Wemyss*, p.346, diary entry for 21 January 1917.
2 Bray, *Shifting Sands*, p.119.
3 TNA, FO 882/27, *Arab Bulletin* 41, 6 February 1917.
4 Bray, *Shifting Sands*, pp.128–9.
5 TNA, FO 882/27, *Arab Bulletin* 41, 6 February 1917.
6 Bray, *Shifting Sands*, p.123.
7 Bray, *Shifting Sands*, p.131.
8 BL, Add 45914, f.7.
9 Lawrence, *Seven Pillars of Wisdom*, 1935, p.163.
10 TNA, FO 141/736, Weldon to Arab Bureau, 25 January 1917.
11 TNA, FO 882/6, Vickery, 'The General Situation in Arabia (Hedjaz) and the Policy and Organisation of the British Mission to Grand Sharif', 2 February 1917.
12 Bray, *Shifting Sands*.
13 TNA, FO 882/26, *Arab Bulletin* 41, 6 February 1917.
14 Winstone, ed. *The Diaries of Parker Pasha*, p.97, quoting notes written by Parker but entitled 'October 1915, TEL Arab Tribes in Arabia'.
15 TNA, FO 882/17, Gertrude Bell, 'Northern Arabia', and FO 882/4, Dmitri Ibrahim, report, after 17 August 1916; Winstone, ed. *The Diaries of Parker Pasha*, p.97.
16 TNA, FO 882/6, Bray, report, n.d. but before 4 January 1917.
17 SAD, Clayton Papers, 694/4, Salmond to Clayton, 12 November 1916.
18 Musbah Haidar, *Arabesque*, p.91; Eugene Rogan, *Frontiers of the State in the Late Ottoman Empire*, Cambridge 1999, p.228; Stitt, *A Prince of Arabia*, p.180.
19 MEC, Hogarth Papers, Hogarth to Laura Hogarth, 3 February 1917.
20 SAD, Wingate Papers, 132/5, 'G', 'The Hedjaz Railway', filed 23 December 1907.
21 A.J.B. Wavell, *A Modern Pilgrim in Mecca*, second edition, London 1918, p.72.
22 IWM, H. Garland Papers, post-war lecture, n.d.
23 IWM, H. Garland Papers, post-war lecture, n.d.
24 TNA, WO 158/987, *Handbook of Hejaz*, Cairo 1917, p.15.

25 TNA, WO 158/987, *Handbook of Hejaz*, p.9.
26 TNA, FO 882/4, Garland's report, 6 March 1917.
27 IWM, H. Garland Papers, post-war lecture, n.d.
28 IWM, H. Garland Papers, post-war lecture, n.d.
29 Winterton, *Fifty Tumultuous Years*, p.8.
30 IWM, H. Garland Papers, post-war lecture, n.d.
31 Touchan et al., 'A 396-year reconstruction of precipitation in Southern Jordan', *Journal of the American Water Resources Association*, Vol.35 No.1 (February 1999).
32 IWM, H. Garland Papers, post-war lecture, n.d.
33 IWM, H. Garland Papers, post-war lecture, n.d.
34 IWM, T. Henderson, *The Hejaz Expedition.*
35 IWM, H. Garland Papers, post-war lecture, n.d.
36 TNA, FO 882/4, Garland's report, 6 March 1917.

9 THE FIRST RAILWAY RAIDS

1 It is impossible to be certain whether the train was travelling north or south. In a lecture after the war Garland claimed it was heading south. However, after the attack, Wingate reported that a train had been mined heading north in the same area (TNA, FO 882/6, Wingate to Robertson, 21 February 1917).
2 IWM, H. Garland Papers, post-war lecture, n.d.
3 IWM, H. Garland Papers, post-war lecture, n.d. and TNA, FO 882/4, Garland's report, 6 March 1917.
4 TNA, FO 882/4, Garland's report, 6 March 1917.
5 TNA, FO 882/4, Garland's report, 6 March 1917.
6 TNA, FO 882/6, Lawrence to Cornwallis, 28 December 1916.
7 IWM, H. Garland Papers, post-war lecture, n.d. and TNA, FO 882/4, Garland's report, 6 March 1917.
8 BL, Add 45914, f.26.
9 BL, Add 45914, f.9.
10 BL, Add 45914, f.19.
11 Alois Musil, *The Northern Hegaz*, New York 1926, p.7.
12 University of Newcastle, Gertrude Bell archive, letter, 25 January 1914.
13 Quoted in Henry Laurens, 'Jaussen en Arabie', *Photographies d'Arabie, Hedjaz 1907–1917*, Paris 1999, p.30.
14 BL, Add 45914, f.21.
15 BL, Add 45914, f.21.
16 TNA, FO 882/6, Lawrence to Clayton, 28 February 1917.
17 *Photographies d'Arabie, Hijaz 1907–1917, p.51.*
18 IWM, Henderson, *The Hijaz Expedition 1916–17.*
19 Stitt, *A Prince of Arabia*, p.177.
20 Stitt, *A Prince of Arabia*, pp.177–8.
21 Stitt, *A Prince of Arabia*, p.178.
22 Stitt, *A Prince of Arabia*, pp.178–9.
23 Musbah Haidar, *Arabesque*, p.102.
24 TNA, FO 882/6, Wingate to Robertson, 19 March 1917; FO 141/736, Wingate to Pearson, 6 March 1917.
25 MEC, Hogarth Papers, Hogarth to Laura Hogarth, 7 November 1917.
26 MEC, Karadogan Papers, Karadogan to Monroe, 17 September 1971.
27 TNA, FO 686/6, Newcombe's report, 12 March 1917.
28 TNA, FO 686/6, Newcombe's report, 12 March 1917.
29 BL, Add 45914, f.23.
30 Garnett, ed. *Letters of T.E. Lawrence*, p.222, Lawrence to Wilson, 9 March 1917.

31 BL, Add 45915, f.22.
32 BL, Add 45915, f.25.
33 Lawrence, *Seven Pillars of Wisdom*, 1935, pp.186–7.
34 Brémond, *Le Hedjaz dans la Guerre Mondiale*, p.72.
35 BL, Add 45983A, entries for 17–25 March 1917.
36 TNA, FO 882/6, Newcombe to Hogarth, 3 April 1917.
37 Quoted in Suleiman Mousa, *T.E. Lawrence: an Arab view*, Oxford 1966, p.55.
38 Graves, ed. *Memoirs of King Abdullah*, p.170.
39 TNA, FO 686/6, Lawrence's report, 24 April 1917.
40 Lawrence, *Seven Pillars of Wisdom*, 1935, p.199.
41 Lawrence, *Seven Pillars of Wisdom*, 1935, p.202.
42 TNA, FO 686/6, Lawrence's report, 16 April 1917.
43 TNA, FO 686/6, Lawrence's report, 24 April 1917.
44 TNA, FO 686/6, Lawrence's report, 24 April 1917.
45 Lawrence, *Seven Pillars of Wisdom*, 1935, p.209.

10 DIFFERENCES OVER TACTICS

1   LHCMA, Joyce 1/78, Joyce to Wilson, 23 March 1917.
2   TNA, FO 882/6, Joyce to Wilson, 1 April 1917.
3   LHCMA, Joyce Papers, 1/125, Joyce to Newcombe, 12 April 1917.
4   LHCMA, Joyce Papers, 1/142, Joyce to Newcombe, 13 April 1917.
5   TNA, FO 686/6, Lawrence's report, 16 April 1917.
6   TNA, FO 686/6, Lawrence's report, 16 April 1917.
7   Lawrence, *Seven Pillars of Wisdom*, 1935, pp.192–3.
8   TNA, FO 686/6, Newcombe's report, 4 May 1917.
9   TNA, FO 686/6, Newcombe's report, 4 May 1917.
10 SAD, Clayton Papers, 470/6, Wilson to Clayton, 16 January 1917.
11 Lawrence, *Seven Pillars of Wisdom*, 1935, p.194.
12 BL, Add 45914, f.13.
13 Lawrence, *Seven Pillars of Wisdom*, 1935, p.239.
14 BL, Add 45915, reverse f.48.
15 Lawrence, *Seven Pillars of Wisdom*, 1935, p.221.
16 Musil, *The Northern Hegaz*, p.7.
17 See, for example, Richard Burton, *Personal Narrative of a Pilgrimage to Al-Madinah and Meccah*, London 1893, p.119.
18 Musil, *The Northern Hegaz*, p.8 and MAE, Guerre 1914–1918, 878, 173–81, Defrance, 'Le mouvement arabe à la frontière du désert syrien' 30 August 1917.
19 Lawrence, *Seven Pillars of Wisdom*, 1935, p.221.
20 TNA, FO 882/7, Lawrence to Clayton, 27 August 1917.
21 MEC, Sykes Papers, Clayton's report on Feisal's plans, 29 May 1917.
22 TNA, FO 686/6, Lawrence's report, late April 1917.
23 TNA FO 882/6, Clayton's note, n.d. but after 5 April 1917.
24 MEC, Sykes Papers, Clayton's report on Feisal's plans, 29 May 1917.
25 TNA, FO 882/6, Lawrence to Wilson, 16 April 1917.
26 BL, Add 45914, f.29.
27 TNA, FO 686/6, Lawrence to Wilson, 8 January 1917.
28 MEC, Sykes Papers, minute of Sykes's interview at 10 Downing Street, 16 December 1915.
29 BL Add 52463, Murray to Robertson, 29 February 1917.

30 MEC, Sykes Papers, note of a conference held at 10 Downing Street, 3 April 1917.
31 MEC, Sykes Papers, note of a conference at 10 Downing Street, 3 April 1917.
32 IOR, L/PS/11/119, Wingate to Balfour, 28 April 1917.
33 TNA, FO 686/6, Lawrence to Wilson, 8 January 1917.
34 TNA, FO 686/6, Lawrence's report, 24 April 1917.
35 IOR, L/PS/10/615, Chamberlain to Chelmsford, 15 February 1917.
36 IOR, L/PS/10/615, piece 1332, Balfour to Wingate, 29 April 1917.
37 MEC, Sykes Papers, Sykes to Wingate, 5 May 1917.
38 MEC, Sykes Papers, Sykes to Wingate, 5 May 1917.
39 Quoted in Adelson, *Sykes*, p.230.
40 MEC, Sykes Papers, Sykes to Wingate, 5 May 1917.
41 Brémond, *Le Hedjaz dans la Guerre Mondiale*, pp.137–8.
42 SAD, Clayton Papers, 693/12, Clayton to Storrs, 7 May 1917.

11 FIGHTING FOR US ON A LIE

1 IWM, W.F. Stirling Papers, letter dated 1 January 1918, Stirling to his sister, 5 November 1918, and Stirling, *Safety Last*, London 1953, p.97.
2 Lawrence, *Seven Pillars of Wisdom*, 1935, p.148.
3 Alec Kirkbride, *An Awakening*, University Press of Arabia 1971, p.51.
4 BL, Add 45983A, 11–12 May 1917.
5 BL, Add 45915, reverse f.47.
6 Lawrence, *Seven Pillars of Wisdom*, 1935, p.237.
7 Lawrence, *Seven Pillars of Wisdom*, 1935, p.30.
8 Lawrence, *Seven Pillars of Wisdom*, 1935, p.30.
9 Lawrence, *Seven Pillars of Wisdom*, 1935, p.496.
10 Lawrence, *Seven Pillars of Wisdom*, 1935, p.348.
11 BL, Add 45903, Lawrence to Charlotte Shaw, 28 September 1925.
12 Lord Vansittart, *The Mist Procession*, London 1958, p.205.
13 Lawrence, *Seven Pillars of Wisdom*, 1935, p.239.
14 Woodrow Wilson, speech to Congress, 2 April 1917.
15 Charles Seymour, ed. *The Intimate Papers of Colonel House*, London 1928, Vol.III, p.47.
16 IOR, L/PS/10/609, Wingate to Balfour, 23 April 1917; Wingate to Balfour, 10 May 1917; Balfour to Wingate, 14 May 1917.
17 MEC, Sykes Papers, Sykes to Wingate, 22 February 1917.
18 MEC, Sykes Papers, Sykes to Wingate, 23 May 1917.
19 IOR, L/PS/11/124, Wemyss's report, 13 June 1917.
20 TNA, FO 882/12, Lawrence to Wilson, 30 July 1917.
21 IOR, L/PS/11/124, Wemyss's report, 13 June 1917.
22 MEC, Sykes Papers, Sykes to Wingate, 23 May 1917.
23 Antonius, *The Arab Awakening*, pp.423–4, McMahon to Husein, 13 December 1915.
24 TNA, FO 371/3054, Wingate to Balfour, enclosing reports from Lawrence, 16 August 1917.
25 SAD, Clayton Papers, 693/13, Clayton to 'George' 2 March 1918.
26 MEC, Sykes Papers, Sykes to Wingate, 23 May 1917.
27 MEC, Sykes Papers, Sykes to Wingate, 23 May 1917.
28 BL, Add 45915, 20 May 1917, f.50 .
29 BL, Add 45915, reverse f.49.
30 BL, Add 45915, reverse f.49.
31 BL, Add 45915, 22 May 1917, f.53.

32 Lawrence, *Seven Pillars of Wisdom*, 1935, p.248.
33 BL, Add 45915, 23 May 1917 reverse f.52.
34 BL, Add 45915, 19 May 1917, f.50.
35 Lawrence, *Seven Pillars of Wisdom*, 1935, p.253.
36 Lawrence, *Seven Pillars of Wisdom*, 1935, p.255.
37 Lawrence, *Seven Pillars of Wisdom*, 1935, p.255.
38 BL Add 45915, f.53.
39 Lawrence, *Seven Pillars of Wisdom*, 1935, p.254.
40 SAD, Clayton Papers, 693/11, Lawrence to Sykes (unsent), 7 September 1917.
41 BL, Add 45915, f.54.
42 Lawrence, *Seven Pillars of Wisdom*, 1935, p.270.
43 Lawrence, *Seven Pillars of Wisdom*, 1935, p.265.
44 BL, Add 45915, f.54.
45 Lawrence, *Seven Pillars of Wisdom*, 1935, p.266.
46 BL, Add 45915, f.55.
47 TNA, FO 882/27, *Arab Bulletin* 44, 12 March 1917.
48 BL, Add 45983A, 5 June 1917.
49 BL, Add 45915, reverse f.55.

12 AQABA

1 MEC, Sykes Papers, Clayton's report on Feisal's plans, 29 May 1917.
2 SAD, Clayton Papers, 693/12, Clayton to Pearson, 2 March 1917.
3 MEC, Sykes Papers, Clayton's report on Feisal's plans, 29 May 1917.
4 IWM, H. Garland Papers, post-war lecture, n.d.
5 TNA, FO 686/6, Newcombe's report on raids of 4–10 May 1917.
6 TNA, FO 686/6, Garland's report, 22 May 1917.
7 TNA, FO 686/6, Garland's report, 22 May 1917.
8 TNA, FO 686/6, Newcombe's report on raids of 4–10 May 1917.
9 Alec Kirkbride, *An Awakening*, p.39.
10 William Facey and Najdat Fathi Safwat, eds. *A Soldier's Story – From Ottoman Rule to Independent Iraq: The Memoirs of Jafar Pasha Al-Askari*, London 2003, p.105.
11 IWM, Henderson, *The Hejaz Expedition 1916–17*.
12 Garnett, ed. *The Letters of T.E. Lawrence*, p.225, Lawrence to Clayton, 10 July 1917.
13 Lawrence, *Seven Pillars of Wisdom*, 1935, p.546.
14 BL, Add 45915, reverse f.57.
15 BL, Add 45915, f.57.
16 Lawrence, *Seven Pillars of Wisdom*, 1935, p.293.
17 LHCMA, Joyce Papers, 1/243, Joyce to Wilson, 3 July 1917.
18 Facey and Safwat, eds. *The Memoirs of Jafar Pasha Al Askari*, p.122.
19 LHCMA, Joyce Papers, 1/245, Joyce to Wilson, 15–16 July 1917. Joyce had ordered 200 pairs of boots in May 1917, asking for '7s, 8s, 9s and a few 10s', Joyce Papers, 1/204.
20 Facey and Safwat, eds. *The Memoirs of Jafar Pasha Al-Askari*, p.122.
21 LHCMA, Joyce Papers, 1/245, Joyce to Wilson, 15–16 July 1917.
22 TNA, WO 339/125412, H.S. Hornby, Army record.
23 IWM, Henderson, *The Hejaz Expedition, 1916–1917*.
24 IWM, Henderson, *The Hejaz Expedition, 1916–1917*.
25 TNA, FO 686/6, Newcombe's report, 18 July 1917.
26 Lawrence, *Seven Pillars of Wisdom*, 1935, p.298.

27 Lawrence, *Seven Pillars of Wisdom*, 1935, p.301.
28 Lawrence, *Seven Pillars of Wisdom*, 1935, p.302.
29 Lawrence, *Seven Pillars of Wisdom*, 1935, p.302.
30 Lawrence, *Seven Pillars of Wisdom*, 1935, p.303.
31 Lawrence, *Seven Pillars of Wisdom*, 1935, p.303.
32 Lawrence, *Seven Pillars of Wisdom*, 1935, pp.311–12.
33 Lawrence, *Seven Pillars of Wisdom*, 1922, p.336.
34 BL, Add 45983A, 7 July 1917.

13 THE IMPACT OF AQABA

1 MEC, Sykes Papers, Clayton's report, 10 July 1917.
2 Lawrence, *Seven Pillars of Wisdom*, 1922, p.347.
3 BL Add 45915, f.59.
4 TNA, FO 882/26, *Arab Bulletins* 53 and 55, 14 and 28 June 1917.
5 TNA, FO 882/7, Clayton to Macdonogh, 5 July 1917.
6 TNA, FO 882/26, *Arab Bulletin* 56, 9 July 1917.
7 IOR, L/PS/11/124, Wingate to Robertson, 10 July 1917.
8 TNA, FO 882/27, *Arab Bulletin* 57, 24 July 1917.
9 Lawrence, *Seven Pillars of Wisdom*, 1922, pp. 295 and 305.
10 T.E. Lawrence, *T.E. Lawrence to his Biographers, Robert Graves and Liddell Hart*, London 1963, pp.88–9.
11 LHCMA, Liddell Hart Papers, 9/13/42, Lawrence to Stirling, 25 September 1917.
12 IOR, L/PS/11/124, Wingate to Robertson, 13 July 1917.
13 MAE, Guerre 1914–1918, 879, 25–57, Defrance to Ribot, enclosing report by Jaussen, 8 October 1917.
14 Jeremy Wilson, *Lawrence of Arabia: the authorised biography of T.E. Lawrence*, London 1989, p.413. Reference to a 'little revolt lately' in the area north of Acre is also made by Jaussen, in a report dispatched by Defrance to Ribot, MAE, Guerre 1914–1918, 879, 25–57, 8 October 1917.
15 Rogan, *Frontiers of the State in the Late Ottoman Empire*, p.231.
16 MEC, Sykes Papers, Wingate to Balfour, 3 July 1917.
17 MEC, Hogarth Papers, Hogarth to Laura Hogarth, 19 January 1917.
18 MEC, Hogarth Papers, Hogarth to Clayton, 11 July 1917.
19 TNA, FO 371/3054, Hogarth's memorandum, 10 July 1917. Disparaging allegations about Britain's ambitions in the Middle East had been made in *Pravda* on 23 April 1917.
20 MEC, Hogarth Papers, Hogarth to Clayton, 11 July 1917.
21 MEC, Sykes Papers, Sykes to Clayton, 22 July 1917.
22 MEC, Hogarth Papers, Hogarth to Clayton, 20 July 1917.
23 MEC, Sykes Papers, Sykes to Clayton, 22 July 1917.
24 MEC, Sykes Papers, Sykes to Drummond, 20 July 1917.
25 MEC, Hogarth Papers, Hogarth to Clayton, 20 July 1917.
26 Garnett, ed. *The Letters of T.E. Lawrence*, pp.228–30, Lawrence to Clayton, 10 July 1917, pp.228–30.
27 MEC, Sykes Papers, Clayton's report, 16 July 1917.
28 MEC, Sykes Papers, Clayton's report, 16 July 1917.
29 LHCMA, Allenby Papers, 1/8/6, Allenby to Lady Allenby, 9 July 1917.
30 Lawrence, *Seven Pillars of Wisdom*, 1935, p.322.
31 Anthony Bruce, *The Last Crusade*, London 2003, p.116.
32 TNA, WO 106/718, Allenby to Robertson, 16 July 1917.
33 MEC, Hogarth Papers, Hogarth to Clayton, 11 July 1917.
34 TNA, WO 158/634, Allenby to Robertson, 19 July 1917.
35 TNA, FO 882/16, Clayton to Sykes, 22 July 1917.

36 LHCMA, Joyce Papers, 1/245, Joyce to Wilson, 15–16 July 1917.
37 Facey and Safwat, eds. *The Memoirs of Jafar Pasha Al-Askari*, p.119.
38 TNA, FO 686/6, Davenport's report, 8 August 1917.
39 Facey and Safwat, eds. *The Memoirs of Jafar Pasha Al-Askari*, p.158.
40 Edward Robinson, *Lawrence the Rebel*, London 1946, p.92.
41 TNA, FO 371/3054, Wingate to Balfour, enclosing reports by Lawrence, 16 August 1917.
42 TNA, WO 158/634, piece 24A.
43 LHCMA, Robertson Papers, 8/1/67, Robertson to Allenby, 1 August 1917.

14 IMPOLITIC TRUTHS

1   TNA, WO 158/611, Robertson to Allenby, 10 August 1917.
2   Quoted in Wilson, *Lawrence of Arabia*, p.427.
3   LHCMA, Robertson Papers, 8/1/69, Robertson to Allenby, 10 August 1917.
4   TNA, WO 158/634, Lawrence's report, 6 August 1917.
5   Lawrence, *Seven Pillars of Wisdom*, 1922, p.355.
6   LHCMA, Robertson Papers, 8/1/70, Allenby to Robertson, 21 August 1917.
7   Brown, ed. *Lawrence of Arabia: the selected letters*, p.123, Lawrence to Sarah Lawrence, 27 August 1917.
8   TNA, WO 158/634, piece 41B, Arab Bureau to GHQ, 16 August 1917.
9   Brown, ed. *Lawrence of Arabia: the selected letters*, pp.126–7, Lawrence to Clayton, 27 August 1917.
10 Facey and Safwat, eds. *The Memoirs of Jafar Pasha Al-Askari*, p.132.
11 TNA, WO 158/634, Macindoe's report, 27 August 1917.
12 TNA, WO 158/634, piece 91A, Joyce to Clayton, 12 September 1917, reported by Clayton to GSO, 20 September 1917.
13 Brown, ed. *Lawrence of Arabia: the selected letters*, p.125, Lawrence to Clayton, 27 August 1917.
14 MEC, Sykes Papers, Sykes to Clayton, 22 July 1917.
15 SAD, Clayton Papers, 693/11, Lawrence to Sykes (unsent), 9 September 1917.
16 SAD, Clayton Papers, 693/11, Lawrence to Sykes, 9 September 1917 (unsent).
17 Quoted in Leonard Stein, *The Balfour Declaration*, London 1961, p.294.
18 SAD, Clayton Papers, 693/11, Lawrence to Sykes, 9 September 1917 (unsent).
19 SAD, Clayton Papers, 693/11, Lawrence to Sykes, 9 September 1917 (unsent).
20 SAD, Clayton Papers, 693/11, Lawrence to Clayton, 7 September 1917.
21 Lawrence, *Seven Pillars of Wisdom*, 1935, p.359.
22 TNA, FO 882/4, Clayton to General Staff, enclosing Lawrence's report, 29 September 1917.
23 Lawrence, *Seven Pillars of Wisdom*, 1922, p.399.
24 Lawrence, *Seven Pillars of Wisdom*, 1935, p.361.
25 Lawrence, *Seven Pillars of Wisdom*, 1935, p.367.
26 A.W. Lawrence, ed. *T.E. Lawrence by his friends*, London 1954, p.167.
27 Lawrence, *Seven Pillars of Wisdom*, 1935, p.368.
28 Garnett, ed. *The Letters of T.E. Lawrence*, pp.237–8, Lawrence to Leeds, 24 September 1917.
29 LHCMA, Liddell Hart Papers, 9/13/42, Lawrence to Stirling, 25 September 1917.
30 BL, Add 45903, Lawrence to Charlotte Shaw, 29 March 1927, with a copy of a letter to Vyvyan Richards, 15 July 1918, on the reverse.
31 MEC, Hogarth Papers, Hogarth to Laura Hogarth, 14 October 1917.
32 Lawrence, ed. *T.E. Lawrence by his friends*, p.167.
33 LHCMA, Joyce Papers, 1/258, Joyce to Clayton, 25 September 1917.
34 SAD, Wingate Papers, 146/3, Lloyd to Wingate, 17 August 1917.
35 Garnett, ed. *The Letters of T.E. Lawrence*, p.236, Lawrence to Wilson, 2 September 1917.

15 DIFFICULT TIMES

1 SAD, Clayton Papers, 693/12, Clayton to Lawrence, 20 September 1917. US President Woodrow Wilson's criticisms would be most forcefully put in his Fourteen Points the following January. Point Twelve proposed the opportunity of autonomy for Arabs and other non-Turks under Ottoman rule.

2 MEC, Sykes Papers, Sykes to Clayton, 22 July 1917.

3 Quoted in Adelson, *Mark Sykes*, p.246.

4 SAD, Clayton Papers, 693/12, Clayton to Lawrence, 20 September 1917.

5 LHCMA, Joyce Papers, 1/254, Joyce to Clayton, 17 September 1917.

6 Brown, ed. *Lawrence of Arabia: the selected letters*, p.125, Lawrence to Clayton, 27 August 1917.

7 LHCMA, Joyce Papers, 1/255, Joyce to Clayton, 18 September 1917.

8 LHCMA, Joyce Papers, 1/255, Joyce to Clayton, 25 September 1917.

9 Lawrence, *Seven Pillars of Wisdom*, 1922, p.98.

10 TNA, WO 158/634, Snagge's report, 1 October 1917.

11 TNA, WO 158/634, Snagge's report, 1 October 1917.

12 TNA, WO 158/634, Snagge's report, 1 October 1917.

13 LHCMA, Joyce Papers, 1/258, Joyce to Clayton, 25 September 1917.

14 Brémond, *Le Hedjaz dans la Guerre Mondiale*, p.179.

15 Brémond, *Le Hedjaz dans la Guerre Mondiale*, p.177.

16 TNA, WO 158/634, Jeddah to Arab Bureau, 26 November 1917.

17 TNA, FO 686/6, Davenport's report, 8 August 1917.

18 TNA, WO 158/611, Robertson to Allenby, 5 October 1917.

19 TNA, WO 158/611, Allenby to Robertson, 9 October 1917.

20 MEC, Sykes Papers, Clayton to Sykes, 20 September 1917.

21 TNA, FO 371/3054, Note on the situation in Egypt, 10 July 1917.

22 SAD, 146/7, FO to Wingate, 19 October 1917; Wingate referred to the report from Berne (dated 25 October) in a telegram on 2 November 1917 (IOR, L/PS/10/609, piece 4396).

23 Kirkbride, *An Awakening*, p.17.

24 Brémond, *Le Hedjaz dans la Guerre Mondiale*, p.215.

25 TNA, FO 882/26, *Arab Bulletin* 66, 21 October 1917.

26 TNA, FO 882/26, *Arab Bulletin* 66, 21 October 1917.

27 Quoted in Christophe Leclerc, 'The French Soldiers in the Arab Revolt', *Journal of the T.E. Lawrence Society*, Vol.IX, No.1 (Autumn 1999).

28 TNA, FO 882/26, *Arab Bulletin* 66, 21 October 1917.

29 Lawrence, *Seven Pillars of Wisdom*, 1922, p.423.

30 SAD, Clayton Papers, 693/12, Clayton to Lawrence, 20 September 1917.

31 LHCMA, Robertson Papers, 8/1/73, Allenby to Robertson, 17 October 1917.

32 LHCMA, Robertson Papers, 8/1/73, Allenby to Robertson, 17 October 1917.

33 TNA, WO 33/935, Allenby to Robertson, 13 October 1917.

34 TNA, FO 371/3054, Hogarth to Ormsby-Gore, 26 October 1917.

35 MEC, Sykes Papers, Clayton to Sykes, 18 October 1917.

16 GAZA AND YARMUK

1 TNA, FO 882/26, *Arab Bulletin* 67, 30 October 1917.

2 TNA, FO 882/26, *Arab Bulletin* 67, 30 October 1917.

3 Facey and Safwat, eds. *The Memoirs of Jafar Pasha Al-Askari*, p.130.

4 MEC, Sykes Papers, extract from Pearson to Clayton, 5 October 1917, in Clayton to Sykes, 18 October 1917.

5 SAD, Clayton Papers, 693/12, Clayton to Joyce, 30 October 1917.
6 IWM, Lawrence Papers, notes on the campaign dictated by Lawrence to Edward Robinson, September 1917.
7 SAD, Clayton Papers, 693/11, Lawrence to Clayton, 24 October 1917.
8 SAD, Clayton Papers, 693/11, Lawrence to Clayton, 24 October 1917.
9 Lawrence, *Seven Pillars of Wisdom*, 1935, p.388.
10 CCC, Lloyd Papers, GLLD 9/10, Clayton to Lloyd, 25 October 1917.
11 SAD, Clayton Papers, 693/12, Clayton to Lawrence, 20 September 1917.
12 SAD, Clayton Papers, 694/5, Lloyd, 'Diary of a journey with TEL to El Jaffer'.
13 SAD, Clayton Papers, 694/5, Lloyd, 'Diary of a journey with TEL to El Jaffer'.
14 SAD, Clayton Papers, 694/5, Lloyd, 'Diary of a journey with TEL to El Jaffer'.
15 SAD, Clayton Papers, 694/5, Lloyd, 'Diary of a journey with TEL to El Jaffer'.
16 SAD, Clayton Papers, 694/5, Lloyd, 'Diary of a journey with TEL to El Jaffer'.
17 Lawrence, *Seven Pillars of Wisdom*, 1935, p.401.
18 CCC, Lloyd Papers, GLLD 9/10, Lloyd's notes, n.d.
19 Lawrence, *Seven Pillars of Wisdom*, 1935, p.398.
20 SAD, Clayton Papers, 694/5, Lloyd, 'Diary of a journey with TEL to El Jaffer', n.d.
21 SAD, Clayton Papers, 694/5, Lloyd, 'Diary of a journey with TEL to El Jaffer', n.d.
22 Lawrence, *Seven Pillars of Wisdom*, 1935, p.401.
23 The bombardment, designed to divert Turkish attention away from Beersheba, where the main thrust of the offensive was aimed, in fact began on 27 October, the previous day.
24 SAD, Clayton Papers, 694/5, Lloyd, 'Diary of a journey with TEL to El Jaffer', n.d. Lloyd was thinking of the failed Gunpowder Plot to blow up Parliament, planned for 5 November 1605.
25 MEC, Hogarth Papers, Hogarth to Laura Hogarth, 11 November 1917.
26 MEC, Hogarth Papers, Hogarth to 'Billy', 2–3 November 1917.
27 MEC, Hogarth Papers, Hogarth to 'Billy', 2–3 November 1917.
28 TNA, FO 882/7, Joyce to Clayton, 4 November 1917.
29 Lawrence, *Seven Pillars of Wisdom*, 1935, p.411.
30 Lawrence, *Seven Pillars of Wisdom*, 1935, p.423.
31 Garnett, ed. *The Letters of T.E. Lawrence*, p.239, Lawrence to Joyce, 13 November 1917,.
32 Lawrence, *Seven Pillars of Wisdom*, 1935, p.425.
33 Lawrence, *Seven Pillars of Wisdom*, 1935, p.428.
34 Lawrence, *Seven Pillars of Wisdom*, 1935, p.431.
35 Brown, ed. *Lawrence of Arabia: the selected letters*, p.140, Lawrence to his parents, 14 December 1917.
36 TNA, FO 158/634, Joyce to Arab Bureau, 25 November 1917.
37 MEC, Hogarth Papers, Hogarth to Laura Hogarth, 26 November 1917.
38 MEC, Hogarth Papers, Hogarth to Laura Hogarth, 29 November 1917.
39 TNA, FO 882/26, *Arab Bulletin* 73, 5 December 1917.
40 Lawrence, *Seven Pillars of Wisdom*, 1935, p.442.

17 DARA OR AZRAK?

1 BL Add 45983A. An unusual change in the style of Lawrence's capital As for 27–8 November (both entries are for 'Akaba') suggests that he wrote up the earlier entries no later than 26 November.
2 Quoted in Lawrence James, *The Golden Warrior*, London 1990, p.252.
3 Brown, ed. *Lawrence of Arabia: the selected letters*, p.175, Lawrence to W.F. Stirling, 28 June 1919.
4 TNA, FO141/510/7.
5 Lawrence, *Seven Pillars of Wisdom*, 1922, p.496.
6 Lawrence, *Seven Pillars of Wisdom*, 1922, p.497.

7 Lawrence, *Seven Pillars of Wisdom*, 1922, p.498.

8 Lawrence, *Seven Pillars of Wisdom*, 1922, p.499.

9 I would never have bothered requesting this test had I already known, as I subsequently discovered, that a similar test had been commissioned by J.N. Lockman during research for his book *Scattered Tracks on the Lawrence Trail*, Michigan 1996. Lockman said his test revealed nothing.

10 Brown, ed. *Lawrence of Arabia: the selected letters*, p.138, Lawrence to Sarah Lawrence, 14 November 1917.

11 Brown, ed. *Lawrence of Arabia: the selected letters*, p.139, Lawrence to his parents, 14 December 1917.

12 BL, Add 45903, Lawrence to Charlotte Shaw, 19 July 1924.

13 BL, Add 45903, Lawrence to Charlotte Shaw, 26 December 1925.

14 Lawrence, *Seven Pillars of Wisdom*, 1935, p.445.

15 Lawrence, *Seven Pillars of Wisdom*, 1922, p.502.

18 THE JEWS AND JERUSALEM

1 Reproduced in Leonard Stein, *The Balfour Declaration*, London 1961, frontispiece.

2 Hugh Strachan, *The First World War*, Vol.I, Oxford 2003, p.957.

3 Robert Gildea, *Barricades and Borders: Europe 1800–1914*, Oxford 1987, p.284.

4 MEC, Clayton Papers, Clayton to Wingate, 3 August 1916. The CUP was the ruling Committee of Union and Progress.

5 MEC, Sykes Papers, 19 July 1917.

6 Quoted in Stein, *The Balfour Declaration*, p.275, Sykes to Sokolow, 12 April 1917.

7 SAD, Wingate Papers, 166/3, Wingate to Allenby, 17 December 1917.

8 Quoted in Stein, *The Balfour Declaration*, p.275, Sledmere Papers, no.66, *c.* September 1917.

9 President Woodrow Wilson, speech to Congress, 2 April 1917.

10 MEC, Sykes Papers, Clayton to Sykes, 28 November 1917.

11 SAD, Clayton Papers, 693/13, Clayton to Bell, 8 December 1917.

12 University of Newcastle, Gertrude Bell archive, Bell to Mary Bell, 25 January 1918.

13 SAD, Clayton Papers, 693/13, Clayton to Bell, 8 December 1917.

14 MEC, Sykes Papers, Clayton to Sykes, 28 November 1917.

15 Brémond, *Le Hedjaz dans la Guerre Mondiale*, p.128; Lawrence, *Seven Pillars of Wisdom*, 1922, p.51.

16 TNA, FO 686/33, Wilson to Husein, 28 October 1916; Brémond, *Le Hedjaz dans la Guerre Mondiale*, p.58.

17 TNA, FO 686/38, Wilson's notes of conversation with King Husein, 6 June 1918.

18 MEC, Sykes Papers, Wingate to Foreign Office, 29 November 1917.

19 IOR, L/PS/10/609, Wingate to Foreign Office, 2 November 1917. Husein was reported to have stopped paying the Harb in *Arab Bulletin* 70, 21 November 1917.

20 IOR, L/PS/10/609, Wingate to Foreign Office, 15 November 1917.

21 IOR, L/PS/10/609, Hirtzel, minute, 15 August 1916.

22 IOR, L/PS/10/609, Foreign Office to Wingate, 6 February 1917.

23 TNA, T 1/12249, piece 33669, note, n.d.

24 TNA, FO 882/26, *Arab Bulletin* 68, 7 November 1917.

25 TNA, WO 33/946, Allenby to Robertson, 15 November 1917.

26 IOR, L/PS/10/609, piece 4753, Foreign Office to Wingate, 17 November 1917.

27 TNA, WO33/946, Robertson to Allenby, 21 November 1917.

28 LHCMA, Allenby Papers, 1/8/32, Allenby to Lady Allenby, 11 December 1917.

29 IWM, H.V. Gilbert Papers.

30 Lawrence, *Seven Pillars of Wisdom*, 1922, p.510.

31 SAD, Wingate Papers, 147/6, Wingate to Allenby, 27 December 1917.

32 *Glasgow Herald*, 'Jerusalem Delivered', 11 December 1917.

33 *The Times*, 'Jerusalem', 11 December 1917.

34 Franz von Papen, *Memoirs*, London 1952, p.80.
35 TNA, FO 686/38, Journal to Feisal, November 1917.
36 TNA, FO, 686/38 Jemal to Feisal, November 1917.
37 Donald M. McKale, *War by Revolution*, Ohio 1998, p.213.
38 SAD, Wingate Papers, 147/2, *El Balagh*, 6 and 12 December 1917, reporting Jemal's speech to the Beirut Club, 5 December 1917.
39 Quoted in Wilson, *Lawrence of Arabia*, p.468.
40 Robinson, *Lawrence the Rebel*, p.123.
41 Quoted in Robinson, *Lawrence the Rebel*, p.119.

19 FIGHTING DE LUXE

1 TNA, WO 158/634, Macauley to EEF, 10 January 1918, forwarded by Campbell on 12 January 1918.
2 LHCMA, Robertson Papers, 4/5/10, Allenby to Robertson, 14 December 1917 and 20 December 1917.
3 IWM, Dawnay Papers, 69/21/2, Allenby to Robertson, 26 November 1917.
4 SAD, Wingate Papers, 148/1, Lt.-Col. for Brig. Gen. Hejaz Ops to Dir. Mil. Int., 5 January 1918.
5 Lawrence, ed. *T.E. Lawrence by his friends*, p.170.
6 Lawrence, *Seven Pillars of Wisdom*, 1922, p.515.
7 Lawrence, *Seven Pillars of Wisdom*, 1935, p.458.
8 Lawrence, *Seven Pillars of Wisdom*, 1922, p.518.
9 TNA, FO 882/27, *Arab Bulletin* 77, 27 January 1918.
10 Siddons in his flight log (IWM, V.D. Siddons Papers) mentions low clouds.
11 David Hogarth, *The Penetration of Arabia*, London 1904, p.46.
12 MEC, Hogarth Papers, Hogarth to 'Mary', 19 January 1918.
13 MEC, Hogarth Papers, Hogarth to 'Billy', 10 January 1918.
14 MEC, Hogarth Papers, Hogarth to 'Billy', 10 January 1918; TNA, FO 882/27, *Arab Bulletin* 77, 27 January 1918.
15 SAD, Wingate Papers, 148/2, Hogarth to Wingate, 19 January 1918.
16 SAD, Wingate Papers, 148/1, Arab Bureau to Bassett, 6 January 1918.
17 Quoted in Stein, *The Balfour Declaration*, p.633.
18 TNA, FO 882/13, Hogarth to Wingate, 15 January 1918.
19 TNA, FO 882/27, *Arab Bulletin* 77, 27 January 1918.
20 Robinson, *Lawrence the Rebel*, p.130.
21 Facey and Safwat, eds. *The Memoirs of Jafar Pasha Al-Askari*, p.154.
22 Lawrence, *Seven Pillars of Wisdom*, 1935, p.472.
23 TNA, WO 158/634, Lawrence to Clayton, 22 January 1918.
24 Rogan, *Frontiers of the State*, p.238.
25 TNA, WO 158/634, Lawrence to Clayton, 22 January 1918.
26 TNA, FO 882/27, *Arab Bulletin* 79, 18 February 1918.
27 Lawrence, *Seven Pillars of Wisdom*, 1935, p.483.
28 Lawrence, *Seven Pillars of Wisdom*, 1935, p.483.
29 Kirkbride, *An Awakening*, p.13.
30 Kirkbride, *An Awakening*, p.14.
31 Lawrence, *Seven Pillars of Wisdom*, 1935, p.500.
32 TNA, FO 882/7, Lawrence to Clayton, 12 February 1918.
33 Lawrence, *Seven Pillars of Wisdom*, 1922, p.568.

20 NEW CONDITIONS

1 MEC, Hogarth Papers, Hogarth to 'Billy', 25 February 1918.
2 MEC, J.W.A. Young Papers, 'A Little to the East', 29 December 1945.
3 Robinson, *Lawrence the Rebel*, p.133.
4 LHCMA, Joyce Papers, 1/265, Dawnay to Joyce, 22 February 1918.
5 Lawrence, *Seven Pillars of Wisdom*, 1922, p.572.
6 Matthew Hughes, *Allenby and British Strategy in the Middle East*, London 1999, p.60.
7 LHCMA, Robertson Papers, 7/5/84, Allenby to Robertson, 25 January 1918.
8 LHCMA, Robertson Papers, 7/5/86, Allenby to Robertson, 23 February 1918.
9 TNA, FO 882/3, Clayton to Wilson, 17 December 1917.
10 Hubert Young, *The Independent Arab*, London 1933, pp.141-2.
11 Young, *The Independent Arab*, pp.141-2.
12 Young, *The Independent Arab*, p.18.
13 Brown, ed. *Lawrence of Arabia: the selected letters*, p.153, Lawrence to Sarah Lawrence, 8 March 1918.
14 Kirkbride, *An Awakening*, p.22.
15 SAD, Clayton Papers, 470/7, Wilson to Clayton, 6 October 1917.
16 Young, *The Independent Arab*, p.150.
17 Facey and Safwat, eds. *The Memoirs of Jafar Pasha Al-Askari*, p.138.
18 Young, *The Independent Arab*, p.160.
19 Facey and Safwat, eds. *The Memoirs of Jafar Pasha al Askari*, p.138.
20 TNA, WO 158/634, Hedgehog Cairo to Jedda, 20 March 1918.
21 Liman von Sanders, *Five Years in Turkey*, p.211.
22 Geoffrey Inchbald, *Imperial Camel Corps*, London 1970, p.107.
23 TNA, FO 882/27, *Arab Bulletin* 84, 7 April 1918, and WO 33/946, Allenby to War Office, 31 March 1918.
24 Quoted in Martin Gilbert, *First World War*, London 1994, p.408.
25 TNA, WO 33/946, War Office to Allenby, 27 March 1918.
26 Young, *The Independent Arab*, p.165.
27 LHCMA, Joyce Papers, 1/270, Dawnay's report, 1 May 1918.
28 MEC, J.W.A. Young Papers, note, 21 April 1918.
29 Kirkbride, *An Awakening*, pp.42-3.
30 Kirkbride, *An Awakening*, p.41.
31 Lawrence, *Seven Pillars of Wisdom*, p.586. See James Elroy Flecker's 'The Golden Journey to Samarkand', 1915.
32 LHCMA, Joyce Papers, 2/6, Joyce to Dawnay, 6 January 1918.
33 TNA, FO 882/27, *Arab Bulletin* 80, 26 February 1918.
34 LHCMA, Joyce Papers, 1/270, Dawnay's report, 1 May 1918.
35 TNA, FO 882/26, *Arab Bulletin* 60, 20 August 1917.
36 LHCMA, Joyce Papers, 1/270, Dawnay's report, 1 May 1918.
37 Young, *The Independent Arab*, p.151.
38 Facey and Safwat, eds. *The Memoirs of Jafar Pasha Al-Askari*, p.139.
39 LHCMA, Joyce Papers, 1/270, Dawnay's report, 1 May 1918.
40 Lawrence, *Seven Pillars of Wisdom*, 1935, p.516.
41 Lawrence, *Seven Pillars of Wisdom*, 1922, p.598.
42 Lawrence, *Seven Pillars of Wisdom*, 1922, p.598. Lawrence gave Ali and Othman the names Daud and Farraj in *Seven Pillars of Wisdom*. In this quote 'Daud' has been replaced with 'Ali'.
43 Quoted in Mousa, *T.E. Lawrence: An Arab View*, p.163.
44 Lawrence, *Seven Pillars of Wisdom*, 1935, p.520.
45 Lawrence, *Seven Pillars of Wisdom*, 1922, p.604.
46 Facey and Safwat, eds. *The Memoirs of Jafar Pasha Al-Askari*, London 2003, p.143.

47 Young, *The Independent Arab*, pp.165–6.
48 IWM, F.G. Peake Papers, DS/Misc/16.
49 Lawrence, *Seven Pillars of Wisdom*, 1935, p.521.
50 Lawrence, *Seven Pillars of Wisdom*, 1935, p.521.
51 Lawrence, *Seven Pillars of Wisdom*, 1935, p.521.
52 Lawrence, *Seven Pillars of Wisdom*, 1935, p.510.
53 IWM, Beaumont Papers 12 December 1936. In his account, written from memory after the events, Beaumont associates this incident with another raid. However, the detail about the stone striking the turret seems to correlate with Lawrence's description of this raid.
54 S.C. Rolls, *Steel Chariots in the Desert*, London 1937, p.176.
55 Lawrence, *Seven Pillars of Wisdom*, 1935, p.522.
56 LHCMA, Joyce Papers, 1/270, Dawnay's report, 1 May 1918.
57 Lawrence, *T.E. Lawrence to his biographers: Robert Graves and Liddell Hart*, p.100.
58 IWM, F.G. Peake Papers, DS/Misc/16.

21 A COMPLETE MUCK-UP

1 MEC, H.W. Young Papers, note, 21 April 1918.
2 Young, *The Independent Arab*, p..166.
3 Young, *The Independent Arab*, p.165.
4 Young, *The Independent Arab*, p.174.
5 TNA, WO 33/946, WO to Allenby, 2 April 1918.
6 IWM, Wilson Papers, HHW 2/33A/2, Allenby to Wilson, 20 April 1918.
7 LHCMA, Robertson Papers 4/4/108, Allenby to Robertson, 7 December 1917.
8 TNA, WO 158/634, Report by E.D. Machray, 24 April 1918.
9 Lawrence, *Seven Pillars of Wisdom*, 1922, p.611.
10 Quoted in C.T. Atkinson, 'General Liman von Sanders on his Experiences in Palestine', *Army Quarterly* 3 (1921–2), p.266.
11 Von Papen, *Memoirs*, p.79.
12 IWM, D.H. Calcutt, diary 6 May 1918, quoted in Rogan, *Frontiers of the State*, p.238.
13 TNA, WO 158/634, Hedgehog to Aqaba, 5 May 1918.
14 TNA, WO 158/634, Joyce's report, 31 May 1918, and LHCMA, Joyce Papers, 1/Q/8, testimony of Ibn al-Najdawi, 8 Shaaban, 1336 [*c.*17 May 1918].
15 TNA, WO 158/634, Joyce's report, 31 May 1918.
16 SAD, Wingate Papers, 148/3, Wingate to Allenby, 7 May 1918.
17 MEC, Sykes Papers, Ormsby-Gore to Sykes, 9 April 1918.
18 Count Bernstorff, *Memoirs*, Berlin 1936, p.179, quoted in Efraim Karsh and Inari Karsh, 'Myth in the Desert, or Not the Great Arab Revolt', in *Middle Eastern Studies*, Vol.33 No.2, April 1997, pp.267–312.
19 TNA, WO 158/634, Jemal to Feisal, reported in intelligence notes, 5 June 1918.
20 TNA, FO 371/3881, quoted in Karsh and Karsh, 'Myth in the Desert, or Not the Great Arab Revolt'.
21 SAD, Clayton Papers, 470/7, Cornwallis to Clayton, 28 November 1917.
22 TNA, FO 686/38, Bassett to Husein, 2 May 1918.
23 LHCMA, Joyce Papers, 1/271, Bassett to Arab Bureau, 8 May 1918.
24 TNA, FO 686/38, Wilson, note on conversation with King Husein, 27 May 1918.
25 MEC, Hogarth Papers, Hogarth to 'Mary', 19 January 1918.
26 TNA, FO 882/27, *Arab Bulletin* 87, 30 April 1918.
27 SAD, Clayton Papers, 693/13, Clayton to Sykes, 4 April 1918.
28 SAD, Wingate Papers, 148/8, Clayton to Wingate, 21 April 1918.
29 LHCMA, Joyce Papers, 1/272, Dawnay to Joyce, 27 May 1918.

30 TNA, FO 686/38, Wilson to Wingate, 5 June 1918.
31 TNA, FO 686/38, Wilson to Wingate, 5 June 1918.
32 IWM, Wilson papers, HHW2/33A/18, Allenby to Wilson, 14 August 1918.
33 TNA, FO 686/38, Wilson, note of meeting with Husein, 28 May 1918.
34 TNA, FO 686/38, Wilson to Wingate, 5 June 1918.
35 LHCMA, Joyce Papers, 1/O/14, Joyce's notes on the Feisal–Weizmann meeting.
36 TNA, FO 882/27, *Arab Bulletin* 93, 18 June 1918.

22 PREPARING FOR THE PUSH

1   TNA, WO 158/634, pieces 123 and 135, for 31 May and 11 June 1918.
2   'The Hijaz Railway 1918: A German Report', in the *Journal of the T.E. Lawrence Society*, Vol.XII No.2 (Spring 2003).
3   Liman von Sanders, *Five Years in Turkey*, p.258.
4   Liman von Sanders, *Five Years in Turkey*, p.231.
5   Sykes, *The Caliphs' Last Heritage*, p.471.
6   Antonin Jaussen, *Mission Archéologique en Arabie*, Vol.II, p.7.
7   IWM, Wilson papers, HHW2/33A/7, Allenby to Wilson, 15 June 1918.
8   IWM, Wilson papers, HHW2/33A/12, Allenby to Wilson, 22 June 1918.
9   IWM, Wilson papers, HHW2/33A/12, Allenby to Wilson, 22 June 1918.
10 SAD, Clayton Papers, 693/13, Robertson to India, copied to Clayton, 14 March 1918.
11 IWM, Wilson papers, HHW2/33A/3A, Wilson to Allenby, 29 May 1918.
12 Bruce, *The Last Crusade*, p.205.
13 Lawrence, *Seven Pillars of Wisdom*, 1935, p.527.
14 LHCMA, Joyce Papers, 1/272, Dawnay to Joyce, 27 May 1918.
15 IOR, L/PS/10/12, F.R. Maunsell, Detailed Report on Hejaz Railway, 1907.
16 LHCMA, Joyce Papers, 1/282, Joyce to Hornby, 2 June 1918.
17 C.S. Jarvis, *Arab Command: the biography of Lieutenant-Colonel F.W. Peake Pasha*, London 1942, p.37.
18 Brown, ed. *Lawrence of Arabia: the selected letters*, p.155, Lawrence to Husein, 25 June 1918.
19 LHCMA, Joyce Papers, 1/300, Dawnay to Joyce, 12 June 1918.
20 LHCMA, Joyce Papers, 1/300, Dawnay to Joyce, 12 June 1918.
21 LHCMA, Joyce Papers, 1/300, Dawnay to Joyce, 12 June 1918.
22 LHCMA, Joyce Papers, 1/308, Joyce to Dawnay, 20 June 1918.
23 TNA, FO 882/27, *Arab Bulletin* 92, 11 June 1918.
24 TNA, FO 882/13, *Arab Bulletin Supplementary Papers*, No.5: Lawrence, 'Tribal Politics in Feisal's area', 24 June 1918.
25 TNA FO 882/27, *Arab Bulletin* 83, 'Palestine Letter', 27 March 1918. Hogarth was the Arab Bureau's representative in Palestine at the time.
26 Antonius, *The Arab Awakening*, p.434.
27 TNA, FO 686/9, Husein to Wilson, 20 June 1918.
28 TNA, FO 686/9, Wilson to Husein, 21 June 1918.
29 TNA, FO 686/9, Wilson to Husein, 28 June 1918.
30 TNA, FO 686/10, Joyce to Lawrence, 28 June 1918.
31 Garnett, ed. *The Letters of T.E. Lawrence*, pp.243–6, Lawrence to Richards, 15 July 1918.
32 LHCMA, Joyce Papers, 1/264, Dawnay to Joyce, 3 July 1918.
33 LHCMA, Joyce Papers, 1/310, Dawnay to Joyce, 3 July 1918.

23 HOLDING OPERATIONS

1 TNA, WO 158/639B, Bartholomew to Chief of General Staff, 15 July 1918.
2 LHCMA, Joyce Papers, 1/311, Dawnay to Joyce, 15 July 1918.
3 Young, *The Independent Arab*, p.203.
4 LHCMA, Joyce Papers, 1/264, Dawnay to Joyce, 3 July 1918.
5 Lawrence, *Seven Pillars of Wisdom*, 1935, p.540.
6 Allenby informed the CIGS of his intention to attack in September on 24 July 1918; IWM, Wilson papers, HHW2/33A/14.
7 Young, *The Independent Arab*, p.203.
8 Lawrence, *Seven Pillars of Wisdom*, 1922, p.642.
9 IWM, Pearman Papers, 78/21/1, Lecture: 'The Imperial Camel Corps with Col. Lawrence', n.d.
10 Robin Buxton, note dated 16 August 1918, quoted in Wilson, *Lawrence of Arabia*, p.537.
11 IWM, H. Garland Papers, post-war lecture, n.d.
12 Laurence Moore, quoted in Inchbald, *The Imperial Camel Corps*, London 1970, pp.131–2.
13 Stirling, *Safety Last*, p.86.
14 Stirling, *Safety Last*, p.87.
15 Moore, quoted in Inchbald, *The Imperial Camel Corps*, pp.133–4.
16 TNA, WO 374/43340, Lyall's Army record.
17 Bodleian Library, Oxford, MS Photogr. c.123/2 f.130.
18 Lawrence, *Seven Pillars of Wisdom*, 1935, p.555.
19 Lawrence, *Seven Pillars of Wisdom*, 1935, p.555.
20 Lawrence, *Seven Pillars of Wisdom*, 1935, p.555.
21 TNA, FO 882/27, *Arab Bulletin* 100, 20 August 1918.
22 Lawrence, *Seven Pillars of Wisdom*, 1935, p.548.
23 Liman von Sanders, *Five Years in Turkey*, p.262.
24 LHCMA, Bartholomew Papers, 1/9, translation of a document dated 29 August 1918, written by a German Army liaison officer attached to the Turkish Eighth Army. Addressed to the Military Plenipotentiary in Constantinople.
25 TNA, FO 686/9, Wilson's report, 19 July 1918.
26 TNA, FO 686/9, Wilson's report, 19 July 1918.
27 TNA FO 686/10, Wilson's report, 21 July 1918.
28 TNA, FO 686/9, Wilson's report, 21 July 1918.
29 TNA, FO 686/10, Bassett to Director, Arab Bureau, 30 July 1918.
30 TNA, FO 686/10, Husein's letter, 28 July 1918.
31 TNA, FO 686/10, Bassett to Arab Bureau, 30 July 1918.
32 TNA, FO 686/10, Bassett to Husein, 3 August 1918.
33 IWM, Wilson papers, HHW2/33A/18, Allenby to Wilson, 14 August 1918.
34 TNA, WO 33/960, Allenby to War Office, 16 August 1918.
35 Quoted in Joseph Kostiner, 'Prologue of Hashemite Downfall and Saudi Ascendancy: A New Look at the Khurma Dispute, 1917–1919', in Asher Susser and Aryeh Shmulevitz, eds. *The Hashemites in the Modern Arab World*, London 1995.
36 Buxton, note dated 4 August 1918, quoted in Wilson, *Lawrence of Arabia*, p.534.
37 Buxton, note dated 16 August 1918, quoted in Wilson, *Lawrence of Arabia*, p.537.
38 Moore quoted in Inchbald, *The Imperial Camel Corps*, p.135.
39 TNA, WO 158/639B, Bartholomew to Chief of General Staff, 15 July 1918.
40 TNA, WO 158/639B, Bartholomew to Chief of General Staff, 15 July 1918.
41 Moore quoted in Inchbald, *The Imperial Camel Corps*, p.136.
42 Kirkbride, *An Awakening*, p.62.
43 Lawrence, *Seven Pillars of Wisdom*, 1935, p.574.
44 Moore, quoted in Inchbald, *The Imperial Camel Corps*, p.137.

45 LHCMA, Bartholomew Papers, 1/9, translation of a document dated 29 August 1918, written by a German Army liaison officer attached to the Turkish Eighth Army. Addressed to the Military Plenipotentiary in Constantinople.

24 THE DARA RAID

1 TNA, FO 882/27, *Arab Bulletin* 104, 24 September 1918.
2 Facey and Safwat, eds. *The Memoirs of Jafar Pasha al-Askari*, p.149.
3 Kirkbride, *An Awakening*, p.47.
4 Kirkbride, *An Awakening*, p.47.
5 Young, *The Independent Arab*, p.204.
6 Young, *The Independent Arab*, p.204.
7 Young, *The Independent Arab*, p.206.
8 Lawrence, *Seven Pillars of Wisdom*, 1922, p.700.
9 Young, *The Independent Arab*, p.197.
10 Young, *The Independent Arab*, p.198.
11 Young, *The Independent Arab*, pp.208–9.
12 Facey and Safwat, eds. *The Memoirs of Jafar Pasha al-Askari*, p.150.
13 Young, *The Independent Arab*, p.211.
14 Lawrence, *Seven Pillars of Wisdom*, 1935, p.576.
15 TNA, FO 882/13 Lawrence via Commandant Aqaba to Hedgehog Cairo, 30 August 1918, quoted in Wilson, *Lawrence of Arabia*, p.540.
16 Lawrence, *Seven Pillars of Wisdom*, 1935, p.577.
17 LHCMA, Joyce Papers, 1/Q/20, n.d.
18 Lawrence, *Seven Pillars of Wisdom*, 1922, p.703.
19 BL, Add 45983B.
20 Winterton, *Fifty Tumultuous Years*, p.179. The comment was made by Lowell Thomas.
21 Kirkbride, *An Awakening*, p.47.
22 Lawrence, *Seven Pillars of Wisdom*, 1922, p.702.
23 TNA, FO 882/27, *Arab Bulletin* 102, 3 September 1918.
24 MEC, Tibawi Papers, Fakhri to Husein, 4 September 1918, and S. Tanvir Wasti, 'The Defence of Medina 1916–19' in *Middle Eastern Studies*, Vol. 27, (4) October 1991.
25 Lawrence, *Seven Pillars of Wisdom*, 1935, p.581.
26 SAD, Clayton Papers, 694/5, Lloyd, 'Diary of Journey with TEL to El Jaffer' n.d.
27 Winterton, *Fifty Tumultuous Years*, p.182.
28 Winterton, *Fifty Tumultuous Years*, p.182.
29 TNA, FO 882/27, *Arab Bulletin* 106, 22 October 1918.
30 TNA, FO 882/27, *Arab Bulletin* 106, 22 October 1918.
31 Winterton, *Fifty Tumultuous Years*, pp.64–5.
32 'The Hijaz Railway 1918: A German Report', in the *Journal of the T.E. Lawrence Society*, Vol.XII No.2 (Spring 2003).
33 Young, *The Independent Arab*, p.219.
34 Lawrence, *Seven Pillars of Wisdom*, 1935, p.594.
35 Jarvis, *Arab Command: the biography of Lieutenant-Colonel F.W. Peake Pasha*, p.48.
36 Lawrence, *Seven Pillars of Wisdom*, 1935, p.594.
37 Liman von Sanders, *Five Years in Turkey*, p.274.
38 Lawrence, *Seven Pillars of Wisdom*, 1935, p.594.
39 Kirkbride, *An Awakening*, p.69.
40 Young, *The Independent Arab*, p.227.

41 Liman von Sanders, *Five Years in Turkey*, p.290.
42 Young, *The Independent Arab*, p.228.
43 Young, *The Independent Arab*, p.228.
44 Young, *The Independent Arab*, p.228–9.
45 Young, *The Independent Arab*, p.230.
46 Kirkbride, *An Awakening*, p.71.
47 Young, *The Independent Arab*, p.231.
48 Liman von Sanders, *Five Years in Turkey*, p.274.
49 TNA, FO 882/27, *Arab Bulletin* 106, 22 October 1918.
50 Kirkbride, *An Awakening*, p.72.
51 Alec Kirkbride, *A Crackle of Thorns*, London 1956, p.8.
52 Lawrence, *Seven Pillars of Wisdom*, 1935, p.608.
53 Atkinson, 'General Liman von Sanders on his Experiences in Palestine', *Army Quarterly* 3, pp.257–75.
54 LHCMA, Allenby Papers, 1/9/1, Allenby to Lady Allenby, 19 September 1918.
55 Lawrence, *Seven Pillars of Wisdom*, 1935, p.612.
56 LHCMA, Joyce Papers, 1/263, Dawnay to Joyce, n.d. but from context 20 September 1918.
57 MEC, H.W. Young Papers, Allenby to Feisal, 20 September 1918.
58 LHCMA, Joyce Papers, 1/263, Dawnay to Joyce, n.d. but from context 20 September 1918.
59 Lawrence, *Seven Pillars of Wisdom*, 1922, p.754.

25 THE ROAD TO DAMASCUS

1 'The Hijaz Railway 1918: A German Report', in the *Journal of the T.E. Lawrence Society*, Vol.XII No.2 (Spring 2003).
2 Kirkbride, *An Awakening*, p.77.
3 'The Hijaz Railway 1918: A German Report', in the *Journal of the T.E. Lawrence Society*, Vol.XII No. 2 (Spring 2003).
4 Vincennes, SS Marine Q86, Jaussen's report, 20 September 1918.
5 Quoted in Wilson, *Lawrence of Arabia*, p.553.
6 Translated in the *Evening Standard*, 25 September 1918.
7 TNA, WO 33/960, DMI to Allenby, 25 September 1918.
8 TNA, WO 95/4371, Allenby to Feisal, 25 September 1918.
9 TNA, WO 95/4551, Special Instruction to the Australian Mounted Division, quoted in Hughes, *Allenby and British Strategy in the Middle East*, London 1999, p.98.
10 Lawrence, *Seven Pillars of Wisdom*, 1935, pp.623–4.
11 Young, *The Independent Arab*, p.245.
12 Kirkbride, *An Awakening*, p.81.
13 Young, *The Independent Arab*, p.248.
14 Lawrence, *Seven Pillars of Wisdom*, 1922, p.770.
15 Lawrence, *Seven Pillars of Wisdom*, 1935, p.631.
16 Lawrence, *Seven Pillars of Wisdom*, 1935, p.631.
17 Lawrence, *Seven Pillars of Wisdom*, 1935, p.631.
18 Lawrence, *Seven Pillars of Wisdom*, 1935, p.631.
19 Lawrence, *Seven Pillars of Wisdom*, 1935, p.633.
20 Liman von Sanders, *Five Years in Turkey*, p.292.
21 TNA, FO 882/27, *Arab Bulletin* 106, 22 October 1918.
22 Young, *The Independent Arab*, p.251.
23 LHCMA, Joyce Papers, 2/20/1, Peake to A.W. Lawrence, 4 August 1965.
24 Young, *The Independent Arab*, pp.251–2.

25 Winterton, *Fifty Tumultuous Years*, pp.71–2.
26 Kikbride, *An Awakening*, p.82.
27 Kirkbride, *An Awakening*, pp.84–5.
28 Sir G. de S. Barrow, *The Fire of Life*, London n.d., p.211.
29 Lawrence, *Seven Pillars of Wisdom*, 1922, p.782.
30 Stirling, *Safety Last*, p.93.
31 Philip Graves, *The Pursuit*, London 1930.
32 TNA, FO 882/27, *Arab Bulletin* 106, 22 October 1918.
33 TNA, WO 33/960, Allenby to WO, 30 September 1918.
34 Liman von Sanders, *Five Years in Turkey*, p.304.
35 Liman von Sanders, *Five Years in Turkey*, p.304.
36 Musbah Haidar, *Arabesque*, p.147.
37 Stirling, *Safety Last*, p.94.
38 Stirling, *Safety Last*, p.94.

26 A HOUSE WITH NO DOOR

1 Lawrence, *Seven Pillars of Wisdom*, 1935, p.645.
2 TNA, FO 882/27, *Arab Bulletin* 106, 22 October 1918.
3 MEC, Allenby Papers, Chauvel to Bean, 8 October 1929.
4 MEC, Allenby Papers, Chauvel to Bean, 8 October 1929.
5 Brown, ed. *Lawrence of Arabia: the selected letters*, p.176, Lawrence to W.F. Stirling, 28 June 1919.
6 IWM, certificate, dated 8 November 1918, accompanying EPH 4338.
7 Lawrence, *Seven Pillars of Wisdom*, 1922, p.799.
8 Lawrence, *Seven Pillars of Wisdom*, 1935, p.651.
9 Stirling, *Safety Last*, p.95.
10 Stirling, *Safety Last*, p.95.
11 Kirkbride, *A Crackle of Thorns*, p.9.
12 Kirkbride, *An Awakening*, p.97.
13 TNA, WO 95/4553, War Diary of ADMS, Australian Mounted Division, for October 1918.
14 MEC, Allenby Papers, Chauvel to Bean, 8 October 1929.
15 IWM, Q12377.
16 TNA, WO 33/960, War Office to GHQ Egypt, 1 October 1918.
17 SAD, Wingate Papers, 170/2, Allenby to Lady Allenby, 3 September [October] 1918. Money was Major-General A.W. Money, the Chief Administrator of the Occupied Enemy Territory (South).
18 This impression was corroborated by Kirkbride, who had heard about the meeting from Tahseen Qadri, an Arab who was present. Kirkbride, *An Awakening*, p.99.
19 MEC, Allenby Papers, Chauvel, note, 31 October 1935.
20 IWM, Wilson HHW2/33A/29, Allenby to Wilson, 9 November 1918.
21 BL, Add 45914, f.42.
22 TNA, WO 33/960, Allenby to WO, 6 October 1918.
23 Stirling, *Safety Last*, p.97.
24 IWM, Stirling Papers, Stirling to his sister, 5 November 1918.
25 TNA, WO 33/960, Allenby to WO, 12 October 1918; WO 33/960, Allenby to WO, 13 October 1918.
26 IWM, Wilson papers, HHW2/33A/28, Allenby to Wilson, 19 October 1918.
27 TNA, FO 882/17, Clayton to FO, 19 October 1918.
28 MAE, Nantes, Jerusalem, B, 114, SS Marine Q86, Jaussen's report, 15 November 1918.
29 *The Times*, 17 October 1918.
30 Garnett, ed. *The Letters of T.E. Lawrence*, p.266, 'The reconstruction of Arabia', 4 November 1918.

31 MEC, Hogarth Papers, Hogarth to Clayton, 1 November 1918.
32 Quoted in Margaret Macmillan, *Peacemakers*, London 2002, p.397.
33 Young, *The Independent Arab*, p.280.
34 Quoted in Hughes, *Allenby and British Strategy*, p.118.
35 TNA, WO 33/960, GHQ to WO, 22 November 1918.
36 Brémond, *Le Hedjaz dans la Guerre Mondiale*, p.310.
37 SAD, Clayton Papers, 694/6, the Weizmann–Feisal Agreement, 3 January 1919.
38 Quoted in Wilson, *Lawrence of Arabia*, p.596.
39 TNA, CAB 27/37, Hirtzel, 'Policy in Arabia', 20 November 1918.
40 TNA, FO 608/97/371/5/3, Intelligence Department of the Naval Staff, 26 February 1919, quoted in Hughes, *Allenby and British Strategy*, p.121.
41 TNA, CAB 21/119, Hankey to Balfour, 1 August 1918, quoted in Hughes, *Allenby and British Strategy*, p.120.
42 Lord Hardinge of Penshurst, *Old Diplomacy*, London 1947, p.232.
43 IWM, W.F. Stirling Papers, letter, 26 April 1919.
44 Quoted in Hughes, *Allenby and British Strategy*, p.158.
45 Ross Burns, *The Monuments of Syria*, London 1992, p.91.
46 TNA, FO 686/6, Lawrence to Wilson, 8 January 1917.

EPILOGUE

1 *Sunday Times*, 'A Report on Mesopotamia', 22 August 1920.
2 BL, Add 45903, Lawrence to Shaw, 18 October 1927.
3 SAD, Clayton Papers, 693/11, Lawrence to Clayton, 8 October 1928.
4 Quoted in Hanna Batatu, *The Old Social Classes and Revolutionary Movements of Iraq*, Princeton 1978, p.25.
5 *The Times*, 20 May 1935.
6 T.E. Lawrence, *Revolt in the Desert*, New York 1927, p.66.
7 Basil Liddell Hart, *'T.E. Lawrence' in Arabia and After*, London 1934, p.438.
8 D.L. Lloyd Owen, *The Desert my Dwelling Place*, London 1957, p.46.
9 Storrs, *Orientations*, p.177.
10 Quoted in Elie Kedourie, *In the Anglo-Arab Labyrinth*, Cambridge 1976, p.119.
11 SAD, Wingate Papers, 171/6, 28 December 1918, quoted in M.W. Daly, *The Sirdar*, Newark 1997, p.27.
12 SAD, Wingate Papers, 148/4, 11 February 1918.
13 LHCMA, Allenby Papers, 1/8/15, Allenby to Lady Allenby, 3 October 1917.
14 Amin Rihani, *Around the Coasts of Arabia*, London 1930, frontispiece.
15 King Abdullah, 'As the Arabs see the Jews', *American Magazine*, November 1947.
16 Hansard, 1 August 1930, cols, 902–3.
17 *The Times*, 8 July 1937.
18 Kedourie, *In the Anglo-Arab Labyrinth*, p.228.
19 IOR, L/PS/12/3349, Memoranda respecting the McMahon–Husein correspondence of 1915 and 1916 and certain subsequent statements made on behalf of his Majesty's Government in regard to the future status of Palestine. December 1939: Lord Chancellor's opinion, circulated to Cabinet on 23 January 1939.
20 Storrs, *Orientations*, p.179.
21 *The Times*, 30 December 1949.
22 Report of a committee set up to consider certain correspondence between Sir Henry McMahon and the Sharif of Mecca in 1915 and 1916, March 16, 1939, Cmd. 5974.
23 *The Times*, 'Lawrence of Arabia's Lessons on the Iraq War', 1 March 2004; *Sunday Times*, 'Lawrence of Arabia Guides US Troops', 22 May 2005.
24 Osama bin Laden, http://news.bbc.co.uk/1/hi/world/south_asia/1585636.stm

BIBLIOGRAPHY

1. ARCHIVES

Bodleian Library, Oxford
T.E. Lawrence Papers

British Library
Egypt 1916–17, Private letters between General Sir William Robertson and General Sir Archibald Murray, privately printed in 1932 (Add 52463)

T.E. Lawrence papers, diaries, letters and photographs (Add 45914, Add 45915, Add 45983A and B, Add 45903, Add 50584)

The Gertrude Bell Project (online archive), Robinson Library, University of Newcastle
G. Bell letters

Churchill College, Cambridge
G. Lloyd Papers

India Office Records, British Library, London
Files from series:

L/PS/10

L/PS/11

L/PS/12

L/PS/18

Mss Eur D660, Sir A.H. Grant Papers

Mss Eur D613, Sir G. Roos-Keppel Papers

Mss Eur E264/7, telegrams between the Viceroy and the Secretary of State for India, 1916

Imperial War Museum
T.W. Beaumont Papers

Sir P.W. Chetwode Papers

G. Dawnay Papers

H. Garland Papers
H.V. Gilbert Papers
F. Hayward Papers
T. Henderson, *The Hejaz Expedition, 1916–17 – A Narrative of the Work done by the Arabian detachment of No 14 Squadron RFC while attached to the Hejaz expedition*
F.G. Peake Papers
D.G. Pearman Papers
V.D. Siddons Papers
W.F. Stirling Papers
Sir H.H. Wilson Papers

Liddell Hart Centre for Military Archives, King's College, London
Sir E.H.H. Allenby Papers
Sir W.H. Bartholomew Papers
P.C. Joyce Papers
Sir W.R. Robertson Papers

Middle East Centre, St Antony's College, Oxford
Sir E.H.H. Allenby Papers
N. Barbour Papers
E. Baring Papers
Sir G.F. Clayton Papers
D.G. Hogarth Papers
I. Karadogan Papers
T.E. Lawrence Papers
S.F. Newcombe Papers
H. St.J. Philby Papers
Sir M. Sykes Papers
A. Tibawi Papers
W. Yale Papers
Sir H.W. Young Papers
J.W.A. Young Papers

The National Archives, Kew
Files from series:
FO 141 Embassy and Consulates, Egypt: general correspondence
FO 371 Political Departments: general correspondence
FO 686 Jeddah Agency papers
FO 882 Arab Bureau papers
T1 Treasury files
WO 33 War Office: Reports, Memoranda and Papers
WO 95 War diaries
WO 106 Directorate of Military Operations and Military Intelligence: correspondence and papers
WO 158 War Office, Military Headquarters' correspondence and papers
WO 374 Officers' service records

Pembroke College, Cambridge
Sir R. Storrs Papers

Sudan Archive, University of Durham Library
Sir G.F. Clayton Papers
Sir F.R. Wingate Papers

2. BOOKS AND ARTICLES

Abdullah, 'As the Arabs see the Jews', *American Magazine*, November 1947

Adelson, R., *Mark Sykes: Portrait of an Amateur*, London 1975

Antonius, G., *The Arab Awakening*, London 1938

Armstrong, K., *Islam: a short history*, London 2001

Arnold, T.W., *The Caliphate*, second edition, London 1965

Asher, M., *Lawrence: the uncrowned king of Arabia*, London 1999

Asprey, R.B., *War in the Shadows*, London 1994

Atkinson, C.T., 'General Liman von Sanders on his Experiences in Palestine', *Army Quarterly* 3 (1921–2)

Ayalon, A., 'The Hashemites, T.E. Lawrence and the postage stamps of the Hijaz', in Susser, A., and Shmuelevitz, A., eds. *The Hashemites in the Modern Arab World: A Festschrift in Honour of the Late Professor Uriel Dann*, London 1995, pp. 15–30

Baker, R., *King Husain and the Kingdom of the Hejaz*, Cambridge 1979

Barrow, Sir G. de S., *The Fire of Life*, London n.d.

Batatu, H., *The Old Social Classes and the Revolutionary Movements of Iraq*, Princeton 1978

Bell, Gertrude, *The Desert and the Sown*, New York 1907

Bernstorff, Count, *Memoirs*, Berlin 1936

Birdwood, Lord C.B.B., *Nuri As-Said*, London 1959

Bray, N.N.E., *Shifting Sands*, London 1934

Brémond, E., *Le Hedjaz dans la Guerre Mondiale*, Paris 1931

Brodrick, A.H., *Near to Greatness: a life of the Sixth Earl Winterton*, London 1965

Brown, M., ed. *Lawrence of Arabia: the selected letters*, London 2005

Bruce, A., *The Last Crusade*, London 2002

Buchan, J., *Greenmantle*, London 1916

Burdett, A.L.P., ed. *Arab Dissident Movements*, Slough 1996

Burns, R., *Monuments of Syria*, London 1999

Burton, R. *Personal Narrative of a Pilgrimage to Al-Madinah and Meccah*, London 1893

Cain, P.J., and Hopkins, A.G., *British Imperialism 1688–2000*, second edition, Edinburgh 2002

Callwell, C.E., *Small Wars*, second edition, London 1899

Charmley, J., *Lord Lloyd and the decline of the British Empire*, London 1987

Chirol, V., *Pan-Islamism*, London 1906

Chirol, V., *Fifty Years in a Changing World*, London 1927

Churchill, W.S., *Great Contemporaries*, London 1937

Clayton, Sir G.F., *An Arabian Diary*, ed. Collins, R.O., Berkeley 1969

Cork and Orrery, Earl of, [Boyle, W.], *My Naval Life, 1886–1941*, London 1942

Daly, M.W., *The Sirdar: Sir Reginald Wingate and the British Empire in the Middle East*, Philadelphia 1997

Daly Metcalf, B., *Islamic Revival in British India: Deoband 1860–1900*, Princeton 1982

Dawisha, A., *Arab Nationalism in the Twentieth Century*, Princeton 2003

Dawn, C.E., *From Ottomanism to Arabism: Essays on the origins of Arab nationalism*, Illinois 1973

Djemal Pasha, *Memories of a Turkish Statesman 1913–1919*, London 1922

Dowson, Sir E.M., *A Short Note on the design and issue of postage stamps prepared by the Survey of Egypt for His Highness Husein, Emir & Sherif of Mecca & King of the Hejaz*, El-Qahira 1918

Douglas-Hamilton, J., *From Gallipoli to Gaza: the desert poets of World War One*, London 2003

Erickson, E., *Ordered to Die: a history of the Ottoman Army in World War One*, London 2001

Erskine, Mrs S., *King Faisal of Iraq*, London 1933

Esin, E., *Mecca the Blessed, Madinah the Radiant*, London 1963

Facey W., with Grant, G., *Saudi Arabia by the First Photographers*, London *c.* 1996

Facey, W., and Safwat, N.F., eds. *A Soldier's Story: The Memoirs of Jafar Pasha Al-Askari*, London 2003

Ferguson, N., *Empire: How Britain made the Modern World*, London 2003

Field, M., *The Merchants*, London 1984

Fisher, J., *Curzon and British Imperialism in the Middle East*, London 1999

Fisher, J., 'The Rabegh Crisis 1916–17: "A comparatively Trivial Question" or "A Self-Willed Disaster"', *Middle Eastern Studies*, Vol.38 No.3, July 2002, pp.73–92

Fisher, J., *Gentlemen Spies*, Stroud 2002

Fitzherbert, M., *The Man who was Greenmantle: a biography of Aubrey Herbert*, London 1983

Fletcher, D., *War cars: British armoured cars in the First World War*, London 1987

Freedman, I., *The Question of Palestine*, London 1973

Fromkin, D., *A Peace to End All Peace*, paperback edition, London 2000

Gilbert, M., *First World War*, London 1994

Gilbert, M., *Israel*, London 1999

Gildea, R., *Barricades and Borders: Europe 1800–1914*, Oxford 1987

Graves, P., *The Pursuit*, London 1930

Graves, P., *Briton and Turk*, London 1941

Graves, P., ed. *Memoirs of King Abdullah of Transjordan*, London 1950

Graves, R., *Lawrence and the Arabs*, London 1927

Grey, Sir E., *Twenty Five Years – 1892–1916*, London 1925

Gubser, P., *Politics and Change in Al-Karak*, Oxford 1973

Haidar, M., *Arabesque*, London 1944

Hardinge of Penshurst, Lord, *Old Diplomacy*, London 1947

Hardy, P., *The Muslims of British India*, Cambridge 1972

Henderson Stewart, F., *Honor*, Chicago 1994

Hogarth, D.G., *The Penetration of Arabia*, London 1904

Hogarth, D.G., 'Mecca's Revolt against the Turk', *Century Magazine*, 100 (1920), pp.403–9

Hogue, O., *The Cameliers*, London 1919

Hughes, M., *Allenby and British Strategy in the Middle East*, London 1999

Hughes, M., ed. *Allenby in Palestine: the Middle East Correspondence of Field Marshal Viscount Allenby, June 1917–October 1919*, Stroud 2004

Inchbald, G., *Imperial Camel Corps*, London 1970

James, L., *Imperial Warrior – the life and times of Sir Edmund Allenby*, London 1993

James, L., *The Golden Warrior: the Life and Legend of Lawrence of Arabia*, revised edition, London 1995

Jarvis, C.S., *Arab Command: the biography of Lieutenant-Colonel F.W. Peake Pasha*, London 1942

Jathar, G.B. and Beri, S.G., *Indian Economics*, London 1933

Jaussen, A., *Coutumes des Arabes au pays de Moab*, Paris 1908

Jaussen and Savignac, *Mission Archéologique en Arabie*, Volume II, Paris 1914

Karsh, E., and Karsh, I., 'Myth in the Desert, or Not the Great Arab Revolt', in *Middle Eastern Studies*, Vol.33 No.2, April 1997

Keay, J., *Sowing the Wind: the seeds of conflict in the Middle East*, London 2003

Kedourie, E., *In the Anglo-Arab Labyrinth*, Cambridge 1976

Khoury, P.S., *Urban Notables and Arab Nationalism*, Cambridge 1983

Kidwai, M.H., *Pan-Islamism and Bolshevism*, London [1937]

Kinross, J.P.D.B., *Ataturk: the rebirth of a nation*, London 1964

Kirkbride, A., *A Crackle of Thorns*, London 1956

Kirkbride, A., *An Awakening*, University Press of Arabia 1971

Knightley, P., and Simpson, C., *The Secret Lives of Lawrence of Arabia*, London 1969

Kostiner, J., 'Prologue of Hashemite Downfall and Saudi Ascendancy: A New Look at the Khurma Dispute, 1917–1919', in Susser, A., and Shmuelevitz, A., eds. *The Hashemites in the Modern Arab World*, London 1995

Landau, J.M., *The Politics of Pan-Islam*, Oxford 1990

Lancaster, W., *The Rwala Bedouin Today*, Cambridge 1981

Larès, M., *T.E. Lawrence, la France et les Français*, Paris 1980

Laurens, H., 'Jaussen et les services de renseignement français (1915–1919)' in Chatelard, G., and Tarawneh, M., eds. *Antonin Jaussen: Sciences sociales occidentales et patrimoine arabe*, Centre d'Études et de Recherches sur le Moyen-Orient Contemporain 1999, pp.23–35

Lawrence, A.W., ed. *T.E. Lawrence by His Friends*, London 1937

Lawrence, B., ed., *Messages to the World: the statements of Osama bin Laden*, London 2005

Lawrence, T.E., *Seven Pillars of Wisdom*, London 1935

The Letters of T.E. Lawrence, ed. Garnett, D., London 1938

Lawrence, T.E., *Letters to his Biographers Robert Graves and Liddell Hart*, London 1963

Lawrence, T.E., *Crusader Castles*, Oxford 1988

Lawrence, T.E., *Seven Pillars of Wisdom* (The Complete 1922 Oxford Text), Fordingbridge 2004

Leclerc, C., 'The French Soldiers in the Arab Revolt', *Journal of the T.E. Lawrence Society*, Vol.IX, No.1 (Autumn 1999)

Lewis, B., *The Crisis of Islam*, London 2003

Lewis, G., 'The Ottoman Proclamation of Jihad in 1914', in *Arabic and Islamic Garland: Historical, Educational and Literary Papers presented to Abdul Latif Tibawi*, London 1977

Liddell Hart, B., *'T.E. Lawrence' in Arabia and After*, London 1934

Liman von Sanders, O., *Five Years in Turkey*, Nashville 2000

Lloyd Owen, D.L., *The Desert My Dwelling Place*, London 1957

Lockman, J.N., *Scattered Tracks on the Lawrence Trail*, Michigan 1996

Lockman, J.N., *Meinertzhagen's Diary Ruse*, Michigan 1995

MacMillan, M., *Peacemakers*, London 2001

McKale, D.M., *War by Revolution*, Ohio 1998

Manual of Field Engineering 1911, GS, War Office (1914 reprint)

Margoliouth, D.S., 'Pan-Islamism', *Proceedings of the Central Asian Society*, 12 January 1912

Massey, W.T., *Allenby's Final Triumph*, London 1920

Meeker, M., *Literature and Violence in North Arabia*, Cambridge 1979

Morgenthau, H., *Ambassador Morgenthau's Story*, New York 1919

Morris, J., *The Hashemite Kings*, London 1959

Mousa, S., *T.E. Lawrence: an Arab view*, Oxford 1966

Mundy, M., and Musallam, B., *The Transformation of Nomadic Society in the Arab East*, Cambridge 2000

Musil, A., *The Northern Hegaz*, New York 1926

Nelson, B., *Azraq: desert oasis*, London 1973

Nevakivi, J., *Britain, France and the Arab Middle East, 1914–1920*, London 1969

Nevo, J., 'Abdallah's memoirs as historical source material', in Susser, A. and Shmuelevitz, A., eds. *The Hashemites in the Modern Arab World: A Festschrift in Honour of the Late Professor Uriel Dann*, London 1995, pp. 165–82.

Nicholson, J., *The Hejaz Railway*, London 2005

Nicolson, N., ed. *Harold Nicolson, Diaries and Letters, 1907–1964*, London 2004

Ochsenwald, W., *The Hijaz Railroad*, Charlottesville 1980

Ochsenwald, W., *Religion, Society and the State in Arabia – the Hijaz under Ottoman control, 1840–1908*, Ohio 1984

O'Dwyer, M.F., *India as I Knew It*, London 1925

Özcan, A., *Pan-Islamism: Indian Muslims, the Ottomans and Britain 1877–1924*, Leiden 1997

Peake, F.G., *History of Jordan and its Tribes*, Miami 1958

Photographies d'Arabie, Hijaz 1907–1917, Paris 1999

Pierard, P., and Legros, P., *Off-Road in the Hejaz*, Dubai 2001

Prasad, Y.D., *The Indian Muslims and World War I: a phase of disillusionment with British rule, 1914–1918*, New Delhi 1985

Reid, F., *The Fighting Cameliers*, Sydney 1934

Robertson, Sir W., *From Private to Field Marshal*, London 1921

Robinson, E.H.T., *Lawrence the Rebel*, London 1946

Rogan, E., *Frontiers of the State in the Late Ottoman Empire*, Cambridge 1999

Rolls, S.C., *Steel Chariots in the Desert*, London 1937

Schatkowski Schilcher, L., 'The Famine of 1915–1918 in Greater Syria', in Spagnolo, J., ed. *Problems of the Modern Middle East in Historical Perspective*, Reading 1996

Segev, T., *One Palestine, Complete*, paperback edition, London 2001

Seymour, C., ed. *The Intimate Papers of Colonel House*, London 1928

Smith, J.A., *John Buchan, A Biography*, London 1965

Stein, L., *The Balfour Declaration*, London 1961

Stevenson, D., *1914–1918: The History of the First World War*, London 2005

Stirling, W.F., *Safety Last*, London 1953

Stitt, G., *A Prince of Arabia, The Emir Shereef Ali Haider*, London 1948

Storrs, R., *Orientations*, London 1937

Strachan, H., *The First World War, Volume I: To Arms*, Oxford 2001

Sykes, M., *The Caliphs' Last Heritage*, London 1915

Tanvir Wasti, S., 'The Defence of Medina' *Middle East Studies* vol. 27, No. 4, October, 1991

Tauber, E., *The Arab Movements in World War I*, London 1993

'The Hijaz Railway 1918: A German Report', *Journal of the T.E. Lawrence Society*, Vol.XII No.2 (Spring 2003)

Thesiger, W., *Arabian Sands*, London 1959

Tibawi, A.L., *A Modern History of Syria*, London 1969

Touchan, R., Meko, D. and Hughes, M.K., 'A 396-year reconstruction of precipitation in Southern Jordan', *Journal of the American Water Resources Association*, Vol.35 No.1 (Feb. 1999)

Tourret, R., *Hedjaz Railway*, Abingdon 1989

Travers, T., *Gallipoli*, Stroud 2001

Travis, A., *Bound and Gagged: A secret history of obscenity in Britain*, London 2000

Vansittart, Lord, *The Mist Procession*, London 1958

Von Papen, F., *Memoirs*, London 1952

Wallach, J., *Desert Queen*, paperback edition, London 1997

Wavell, A.J.B., *A Modern Pilgrim in Mecca*, second edition, London 1918

Weldon, L.B., *Hard Lying*, London 1925

Wemyss, V. Wester, *The Life and Letters of Lord Wester Wemyss*, London 1935

Westrate, B., *The Arab Bureau: British Policy in the Middle East, 1916–1920*, Pennsylvania 1992

Wilson, J., *Lawrence of Arabia: the authorised biography of T.E. Lawrence*, London 1989

Wilson, M.C., *King Abdullah of Jordan: a political biography*, Oxford 1983

Wilson, M.C., *King Abdullah, Britain and the making of Jordan*, Cambridge 1987

Winstone, H.V.F., ed. *The Diaries of Parker Pasha*, London 1983

Winterton, Earl, [Turnour, E.], *Fifty Tumultuous Years*, London 1955

Woodward, D.R, *Lloyd George and the Generals*, Newark 1983

Wyman Bury, G., *Pan-Islam*, London 1919

Yapp, M.E., *The Making of the Modern Near East, 1792–1923*, London 1987

Young, H., *The Independent Arab*, London 1933

Zeigler, P., *Edward VIII*, London 1990

Zeine, Z.N., *The Emergence of Arab Nationalism*, Beirut 1966

ACKNOWLEDGEMENTS

For permission to quote from copyright published and unpublished records I would like to thank: Omar Ziad al Askari for Jafar Pasha al Askari; Patricia Bettany for D.H. Calcutt, Patience Marshall for Sir Gilbert Clayton; Mena Garland O'Connor for Herbert Garland; Dr Caroline Barron for David Hogarth; The Seven Pillars of Wisdom Trust for T.E. Lawrence; Sir Tatton Sykes for Sir Mark Sykes and Martin Dane for Sir Reginald Wingate. Extracts from Gertrude Bell's letters are included by permission of the Special Collections Librarian, Robinson Library, University of Newcastle upon Tyne, and for Sir Ronald Storr's papers by permission of the Master and Fellows of Pembroke College, Cambridge. I would like to thank the Trustees of the Liddell Hart Centre for Military Archives and the Imperial War Museum for permission to quote from papers held in their respective archives. Quotations from Crown copyright reocrds held by the India Office Records, The National Archive, the Sudan Archive and the British Library appear by permission of Her Majesty's Stationery Office. Extracts from *Arab Command: the Biography of Lt Col FW Peake Pasha* and *My Naval Life* by the Earl of Cork and Orrery, both published by Hutchinson, and the *Memoirs of King Abdullah of Jordan*, edited by Philip Graves and published by Jonathan Cape, are all reprinted by permission of The Random House Group Ltd.

This book would not exist were it not for the enthusiasm and efforts of Catherine Clarke and George Lucas, and my editors Sarah Marcus and Bill Swainson at Bloomsbury and Maria Guarnaschelli at W.W. Norton. I am very grateful to them all. I would also particularly like to thank

Richard Spring for his constant encouragement since our visit to Syria in 2002, which sparked my interest in Britain's involvement in the Middle East, and Steve Boyle and Tom Tugendhat, who were game enough to accompany me into the desert on the field trips to Jordan and Saudi Arabia. For a wide range of help during my research, including expertise, research, recolletions, suggestions and hospitality, I would like to thank Attayak Ali, the last St Jon Armitage, Ray Benitze, Michael Binyon, Jenny Carter-Manning, Anna Checkley, Derek Cooper, Rob Crothers, Richard Drayton, Baroness Elles, Elizabeth Elliott, Ed Erickson, William Facey, Mark Goodwin, David Grisenthwaite, Jane Hogan, Patrick Kidd, Robert Knight, Henri Laurens, Alysa Levene, Sami Nawar, Tamsin O'Connell, Patrick Pierard, Andrew Reynolds, Eugene Rogan, Charlie Sykes, Ramzi Touchan, Mesut Uyar, Debbie Usher, George Williamson and Harvey Woods. That I was able to enter Saudi Arabia at all was due largely to the British Ambassador, Sir Sherard Cowper-Coles. I am very grateful to him and his wife, Bridget, for welcoming me to Riyadh. I must also thank the staffs of the India Office Library, The National Archive, the Liddell Hart Centre for Military Archives, the Imperaial War Musuem, the Sudan Archive, the Middle East Centre and the Modern Papers Reading Room at the Bodleian Library for their help. Dr Christopher Wright and Dr Barry Knight at the British Library enabled me to have T.E. Lawrence's diary forensically examined by George Jenkinson. I would like to thank all three for their time and I should add that my interpretation of the films that resulted is my own.

Finally I would also like to thank my colleagues, especially Meladie Blackshaw, Caroline Denton, James Dunseath and Juliette Proudlove, for their forbearance, and my parents, Valerie and Stuart, for their endless support.

INDEX

A NOTE ON THE AUTHOR

James Barr graduated from Oxford with a first in Modern History, went on to write leaders for the *Daily Telegraph* and now works in the City. *Setting the Desert on Fire* is his first major work.

A NOTE ON THE TYPE

Linotype Garamond Three – based on seventeenth-century copies
of Claude Garamond's types, cut by Jean Jannon. This
version was designed for American Type Founders in 1917,
by Morris Fuller Benton and Thomas Maitland Cleland and
adapted for mechanical composition by Linotype in 1936.